Fractured China

Is China's rise a threat to international order? *Fractured China* shows that it depends on what one means by 'China', for China is not the monolithic, unitary actor that many assume. Forty years of state transformation – the fragmentation, decentralisation and internationalisation of party-state apparatuses – have profoundly changed how its foreign policy is made and implemented. Today, Chinese behaviour abroad is often not the product of a coherent grand strategy, but results from a sometimes-chaotic struggle for power and resources among contending politico-business interests, within a surprisingly permissive Chinese-style regulatory state. Presenting a path-breaking new analytical framework, *Fractured China* transforms the central debate in International Relations and provides new tools for scholars and policymakers seeking to understand and respond to twenty-first century rising powers. Drawing on extensive fieldwork in China and Southeast Asia, it includes three major case studies – the South China Sea, non-traditional security cooperation, and development financing – to demonstrate the framework's explanatory power.

LEE JONES is Reader in International Politics at Queen Mary University of London. His other books include *ASEAN, Sovereignty and Intervention in Southeast Asia* (2012), *Societies Under Siege: Exploring How International Economic Sanctions (Do Not) Work* (2015), and *The Political Economy of Southeast Asia: Politics and Markets under Hyperglobalisation* (2020).

SHAHAR HAMEIRI is Australian Research Council Future Fellow and Associate Professor of International Politics in the School of Political Science and International Studies, University of Queensland. Among his recent books are *Governing Borderless Threats* (2015), *International Intervention and Local Politics* (2017), and *The Political Economy of Southeast Asia* (2020).

Fractured China

How State Transformation Is Shaping China's Rise

LEE JONES
Queen Mary University of London
SHAHAR HAMEIRI
University of Queensland

CAMBRIDGE
UNIVERSITY PRESS

University Printing House, Cambridge CB2 8BS, United Kingdom

One Liberty Plaza, 20th Floor, New York, NY 10006, USA

477 Williamstown Road, Port Melbourne, VIC 3207, Australia

314–321, 3rd Floor, Plot 3, Splendor Forum, Jasola District Centre,
New Delhi – 110025, India

103 Penang Road, #05–06/07, Visioncrest Commercial, Singapore 238467

Cambridge University Press is part of the University of Cambridge.

It furthers the University's mission by disseminating knowledge in the pursuit of
education, learning, and research at the highest international levels of excellence.

www.cambridge.org
Information on this title: www.cambridge.org/9781316517796
DOI: 10.1017/9781009047487

© Lee Jones and Shahar Hameiri 2021

First published 2021

A catalogue record for this publication is available from the British Library.

Library of Congress Cataloging-in-Publication Data
Names: Hameiri, Shahar, author. | Jones, Lee, 1981– author.
Title: Fractured China : how state transformation is shaping China's rise / Shahar
Hameiri, University of Queensland, Lee Jones, Queen Mary University of London.
Description: 1 Edition. | New York : Cambridge University Press, 2021. | Includes
bibliographical references and index.
Identifiers: LCCN 2021011674 (print) | LCCN 2021011675 (ebook) | ISBN
9781316517796 (hardback) | ISBN 9781009047487 (ebook)
Subjects: LCSH: Capitalism – Political aspects – China. | Globalization – Political
aspects – China. | China – Economic policy – 2000– | China – Foreign relations. |
BISAC: POLITICAL SCIENCE / International Relations / General | POLITICAL
SCIENCE / International Relations / General
Classification: LCC HC427.95 .H336 2021 (print) | LCC HC427.95 (ebook) |
DDC 327.51–dc23
LC record available at https://lccn.loc.gov/2021011674
LC ebook record available at https://lccn.loc.gov/2021011675

ISBN 978-1-316-51779-6 Hardback
ISBN 978-1-009-04846-0 Paperback

*For Rosemary Foot, Andrew Hurrell, Kanishka Jayasuriya
and Garry Rodan*

Contents

Figures

Maps

Tables

Acknowledgements

Fractured China is the culmination of a six-year research project and, like all books, it is the work of many more people than those whose names appear on the cover. The underpinning research, particularly the all-important fieldwork, would have been impossible without the financial support of the Australian Research Council (DP1701102647). We also received funding from the UK's Independent Social Research Foundation (POLP1A3 R), the British Academy's Newton Fund (AF150300) and our respective academic departments. We thank all of these funders for their support. Lee is also very grateful to the National University of Singapore and Stanford University for appointing him to the Lee Kong Chian Distinguished Visiting Fellowship in 2014–15, during which the groundwork for this project was laid.

We also owe a great deal to Shaun Breslin, who accompanied us on our first fieldtrip to China and helped us get this project off the ground, and to our Chinese friends and colleagues who sustained us thereafter. We are particularly grateful to Ren Yuanzhe, Zhang Biao, Zou Yizheng and Su Hao for their support. We also thank colleagues at Peking and Renmin Universities, the China University of Political Science and Law and China Foreign Affairs University, for their early feedback on our project. At a time of rapidly deteriorating relations between China and the West, these friendships sustain our hope for a better future. We are also deeply grateful to the many individuals in China and Southeast Asia who gave up their time to be interviewed. Above all, we are indebted to our research assistants: Zhou Yuping, Yang Kejia, Kham Lin Thu, Ang Len, Ryan Smith, Jan Mairhoefer and Monica DiLeo. Without their help, particularly during our long periods of fieldwork, we simply could not have completed this project successfully.

We would also like to thank the many colleagues who gave us feedback on our work in progress, including those who invited us to give talks at their institutions, and the anonymous reviewers of our earlier publications. We are especially grateful to Cambridge University

Press's two anonymous reviewers, whose detailed, thoughtful comments greatly improved the book. We also thank John Haslam and Tobias Ginsberg at Cambridge University Press for their help in bringing the book to press, as well as our copy editors, Paula Bownas and Alice Stoakley, our indexer, Rohan Bolton, and our cartographer, Avik Nandy.

Of course, none of the individuals we mention, or anyone to whom we spoke, are remotely responsible for the arguments we have developed: this book reflects our judgements alone. Sadly, this is an important caveat in light of ever-diminishing academic freedom in China. We could keenly sense this during our fieldwork and, as it was drawing to a close, we were appalled to see the arrest of Canadian researchers Michael Kovrig and Michael Spivor, in apparent retaliation for the Canadian government's arrest of Huawei executive Meng Wanzhou. They remain in arbitrary detention today. Like many others, we support calls for their immediate release. But we also hope that the Chinese government will recognise the self-defeating nature of limits on academic freedom. If detailed, fine-grained scholarship on the realities of Chinese governance becomes impossible, the world becomes not just intellectually poorer, but also more dangerous. If the only picture of China available to outsiders is that of a closed, monolithic, unitary actor, international suspicion and conflict will only become more likely.

Finally, we would like to thank those who support us on a daily basis. For their moral, professional and intellectual support over the last six years, we would like to thank our immediate colleagues, particularly Nick Hostettler, Ray Kiely, Sophie Harman, Madeleine Davis, Kim Hutchings, Chris Reus-Smit, Andrew Phillips, Stephen Bell, Melissa Curley, Richard Devetak and Kath Gelber, and the members of the Australian International Political Economy Network. In a university sector increasingly characterised by thuggish managerialism and the debasement of education and research, they have provided a vital lifeline. So, too, have our good friends Philip Cunliffe, George Hoare, Chris Bickerton, Peter Ramsay, Toby Carroll, Tom Chodor and Fabio Scarpello. Over several years when many in our social milieu were losing their minds, they enriched ours. Finally, we are deeply grateful to our spouses, Chang and Meggan, for tolerating our lengthy absences during fieldwork and, more importantly, for their boundless love, patience and support. It is not easy to be married to an academic. Shahar would also like to thank his children, Josh, Theo and Nina, for putting up with his dad jokes (not hard, they're brilliant!), and for the love and joy they bring to his life every day (apart from Sunday mornings before 9 am).

We dedicate this book to our graduate school mentors, Rosemary Foot, Andrew Hurrell, Kanishka Jayasuriya and Garry Rodan. We have always been grateful for the way they supported us through our postgraduate degrees, and far beyond, with wisdom and generosity. We hope that this book lives up to what they have tried to teach us.

Abbreviations

9DL	Nine-dash line
AD	Alternative development
AIIB	Asian Infrastructure Investment Bank
ASEAN	Association of Southeast Asian Nations
ATS	Amphetamine-type stimulants
BFA	Bureau of Fisheries Administration (China)
BOT	Build, Operate, Transfer
BRI	Belt and Road Initiative
BRICS	Brazil, Russia, India, China and South Africa
BSPP	Burmese Socialist Programme Party
CCDAC	Central Committee for Drug Abuse Control (Myanmar)
CCG	China Coastguard
CCP	Chinese Communist Party
CDB	China Development Bank
CDC	Council for the Development of Cambodia
CDCP	Centre for Disease Control and Prevention (China)
CIDCA	China International Development Cooperation Agency
CMC	Central Military Commission (China)
CMP	China Maritime Police
CMS	China Marine Surveillance
CNOOC	China National Offshore Oil Company
CNPC	China National Petroleum Corporation
CNRP	Cambodian National Rescue Party
COM	Council of Ministers (Cambodia)
CPEC	China-Pakistan Economic Corridor
CPI	China Power International
CPP	Cambodian People's Party
CPPCC	Chinese People's Political Consultative Conference
CRC	Conditional Registration Certificate
CSO	Civil society organisation
CSR	Corporate social responsibility

DAC	Development Assistance Committee (Organisation for Economic Co-operation and Development)
DCB	Drug Control Bureau (China)
DF	Development financing
DfID	Department for International Development (Britain)
DOC	Department of Commerce (China)
EAG	Ethnic-minority armed group
EDC	Electricité du Cambodge (Cambodia)
EEZ	Exclusive economic zone
EIA	Environmental impact assessment
ESIA	Environmental and social impact assessment
EVN	Electricity Vietnam
EXIM Bank	Export-Import Bank (China)
FAC	Foreign Affairs Commission (China)
FALSG	Foreign Affairs leading small group (China)
FLEC	Fisheries Law Enforcement Command (China)
FPA	Foreign Policy Analysis
GAC	General Administration of Customs (China)
GDP	Gross domestic product
GFC	Global Financial Crisis
GMS	Greater Mekong Subregion
GWD	Great Western Development
ILD	International Liaison Department (China)
IR	International Relations
KIA	Kachin Independence Army
KIO	Kachin Independence Organisation
LM-LESC	Lancang-Mekong Integrated Law Enforcement and Security Cooperation Centre
LPRP	Lao People's Revolutionary Party
LS2	Lower Sesan 2 Dam (Cambodia)
LSG	Leading small group (China)
MDB	Multilateral development bank
MEP	Ministry of Electric Power-1 (Myanmar)
MFA	Ministry of Foreign Affairs (China)
MIME	Ministry of Infrastructure, Mines and Energy (Cambodia)
MLEA	Maritime law enforcement agency
MLNR	Ministry of Land and Natural Resources (China)
MNDAA	Myanmar National Democratic Alliance Army
MoA	Ministry of Agriculture (China)

MoD	Ministry of National Defence (China)
MOE	Ministry of the Environment (Cambodia)
MoF	Ministry of Finance (China)
MOFCOM	Ministry of Commerce (China)
MOU	Memorandum of Understanding
MPS	Ministry of Public Security (China)
MSA	Maritime Safety Administration (China)
NDA-K	National Democratic Army-Kachin
NDB	New Development Bank
NDRC	National Development and Reform Commission (China)
NGO	Non-governmental organisation
NLD	National League for Democracy (Myanmar)
NNCC	National Narcotics Control Commission (China)
NOC	National oil company
NPC	National People's Congress (China)
NTS	Non-traditional security
ODA	Official Development Assistance
OOF	Other Official Financing
OSP	Opium substitution programme (China)
PAP	People's Armed Police (China)
PBC	People's Bank of China
PLA	People's Liberation Army (China)
PLAN	People's Liberation Army Navy (China)
RCC	Rivers Coalition in Cambodia
RG	Royal Group (Cambodia)
SASAC	State-owned Assets Supervision and Administration Commission (China)
SCS	South China Sea
SLORC	State Law and Order Restoration Council (Myanmar)
SOA	State Oceanic Administration (China)
SOC	State Oceanic Commission (China)
SOE	State-owned enterprise
SPDC	State Peace and Development Council (Myanmar)
UN	United Nations
UNCLOS	United Nations Convention on the Laws of the Sea
UNODC	United Nations Office on Drugs and Crime
USDP	Union Solidarity and Development Party (Myanmar)
UWSA	United Wa State Army
WTO	World Trade Organization

Introduction

Consider the following three vignettes. First, in 2011, documents found in Tripoli revealed that Chinese state-owned enterprises (SOEs) had agreed to sell US$200 m worth of arms, including rocket launchers and anti-tank missiles, to the embattled Muammar Gaddafi regime. This was in breach of a United Nations (UN) embargo, to which China was ostensibly committed. Beijing's Ministry of Foreign Affairs (MFA) was totally unaware of the arms deal (Zhang 2013). It insisted that it had asked all government agencies to implement the UN resolution, and denied that any contracts had actually been signed or that any weapons had been delivered. However, the anti-Gaddafi rebels claimed that the arms had been supplied and used against rebel forces (Branigan 2011). This naturally damaged China's official policy of improving relations with Libya's National Transitional Council (Branigan 2011; Taylor and Wu 2013).

Second, in September 2014, 200 Chinese People's Liberation Army (PLA) soldiers entered Indian-claimed territory in the western Himalayas and constructed a 1.9 km road. Indian troops challenged them, leading to a two-week standoff. Though such confrontations along the Sino-Indian border are common, this one occurred just one day before China's President Xi Jinping was to meet Indian Prime Minister Narendra Modi in Delhi, the first visit to India by a Chinese leader in eight years, scotching hopes for rapprochement (Burke and Branigan 2014). Many Indian observers questioned China's sincerity, not least because another border incident had occurred shortly before Premier Li Keqiang's visit to India in 2013 (Tiezzi 2014).

Third, consider China's record on nuclear non-proliferation. Since 2006, Beijing has ostensibly supported tightening sanctions on North Korea in response to its nuclear programme. The Ministry of Transport has directed local governments to implement UN resolutions mandating stricter supervision of cargoes and the prevention of trans-shipment to North Korea. China's big four state-owned banks also stopped dealing with North Korea, and China closed its account with North

Korea's Foreign Trade Bank. Following North Korea's third nuclear test in 2013, Beijing abandoned large-scale bilateral economic cooperation, and subsequently Pyongyang was not included in China's Belt and Road Initiative (BRI), nor invited to join the new China-led Asian Infrastructure Investment Bank (AIIB) (Gray and Lee 2018: 122–3). Simultaneously, however, Chinese investment in North Korea increased. From 2003 to 2012, approved investment grew from US$1.12m to US$109.5m, spanning mineral resources, manufacturing, logistics, retail and transportation. Investment only started to decline after 2012, and even then, US$209.1m was officially recorded in the period 2013–17.[1] By offshoring labour-intensive manufacturing, Chinese investors have increasingly integrated North Korean factories into regional and global production networks, boosting apparel exports to China from US$186.42m in 2010 to US$799.3m in 2015, comprising around a third of North Korean exports to China (Gray and Lee 2018: 124–5). Chinese local authorities bordering North Korea have also periodically eased curbs on tourism and trade, cracking down only in response to US pressure (Wong 2017; Daekwon 2018). Unsurprisingly, Beijing has been blasted for undermining UN sanctions, with President Trump tweeting that China had been 'caught red handed'.

These vignettes, though superficially different, each demonstrate inconsistent behaviour in China's foreign and security policymaking and implementation. Indeed, such inconsistent, or even contradictory, international behaviour is very common, including in high-profile issue areas. Yet International Relations (IR) scholars have either ignored or neglected to explain this. Notwithstanding their many differences, all IR approaches view China as a unitary actor in international politics. Consequently, they shoehorn inconsistent behaviour into existing frameworks geared around identifying China's overall, 'real' underlying objectives. Since evidence is mixed, and because the inner workings of China's political system are obscure, observers project the expectations of their preferred theoretical models onto Chinese behaviour.

For example, realists explain the gap between China's formal commitments on North Korean sanctions and their implementation as

---

[1] Much Chinese investment is not officially approved and so is not recorded in government data.

reflecting Chinese grand strategy: in the context of Sino-US geopolitical rivalry, Beijing seeks to avoid North Korea's collapse to maintain a 'buffer' state between itself and American forces in South Korea (Moore 2007; Habib 2016; Kong 2018). However, closer inspection reveals that deepening trade and investment relations with North Korea have actually been driven by profit-seeking companies and individuals based in border provinces seeking to find new markets, or exploit a lower-cost, more disciplined labour force. Their activities are often encouraged and aided by subnational governments keen to boost their local economies. Rather than directing this activity, Beijing has been largely reactive (Gray and Lee 2018: 124–7). Consequently, even relations with North Korea – a neighbouring, strategically critical country – cannot be aggregated into a single, unified Chinese position under tight central control. Rather, they encompass diverse, potentially contradictory activities by a range of actors operating at different scales – local, provincial, national – within the Chinese party-state.

At its core, this book's argument is simple: China's international engagements often exhibit inconsistent or even contradictory behaviour because China today is not a unitary international actor. Decades of state transformation, involving the fragmentation, decentralisation and internationalisation of party-state apparatuses, mean that many Chinese actors, with often differing interests and agendas – including national ministries, regulatory agencies, law enforcement bodies, provincial and local governments and SOEs – now operate internationally with considerable autonomy and limited coordination and oversight. This produces outcomes that do not necessarily reflect top leaders' agendas – which may themselves be unclear. To many China experts, these claims may seem uncontroversial (e.g. Su 2012; Christensen 2013; Shirk 2014: 401; Jakobson and Manuel 2016). Yet IR debates on China's rise have largely ignored their insights, continuing to treat China as a unitary actor (see Hameiri and Jones 2016). This is due to China experts' overwhelming empiricism – their descriptive approach, treating China as a unique case, and their failure to develop theories and frameworks capable of conveying their important empirical insights into IR-theoretical debates. It also reflects IR theorists' failure to develop suitable frameworks for China scholars to use. Our book aims to bridge this gap. We seek to intervene in IR debates over China's rise by developing and deploying a conceptual framework that foregrounds the changes in China's party-state and their international ramifications, building on decades of superb empirical scholarship in China studies.

This research agenda has put us in the peculiar position of being simultaneously criticised by China experts for restating the obvious, and by IR scholars for making outlandish claims about the autonomy enjoyed by Chinese agencies. We have dubbed this 'Schrödinger's China': China is simultaneously 'obviously' fragmented and 'obviously' unitary. This experience only underscores that, in reality, China experts' 'common sense' has yet to connect with mainstream IR debates. Indeed, the gulf between the disciplinary subfields is so profound that it even appears within single volumes: sections on domestic politics discuss fragmentation and multiplicity, but those on international politics revert to treating China as a unitary actor (e.g. Hsiao and Lin 2009; Foot 2013). Another critique we have encountered is that, while the party-state was more fragmented in the past, everything has changed under the 'new Mao', Chinese Communist Party (CCP) Chairman Xi Jinping. Yet, as our case studies show, many pre-existing dynamics persist under Xi. The framework we develop can explain both this *and* the recentralisation observed since 2013.

This book therefore builds on – indeed, could not exist without – extensive empirical research by China specialists, including by authors writing in the Chinese language, but it also surmounts the limitations of this work. It does not merely demonstrate the pluralisation of China's foreign policymaking and implementation processes empirically. Rather, it elaborates a framework that allows us to explain how state transformation processes in China shape China's international engagements and their outcomes in important policy domains. While we focus on China, this basic framework has been applied to several other 'rising powers'; indeed, it could potentially be applied to any state (see Hameiri, Jones and Heathershaw 2019). Our principal aim is thus to reshape the crucial IR debate over the nature and implications of the rise of China and other emerging powers today. Given the real and growing risk of conflict and even war between major powers, this is an urgent and critically important task.

China's Rise: The Misguided Statism of Existing Debates

China's rapid economic rise in the era of 'reform and opening up' is without historical precedent. From 1978 to 2019, China's gross domestic product (GDP) grew from US$218bn to US$14.14tr (IMF 2019). In 2019, China's nominal share of world GDP, at 16.1 per cent, was second only to the US's 24.4 per cent (Statistics Times 2018). In the second quarter of 2020, amid the economic catastrophe accompanying the coronavirus pandemic, China's economy may have even become the world's biggest in nominal terms, at least temporarily, for the first time in two centuries. Measured by purchasing power parity, China has been the world's biggest economy since 2014, accounting for 19.2 per cent of global GDP in 2019 (versus just 2.3 per cent in 1980), against the USA's 15 per cent (IMF 2019). China also contributes 27.2 per cent to global growth, more than any other state, suggesting the nominal GDP gap with the USA will narrow further (Tanzi and Lu 2018). Chinese trade and outbound investment has also boomed. The value of China's trade rose from US$1.02tr in 2000 to US$5.92tr in 2013, making it the largest trading partner for 124 countries (UNCTAD 2018). From 2000 to 2019, China's outward direct investment flows rose from US$2.3bn to US$129.8bn, taking the total stock from US$27.8bn to US$1.94tr (UNCTAD 2001: 298; 2019a: 213, 217). China has also become a major source of development financing, disbursing an estimated US$354.4bn in the period 2000–14, just US$40bn less than the USA (Dreher et al. 2017).

The implications of this astounding economic rise have generated a heated debate among IR scholars, policymakers and the wider public. The IR literature on China's rise is enormous, but the debate has consolidated and stalled around two basic positions. The first, 'revisionist' camp, led by realists, argues that a rising China is intent on harnessing its economic might to expand its national power and ultimately supplant the USA as the dominant global power. The alternative, 'status quo' camp, led by liberals and constructivists, argues that although China dislikes some aspects of the USA-led international order, it has benefited greatly from it and will therefore seek to broadly preserve existing arrangements, even as its power grows.

Unfortunately, ample evidence exists to support both positions (Goldstein 2007). For example, while China has signed the United Nations Convention on the Laws of the Sea (UNCLOS) and incorporated it into domestic law, displaying apparent convergence with international law, Beijing rejected the jurisdiction of a special tribunal in The Hague, established under UNCLOS, to examine the Philippines' challenge to Chinese territorial claims in the South China Sea.

Likewise, while the China-led AIIB resembles other multilateral development banks and thus does not overturn the status quo (Chin 2016; Wilson 2019), other forms of Chinese development financing clearly diverge from, and weaken, global norms, as we discuss in Chapter 4 (see also Hameiri and Jones 2018).

The existence of such discrepant evidence is reflected by disagreements within IR-theoretical schools, as some scholars slide into the 'revisionist' camp and others into the 'status quo' camp. For example, some realists think China is moving to challenge US hegemony, others that it remains weak and can be contained (Mearsheimer 2014a; cf. Kirshner 2012). Similarly, some Marxists detect evidence that China is mounting a counter-hegemonic challenge to the USA and the two states may enter an inter-imperialist war, while others maintain that China is rising within a US-led capitalist system (Arrighi 2007; Callinicos 2009; cf. Saull 2012; Hung 2016). Some liberals and English School adherents argue that China is challenging the liberal global order, others that it is seeking only minor revisions within an order that can survive relative US decline (Friedberg 2005; Chin and Helleiner 2008; cf. Ikenberry 2008; Buzan 2010). Likewise, some constructivists suggest Beijing is being socialised into the prevailing system of rules, others, that Chinese culture entails a revisionist orientation (Johnston 2003; Acharya 2006; cf. Johnston 1998; Kang 2003; Wang, Yuan-Kang 2013).

As neither side has managed to conclusively settle the argument with the available evidence, the debate has stalled and become speculative, turning less on what China is actually doing now than on claims about what it will do or become in the future (Breslin 2013). The content of this speculation is largely determined by scholars' preferred theoretical models, refracted into the worldviews of policymakers and others. For example, because of their 'zero-sum' theorising of international relations, realists see rising powers as naturally revisionist. As rising powers become stronger relative to traditional powers, they will invariably seek to challenge them, while the latter will try to restrain their rivals' rise. This leads 'offensive' realists and power transition theorists to anticipate conflict and war (Gilpin 1981; Kennedy 1988; Mearsheimer 2014b). 'Defensive' realists are less pessimistic: because they assume that states seek security, not domination, they believe that rising powers can be contained by balance-of-power policies (Kirshner 2012). Nonetheless, because all realists expect China to be revisionist, they explain away inconsistent behaviour as only a temporary accommodation with the status quo: Beijing is merely 'biding its time'.

Unlike realists, liberals believe that durable international cooperation is possible when states have shared interests, especially when international institutions lock in mutually beneficial arrangements. They maintain that China has benefited enormously from the US-led, post-war 'liberal international order', with its deep enmeshment in the global economy creating strong incentives to cooperate (Ikenberry 2008; Shambaugh 2013; Gu 2017). Accordingly, they interpret and explain revisionist behaviour by China as merely an attempt to improve its position within the existing order, rather than a 'revolutionary' attempt to overthrow it (Kahler 2013; Ikenberry and Lim 2017).

Because constructivists and English School scholars see rising powers' orientation towards the existing order as rooted in potentially shifting identities and norms, they can more easily fall into either camp in the rising China debate (e.g. Acharya 2011; Loke 2017; Pu 2017). Nonetheless, they fare no better in explaining the co-existence of revisionist and status quo behaviours. For example, while Zhou (2003) explains China's increasingly constructive participation in global nuclear governance by reference to its shifting identity from a 'special nuclear state' to a 'normal nuclear state', this cannot explain why Chinese behaviour actually displays revisionist and status quo orientations simultaneously. Indeed, while China has become increasingly willing to commit itself to nuclear non-proliferation treaties, its nuclear cooperation with countries such as Iran and Pakistan has been undermining the credibility of its promise (Hameiri and Zeng 2020).

Recent rising tensions between the USA and China, especially over trade and technology, have also been understood through this limited debate. For those who already thought China was a revisionist power, the conflict supplies further proof for their original thesis (Friedberg 2018; Mearsheimer 2019). For those on the status quo side, growing geopolitical frictions are largely understood to result from US provocations under the Trump administration (Ikenberry 2018; Fravel et al. 2019). Thus, although rising Sino-US hostility has undoubtedly boosted the revisionist position in Western policymaking circles and beyond, the underlying impasse in the debate has not been resolved.

This selective approach to evidence and paralysed debate reflect a shared weakness of IR approaches: their view of China as a unitary

actor in international politics. This sometimes reflects the generic statism of many IR theories, which simply assume that states are unitary
actors as a basic axiom, and sometimes a perception that China, like the
other so-called BRICS (Brazil, Russia, India and South Africa), is
a 'Westphalian' state, protective of its national sovereignty (Laïdi
2012; Cooper and Flemes 2013). In China's case, this view is reinforced
by its authoritarian, one-party political system, which appears to outsiders as a monolithic, top-down system that ensures coherent, strategic policymaking.

Most IR theories are ontologically predisposed to viewing states as
unitary actors, even those that take account of domestic factors in
policy formation. For mainstream 'third image' theorists like neore-
alists and neoliberal institutionalists, it is unnecessary to consider
states' internal structures as the international system drives all states
to behave in similar ways (e.g. Keohane 1984; Mearsheimer 2014b).
Constructivists may have challenged the idea of states as rational
actors, but they have largely maintained a view of states as coherent
'units' possessing identities as well as interests – even theorising the
state as a 'person' (Wendt 2004). Importantly, even approaches that
ostensibly accept that states are not unitary actors, such as liberalism
and foreign policy analysis, ultimately see states as behaving as such,
after internal contestation is authoritatively resolved into a singular
policy decision (e.g. Putnam 1988; Legro and Moravcsik 1999; Hill
2016). This leaves these IR approaches unable to reckon with contradictory behaviour by states, leading analysts to cherry-pick or interpret evidence in ways that support their preferred theory. Thus, for
realists, for example, Chinese behaviour that seems irrational and
counterproductive – such as investing in white-elephant projects like
loss-making ports – is rationalised as serving a cunning strategic plan:
extending China's strategic reach through 'debt trap diplomacy' (cf.
Jones and Hameiri 2020).

The validity of these statist frameworks has been challenged by
historical sociologists and historians, who have long argued that
empires in Europe, Asia and Africa, including China (as we discuss in
Chapter 1), were administratively decentralised and sprawling, challenging the assumption that the 'units' of international politics have
always resembled the territorialised 'power containers' of IR's nation-
states (e.g. Nexon 2009; Phillips and Sharman 2015). Indeed, territorially bounded Westphalian statehood really only consolidated in

Europe and European settler societies in the nineteenth and early twentieth centuries, spreading globally only with decolonisation after World War II (e.g. Hobsbawm 1987; 1994; Van Creveld 1999; Reus-Smit 2013; Teschke 2003; Sassen 2006). As most IR theories developed in this period of state consolidation, unsurprisingly they have tended to naturalise Westphalian statehood as a trans-historical fixture of international politics (Walker 1993; Buzan and Lawson 2015).

A further challenge to the statism of IR's rising powers comes from studies on contemporary processes of state transformation, which are related to the intensification and deepening of economic globalisation. Many scholars have noted the growing fragmentation of the traditional Westphalian state and the associated rise of novel modes of governance (Sassen 2006). These include, amongst other things: global and multilevel governance (Hooghe and Marks 2003; Rosenau 2003; Coen and Pegram 2018); transgovernmental networks (Slaughter 2004); networked polities (Ansell 2000); 'neo-medievalism' and 'transnational neo-pluralism' (Cerny 2010); state rescaling (Keating 2013); subnational 'paradiplomacy' (Aldecoa and Keating 1999); 'local internationalism' (Massey 2007); and new scalar governance arrangements (Jessop 2002; Brenner 2004). Though varying in their focus and theoretical orientation, these studies share a broad concern with understanding shifts in statehood from Weberian 'command and control' models to more fragmented, networked and regulatory modes of statehood. Such transformations are seen to have blurred the distinction between the domestic and international domains, while greatly expanding the range of state, non-state and intergovernmental actors involved in the making and implementation of policies with international implications, and the variety of modes of governance through which these actors interact with each other across borders (Jayasuriya 2001; 2012).

While not always oblivious to these intellectual developments, the IR literature on rising powers, and on China specifically, has assumed that while state transformations may perhaps have occurred in 'post-Westphalian' regions like Europe, non-Western rising powers have resisted such processes (Sørensen 2004). The latter are typically portrayed as more tightly controlled internally, entailing external resistance to transnational governance and 'a neo-Westphalian commitment to state sovereignty and non-intervention' (Cooper and Flemes 2013: 952). They are 'a coalition of sovereign state defenders', united by the desire to erode 'western hegemonic claims by protecting ... the political sovereignty of states' (Laïdi 2012: 614–15). China has thus been described as a 'unitary, Westphalian state' (Tubilewicz 2017: 933); 'a unitary or monolithic entity' (Taylor 2014: ch. 1); and an authoritarian, top-down system where, '[o]nce the general secretary gives orders, factions salute and do their job with only minimal passive resistance at the margins' (Norris 2016: 49). Accordingly, China is a 'conservative power' (Johnston 2003: 14–15), with a 'rather traditional' approach to sovereignty (Kang 2007: 79), seeking to 'reaffirm sovereignty and internal autonomy against challenges from evolving concepts of human rights, domestic governance, and humanitarian intervention' (Buzan 2010: 14; also Etzioni and Ikenberry 2011; Harris 2014: ch. 3). Even self-proclaimed 'critical scholars' concur that China is a clear case of Westphalian sovereignty in which 'despotic and infrastructural power [are] still deployed within a bounded state territory' (Agnew 2009: 130; see also Rolf and Agnew 2016: 264–5).

For many, therefore, China is actively reversing earlier state transformation trends globally, dragging the world 'back to Westphalia' (Flemes 2013: 1016). As Ginsburg (2010: 27) argues, 'any "Eastphalian" world order will mean a return to Westphalia ... [emphasising] principles of mutual non-interference ... sovereignty, and formal equality of states ... [and] putting an end to the brief interlude of European universalism and global constitutionalism'. This cyclical view of international politics is also reflected in works with titles like 'Will Asia's Past Be Its Future?' (Acharya 2006), and predictions of the international system going 'Back to the Future' (Mearsheimer 1990; Jervis 1991; Auslin 2013). Indeed, some have explicitly argued that, given the nature of its state, China offers 'no viable alternative to the Cold War structure of international relations based on absolute sovereignty, non-interference and traditional power balancing' (Odgaard 2007: 216), with a 'new cold war' thus developing between the USA and China (Shearman 2014), a sentiment endorsed by US Vice-President Pence in late 2018 (in Mead 2018).

China's authoritarian system of government has certainly reinforced this perception that it is a unitary actor. The hierarchical structures of the CCP, which has ruled China since 1949, appear to allow top leaders near-absolute control over all state apparatuses, from Beijing down to the remotest village, while the private sector and civil society enjoy scant political space or autonomy (McGregor 2010). Analysts have thus asked, 'what does China think?' (Leonard 2008), implying that it possesses a single mind, or have attempted to decipher 'Xi's true intentions', implying that China's international behaviour simply reflects one man's wishes (Economy 2018: x). They have also endeavoured to uncover China's 'grand strategy' or 'global strategy' (Johnston 1998; Goldstein 2005; Clegg 2009; Ye 2010; Tellis 2013; Zhang 2015). The party-state is assumed to be so coherent that one observer even suggests it has a 'secret strategy' to supplant US hegemony spanning an entire century (Pillsbury 2014). China is often contrasted favourably to democratic states in this respect: for example, Dan Coats (2020), a former US senator and director of national intelligence, complains that while US policy towards China is driven by short-term political goals, 'the Chinese are clearly pursuing their foreign policy goals according to a carefully calculated long-term strategy'. Thus, for instance, analysts speak of the globalisation of Chinese state-owned and private businesses as a monolithic 'China Inc.' (Fishman 2005), a form of economic statecraft expressing 'effective use of all the cogs in the state's machinery ... it is the Communist Party that provides the score for the orchestra (banks, corporations, diplomats), in order to play out their symphony' (Cardenal and Araújo 2013: 110; see also Holslag 2019: ch. 3). Many studies, and much more policy and popular discourse, portray China's external behaviour as being directed by tightly controlled, highly strategic, clear-eyed, singular intelligence: Xi Jinping as a sort of real-life comic-book mastermind.

This view of China as a monolithic state in both the IR rising powers debate and non-academic discourse is contradicted by decades of research in the subfield of Chinese politics. For instance, despite noting some streamlining under Xi, Shirk (2014: 401) argues that Chinese international behaviour is driven by 'insecure leaders' desperate to maintain economic growth and nationalist support, and a 'dysfunctional policy process dominated by powerful interest groups, many of them within the state itself', often 'parochial' actors which may promote 'international risk taking' for their own 'short term' benefit. For Norris (2016: 46), political decision-making in China, 'as is the case with most other nations ... involves multiple actors, many of which are frequently motivated by their own narrow interests. The result ... is often a seemingly incongruous pattern of foreign policy behaviour'. Christensen (2013: 24, 27–8) likewise states: 'Beijing's foreign policy system seems relatively poorly structured to manage the complex challenges created by China's newfound influence, let alone craft a new grand strategy'; accordingly, 'foreign countries interacting with China ... face a different set of problems than would be posed by a unified and assertive new Chinese strategy'. Su (2012: 504) concurs: 'We cannot treat the Chinese state as monolithic, or "China Inc.", in which everything works in harmony ... The Chinese state's functionality is riddled with competing state agencies, problems of cross-departmental coordination, and mismatch between central and local policies.' China experts also refute the supposed external manifestation of China's allegedly Westphalian state. Carlson (2008: 4), for example, argues that 'Chinese sovereignty is not as unyielding and monolithic as is commonly asserted', while others note the withering of the non-interference principle as Chinese actors move to protect burgeoning overseas interests, becoming embroiled in foreign peace processes, global anti-piracy efforts and peacekeeping missions (Duchâtel, Bräuner and Hang 2014; Parello-Plesner and Duchâtel 2015; Chen 2016; Zou and Jones 2020).

Building on these and similar insights, we argue that a first step in explaining apparent contradictions in China's international behaviour is to drop the unitary actor assumption. Indeed, far from being a Westphalian throwback, the Chinese party-state has undergone considerable post-Westphalian transformations during the reform era, involving the uneven and contested fragmentation, decentralisation and internationalisation of state apparatuses (Hameiri and Jones 2016). Subject to ongoing piecemeal restructuring, central state agencies have reduced in size, and decision-making authority has become fragmented, overlapping and incoherent. Multiple central party and state bodies are responsible for the same policy domain, often with limited direct authority over implementing agencies. State-owned enterprises, for example, remain formally state-owned, but in practice operate with considerable autonomy, especially overseas. To facilitate pro-market experimentation and development, Beijing has also decentralised responsibilities to subnational governments (Ang 2016). Over time, this generated '*de facto* federalism' (Zheng 2007), with extensive centre–local bargaining occurring throughout the policy formation and implementation process. Party-state apparatuses have often also internationalised, as formerly domestic agencies have increasingly acquired international roles, typically with limited central oversight: provincial governments now control their foreign economic relations, signing international treaties to promote local economic interests; SOEs have been encouraged to 'go out' from the late 1990s, with some becoming major global actors; regulators have joined transnational regulatory bodies; and law enforcement agencies have internationalised to manage transnational security problems, like piracy and narcotics. Indeed, where dynamics of fragmentation or decentralisation intersect with internationalisation, as occurs in many policy domains, China no longer operates as a unitary actor internationally.

However, as we elaborate in Chapter 1 and demonstrate in the following case studies, what has emerged is not an anarchic free-for-all, but a dynamic and evolving 'Chinese-style regulatory state' (Jones 2019). Central leaders rarely control outcomes directly, but primarily use mechanisms to 'steer' other actors in the wider party-state in favoured directions. This involves issuing broad policy guidelines and establishing coordinating mechanisms, like 'leading small groups' (LSGs) or Central Party Commissions, as well as attempting to audit subordinates' conduct. In turn, subordinates engage with policymaking and implementation by influencing, interpreting and, more rarely, ignoring central directives, injecting their own interests and agendas into the process (Jones 2019). This enables conduct that would be inexplicable using approaches that expect all domestic contestation to end once an authoritative foreign policy decision is made.

This approach does *not* imply that we consider the top Chinese leadership or central agencies to be powerless or weak. Senior leaders retain important mechanisms, primarily via the CCP, to rein in subordinate actors that stray too far from their intended policies, or produce adverse outcomes. They can discipline or purge cadres, issue tighter guidelines and recentralise authority. They also use party doctrines, like 'Xi Jinping Thought' or the 'three represents', to promote ideological coherence among cadres, officials and wider society. Xi has been the manipulator *par excellence* of these mechanisms – though none of them are new. Moreover, these mechanisms can never fully eradicate the problems associated with the party-state's fragmentation, decentralisation and internationalisation. Accordingly, though the Chinese party-state may, in some cases, operate coherently to implement leaders' wishes, the policymaking and implementation process often generates outcomes that were neither foreseen nor desired by central leaders, prompting further attempts to rein in subordinates, clarify guidelines, or recentralise authority. Chinese foreign and security policy is shaped by these ongoing complementary or competitive interactions between actors within the transformed party-state, which are never decisively resolved (Jones 2019). Thus, China's party-state is 'fractured': it is neither a smoothly unified whole, nor a collection of broken pieces. Our model, described in Chapter 1, seeks to explain the full spectrum of policy outcomes, from behaviours that approximate unitary agency to those approximating radical fragmentation, and, more commonly, everything between these extremes.

However, in this book we are not only interested in understanding how Chinese policy outputs emerge, as in Foreign Policy Analysis frameworks, but also in explaining their outcomes, which are produced through the interactions of China's transformed party-state with other states and societies. Our case studies focus on Chinese engagements in Southeast Asia. International Relations scholars typically argue that rising powers' influence and challenge to the established order are felt first in their nearby regions (Friedberg 1993; Buzan and Wæver 2003). Accordingly, China's conduct in East and Southeast Asia is seen to portend how it will behave when it becomes powerful enough to project its power globally (Breslin 2009), making the region an unparalleled 'laboratory' for understanding China's rise. Existing IR studies typically emphasise Southeast Asia's strategic reactions to intensifying Sino-US rivalry, focusing on 'hedging' tactics vis-à-vis China, responses to the US 'pivot' to Asia or Trump's 'America First' approach, or the Association of Southeast Asian Nations' difficulties in managing regional order (e.g. Goh 2013; Foot 2014; Kuik 2016). Yet, just as China is not monolithic, nor are the states that Chinese actors engage. Different socio-political forces react differently to different Chinese practices: while some accept and support Chinese initiatives, others contest and resist them. Hence, the outcomes of China's international engagements are shaped both by China's state transformation processes in particular policy domains, and by how these dynamics interact with struggles for power and resources in recipient societies. Actors in these other societies, especially the powerful interests represented in ruling coalitions, play a pivotal role, even in ostensibly weak and impoverished states like Cambodia and Laos, often seen as China's closest allies in Southeast Asia (Rice and Patrick 2008; Ciorciari 2015; Pang 2017).

As discussed in Chapter 1, this research focus has produced a methodological innovation in the study of China. We could only understand how state transformation is shaping China's rise through in-depth case studies. This involved several research trips and over 100 interviews with individuals and groups in Beijing, Shanghai, Haikou (Hainan province) and Kunming (Yunnan province), plus Myanmar, Laos and Cambodia. Although we were able to gain some access to interviewees in China with good knowledge of particular policy domains, the Chinese party-state is notoriously opaque, especially at the highest levels of government, a challenge that has worsened under Xi Jinping. However, the party-state's internationalisation provides novel opportunities to learn about its inner workings, because more – and more accessible – foreign actors are interacting with Chinese party-state officials. By interviewing these individuals, we gained insights that would have been virtually impossible to obtain within China itself. This 'outside-in' method provides a useful way to unpack the Chinese 'black box' amid intensifying secrecy and repression.

Structure of the Book

Following this introductory chapter, Chapter 1 elaborates our theoretical and methodological approach. Building on Gramscian state theory, we trace the rise of a powerful, though divided, cadre-capitalist class from 1978, and the associated, uneven and contested fragmentation, decentralisation and internationalisation of China's party-state. Having sketched these wider dynamics, Chapter 1 describes a model for understanding how power is exercised in the Chinese-style regulatory state that has emerged, and how this shapes the making and implementation of Chinese foreign and security policies. Finally, we explain our method and case selection, and respond to predictable challenges to our argument – that China's state transformation is nothing new, and that recentralisation under Xi Jinping has made the state transformation argument outdated.

The next three chapters provide detailed case studies that use our theoretical framework to explain the outcomes of Chinese foreign and security policies. To demonstrate the broad applicability of our approach, we have chosen cases from both so-called high politics and low politics. Chapter 2 examines Chinese engagements in the South China Sea (SCS). This is often portrayed as one of the world's most dangerous geopolitical hotspots, where great-power war could begin (Kaplan 2014; Taylor 2018). China has increasingly militarised its SCS territories while confronting Southeast Asian claimants, and the USA and its allies have stepped up military assistance to the latter and intensified naval patrols. The SCS thus appears to be a prominent 'traditional' security issue, touching directly on military matters and questions of territory and sovereignty, where IR scholars would typically expect central states to retain tight control. Yet, we show that for decades Chinese policy has been steered only loosely by exceedingly vague sovereignty claims and slogans, permitting a host of fragmented, decentralised and internationalised actors to jockey for power and resources around this issue. Although this has enhanced China's dominance in the SCS, it has also generated unanticipated and undesirable conflicts with neighbouring states and their allies, and damaged China's wider foreign policy goals. Xi's recent efforts to discipline these various actors and recentralise control have gradually imposed greater order, though not without resistance, and at the price of empowering hawkish elements within the Chinese-style regulatory state.

Chapters 3 and 4 develop the state transformation approach to its fullest extent by considering how Chinese activities intersect with forces within Southeast Asian societies. Chapter 3 examines Chinese efforts to manage 'non-traditional' security (NTS) issues in the Greater Mekong Subregion (GMS). Issues of NTS like climate change, pandemic disease, transnational terrorism and organised crime have become increasingly prominent on the security agendas of many states and international organisations in recent decades, and will likely become even more so following the devastating COVID-19 pandemic. As NTS threats easily traverse borders, they are widely seen to require novel forms of transnational cooperation, including efforts by powerful states to extend their governance frontier into territories where threats originate, and to network state apparatuses into new transboundary regimes (Hameiri and Jones 2015). Reflecting the Westphalian optic of IR theory, rising powers like China are typically seen as blocking progress on NTS issues given their absolute commitments to state sovereignty (e.g. Patrick 2010). Conversely, we show that, as China's economy has transnationalised, intensifying NTS problems and China's vulnerability to them, Beijing's 'noninterference' stance has softened and Chinese actors are increasingly extending their reach beyond China's borders to manage NTS problems.

Chapter 3 focuses on the challenges of illegal narcotics and associated criminal activity, particularly banditry on the Mekong river.[2] China's 'reform and opening up' have re-exposed its population to drug flows from the golden triangle. Chinese agencies have moved to tackle this problem at source by sponsoring opium substitution programmes and transboundary law enforcement projects in Laos and Myanmar. The outcomes of these interventions are shaped by how Chinese party-state transformation dynamics interact with sociopolitical conflicts in these target states. The key actors involved in governing this security problem are, on the Chinese side, local governments and companies with primarily pecuniary motives, and, on the recipient side, state security forces and (in Myanmar's case) ethnic-minority armed groups. These interests have skewed counter-narcotics governance towards profiteering, generating considerable social unrest while failing to resolve the underlying NTS challenge.

The transnationalisation of Chinese corporate actors has also exposed them to political instability and criminal activity, necessitating a response from the party-state. In the GMS, the main focus has been banditry affecting Chinese shipping along the Mekong. In response, Chinese law-enforcement agencies have extended their governance frontier into the GMS, spearheading riverine patrols to make the Mekong safe for Chinese capitalism. These patrols have recently been institutionalised into a new Chinese-led international organisation.

Chapter 4 examines Chinese development financing (DF). China's rapidly growing DF portfolio is widely assumed to be a form of economic statecraft, directed at achieving geostrategic objectives (Cardenal and Araújo 2013: 151; Reilly 2013). However, as so often, no conclusive evidence has emerged to show that China is using DF either for revisionist purposes or in line with the status quo, with evidence available on both sides (Hameiri and Jones 2018). Chapter 4 shows that state transformation has profoundly shaped DF policymaking and implementation. Thanks to state fragmentation, authority and policymaking are contested among central agencies, producing weak oversight for implementing SOEs, which primarily seek pecuniary benefits with scant regard for official Chinese diplomatic goals,

---

[2] Legally speaking, piracy only occurs on the high seas. Banditry is the preferred term for riverine criminality.

militating against the coherent, strategic direction of flows for geopolitical or diplomatic ends.

The impact of Chinese DF turns on the interaction of these dynamics with host-state structures and struggles, as we demonstrate through case studies of hydropower dam development in Cambodia and Myanmar. We show that projects are not strategically directed from Beijing, but emerge 'bottom-up' from lobbying by SOEs and recipient governments, while China's fragmented DF governance regime permits widespread malpractice. However, final outcomes vary starkly across the two cases given the very different recipient societies. In Cambodia, Chinese DF was managed by a dominant-party regime in ways that bolstered its domination, generating warmer ties with Beijing. In Myanmar, however, socio-political fragmentation meant that similar projects exacerbated social conflict and even sparked renewed civil war, prompting a crisis in bilateral relations.

Our concluding chapter summarises and elaborates on our findings. This is the first book to systematically study how state transformation dynamics shape China's external relations; consequently, it has an exploratory character, seeking to understand how this plays out in different policy areas. The Conclusion reflects on overall patterns, seeking to discern when we might expect more or less coordinated/ fragmented behaviour on China's part. Our case studies show that the answer cannot be whether an issue concerns 'high' or 'low' politics, as considerable fragmentation abounds in both. Nor can questions of geography or the presence of 'core' interests explain variation. Rather, we suggest that the alignment of important interests, coupled with the specific institutional arrangements within the party-state, are the key issues. This hypothesis can be tested as part of a longer-term research agenda.

The Conclusion also provides broad policy recommendations for those seeking to engage China. Many foreign governments, international organisations, civil society actors and businesses increasingly worry about China's rise and its impact on them; this is manifesting in growing hostility towards Beijing in various ways. While we agree that Chinese behaviour is often troubling, our analysis shows that it is wrong to assume that it is always the result of an intentional grand strategy. Accordingly, responding to China as a monolithic entity is misguided and counterproductive. Instead, a more sophisticated approach is needed, which recognises the multiplicity of actors and interests operating within specific issue areas, and engages in ways that support those pursuing more positive outcomes.

Finally, although this book was researched and mostly written before the COVID-19 pandemic, the Conclusion offers some tentative thoughts about how our framework might explain these events.

1 | *State Transformation and Chinese Foreign Policy*

If we want to understand China's international behaviour, we have to open the black box ... State authority is fragmenting, more and more actors are involved in the making of foreign policy, and implementing it. Authority is increasingly decentralised, and the players are increasingly internationalised.

> Researcher, Chinese Ministry of Public
> Security (Interviewee A32 2018)

This chapter sets out the three main vectors of state transformation – the fragmentation, decentralisation and internationalisation of state apparatuses – and theorises their impact on China's foreign relations, establishing the framework that we deploy in the following empirical chapters. We argue that China's state transformation has shaped, and been shaped by, the post-1978 shift from the Maoist command economy to a capitalist economy. After describing the party-state's transformation, we theorise how Chinese foreign policy 'works' in this new era. Rather than arguing that central authorities have simply lost power, we explore *how* power is exercised within the transformed party-state. We argue that a Chinese-style regulatory state has emerged, wherein top leaders rarely control state outputs directly, but rather seek to 'steer' and coordinate a diverse array of actors towards often vaguely defined ends (Jones 2019). The mechanisms they use include the promulgation of party doctrine; speeches and slogans; the Chinese Communist Party's (CCP) powers of appointment, appraisal and discipline; discretionary fiscal and policy concessions; and coordinating institutions. In turn, however, actors within the disaggregated party-state and state–society complex may influence, interpret or even ignore central directives. Political outcomes depend on evolving struggles for power and resources within the Chinese-style regulatory state, which may involve both complementary and competitive interactions between actors within different agencies and located at different territorial scales. These struggles are rarely, if ever, decisively resolved, but continue throughout, and strongly influence, the implementation of foreign and security policies. Moreover, they interface with struggles for power and resources in other societies. These dynamics generate outcomes that are often at odds with what top Chinese leaders anticipated or desired. The chapter then discusses methodological issues and rebuts two predictable objections to our argument: that state transformation is nothing new in China, and that the re-centralisation of policymaking under Xi has made a state transformation approach redundant.

First, however, we must clarify our conceptualisation of the state. There are several ways to theorise state transformation, corresponding to different state theories (vom Hau 2015). Ours is rooted in Gramscian state theory (Gramsci 1971), as developed by Poulantzas (1978) and Jessop (1990; 2008). From this perspective, states are not separate from society, as in Weberian political science (Cammack 1989; Mitchell 1991). States are condensations of social relations and conflicts rooted in evolving political-economy contexts. State institutions' form, evolution and operation are bound up in struggles for power and control over resources among socio-political groups, especially classes and class fractions. State apparatuses are never neutral: they always distribute power and resources unequally across social groups and, accordingly, they are always the site of – sometimes ferocious – political struggles. Moreover, states' institutional forms are always more accessible to some forces pursuing certain strategies than others – an attribute that Jessop (2008) calls 'strategic selectivity'. A corporatist institution, for example, provides routinised access for labour unions and business owners; a business advisory council does not. Accordingly, socio-political forces seek to mould state apparatuses in ways that advance their and their allies' interests and agendas. Social forces' evolving composition and power, and their alliances and strategies, thus generate efforts to reshape state institutions, to advance or stymie emerging interests and agendas. Their efforts are often contested by those standing to lose out. What emerges from these struggles is what we label 'state transformation'.

Importantly, this approach does not see states as necessarily unified entities. On the contrary, different state apparatuses may have different relationships with different social groups and, reflecting this, are frequently at odds with one another. As Migdal (2001: 20) puts it:

The sheer unwieldy character of states' far-flung parts, the many fronts on which they fight battles with groupings with conflicting standards of behaviour, and the lure for their officials of alternative sets of rules that might, for example, empower or enrich them personally or privilege the group to which they are most loyal, all have led to diverse practices by states' parts or fragments ... [These] have allied with one another, as well as with groups outside, to further their goals ... [producing outcomes] often quite distinct from those set out in the state's own official laws and regulations.

Certain political forces may struggle to cohere a state's 'far-flung parts' but, as Jessop argues, this 'cannot guarantee its *substantive* operational unity. For the state is the site of class(-relevant) struggles and contradictions and rivalries among its different branches'. Accordingly, rather than presupposing the state's coherence, 'we must examine the different strategies and tactics that state managers develop to impose a measure of coherence on the activities of the state', and trace their political effects (Jessop 2008: 36–7). This makes a Gramscian approach far more useful for analysing the impact of the fragmentation, decentralisation and internationalisation of state apparatuses on foreign policy than traditional International Relations (IR) or Foreign Policy Analysis (FPA) approaches, which typically assume either that states are unitary actors or that internal contestation ultimately resolves into a 'decision' that then authoritatively determines all of the state's subsequent activity (see Jones 2019: 581–3).

The Social Basis of China's State Transformation

From a Gramscian perspective, to understand the Chinese party-state's transformation we must first grasp the socio-economic changes undergirding it. The fragmentation, decentralisation and internationalisation of China's party-state are bound up with the post-1978 'reform and opening up' process: the contested transition from Maoist state-socialism towards capitalism, within the carapace of a one-party regime. This has produced a colossal shift in power towards the fractious 'cadre-capitalist' class that now dominates the Chinese polity.

Maoism's disastrous failures led, from 1979, to a dramatic pro-market passive revolution (Wang, Hui 2011).[1] Notwithstanding

---

[1] For Gramscians, a passive revolution involves a fundamental shift in socio-political relations without mass participation, that is, one imposed 'from above'. See Hui (2016).

continued doctrinal adherence to 'socialism', the CCP embarked on piecemeal reforms that, gradually and with stumbling reversals in the face of sporadic opposition, dismantled key aspects of China's command economy and unleashed market forces. Through the 1980s, local governments were permitted to experiment with pro-market reforms (Ang 2016). Foreign investment was courted, and China's seaboard was inserted into global markets as a site for low-cost, labour-intensive production, becoming the 'factory of the world' after China's World Trade Organization (WTO) accession in 2001. In the 1990s and early 2000s, small and medium-sized state-owned enterprises (SOEs) were privatised, while larger ones were consolidated and 'corporatised' – shorn of their previous social welfare responsibilities and turned into profit-oriented entities under arms-length control. The private economy quickly boomed, already comprising around two-thirds of GDP and 80 per cent of growth by 2000 (Fan 2000). SOEs' share of industrial output fell from 78 per cent in 1980 to just 16 per cent by 2015, while their share of urban employment declined to just 11 per cent (Lardy 2018: 333–4). From 2000, Chinese enterprises were encouraged to 'go out', sending outbound investment surging, from US$2.3bn in 2000 to US$129.8bn by 2019, taking China's total stock of out-bound investment from US$27.8bn to US$1.94tr (UNCTAD 2001: 298, 309; 2019a: 213, 217).

This remarkable transformation has occurred within, and thus been powerfully mediated by, an authoritarian one-party regime, producing a dominant bourgeoisie that has largely emerged from within, and remains interpenetrated with, the CCP. Local CCP leaders exploited the reform process to privatise state assets into the hands of themselves and their relatives and/or clients (Oi 1999; Dickson 2003). The continued vagueness of private property rights, coupled with enduring political control over capital allocation and the judiciary, also allows officials considerable discretion to advance allied business interests (Zhang, Jun 2010: 53–4). This has led to the strong permeation of state and private capital, with SOEs owning an estimated quarter of private firms, while many SOEs have private shareholders, and CCP committees are present in both private and state companies (Goodman 2014: 75; see also Huang 2008; McGregor 2010). Coupled with extensive land-grabbing by local governments, China's reforms have thus entrenched a highly predatory mode of local governance and extensive corruption, with political, bureaucratic and judicial power routinely used to support particular business interests (Pei 2016).

Since 1978, the party-state has morphed around the emerging capitalist class, through mounting constitutional recognition and protection of private property and the market, as well as President Jiang Zemin's 'three represents', an ideological contortion which admitted businesspeople into the CCP and, subsequently, legitimised their direct incorporation into state structures (Liu 2011: 58; see also Dickson 2008). A third of businesspeople, including the 500 richest individuals, quickly joined the CCP after Jiang's reforms (Li 2009: 20). By 2003, fifty-five businessmen sat in the National People's Congress (NPC), the national legislature, while businesspeople also comprised 17 and 35 per cent of the membership of local legislative and consultative bodies, respectively (So 2013: 62–3). By 2012, 160 of China's 1,024 richest people were NPC members or in a prominent advisory group (So 2013: 63). The net worth of the seventy richest NPC members exceeded US$89.9bn, vastly exceeding the combined wealth of the richest 600 US officials, at US$7.5bn (Bloomberg 2012a). President Xi's own family's assets reportedly total US$1bn (Bloomberg 2012b), while former premier Wen Jiabao's top US$2.7bn (Barboza 2012).

The emergent business class now manifests in practically every party-state agency, from local governments and national ministries to party organisations and universities, all of which pursue profit-making activities. Even the People's Liberation Army (PLA) 'has become one of China's largest business conglomerates' (So 2013: 58–9), while the CCP's own party schools engage in marketised competition and money-making schemes, bringing 'market forces into the party' (Lee 2017: 90). As Goodman (2014: 66) observes, 'cadres have become embourgeoisied and ... capitalists have been politicized'. Through this dramatic transformation, social and political power has shifted from workers and peasants, the bedrock of Mao's regime, towards a narrow elite – perhaps 3 per cent of the population (Goodman 2014: 90–1) – variously described as a 'cadre-capitalist' (So 2013), 'bureaucratic capitalist' (He 1998), or 'crony capitalist' class (Pei 2016; see also Wang, Hui 2011). Some scholars suggest that 'the government was "kidnapped" by corporate power' (Zhang, Jun 2010: 9–10), or even posit an 'enterprise-owned state' in place of the state-owned enterprise (Groombridge, in Chen 2009: 255). Though exaggerated, these descriptions capture the stark shift in the state's class basis, the rise of powerful politico-business interests, and the Chinese party-state's dependence on maintaining capital accumulation in order to survive.

Although overlapping business and political elites now form a tight alliance against challenges from below, including the increasingly faint prospect of democratisation (Chen and Dickson 2010), this class is not a unitary actor. Rather, it is highly fractious, factionalised and internally competitive. Given its interpenetration with different parts of the party-state, this manifests in struggles within and among state apparatuses. Through the 1980s and early 1990s, local governments exploited their newfound freedoms to launch private enterprises, erecting trade and investment barriers against their rivals that approached those between sovereign states, shattering the national command economy into rival 'economic dukedoms' (Zhou 2010: 202–3; see also Zheng 2004: 111–12). Despite central efforts to abate this competition, local protectionism and project duplication remain rampant, creating vast industrial and infrastructural overcapacity. The 2004 airport construction 'war', for example, means that China now has more airports per square kilometre than the US (Zhou 2010: 207). This 'transformation of the local state', Pei (2016: ch. 6) argues, has entailed the 'privatisation of state power'. Xi's anti-corruption campaigns have revealed dense state–business networks, with local elites – as senior as provincial party secretaries – running competing 'mafia states' (Pei 2016: Introduction). Moreover, the highly uneven insertion of parts of China's economy into global flows of investment, production and trade has generated a 'substantial degree of internal (regional) heterogeneity': 'regional styles of capitalist development ... remain distinct from one another, and [are] deeply networked into a range of [different] global production networks, and "offshore" economies' (Zhang and Peck 2016: 52; see also Mulvad 2015). In coastal areas in particular, foreign capital has become an important social base for the regime, with a documented influence on policy outcomes (Hui and Chan 2016). Conversely, the cadre-capitalist class in more economically backward, landlocked regions tends to be more domestically oriented, with interests in protecting uncompetitive domestic industries or predatory cross-border ventures in the infrastructure and extractive sectors (Hameiri, Jones and Zou 2019). Alliances can also span several scales, localities and state institutions, such as the powerful 'petroleum faction' headed by former internal security tsar Zhou Yongkang, which Xi spectacularly dismantled in 2014–15.

Recent anti-corruption campaigns reflect the regime's struggle to maintain societal consent in the wake of China's passive revolution from Maoism to authoritarian capitalism. Urban resistance to predatory reform manifested in the 1989 Tiananmen uprising, with brutal repression required to restore order and advance marketisation (Wang, Hui 2011). Subsequently, peasant resistance to land-grabbing and labour unrest also increased sharply. This has yielded some concessions, like the legalisation of trade unions, the creation of tripartite institutions to address workers' grievances and the modest expansion of social welfare (So 2013: ch. 5; Goodman 2014: chs. 5–6; Chan and Hui 2017). However, the CCP has cultivated the urban middle class as its main social base. Reflecting its origins in state-led development and its direct and indirect dependence on state employment, China's middle class is largely pro-authoritarian, albeit increasingly desirous of 'good governance'. The CCP has thus been spurred to curtail corruption, deepen the 'rule of law', promote urban consumption and develop bourgeois ideology, like Xi's 'China dream' and the pursuit of 'national development' (So 2013: ch. 3; Goodman 2014: 25–7, ch. 4; Brown 2018: 48–9, 57–8, 116). Coupled with the cadre class's particular interests, and the need to maintain mass employment, this generates an overriding imperative to maintain rapid economic growth. Chinese nationalism is also broadly promoted, while dissent is policed through the coercive promotion of ideological conformity and mounting state surveillance and repression.

The Transformation of China's Party-State

These epochal social, political and economic transformations have been facilitated by – and, in turn, have further spurred – deep, unprecedented changes in the form and operation of the Chinese party-state. These changes are frequently interrelated, but for analytical purposes, we distinguish three main vectors: fragmentation, decentralisation and internationalisation. Our account concisely synthesises decades of scholarship by Chinese politics specialists documenting the emergence of 'fragmented authoritarianism' (Lieberthal and Oksenberg 1988). We then draw out the implications for China's foreign affairs.

Fragmentation

Fragmentation refers to the horizontal dispersal of power and authority across multiple agencies at a given governance scale. Fragmentation is not entirely new in China. Prior to the communist revolution, Chinese territory was highly fragmented between competing warlords and armies. Afterwards, governance was reorganised into three pillars: the party, the military and the state. Although the party also penetrates military and state agencies, this 'stove-piping' led to frequent coordination problems. Nonetheless, fragmentation intensified considerably after 1978 through the piecemeal reform of party-state agencies in pursuit of capitalist transformation.

The numerical proliferation of party-state agencies clearly conveys growing fragmentation and struggles to manage the coordination problems arising therefrom. In 1979, China had around thirty-five national-level agencies. This ballooned to around 100 by 1981, as well as over forty coordinating bodies. Abolitions and mergers in 1982 yielded only modest results: by 1986 there were seventy-one agencies and sixty coordinating bodies. Subsequently, the number of agencies was cut to sixty-five, but only through decentralising some government functions and corporatising SOEs – as discussed further below (Gong and Chen 1994: 70–3). The 1990s saw a more concerted effort, with many economic ministries abolished or transformed into SOEs, more SOEs being corporatised and a super-ministry absorbing several agencies to spearhead market reforms, reducing the total number of ministries to twenty-nine (Zheng 2004: 91–106). However, following Xi Jinping's latest reshuffling of state apparatuses in March 2018, China still had twenty-six ministries and forty-seven other ministerial-level agencies (Economist 2018), while the committees designed to coordinate these – typically known as 'leading small groups' (LSGs) – numbered over eighty (Johnson, Kennedy, and Qui 2017).

This constant reform of party-state apparatuses has created many overlapping jurisdictions. For example: as of 2011, eleven different national-level agencies had some jurisdiction in maritime governance; eleven were involved in energy matters; and forty-one had some role in counter-narcotics (Meidan, Andrews-Speed and Xin 2009: 596–97; ICG 2012: 8; China Anti-Narcotics Network 2015). Since units with equal bureaucratic rank cannot issue binding instructions to one another, this creates enormous scope for interagency conflict and for party-state apparatuses to operate at cross purposes.

Leading small groups are intended to solve this coordination problem, but their sheer proliferation indicates their limited efficacy. Their remits frequently overlap, making it unclear which LSG should resolve problems or formulate policy. For instance, thirteen LSGs deal with external affairs and security, nine in the party and four in the state (Johnson, Kennedy and Qui 2017). As Lampton (2015: 767) wryly comments on such coordinating bodies, 'they too need coordination'! Furthermore, LSGs do not sit 'above' other agencies; unless they are chaired by individuals ranked above those they seek to coordinate, they cannot issue authoritative 'decisions', but operate by consensus. This often results in loose policy frameworks that try to accommodate competing actors, enabling them to pursue their own interests in practice. Even when LSGs do make decisions, particular agencies must still implement them and may drag their feet or interpret orders in unintended ways. Naughton (2016: 41) argues that the proliferation of LSGs chaired by Xi himself, far from securing centralised control, has actually made 'policy-making ... more erratic', with continued struggles among implementing agencies rendering outputs 'fragmentary, disappointing, and ... incoherent', with key decisions 'frequently not [being] implemented' (Naughton 2016: 41, 43). Where conflicts among rival agencies become critical, they may be referred upwards, typically to the State Council (China's cabinet), the CCP Politburo or its Standing Committee, or even the CCP Chairman. However, these heavily overloaded generalists prefer lower-level units to work out their differences. In practice, this leads to the toleration of considerable pluralism among party-state agencies.

Marketisation and SOE corporatisation have also fragmented authority. Corporatisation involves SOEs being removed from direct ministerial control and turned into quasi-autonomous firms that must generate profits to survive and to advance their employees' careers, especially those of senior managers, who are often ambitious party apparatchiks. While corporatised SOEs dominate strategic sectors, and many have become major global players, their regulation is fragmented and weak. In 2003, centrally owned SOEs were placed under the State Council's State-owned Assets Supervision and Administration Commission (SASAC), which primarily seeks to maximise state assets' value, strengthening SOEs' profit-seeking orientation. Some SOEs and/

or their 'private' subsidiaries are listed on national and international stock markets, making them also answerable to private shareholders. The Ministry of Commerce (MOFCOM) and the National Development and Reform Commission (NDRC) also have some jurisdiction over SOEs' international activities, while other regulators and ministries seek to regulate SOEs in their particular sectors (Pearson 2005). Complicating matters further, because some centrally owned SOEs were formerly government ministries, their chairmen retain vice-ministerial rank, giving them extensive access to state power and the ability to defy all but the most senior officials (Zhang, Jun 2010: 142–5). This fragmented oversight gives SOEs enormous practical autonomy, especially when operating overseas, including the capacity to violate Chinese policies, laws and regulations in the pursuit of profit (Jones and Zou 2017).

Decentralisation

Since 1978, power and control over resources have also been extensively devolved to subnational agencies. Again, while some decentralisation did occur previously, its contemporary extent is unprecedented under CCP rule. Under Mao, the Chinese state became heavily centralised after decades of territorial fragmentation. There were several experiments with decentralisation: from 1957–8, as part of the Great Leap Forward, and from 1964–71 as part of the 'third front' campaign and the Cultural Revolution. However, these experiments were limited and disastrous, resulting in rapid re-centralisation (Joffe 1994; Zhao 1994). Provincial governments functioned largely 'as a conduit for central decrees' (Donaldson 2010: 22–3), and had to seek Beijing's approval for even such petty matters as making purchases over RMB100 (Zhao 1994: 26). By 1978, the central government thus dominated a hierarchical, command-and-control system through the physical planning of production, centralised resource allocation and SOE ownership, leaving 'little room for . . . local governments to function autonomously' (Gong and Chen 1994: 69–70).

After 1978, however, power and resource control were significantly decentralised to promote China's economic transformation. In the 1980s, local governments were permitted to establish 'private' enterprises and local markets, generating an entrepreneurial boom involving many local officials (Huang 2008). Coastal areas were allowed to create experimental special economic zones, trialling market reforms that subsequently spread nationwide. Subnational legislatures were empowered to adapt national laws to local conditions, while provincial governors – who rank alongside government ministers and consequently cannot be directly instructed by them – gained majority control over resource allocation, investment and SOE management (Gong and Chen 1994: 77–9). Responsibilities for vast swathes of public policy were also decentralised, including the economy, education, health, rural and urban construction, security and the judiciary (Chen 2005: 191).

As noted above, local leaders exploited these opportunities to pursue 'their own political and economic agendas rather than following orders from Beijing ... sometimes in open defiance of the top leadership' (Lieberthal 2004: 297–8). Crucially, the appointment of all personnel below the rank of vice-governor was decentralised in 1984, with each local party-state tier empowered to make appointments to the one beneath it (Gong and Chen 1994: 79). Theoretically, local agencies belonging to line ministries are accountable to both the national ministry and the local leadership. In practice, because the latter control their appointment and career prospects, their loyalty is predominantly to local party-state bosses (Zhong 2003: 79–85). In some cases, local state reforms have also delinked subnational and national institutions, further weakening Beijing's control (Gong and Chen 1994: 74–5). This has allowed local party chiefs to create 'independent kingdoms' by packing party-state apparatuses with kin and business associates, facilitating the widespread sale of offices, looting and crony capitalism, with officials enjoying 'the latitude to disobey higher administrative authorities or to drag their feet in implementing the centre's policies' (Zhong 2003: 61; see also Pei 2016).

By the early 1990s, power had decentralised to such an extent that scholars were identifying 'a nascent form of federalism' (Zhao 1994: 29–31), or even the 'deconstruction' of the Chinese state (Goodman and Segal 1994). However, the partial re-centralisation of fiscal control in 1994 and of some governmental functions in the 2000s re-centralised power somewhat, while President Xi's anti-corruption purges and the tightening of party discipline have also reined in some of the worst local abuses. Moreover, decentralisation remains uneven, with some provinces exercising considerable practical autonomy while others, like Xinjiang, are kept on a much tighter leash due to fears of social unrest (Cornago 1999: 45). Nonetheless, local governments retain enormous formal and informal authority, resources and leeway to interpret and adapt central directives, making Zheng's (2007) description of China's political system as '*de facto* federalism' still not too far-fetched. Certainly, the provinces are no longer simply conduits for the central government's will. On the contrary, vast amounts of research shows that they frequently: pioneer policies without central authorisation; lobby central authorities vociferously for political and economic concessions; warp central policies to suit local interests; and ignore and defy central regulations and instructions (e.g. Oi 1999; Zhong 2003; Zhou 2010; Hameiri, Jones and Zou 2019). Arguably, China's polity is best described as a complex form of multi-level governance, where vertical bargaining and contestation characterise the entire policy process, from inception through to implementation, and where inter-scalar conflict is common, in a constant power struggle among different party-state tiers (ten Brink 2013).

This continues even under Xi, despite his superficial appearance of omnipotence. For example, local authorities in Liaoning province have clearly colluded in the violation of international sanctions on neighbouring North Korea – sanctions which Xi notionally supports (Wong 2017). Local governments have also defied central instructions to cease illicit borrowing to finance infrastructure spending, with just six provinces borrowing RMB15.4bn (US$2.5bn) in the fourth quarter of 2017 alone (Wang and Cheng 2018). They have also ignored Xi's direct instructions to cut industrial capacity and reduce pollution to meet China's international climate change obligations (Chen 2017). Far from being ruthlessly punished, as one might expect, the recalcitrant are often bargained with and even rewarded. For instance, Hebei province ignored central government instructions to cut steel overcapacity from 2014 to 2017, prompting threats of punishment, but this actually led to a negotiated agreement on capacity reduction backed by US$8bn in central grants to help modernise the sector and offshore polluting factories (Holslag 2019: 120–1).

Crucially for our purposes, provincial governments are now empowered to manage their own foreign economic relations. Before 1979, the central government had total control over foreign trade and investment. However, by 1992, control was extensively decentralised (Zhang and Zou 1994: 155–8; Chen 2005: 192–3). Subnational governments subsequently developed their own foreign affairs and commerce bureaus, notionally accountable to both the national Ministry of Foreign Affairs (MFA) and MOFCOM and local leaders but, in practice, primarily responsive to the latter. These units now engage in 'paradiplomacy', striking deals with foreign governments as far afield as Africa (Chen and Jian 2009; Chen, Jian and Chen 2010; Li 2014). Local governments have also developed their own Overseas Chinese Affairs Offices and Taiwan Affairs Offices, which in some provinces are larger than their foreign affairs bureaus (Cheung and Tang 2001; Swaine 2001). The Special Administrative Regions of Hong Kong and Macao have enjoyed even greater autonomy in conducting their 'external affairs' (Shen 2016), though Hong Kong's autonomy has been curbed substantially of late, following years of anti-Beijing protests. Subnational governments have become leading actors in new regional bodies and even developed their own international cooperation mechanisms. For instance, Yunnan province (joined by Guangxi Zhuang Autonomous Region in 2005) was China's lead representative in the Asian Development Bank's Greater Mekong Subregion from 1992, and launched the Bangladesh–China–India–Myanmar cooperation forum in 1999, which it is now developing further as part of the Belt and Road Initiative (BRI) (Summers 2013: 87–93). Guangxi has promoted its own rival grouping, the Beibu Gulf cooperation forum, since 2006, which has also been incorporated into the BRI (Li 2010: 302–3).[2] As one MFA researcher laments, these provinces now 'compete with each other' to cultivate trade and investment partnerships with Southeast Asian states (Interviewee A02 2017).

Some scholars suggest that this subnational paradiplomacy, being 'perfectly integrated' into national diplomacy, 'almost completely avoids controversies' (Cornago 1999: 45; see also Cabestan 2009: 87; Ptak and Hommel 2016; Tubilewicz 2017). The reality is quite different. Reflecting the tight imbrication of state and business power, subnational governments are primarily concerned to promote local economic interests. They have little understanding of or regard for China's wider foreign policy objectives or the diplomatic context. As an analyst under the State Council states, 'our central leaders [may] have an idea [about foreign policy], but if you talk to enterprises or

---

[2] For a survey of other provincial subregional initiatives, see Lokshin and Shkurko (2014).

local governments, they don't care ... not all of them understand the meaning of President Xi's words ... They are more concerned about direct, short-term benefits ... their economic benefits' (Interviewee A25 2018). Moreover, although foreign affairs bureaus may try to 'lead ... other departments also fight for leadership', and since local governments' priority is 'local development ... how to make use of [national] policy to serve the local economy', commerce bureaus typically dominate in practice (Interviewee A16 2018). Accordingly, as Lampton (2001a: 19) argues, decentralisation means that 'Chinese behaviour may ... be predatory or unmindful of international rules'. Although local and national interests and agendas may align in some cases, producing smooth policy implementation, where they do not, local agency often generates 'problems for [the] national government ... [it] creates turmoil and sends a very bad signal to the outside world' (Interviewee A25 2018).

For example, as discussed in Chapter 3, Yunnan province has supported the expansion of Chinese businesses into neighbouring Myanmar, including rapacious extractive investments and illicit deals with ethnic-minority rebel groups, violating Chinese regulations, generating widespread anti-Chinese sentiment and sparking a bilateral diplomatic crisis in 2011 (Hameiri, Jones and Zou 2019). As we show in Chapter 2, Hainan province has backed its fishing industry to expand into the South China Sea, along with tourism operations, causing tensions with other claimant states (ICG 2012: 22, 10). In 2013, a major Sino-Ghanaian spat emerged after just one Chinese county from Guangxi had promoted the relocation of over 30,000 gold miners to Ghana, who then engaged in widespread illegal and environmentally devastating mining, causing a huge domestic political backlash. Guangxi officials tried to protect the miners from deportation, contributing to a bilateral crisis that 'threatened many of China's diplomatic objectives' (Hess and Aidoo 2016: 322–3). Provinces have even undermined national policy on key issues, sometimes compelling Beijing to change tack. For instance, when the central government imposed de facto economic sanctions on Taiwan in the late 1990s, Fujian officials refused to implement them; by 2004 the central government had shifted to a policy of economic inducement (Norris 2016: chs. 6–7, esp. 123–7). Similarly, during the 1997–8 Asian financial crisis, the central government rejected a policy of devaluation to curry favour with Southeast Asian neighbours, but provinces adopted 'defiantly creative' responses, like subsidising exports and hoarding export earnings overseas, which eventually forced Beijing to implement capital controls, outraging foreign governments (Moore and Yang 2001).

Chinese regions' uneven integration into different transnational investment, production and trade networks generates contrasting outlooks and interests among local elites, complicating national policymakers' efforts to create a coherent external affairs framework (Interviewee A02 2017). By the 1990s, eastern seaboard provinces were already displaying a more internationally oriented outlook than the 'conservative' less-developed regions (Goodman and Segal 1994). This entails conflicting preferences on particular issues. For example, on the South China Sea, the relatively underdeveloped Hainan province stridently promotes sovereignty claims to benefit its fishing and tourism industries, but free-trading Shanghai is more interested in maintaining open sea lanes (Interviewees A10 2018). As a State Council analyst claims:

Chinese east coast provinces ... have similar values to South Korea and Japan, because they rely on international markets and are richer, [but inland provinces] have much less interaction with international markets ... [and] have less willingness, or could not understand very well why a positive relation between China and outside countries is important to their interests. (Interviewee A25 2018)

Since 'the gap between these groups has widened' due to uneven capitalist development, 'it's very difficult to coordinate these different levels' (Interviewee A25 2018).

Internationalisation

Internationalisation involves domestic agencies acquiring an international presence or function, thereby increasing the number of actors involved in a country's international relations. Diverse Chinese agencies which 'were originally established to implement domestic policies ... now play a foreign policy role. They have almost no knowledge of the diplomatic landscape and little interest in promoting the national foreign policy agenda' (ICG 2012: 12).

This is an even more novel development than fragmentation or decentralisation. Under Mao, 'tight central control over foreign affairs at all levels was maintained' (Cheung and Tang 2001: 93). Scholars generally concur that Premier Zhou Enlai monopolised Chinese foreign policy under Mao's close direction (Lu 2001; Teiwes and Sun 2008: 85; Gong, Men and Sun 2010). Asked about internal policy debates in this era, one top MFA official retorted: 'What policy debate? It was just a matter of doing what Mao decreed' (cited in Teiwes and Sun 2008: 85). Institutionally and substantively, Chinese policy was narrowly focused until the 1980s, initially on supporting allied revolutionary movements through party-to-party relations, and later on combating Soviet 'hegemonism'. Remarkably, by 1967 China had just one ambassador serving overseas (Brown 2018: 35).

Institutionalised contact with foreign actors vastly increased and pluralised in the reform era. From 1978 to 1999, the number of states with which China had established bilateral relations increased from 113 to 161, while its membership of international organisations and international non-governmental organisations increased from 21 to 52 and from 71 to 1,163, respectively (Lampton 2001a: 20). To manage these international relationships, 'all central ministries and agencies' – and their subnational counterparts – have established 'international units', which now liaise directly with foreign actors (Harris 2014: 28).

The MFA, never a particularly strong institution,[3] has seen its notional monopoly over foreign policy eroded substantially, as economic and functional agencies gained an international role (see Table 1.1). Crucially, none of these agencies are subordinate to the MFA. In the Chinese political system, one unit may only command another if it is inferior in terms of its bureaucratic rank and if it exercises direct leadership authority over it (see Figure 1.1 and Table 1.2). The MFA cannot therefore give direct instructions to any other ministerial-level agency, which includes provincial governments. As with many other national ministries, the MFA does not directly command subnational offices in charge of foreign affairs; they instead answer to local governments. Moreover, as a state institution, the MFA cannot control the various party organs involved in foreign affairs.

This makes it effectively impossible for the MFA to coordinate, let alone formulate, Chinese foreign policy. As one MFA scholar laments: 'the MFA is not strong enough to manage our foreign affairs ... It has

---

[3] Its pre-eminence under Mao reflected the fact that Premier Zhou served concurrently as foreign minister. Since then, the MFA has been led by individuals ranked far lower in the party-state hierarchy.

Table 1.1 *Party-state agencies involved in China's international affairs*

Agency (abbreviation)	Role in China's international affairs
State institutions	
Ministry of Foreign Affairs (MFA)	Primarily responsible for formal diplomatic relationships.
Ministry of Commerce (MOFCOM)	Primarily responsible for China's foreign economic relations including inbound and outbound trade and investment, China's foreign aid programme and the regulation of SOEs overseas.
National Development and Reform Commission (NDRC)	Approves large-scale foreign investments. Primarily responsible for international climate change negotiations. Lead BRI agency.
People's Bank of China (PBC)	Regulates China's currency including its internationalisation. Participates in the Basel Banking Commission, which regulates global finance.
Ministry of National Defence (MoD)	Has relations with other states' defence establishments.
Ministry of Public Security (MPS)	Responsible for law enforcement cooperation and border security.
Ministry of Finance (MoF)	Defines budgets for other departments, e.g. foreign aid. Sets tariffs policy, influencing international trade.
Ministries of Culture and Education	Involved in international efforts to cultivate 'soft power'.
Other functional ministries	Engaged in international cooperation/regulatory arrangements. Seek to regulate overseas SOEs in their areas.
State-owned enterprises (SOEs)	Invest and trade overseas; implement development financing/aid projects.
State-owned Assets Supervision and Administration Commission (SASAC)	Regulates SOEs, including those operating overseas.
Taiwan Affairs Office	Oversees all relations with Taiwan.
Subnational governments	Provincial governments manage their own foreign economic relations. All subnational governments promote and regulate local SOEs and private firms' internationalisation.

Table 1.1 *(cont.)*

Agency (abbreviation)	Role in China's international affairs
Military institutions	
People's Liberation Army (PLA)	Enjoys extensive bilateral defence ties including inter-military hotlines. Various branches engaged in international defence cooperation, maritime law enforcement and border security. NB: not under MoD command.
Party institutions	
International Liaison Department	Responsible for international party-to-party relations. Traditionally dominant in relations with other communist states.
Department of Propaganda	Involved in international efforts to cultivate 'soft power'.
Overseas United Work Front	Involved in cultivating overseas influence, particularly through the co-optation of 'overseas Chinese'.

Note: Excludes coordinating bodies, which are discussed separately.
Sources: Lampton (2001b); Cabestan (2009); Jakobson and Knox (2010); Christensen (2013); Harris (2014); Lai and Kang (2014); Shirk (2014).

a fake role. Others have their own ways' (Interviewee A02 2017). Sometimes the MFA is not even aware of other agencies' activities until they cause diplomatic crises that the MFA must then try to defuse. For example, in 2009 when Chinese ships harassed USNS *Impeccable* in the South China Sea, the MFA initially denied the presence of PLA Navy vessels, apparently being misled by the Ministry of Agriculture, whose coastguard units were also present (US Embassy 2009). The then US Assistant Secretary of State for the Asia-Pacific describes 'often' having to 'work carefully behind the scenes' with his Chinese counterparts 'to untangle the mess created by nationalist and poorly coordinated elements' (Campbell 2014). Similarly, the MFA had to repair bilateral relations with Myanmar after 2011, when the unscrupulous and sometimes illegal activities of Yunnanese agencies and allied SOEs plunged ties with China into crisis (Hameiri, Jones and Zou 2019).

Table 1.2 *Spatial and bureaucratic hierarchy in the Chinese state*

Bureaucratic rank	Spatial tier				
	National	Provincial (provinces, provincial-level municipalities, autonomous regions, special administrative regions)	Prefectures	County (rural)/District (urban)	Town/Township/Village
1 (highest)	State Council				
2	Commission				
3	Ministry	Provincial Government			
4	Bureau		Prefectural Government		
5	Department	Provincial Government Agencies		County/District Government	
6	Office				Town Government
7			Prefectural Agencies		
8				County/District Government Units	
9 (lowest)					Town-Level Functional Units (rare)

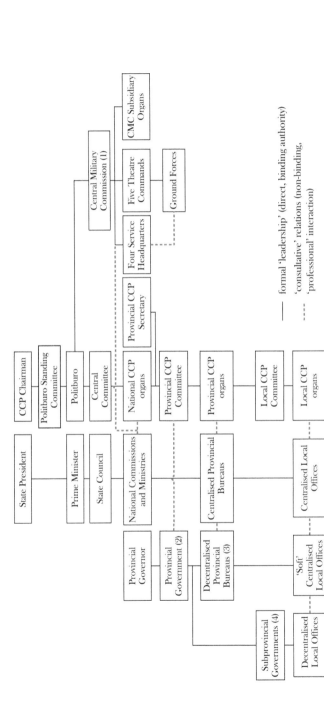

Figure 1.1 The Chinese party-state

Notes

1. The state Ministry of Defence must try to cooperate with the Central Military Commission and its organs.
2. Provincial level units include provinces, provincial level municipalities, autonomous regions, special administrative regions.
3. The vast majority of subnational units are decentralised.
4. Subprovincial units include (in descending rank order) prefectures, counties/districts, towns, townships, villages and hamlets. The division between centralised, 'soft' decentralised and decentralised units is mirrored down to the town level.

An exhaustive survey of all the actors and activities involved in China's foreign affairs would require its own book, but a few key examples are illustrative. The PLA is clearly the most prominent agency. Organisationally, it is subordinate only to the top party leader through his chairmanship of the Central Military Commission (CMC), making it autonomous from state control – a source of constant friction (Lampton 2015: 765). Since 2004 the PLA has acquired 'new historic missions' associated with China's burgeoning transnational economic relations, including counter-piracy, counterterrorism, and the protection of overseas Chinese nationals and assets, which increasingly clash with the MFA's traditional insistence on non-interference in other states' internal affairs (Duchâtel, Bräuner and Hang 2014; Parello-Plesner and Duchâtel 2015; Ghiselli 2021). The PLA is also increasingly involved in multilateral institutions like the ASEAN Regional Forum and the Shanghai Cooperation Organisation, and participates in joint training exercises, extensive military-to-military exchanges and institutionalised defence dialogues with major foreign powers, while also maintaining hotlines to the US and Russia (Li 2010). The navy is frequently seen as particularly freewheeling, giving limited or no notice of foreign patrols or military tests and being backed by a large 'navy lobby' of industrialists and academics, which constantly demands more power and resources and promotes an expansionist foreign policy (Harris 2014: 33, 36; Yung 2015). The PLA also maintains close ties with the arms industry. Cabestan (2009: 75) argues that arms exporters 'tend to follow their respective interests and do not always toe the government line', as exemplified by the Libyan deal mentioned in the Introduction of this book.

Chinese functional agencies have also joined transnational governance networks to manage transboundary issues, particularly those affecting China's capitalist development. These quiet forms of international cooperation typically continue during political or even military tensions. For example, China's environmental agency (now a ministry) has networked with Japan and South Korea since 1999, collaborating on issues like earthquakes and marine pollution, and similar cooperation was launched with the Philippines, Thailand and Indonesia in 2007 (Li 2010: 297–8). China's civilian maritime agencies joined the North Pacific Coastguard Forum in 2004, participating in joint exercises and actions against drug trafficking and illegal migration (Li 2010: 299). China's Ministry of

Transport has also become involved in maritime security initiatives, implementing the US-led Container Security Initiative, and joining the Regional Cooperation Agreement on Combating Piracy and Armed Robbery Against Ships in Asia in 2004 (Ho 2009). Chinese agencies have provided capacity-building support to states around the Malacca Straits, previously a piracy hotspot (Khalid 2009: 432). Chinese and ASEAN phytosanitary regulators are also engaged in transboundary cooperation to harmonise standards and integrate systems relating to the assessment, monitoring and control of animal and plant diseases (Wang 2016). Yunnan health officials joined the Mekong Basin Disease Surveillance network in 2008, designed to build pandemic preparedness and response capacity and implement the World Health Organization's Asia Pacific Strategy for Emerging Diseases. The network has tackled transboundary outbreaks of dengue fever, typhoid, avian influenza and swine influenza, and deployed teams to Myanmar after Cyclone Nargis (Long 2011).

In some cases, Chinese agencies have extended their own 'governance frontier' beyond China's borders to manage transboundary problems. As detailed in Chapter 3, since 2011 China's Ministry of Public Security (MPS) has coordinated and led multinational patrols on the Mekong River to combat banditry and drug trafficking, as well as training and equipping neighbouring states' police forces and mounting joint law enforcement operations. This culminated in December 2017 with the formation of a new MPS-led international organisation, the Integrated Law Enforcement and Security Cooperation Centre. Local governments and agribusiness enterprises in Yunnan province have also worked in Myanmar and Laos to reduce opium production.

As in other states, Chinese agencies sometimes pursue internationalisation as a way of strengthening their hand against domestic rivals and promoting further state transformation to advance their interests and agendas. For example, MOFCOM, the NDRC and other reformist agencies used China's WTO accession to promote deeper marketisation, against the resistance of protectionist interests in local governments and SOEs (Pearson 2001). Similarly, the People's Bank of China (PBC) has joined the Basel Banking Commission, a network of central banks regulating global finance, promoting the implementation of the Basel Banking Accords to liberalise domestic banking, in an (unsuccessful) attempt to overcome opposition from the Ministry of Finance and others keen to retain government control over credit allocation (Brehm and Macht 2004). Similarly, China Investment Corporation, a corporatised sovereign wealth fund, led in the development of the Santiago Protocols, which govern sovereign wealth funds, to 'lock in a purely commercial orientation' against those seeking to use it for political purposes (Norris 2016: 218). In such cases, state apparatuses' internationalisation may spur further, potentially contested, rounds of state transformation, as domestic institutions are reconfigured to implement international obligations. For example, a 'vast bureaucracy' was created across fourteen agencies to comply with the Montreal Protocol, though this was resisted by the MPS, whose local bureaus 'derived substantial income' from polluting activities, until it received compensatory funding (Economy 2001). China's accession to the Financial Action Task Force's global anti-money-laundering regime was also promoted by reformists to reorient state institutions, but resistance from vested interests has again slowed implementation (Heilmann and Schulte-Kulkmann 2011).

Perhaps the most prominently internationalised elements of China's party-state are the many SOEs that have gone abroad, backed by local governments and often accompanied by Chinese workers. Initially, SOEs were developed, typically under functional ministries, to pursue domestic developmental goals. However, after being corporatised and outgrowing domestic markets, they have increasingly internationalised, particularly since 2000 when the government formally encouraged them to 'go out'. Having previously operated exclusively within the domestic party-state, in a sheltered market, many SOEs lack international experience, commonly develop corrupt relations with local officials to further their business objectives, have scant knowledge of or respect for China's wider diplomatic goals, and pursue profit ruthlessly, often competing ferociously against one another (Jones and Zou 2017). As latecomers to foreign markets, they are often forced to operate in riskier locations shunned by investors from developed economies, and thus often become embroiled in environmental degradation, forced displacement and other negative activities (Wang and Zadek 2016). Although SOEs are actually quasi-autonomous, profiteering entities, they are widely seen as arms of the Chinese government, turning corporate expansion into apparent evidence of Chinese 'imperialism', and corporate malfeasance into sometimes-serious diplomatic crises (Gill and Reilly 2007; Jones and Zou 2017).

These situations may be exacerbated by the uneven internationalisation and conflicting objectives of other subnational and national agencies, as discussed fully in Chapter 4. As mentioned, local Chinese governments often disregard the potential negative impacts of their SOEs' overseas activities. The policy banks that usually finance SOE-led projects have no capacity to inspect these to ensure regulatory compliance, and nor do regulators concerned with matters like forestry and environmental protection. The only regulatory agency with an international presence is MOFCOM, which staffs the economic offices in Chinese embassies. However, MOFCOM personnel primarily see their role as promoting Chinese business's expansion, not curbing its excesses. They also generally outclass the embassies' MFA representatives, treating them as 'problem-solvers' when diplomatic frictions emerge from corporate malpractice (Bräutigam 2009; Corkin 2011).

Theorising Foreign Policy amid State Transformation

The Chinese party-state is clearly not a unitary actor. Since the 1980s, it has become unevenly fragmented, decentralised and internationalised and, reflecting the different societal (especially class-fractional) interests imbricated with the party-state's different elements, it is conflict-ridden, with different parts sometimes pursuing contradictory agendas. If IR's unitary actor assumptions cannot hold, what theoretical model can we use to explain China's external relations? This section surveys but rejects existing approaches before developing the Chinese-style regulatory-state model, which is used in the remainder of this book.

The Limits of Existing Approaches

Why have mainstream IR scholars (i.e. those who are not China specialists) been able to ignore four decades of scholarship on the transformation of the party-state and its clear implications for China's external relations? Beyond the resilience of simplistic unitary actor models, the answer is that sinologists have mostly been confined to a China studies silo, either neglecting entirely to theorise their insights or trying to apply inappropriate theoretical models derived from mainstream IR and FPA.

Many China experts are empiricists: they do not theorise their insights, treating them implicitly as *sui generis*, writing descriptively, and largely for fellow specialists. Accordingly, treatments of China's state transformation and foreign policy are overwhelmingly descriptive-empirical, containing little or no theory building or application (see Liu and Teng 2006; Song and Zhang 2015). Even the most innovative work – including major inspirations for this book – is atheoretical, describing but not theorising state transformation's impact (Lampton 2001b; Hao and Lin 2007; Su 2007; Li 2012; Wang 2012). Implicitly, developments are treated as unique manifestations of China's peculiar reform process, neglecting parallel state transformation processes found in many other contexts (see Hameiri, Jones and Heathershaw 2019). Naturally, this has limited the exposure of China specialists' empirical insights to a wider audience.

Where China scholars do deploy theory, they have had to rely upon frameworks that neglect state transformation, such as Putnam's (1988) 'two level games', or bureaucratic politics models drawn from FPA (e.g. Zhong and Wang 2007; Lai and Kang 2014; Long 2016). These approaches, while usefully foregrounding the domestic constitution of foreign policy, still problematically assume that internal contestation always resolves into a singular policy, which then determines the entire state's behaviour. In neoclassical realism, this function is performed by a 'foreign policy executive' (Taliaferro, Lobell and Ripsman 2009; Ripsman, Taliaferro and Lobell 2016), while for liberals this role falls to pluralist state institutions (Solingen 2009). Deviation from top leaders' decisions is understood merely to involve technical problems with policy communication and implementation (Brighi and Hill 2012). This neglects the potential for serious incoherence under contemporary conditions of state transformation.

Recently, a few scholars have started to recognise the importance of state transformation, and to lament its neglect in IR/FPA. Alden and Aran, for instance, rightly criticise FPA for having 'no *theory of the state*, no meaningful incorporation of the systemic changes provoked by *globalization*', and thereby incorrectly presenting states 'as given and timeless, subject to no more than incremental change' (2012: 91–2, emphasis added). Similarly, Hill (2016: 86, 101) admits that changes in statehood have created 'new problems of coordination and control', with the risk of foreign policy being 'splintered by powerful internal elements running their own line' (see also Webber and Smith 2013:

35–7). However, such recognition is rare and has not been followed by the development of new theoretical models. This reflects FPA's primary focus on explaining foreign policy 'decisions', which rules out in advance any incoherence or contradictions among state apparatuses. For instance, Hill quickly banishes the spectre of 'splintered' policy by defining foreign policy as *intrinsically* involving 'coherence' and 'coordination', generating 'purposive action, on behalf of a single community' (Hill 2016: 4–6, 295). Therefore, he simply dismisses the possibility that state apparatuses might act autonomously, or that foreign policy could fail or generate undesired outcomes due to poor coordination (Hill 2016: 206, 238ff, 298–9, 108). Hill insists that decision-making groups remain small – around twenty people – and that foreign ministries or government leaders are 'ideally placed' to coordinate these smoothly, theorising the process using a traditional bureaucratic politics model (Hill 2016: 80–1, 102–9). Similarly, despite recognising the broadening of the foreign policy domain, Webber and Smith (2013: ch. 3) cling to existing FPA models without amending them to incorporate state transformation.

This simply does not capture the complex realities of foreign policy amid state transformation. As many aforementioned examples show, in China, different elements of the party-state often operate at cross-purposes, even under the notional guidance of central policy frameworks. Moreover, far from following a 'bureaucratic politics' model, whereby differences are resolved authoritatively into a binding 'decision', national-level policy frameworks are frequently vague and imprecise – 'Delphic pronouncements', as Fingar (1987: 212) puts it. As Lampton (2001a: 21) remarks, '[s]ometimes, the central government may not even "know" what "it" wants'. This allows for – indeed, it actually requires – interpretation by diverse actors, with bargaining and contestation occurring throughout the shaping *and* implementation of policy.

Alden and Aran are more inventive, sketching several ideal types. In 'clustered states' (Western states that pool sovereignty, capabilities and policymaking), 'agency exists at multiple sites and involves numerous players', whereas in 'institutional states' (traditional Westphalian/Weberian states), foreign policy elites remain autonomous, using 'policy tools that accompanied the rise of the modern state' (Alden and Aran 2012: ch. 5; see also Robertson 2012). However, they provide no theoretical guidance on how 'clustered states' operate. Moreover, IR/

FPA scholars who recognise state transformation's existence generally see it as limited to Western countries; China would inevitably be characterised as an 'institutional state'. Hill's (2016: 243) description of China as a 'highly centralised country' whose political structure 'ensures top-down decision-making' exemplifies this misunderstanding.

A New Model: The Chinese-Style Regulatory State

A new framework is therefore necessary. In building it, we must avoid overly simplistic, binary positions. Much scholarship on Chinese policymaking essentially falls into two camps: one emphasises the processes we collectively identify as state transformation, and the problems arising therefrom; the other emphasises the central government's continued power and control. *Either* power has dispersed to diverse actors at multiple scales, *or* the central government remains dominant. Since China's central government clearly *can* exercise considerable power, this binary framing privileges the latter position, marginalising evidence of incoherence and reasserting traditional notions of statecraft and grand strategy. It also facilitates a dismissive approach to evidence of fragmentation, as those presenting it are easily caricatured as claiming that the Chinese party-state is in total chaos.

We surmount this sterile debate about *whether* China's central government has 'lost' power by focusing on *how* power is exercised in the transformed party-state. Our claim is emphatically not that top leaders have 'lost control' of foreign policy. Rather, we suggest that their means of control are qualitatively different to the Maoist era's top-down, command-and-control mechanisms, or FPA's bureaucratic politics models. We argue that a Chinese-style regulatory state has emerged, wherein top leaders use a range of mechanisms to define broad policy platforms and steer a diverse array of actors towards often loosely defined goals. These other actors may respond by seeking to *influence* policy frameworks, *interpret* them, or *ignore* them. We therefore see policy formulation and implementation as shaped by ongoing complementary or competitive interactions between different actors, which are never resolved decisively into a binding decision or singular policy, but continue throughout the entire process. This is a dynamic model, emphasising evolving power struggles, rather than a static one, which seeks to identify whether power is concentrated or dispersed. Rather than assuming the state's unity, it responds to the Gramscian imperative to 'examine the different strategies and tactics that state managers use to impose a measure of coherence on the activities of the state' (Jessop 2008: 36–7), and traces effects to the contested reception of these measures. Thus, our model can account for instances where policy implementation and outputs appear highly coherent or entirely fragmented, but also for the more common range of options between these extremes.

Politics in the Regulatory State

We begin by specifying how political conflict and coordination has changed through state transformation. Traditionally, states are understood to function through a top-down system of control: senior leaders make a decision, which cascades down the state apparatus to be implemented. In this model, central authorities command and control subordinates directly to secure desired policy outcomes – 'positive coordination'. While never problem-free, this model broadly prevailed under Mao. In a regulatory state, however, power and resources are far more dispersed, and central government shifts to 'negative coordination', elaborating broad regulations and guidelines designed to steer a diverse array of public, private and hybrid actors towards generally defined ends (Majone 1994; Jayasuriya 2001). Several studies of Chinese economic policymaking chart the emergence of regulatory statehood (Pearson 2005; Collins and Gottwald 2011; Hsueh 2011). They show that national ministries no longer make authoritative decisions on investment, production and distribution, but rather set broad guidelines for SOEs and private entities. We argue that China's external policy operates through similar processes.

The shift to regulatory statehood implies a qualitative change in the nature of political struggles. In command-and-control systems, political competition focuses on capturing the commanding heights of the state apparatus. In regulatory states, conflict is more diffuse, focusing on the formation of national-level policy guidelines, and their further interpretation and implementation (Jarvis 2012; Rosser 2015). First, actors may seek to *influence* central guidelines to advance their sectional interests and agendas, through direct participation in policy planning or coordination bodies, or indirect approaches like lobbying. National foreign policy guidelines are shaped by these struggles, reflecting actors' strategies, power, resources and access to decision-making processes. Crucially, we cannot assume that this contestation resolves into a clear, final and binding decision. National-level guidelines may be left broad and vague, particularly when competing interests make incompatible demands, the stakes appear low and/or coordinating agencies cannot resolve conflicts decisively. Moreover, in regulatory states, central guidelines typically require subsequent interpretation by diverse actors tasked with implementing them. We also cannot assume that central coordination mechanisms are effective. These mechanisms are themselves potential sites of contestation and their impact depends on constant political struggle. Accordingly, state coherence is always 'tendential ... failure is an ever-present possibility' (Jessop 2008: 47).

Second, actors may struggle or bargain over the implementation of national guidelines, reflecting their own interests and agendas. Two broad strategies exist. First, actors might simply *ignore* or not implement national guidelines, possibly even 'going rogue' and pursuing their own policies instead. This is likely only when the costs of open defiance are low, for example, when disaggregated actors are stronger than those seeking to coordinate them, or the stakes are limited. Second, and probably more commonly, agents may *interpret* national guidelines in ways that serve sectional interests. Where guidelines are closely specified, and/or where material or political support is needed from central authorities, actors may reframe their existing preferences and programmes as expressions of central directives. This will be easier where guidelines are general or vague, where the actors concerned participated in their formulation, or where coordinating agencies are relatively weak. This may generate outcomes that diverge substantially from central actors' original intentions. Hence, they may react by struggling to intensify policy coordination and control, as we explain in the following section.

Thus, state transformation has shifted the policy process away from 'activating a "chain of command" towards ... "coalition building" where politics is central'; it becomes 'a continuous act of negotiation on several fronts, with no final resolution of the central issues' (Webber and Smith 2013: 87, 102). We are less interested in seeking a potentially non-existent final decision than in tracing how contending interests within the Chinese-style regulatory-state shape the policymaking and implementation process, from inception to outcome.

The Chinese-Style Regulatory State

How do these dynamics play out in China? We identify the existence of a Chinese-style regulatory state because, although regulatory statehood has emerged across the world, as Gramscian state theory emphasises, each state has peculiar features, reflecting its imbrication with its own unique social formation. Because China's passive revolution and state transformation have occurred within a one-party regime, the central government retains authoritarian controls absent in Western regulatory states. Moreover, the emergence of truly independent regulators has been contested by vested interests, resulting in continued political interference, regulations skewed towards dominant economic interests and frequent legal and regulatory violations (Pearson 2005; Hsueh 2011; Jones and Zou 2017).[4] This section outlines the politics of regulatory statehood in China, beginning with the steering mechanisms available to top leaders, then describing how influencing, interpreting and ignoring work in practice.

If Chinese leaders no longer use command-and-control systems to control party-state power, how do they exercise power today? We identify five coordinating mechanisms: party doctrine; broad policy statements; coordinating institutions; fiscal and policy concessions; and the CCP's powers of appointment, appraisal and discipline. These are described in detail, and their various limitations identified.

The first steering mechanism is ideology, specifically the use of CCP doctrine. Party doctrine articulates in broad terms the leadership's worldview, main political objectives and desired mode of rule. It can define general policy and political goals, help instil a common purpose and language among cadres, officials and wider society ('unify thought' in official CCP jargon), and promote loyalty among subordinates (Heath 2018: ch. 6). Doctrine, therefore, can help cohere the party-

---

[4] Importantly, this does not demonstrate that China does not (yet) have a regulatory state (cf. Hsueh 2011). This misconception stems from a Weberian approach to state theory, which establishes ideal types and then measures deviations from these. Critical scholars have long pointed out that even in the ideal-typical Western regulatory states, regulation is systematically biased towards the interests of large-scale capital, with regulatory capture and a 'revolving door' between regulators and regulated being commonplace. For Gramscians, this interpenetration of powerful social forces with state apparatuses is considered to be routine; the analytical task is not to chart compliance/deviation with idealised models but to understand and explain how specific state apparatuses actually function in practice.

state's thinking and activity. In the reform era, doctrinal changes have often been used to steer China's development and grapple with the challenges resulting from capitalist transformation. Deng Xiaoping's 'socialism with Chinese characteristics' opened the door to economic reforms and marketisation, while Jiang's aforementioned 'three represents' welcomed China's new capitalists into the party. Hu Jintao's 'scientific outlook on development' and 'harmonious society' sought to direct effort towards redressing the social ills arising from China's unequal economic development, as part of the CCP's wider shift from 'a revolutionary to a governing' party (Heath 2018: 2). Xi Jinping has deployed doctrine more forcefully than any post-Mao leader. His 'Xi Jinping Thought on Socialism with Chinese Characteristics for a New Era' calls for re-centralising power in the CCP and in the hands of Xi himself. Incorporated into China's constitution in 2018, its propagation has been relentless, with cadres and military personnel being tested for their familiarity with the doctrine. It is taught in schools, universities and workplaces, and displayed widely in public spaces and online. It has also internationalised, most notably in the work of the CCP's secretive United Front Works Department to shape discourse and policies in other countries, including by intimidating critics (Joske 2020).

However, it is important not to overestimate the coherence of CCP ideology or its efficacy in determining Chinese behaviour. This mistake is often made by those who depict ideology as the key driver of Chinese conduct, portraying China as a static monolith driven by an 'underlying Marxist-Leninist-Stalinist-Maoist logic [which] remains the same' as under Mao (Garnaut 2019). However, the evidence provided in this book and elsewhere suggests that official ideology is not uniformly adhered to. Chinese leaders presumably recognise this; otherwise, their relentless efforts to reinforce CCP doctrine would appear superfluous. Moreover, recent doctrinal changes have created 'a much more porous filter than Maoism permitted', admitting diverse intellectual influences (Heath 2018: 42). There is considerable ideological diversity within the party and among China's intellectual elites, with liberalism, neo-authoritarianism, the 'new left', democratic socialism and Confucianism all jostling for influence (Shambaugh 2013; Mulvad 2018; Pan and Xu 2018; Veg 2019), notwithstanding the narrowing of space for open debate under Xi (Lam 2015).

Thus, rather than simply assuming that ideology drives behaviour, it is better to see it as one of several regulatory measures that top leaders use to try to steer the party-state, and wider society, in preferred directions. Moreover, party doctrine is often vague and open to different interpretations. As Patapan and Wang (2018: 59) argue, CCP doctrines

are not strictly speaking 'ideologies', to the extent that they do not seek the exactness or technical jargon of the preceding forms of scientific socialism. Indeed, in their generality and vagueness, they aspire more to be overarching 'narratives' that seek to combine what is obviously in profound tension in contemporary China.

Consequently, although cadres and officials rarely defy CCP doctrine openly, they often interpret it in quite different ways, while nonetheless claiming to be faithful followers of the party line. Thus, as with other regulatory-state mechanisms, doctrine needs to be understood as a possible means of coordination, whose practical efficacy must be investigated in concrete situations, rather than simply being assumed.

A second, and related, steering mechanism involves senior leaders' issuing of broad policy statements at major state events, on foreign visits, or at ad hoc diplomacy work conferences. These communicate top leaders' views of world order and China's place within it, define foreign policy's overall tone and contours, and can initiate substantial policy change. Following such speeches, junior actors often race sycophantically to be seen as complying with top leaders' supposed wishes, creating the impression of awesome top-down control. In reality, these speeches are typically 'full of platitudes, slogans, catchphrases, and generalities' providing mainly 'atmospheric guidance' (Norris 2016: 52), which others must then interpret. Examples include: Deng Xiaoping's famous dictum *tao guang yang hui*,[5] whose meaning is highly debatable (Chen and Wang 2011); Hu's 'harmonious world' – 'more of a narrative than a grand strategy, with no indication of what operational measures would lead to this end' (Harris 2014: 53); Xi's 'new type of great power relations', a vague slogan 'subsequently filled with real meaning [by others], in an incremental manner' (Zeng 2016: 422); Xi's slogan *fenfa youwei*,[6] which has been interpreted to mean

---

[5] Deng's twenty-four-character phrase is usually translated as 'observe calmly, secure our position, cope with events calmly, hide our capacities and bide our time; maintain a low profile; and never claim leadership'.
[6] Usually translated as 'striving for achievement'.

everything from totally disregarding other countries' interests to a modest increase in proactivity (Yamaguchi 2014: 2); or his 'one belt, one road' concept, whose meaning was exceedingly vague until fleshed out by scholars, ministries, SOEs and provinces (Jones and Zeng 2019).

These policy slogans and platforms are kept deliberately vague to accommodate the diverse, competing interests now operating in China's party-state and society, and to facilitate the experimental pursuit of economic growth. Moreover, as Lampton (2015) points out, top leaders may not even know what they wish to achieve, beyond broad brushstrokes. They rely heavily on disaggregated bureaucracies, state-linked think tanks and academics to turn slogans into policies, even on seemingly crucial matters like defining China's 'core interests', allowing them to shape national policy frameworks to benefit sectional interests (Zeng, Xiao and Breslin 2015a). Even when leaders' vague pronouncements are fleshed out into policy frameworks, these can still be rather loose. Reflecting the regulatory-state model, central agencies seek to 'guide lower levels with ... broad policy statements', 'slogans or formulations (*tifa*)', which 'set a general tone or direction' but typically lack substantive detail and require yet further interpretation by those they ostensibly seek to guide (Lieberthal 2004: 189–90). Central agencies very rarely issue 'orders' (*mingling*) that must be implemented stringently. Partly because authority is so fragmented and line control so disrupted by decentralisation, far more common are 'instructions' (*zhishi*) that can be adapted to local conditions, or 'circulars' (*tongzhi*) or 'opinions' (*yijian*) that are merely for 'guidance' (Lieberthal 2004: 195). The State Council's remarkably loose policy documents for the BRI exemplify this approach in the realm of foreign policy (Jones and Zeng 2019).

The third coordinating mechanism in the Chinese-style regulatory state is the use of multiagency committees, often called commissions or the 'leading small groups' (LSGs) mentioned earlier, to coordinate agencies in given policy areas. These exist at the national level – most often beneath the CCP Central Committee or the State Council – but also subnationally, in local regulatory states (e.g. Brødsgaard 2009: ch. 8). Historically, the Foreign Affairs LSG (FALSG) ostensibly oversaw foreign policy. However, as the only LSG lacking a nationwide domestic bureaucracy, it was weak (Lieberthal 2004: 215), meeting 'only infrequently, if ever' (Shirk 2014: 404; also Christensen 2013:

25). It also overlapped with other bodies, including the Politburo Standing Committee, the National Security Commission[7] and LSGs on Taiwan, maritime interests, financial and economic affairs, energy, climate change and so on. Thus, the very institutions developed to counter state fragmentation are themselves fragmented. Furthermore, as noted earlier, LSGs have no formal capacity to instruct the high-ranking agencies they seek to coordinate, operating largely by consensus, unless chaired by the most senior personnel. As one researcher under the State Council explains, the FALSG was merely an 'informal and coordinating body', an 'advising institution' that did not take decisions but generated 'dozens of policy suggestions' for top leaders (Interviewee A28 2018). Understandably perhaps, 'some executive agencies simply bypass [it] and go straight to the top leadership. There is a lack of effective and authoritative coordination' (Li Mingjiang in Ng 2018). Indeed, there are many documented failures of LSGs to coordinate competing foreign policy actors (Cabestan 2009: 88–90).

Xi's own recognition of this fact – a full five years into his re-centralisation drive – explains his creation of a new CCP Foreign Affairs Commission (FAC) in March 2018. The FAC apparently merged the FALSG, the CCP's International Liaison Department (ILD), the Protection of Maritime Rights LSG and the Central Committee's Foreign Affairs Office. It is chaired by State Councillor for Foreign Affairs Yang Jiechi, now a full Politburo member, ostensibly giving it considerable clout. However, according to an individual who advised the regime on creating the FAC, it essentially remains a coordinating body for consultation and discussion, mostly just narrowing down proposals emerging from below, to streamline top leaders' decision-making. 'The bureaucratic struggle for power' within the FAC continues, and decision-making is still heavily influenced by 'the relationship between the guy in charge and Xi Jinping' (Interviewee A28 2018; also Interviewee A01 2018). Moreover, overlaps with many other LSGs remain, while independent agencies apparently persist. The

---

[7] Although this was apparently intended to be an analogue of the US National Security Council, with a strong foreign policy role, its supremacy was never established and its focus seems to have narrowed to domestic regime security, overlapping with other bodies overseeing matters relating to the military, foreign affairs and the economy (Interviewee A28 2018; see also Johnson, Kennedy and Qui 2017; Lampton 2015: 771–2).

ILD, for example, was supposed to have been merged into the new FAC, but actually remains active in promoting international party-to-party relations (Hackenesch and Bader 2020).

A fourth steering mechanism is central agencies' discretionary control over laws, regulations and finance (Donaldson 2010: 33). For example, MOFCOM and the NDRC control important permits and licences, while the policy banks, Ministry of Finance and others control the purse strings. If actors need such resources to pursue their objectives, they are constrained at least to act as if their goals are commensurate with formally agreed national policy. However, given the decentralisation of considerable regulatory power and resources, only the largest schemes require such appeals to Beijing. Moreover, weak oversight means that permits and funding can often be granted for projects that end up undermining official foreign policy objectives (Jones and Zou 2017).

The fifth and most important coordinating mechanism is the CCP itself, specifically its powers of appointment, appraisal and discipline. Although most appointments are now controlled locally, the CCP's central Organisation Department still controls around 4,000 top posts in the party-state, down to the level of provincial governor (McGregor 2010: ch. 3). This constrains senior appointees to toe the party line, particularly if they seek future promotion. The centre can also appoint super-loyalists to oversee particularly troublesome issues, such as restive provinces like Tibet and Xinjiang (Sheng 2011), or the response to COVID-19 in Wuhan and Hubei province (Yang and Mitchell 2020). The CCP's 'cadre responsibility system' regularly assesses CCP personnel against centrally determined 'soft', 'hard' and 'priority' targets. Again, its efficacy varies, not least because these targets are often contradictory – for example, promote economic growth while preserving the environment. Research shows successes and failures in controlling cadres' behaviour, often observing limited punishment for malpractice (Landry 2008; Heberer and Schubert 2012; Mei and Pearson 2014; Ahlers and Schubert 2015). Kostka (2016) dubs this 'command without control'. Moreover, reflecting the state's underlying class basis, there is a strong privileging of economic growth targets, with evidence that violation of central directives is overlooked if growth targets are met (O'Brien and Li 1999; Zhou 2010: 189–90). Officials going seriously astray, however, risk disciplinary procedures that might result in demotion, imprisonment, or even execution. Xi's anti-corruption drive, which has disciplined over one million cadres, is the case *par excellence*.

Clearly, the Chinese party-state's steering mechanisms, while more authoritarian than those in Western regulatory states, all have short-comings, requiring constant struggle to make them effective. This does not mean that the centre has no control or only weak influence over subordinates. Its steering mechanisms clearly have very real effects, even if they only partially achieve their objectives. As Lieberthal (2004: 189) remarks: '[n]one of these remedies has fully resolved the [coordination] problems, but all have affected the way the system has worked'.

Moreover, actors within the party-state are not simply the passive objects of these coordinating mechanisms, but can use three strategies to pursue their own interests and agendas. The first is to *influence* emerging policy frameworks, through participation in formal policy networks or lobbying. The aforementioned coordinating mechanisms often include the very actors they ostensibly seek to coordinate, pro-viding an important channel for influencing emerging policy platforms. For example, the foreign minister may sit on the FALSG/FAC, but so, too, do equally or more powerful representatives from the CCP, MoD, MPS, MOFCOM, PLA and so on (Miller 2015). In other LSGs dealing with internationally relevant issues, like economy and finance, energy or climate change, many functional agencies also participate. Neither the MFA nor any other equally ranked agency can issue binding instructions to one another; rather they must bargain horizontally, seeking to promote guidelines that advance, or at least do not damage, their interests and agendas. Those excluded from such bodies can engage in 'lobbying with Chinese characteristics', using personal net-works and allies in the NPC, the Chinese People's Political Consultative Conference (CPPCC), sectorial ministries, policy banks and state-based policy institutes (Pearson 2001; also Holbig 2004; Li 2012; Yung 2015). While pursuing their 'own specific interests', they portray these as 'national', 'major' or even 'core' interests to attract political and economic support (Wang, Yizhou 2011: 132–3; also Zeng, Xiao and Breslin 2015a).

Thus, apparently 'central' guidelines often emerge 'bottom up', and are typically shaped by contestation and compromise between different forces and interests, explaining why they are so often left vague. An example is the 'going out' policy, which encourages Chinese firms to internationalise. This was only adopted in 2000, effectively rubber-stamping what various SOEs, notably in the oil sector, had been doing since the early 1990s, using the vague policy of opening up as cover (Taylor 2014: ch. 6). Corporate strategy thereby became national policy. Another example, demonstrating the continuity of this phenomenon under Xi Jinping, is the BRI, Xi's signature foreign policy. Rather than emerging 'top down', from Xi's brilliant imagination, the slogan 'one belt, one road' has been developed into a platform that agglomerates two decades of pre-existing cross-border infrastructure-building and regional integration efforts, many of which were developed by provinces and SOEs, not the central government (Summers 2016). The idea of incorporating these into a general platform emerged in the NDRC, not with Xi (Interviewee E05 2018). And, as his slogan was fleshed out into a loose policy platform, ministries, provinces and SOEs competed fiercely to insert their pet projects and interests into the framework, resulting in a baggy 'policy envelope', not a detailed 'grand strategy' (Jones and Zeng 2019).

The second way that Chinese actors can respond to central steering is *ignoring*, that is, disregarding central directives. That this is possible may surprise some, but China specialists have documented many cases, using terms like 'obstruction', 'non-compliance', 'defiance', 'evasion', 'resistance', 'boldly ignoring' and 'circumvention' (respectively: Andrews-Speed 2010; Van Aken and Lewis 2015; Lieberthal 2004: 297–8, 181; Zhou 2010: 13; Li and Wu 2012). This extends to foreign and security policy. State-owned enterprises operating overseas have violated many Chinese regulations, directly undermining and even forcing changes in MFA policy (Jones and Zou 2017). State-owned enterprises have violated UN embargoes despite Beijing's commitments to them (Cardenal and Araújo 2013: 57–8, 116; Zhang 2013; Lampton 2015: 765). Subnational governments have also supported illegal overseas activities by local business interests, damaging interstate relations (Hess and Aidoo 2016; Hameiri, Jones and Zou 2019). The PLA has conducted military tests and aggressive manoeuvres coinciding embarrassingly with presidential visits to target countries (Cabestan 2009: 89; Moore 2014; Cheung 2015; Lampton 2015: 765), and engaged foreign vessels without even informing the MFA or Ministry of Defence (Saunders and Scobell 2015). The autonomous actions of multiple, overlapping Chinese maritime agencies have frequently generated significant international conflict (ICG 2012; Jakobson 2014).

However, given the centre's capacity to discipline subordinate actors who stray too far, '*open* defiance is [relatively] rare' (Zhong 2003: 129–30, emphasis added). Instead, actors quietly subvert central policies, hoping to get away with deviant behaviour without higher authorities noticing, citing implementation difficulties, or exploiting the fragmentation and decentralisation of responsibilities, or contradictions between (or the sheer vagueness of) central policies, to claim that they were loyally trying to follow central instructions all along.

A third response to central guidelines, arguably the most common, is to *interpret* them in ways that favour actors' own interests and agendas. Here, party-state agencies and their societal allies respond to new policy steers by repackaging their existing preferences and policies as being essential for implementing the new initiative. They do not necessarily even wait for leaders' vague pronouncements to be elaborated into something more concrete before doing this; they often start interpreting them immediately, with swift 'resistance' against unfavourable aspects and 'distortion' of others (Zhong 2003: 129). Reflecting the class basis of the transformed party-state, this often involves harnessing pet economic projects to emerging policy themes. For example, well before Xi's 'one belt, one road' concept was developed into a still-loose policy platform in 2015, provinces and SOEs were pushing state banks to subsidise their pre-existing plans in the name of obeying Xi's wishes (Jones and Zeng 2019). Likewise, national oil companies, shipbuilders, the Hainan provincial government and even village-level administrations have all exploited Xi's vague statements around protecting maritime rights to advance their sectional interests (ICG 2016; Kennedy and Erickson 2016). As discussed in Chapter 2, this has created frictions with rival claimants in the South China Sea, even as the MFA ostensibly pursues diplomatic approaches to sovereignty disputes.

In response to these strategies from 'below', central actors may try to use their coordinating mechanisms to steer or rein in others, particularly if their conduct diverges from what was intended and/or creates serious negative consequences. In extreme cases, they may even seek to re-centralise policy control altogether. For example, in the wake of the crisis in Sino-Myanmar relations in 2011, caused in part by the malfeasance of Yunnan province and national and local state-owned and private enterprises, the MFA sought to assert its authority, while the Central Commission for Discipline Inspection cracked down on the worst miscreants (Jones and Zou 2017; Hameiri, Jones and Zou 2019). However, as should be clear by now, truly re-centralising power and control is neither straightforward nor necessarily successful: it can be resisted, entailing struggles for power and resources between actors across different tiers of the party-state. Moreover, 'success' can create mixed results: since the centre lacks the capacity to control policy output in detail, it must leave some space to interpret and implement guidelines to subordinate actors, or risk total paralysis as cadres fear taking any action that might arouse displeasure – as seen following Xi's anti-corruption crackdown (Economy 2018: 29–33).

Therefore, rather than seeing power as *either* dispersed *or* concentrated, a *processual* conceptualisation is more accurate, foregrounding constant, dynamic and evolving interactions between forces located in different parts of the party-state and society. The formation and implementation of foreign and security policy, and the behaviours arising therefrom, are the result of this ongoing process. Where actors' interests align, contestation may be very low, giving the appearance of a monolithic entity; where they do not, however, policy outcomes are likely to be considerably more fragmented.

Does this fractured policy process allow the Chinese party-state to act strategically? This depends on how strategy is defined. If it is understood to mean a clear specification of the goals to be achieved and through what steps, combining directions and priorities for specific actors with appropriate resource commitments, then the vast majority of China's international engagements, including signature policies like the BRI, are not 'strategic' (Jones and Zeng 2019). It is in this sense that this book argues that China's international interactions are generally non-strategic in nature. Conversely, if strategy is defined far more loosely – a general sense of the direction of travel, with relevant actors urged to move in that direction – then the Chinese party-state is capable of pursuing strategic action. However, this is what we describe as the normal operation of the 'Chinese-style regulatory state', which functions through central agencies issuing broad policy guidelines that are fleshed out and interpreted by others. This sometimes generates the desired results but, especially when actors' interests do not align, it often does not.

Many IR scholars try to elide these two definitions by using the rather nebulous concept of 'grand strategy' (see Silove 2018). This allows them to retain the notion that China acts strategically, despite contradictory evidence. Goldstein (2020: 166), for example, claims that: 'a state's grand strategy [may] not [be] explicitly outlined. Sometimes it is only possible to identify ... as it becomes evident over time that leaders' foreign policy statements and choices reflect a distinct vision guiding them as they decide on the appropriateness of military, economic, or diplomatic initiatives'. He argues that China's grand strategy consistently entails pursuing 'national rejuvenation', albeit shifting in approach from Deng's 'biding time' to Xi's assertive defence of China's 'core interests' (Goldstein 2020; see also Heath 2018).

However, this perspective neglects the important implications of this loose approach to 'grand strategy' by Chinese leaders. What does it mean, for example, to say that Chinese actions reflect a quest for 'national rejuvenation'? Aside from specifying that China should be 'prosperous and powerful' by 2049 (Goldstein 2020: 167), it is an exceedingly vague goal that can be interpreted in diverse ways. Likewise, even China's 'core interests' were never clearly specified by the top leadership; rather, they were proposed, contested and interpreted by a wide range of other actors (Zeng, Xiao and Breslin 2015b). When the content of strategy is so vague, almost everything that Chinese actors do can be interpreted as strategic. This may be useful in sustaining a realist outlook, which depends on the existence of monolithic state behaviour, but not necessarily in understanding why Chinese actors behave in the way they do. In our view, rather than assuming that some unstated grand strategy determines all Chinese actors' behaviour, or even retrospectively identifying that strategy from the behaviour, it is better to investigate how policy is formed and implemented in practice. This entails remaining open to the possibility that while top leaders' pronouncements may shape some other actors' behaviour, they can also be shaped, interpreted or even ignored by others.

The Impact of Chinese Engagements on Other Countries

Our view of the state implies an understanding of international relations very different to that found in traditional IR theory. Although no other state is organised exactly like China's, the same broad state-theoretical insights apply everywhere, such that we cannot assume the unity and common purpose of policymaking in any state. Accordingly, to explain the political, social and diplomatic outcomes of Chinese international engagements, we must consider exactly which parts of its state–society complex are engaging which parts of another country's in a given issue area, why, how, and to what effect. An issue-specific approach is important because different sets of actors, interests and agendas operate in each area: the eleven Chinese agencies involved in energy policy are not the same as the forty-one involved in counter-narcotics, for instance; and the same is often true on the receiving end of Chinese behaviour.

The first analytical task is to identify the key actors, interests and agendas at play in recipient societies, and to understand how Chinese actors and their initiatives relate to these. This involves a Gramscian analysis of state–society relations, identifying: the key social forces struggling over power and resources; how these forces relate to general patterns of ownership, control, investment, production and trade; and how social forces are organised into ruling coalitions and opposition forces, in what sort of hierarchical arrangement and through what means (particularly economic concessions, coercion and ideological projects). Issue-specific dynamics are located within the wider context of social power relations and conflict, as these structural contours typically shape the key actors, dynamics and possibilities within a given policy domain.

The next step is to trace out empirically how the Chinese and non-Chinese actors interact with one another, and identify the outcomes arising from this interaction. Chinese initiatives are likely to be con-tested in recipient societies, because they typically involve highly unequal distributions of costs and benefits among different societal groups. For example, despite Beijing's rhetoric of 'win-win' cooper-ation and 'harmonious development', Chinese development financing may be attractive to ruling elites and local companies seeking to develop large-scale infrastructure projects, but deleterious for the local populations likely to suffer land-grabbing, forced displacement, environmental degradation and militarisation around project sites (Hameiri, Jones and Zou 2019). Hence, in many cases, struggles arise over how best to engage Chinese actors. This is also a complex, dynamic and evolving process, though one in which the forces enjoying the greatest power and control over resources and access to key sites of decision-making are best placed to win. Dominant groups will likely try to exploit Chinese initiatives to further their own social, political and economic projects and strategies. This may result in a bargaining process that can further adapt Chinese behaviour, shaping the eventual outcome. For example, in development financing, recipient governments are heavily involved in selecting and initiating projects, thereby harnessing Chinese capital and expertise to pursue their preferred development agenda and, possibly more importantly, funnel resources to their supporters (see Chapter 4). However, where opponents of engagement are well placed, or successfully mobilise societal opposition, they may be able to compel ruling elites to reject Chinese engagement. For example, resistance in countries including Ghana, Zambia, the Philippines and Myanmar has sometimes led to the election of forces hostile to Chinese policies, resulting in a crisis in bilateral relations (Wong et al. 2013; Hess and Aidoo 2014; Hess and Aidoo 2016; Hameiri, Jones and Zou 2019).

Notes on Method

This section elaborates how our state transformation approach is used in the empirical chapters that follow, explains our case selection, and discusses methodological challenges and how we addressed them.

Since we have characterised the making, implementation and outcomes of Chinese foreign and security policy as arising from a contested, constantly evolving process, mechanismic analysis is the most suitable approach. This involves identifying the causal mechanisms through which particular outcomes arise. We begin by specifying the relevant context, guided by theory, then trace the process by which outcomes are produced (Bunge 1997). This involves the following steps, beginning with the Chinese side:

1. Identify how state transformation dynamics have developed in a particular area. Who are the key actors in this domain? What are their interests and agendas? How do they relate to one another, in what patterns of power and hierarchy?
2. Identify the mechanisms central actors use to delineate policy guidelines and steer other actors in this area. What mechanisms and actors are involved? Uncover any contestation – influencing attempts – in the formation of policy guidelines and identify the guidelines emerging from this.
3. Study how relevant actors interpret or ignore these guidelines in their actual behaviour vis-à-vis non-Chinese entities.

These three steps explain Chinese policy behaviour. For cases where we are interested in developing a comprehensive explanation of policy *outcomes*, we must also examine dynamics on the receiving end of this behaviour:

4. Identify the key socio-political forces within the target state, and the key interests surrounding the specific policy domain in question. Examine how these groups experience and evaluate Chinese initiatives in relation to their own interests and agendas.
5. Explore how these groups interact and contest engagement by Chinese actors, and trace the outcomes arising from this contestation.

This sort of detailed process-tracing is possible only through case studies. We have chosen three, all located in China's near-abroad, in Southeast Asia. As outlined in the Introduction, this region is the one most exposed to Chinese influence, providing an excellent 'laboratory' to understand how state transformation dynamics are shaping China's international relations. These processes would not unfold identically everywhere, but our mid-range framework deliberately factors in local specificities, making it generally applicable. Moreover, literature on Chinese engagement in Latin America, Africa and Europe, some of which has been cited in this chapter, provides *prima facie* evidence of similar dynamics elsewhere. We acknowledge that a small-*n* approach is vulnerable to well-known criticisms: three cases in one region simply cannot be assumed to represent the full gamut of China's rise. However, it is the only method capable of testing and demonstrating the impact of state transformation as we have theorised it. Moreover, for robustness and to demonstrate the framework's broad applicability, we have deliberately selected cases that are highly significant policy issues and range across 'high' and 'low' politics. We also engage in intra-case comparison: our explorations of development financing and non-traditional security cooperation each involve two different target countries and different outcomes, which helps to identify the causal significance of contestation within recipient states.

The methodological challenges of this approach are nonetheless formidable. Studying China is extraordinarily difficult; unpacking the party-state, especially amid today's increasing paranoia and secrecy, is even harder. Chinese officials are typically (and increasingly) inaccessible, even to seasoned China experts, while official statistics are often unreliable. This is surely one reason why the 'unitary actor' model and notions of 'grand strategy' persist: in the absence of fine-grained data, they allow us to discuss 'China' in an apparently meaningful way, albeit at a very high degree of abstraction. This is not merely a problem for foreign scholars. James Palmer (2018), a senior journalist who covered China for many years, compellingly argues that 'nobody knows anything about China' – 'including the Chinese government'. In every field of party-state activity, 'virtually every piece of information issued from or about the country is unreliable, partial, or distorted … for both propaganda reasons and individual career ambitions', in addition to 'paranoia', 'fear and greed'. The resultant uncertainty 'goes as much for Chinese as it does for foreigners', with high-level officials repeatedly bemoaning a lack of reliable information. Palmer states bluntly: 'We don't know *anything* about high-level Chinese politics. At best, we can make … informed guesses'. Naturally, these problems multiply when one wishes to uncover behaviour that the party-state seeks to conceal, such as uncoordinated or even rogue conduct.

We address these profound challenges in five main ways. First, we freely admit – as should everyone studying China – that our analysis is necessarily tentative and subject to revision in the face of fresh evidence. Second, unlike some China experts, we do not attempt to engage in 'Kremlinology', that is, the study of elite politics within the government compound of *Zhongnanhai*.[8] This is partly because our understanding of the state implies that such a focus is deficient, since squabbles among a handful of powerful men do not dictate what the party-state does in practice. Kremlinology's failure to foresee the Soviet Union's collapse indicates the weakness of an approach focused exclusively on the state's apex, rather than on the contradictions within the system and its relation to broader political economy dynamics. We also reject Kremlinology because, in the context of radical information shortages, it is unreliable and frequently highly speculative. Widening our gaze to include multiple actors and scales increases the amount of useful information – it can be easier to access subnational officials and data than national ones, for instance – and produces a more holistic picture of what is actually happening. Thirdly, we use triangulation wherever possible, trying to find

---

[8] This work typically focuses on the career trajectories/biographies of individual elites and their supposed factional membership as clues to how they might behave in office (e.g. Li, Cheng 2016).

multiple sources of evidence to support key claims, and being open about when this is impossible. Notwithstanding increasing secrecy and paranoia, there is a growing amount of open-source documentation, official websites and press reportage in China, which foreign scholars are only just beginning to harness.[9] A vast secondary literature also provides valuable data; indeed, as should now be clear, this book would not exist without the extensive prior research of hundreds of China specialists, writing in both English and Chinese.

Our fourth approach is also a standard convention in China scholarship. Since we could directly access policymakers and implementers only rarely, we approached them indirectly. Virtually every part of the Chinese party-state has associated research institutes, often misleadingly called 'think tanks'. In Western contexts, think tanks are usually independent of government, seeking to channel ideas and interests located elsewhere in society into the policymaking process. Chinese think tanks, however, are located beneath particular agencies and ministries; their employees are party-state officials and work on behalf of their overseers. Accordingly, they frequently interact with powerful officials and have valuable insights into how they think and behave. Their comments in private are also frequently franker than (or even contradict) their public writings. Interviews with these officials thus provide a crucial 'way in' to the opaque party-state. We also interviewed a number of university-based scholars. Some of their universities are again directly linked to particular parts of the party-state, such as the MFA or provincial governments, providing research, training and policy advice. Other scholars to whom we spoke had advised senior policymakers, up to and including Xi Jinping. It might be objected that these interlocutors agreed to be interviewed in order to feed us misleading, regime-sanctioned narratives, for example, that any aggressive behaviour by Chinese actors does not reflect central government policy. However, if this was really the motivation of these researchers, officials' refusal to engage with foreign researchers would make little sense, since they could also have used these opportunities to propagate such narratives. Ultimately, we have tried to avoid relying on any one source to make big claims, always endeavouring to triangulate interview data wherever possible.

---

[9] An excellent example is recent work by Andrew Erickson, Connor Kennedy and others on China's maritime militias (discussed in Chapter 2).

Our fifth approach is innovative: we have studied China from the 'outside in'. The internationalisation of Chinese party-state apparatuses means that more are interacting with actors in other countries than ever before. Although Southeast Asian states like Cambodia, Laos and Myanmar are themselves hardly paragons of transparency, we were nonetheless able to interview numerous policymakers, officials, business people, civil society groups and others who interact closely and sometimes routinely with Chinese actors. This was not only important in gathering data about the interactions between Chinese and local actors and how this shaped policy outcomes. It also provided valuable insights into the relations among and behaviour of different party-state entities, both inside China and on the ground in other countries, which would have been impossible to obtain first-hand within China itself. This outside-in approach offers an increasingly important way of unpacking the 'black box' of China's party-state as conditions for research within China deteriorate.

In total, we conducted over 100 interviews with individuals and groups in China, Laos, Myanmar and Cambodia, at both national and subnational scales. In China, our main fieldwork sites were Beijing, Shanghai, Haikou (Hainan) and Kunming (Yunnan), while in the Southeast Asian states we interviewed actors in national capitals and major economic centres and in areas bordering China. To protect our interviewees, we have anonymised them all. By the standards of the field, we have assembled an extremely strong evidence base to demonstrate the impact of state transformation on China's rise.

Predictable Objections

Finally, we want to canvass and rebut two predictable objections to our framework, to clarify any potential misunderstandings and encourage readers to evaluate our argument on its merits. Since these objections have frequently arisen during the course of our research, as we presented our findings or sought to publish them, we felt it was important to address them directly and early.

First, some contend that the fragmentation of state apparatuses, and associated coordination problems, are nothing new: the Chinese state was even more fragmented before 1949, and policy implementation problems existed even under Mao. This is true, but identifying antecedents does not show that state transformation does not matter today, nor does it reckon with what is actually historically unprecedented. As described in the Introduction, from a *longue durée* perspective, one can identify a *generalised* process of the consolidation of national states, societies and economies in the nineteenth through mid-twentieth centuries. The post-war period was the high point of this consolidation, as the Keynesian-Fordist global economic order and Cold War dynamics supported ruling elites in knitting together disparate socio-political forces and markets and establishing dominion over the entire national space (Jessop 2009). In retrospect, this was clearly the high tide of the Westphalian-Weberian state of mainstream IR theory. In the Chinese context, this period saw the CCP defeat its rivals, establish control over outlying areas in Tibet and Xinjiang, establish a centralised political authority and planned national economy, and re-route peripheral areas 'inwards'. However, from the mid-1970s onwards, this system began to unravel globally: a series of capitalist crises (the collapse of the gold standard, the oil crises, stagflation and intensifying social unrest) led to the destruction of the post-war settlement, as states were reconfigured from pursuing national development to securing competitiveness within a global marketplace (Cerny 1997). The exhaustion of state-led development in the Global South, coupled with debt crises and structural adjustment in the 1980s, promoted a similar reconfiguration there (Harrison 2004). China underwent its own structural adjustment process after 1978, with attendant fragmentation, decentralisation and internationalisation of party-state apparatuses. As Gramscians always insist, there are important national variations to this general story, but China is not *sui generis*. There is undoubtedly a generalised tendency of state consolidation followed by fragmentation, both producing and mirroring broad developments in the global political economy.[10]

However, the current era is neither simply a return to pre-Maoist dynamics, nor a continuation of the problems of consolidating statehood that Mao himself grappled with. Thirty years of communist rule profoundly shaped China's state, society and economy, making it a very different polity to that existing prior to 1949. It is the 'fundamental transformations' of *this* system – involving a powerful party-state

---

[10] The COVID-19 pandemic might entail changes in this trajectory, but this was impossible to know at the time of writing.

machinery and large-scale state-owned capital that did not exist before 1949 – via its engagements with globalised capitalism, that characterises the present era (Womack 1994). Even those who try to locate the origins of the present system in the Qin and Han dynasties are compelled to admit that the post-Mao 'reforms were not simply the restoration of the traditional system, because they … introduced many new elements' – most crucially, marketisation – which 'entirely changed the behaviour and incentives of Chinese local officials' (Zhou 2010: 27, 185). The emergence of a cadre-capitalist class dominating state and society is historically unprecedented, as is its imbrication into different, competing circuits of international capitalism. Historical accounts noting pre-1949 fragmentation and centre–periphery frictions under Mao nonetheless rightly insist that China's capitalist transformation has 'fundamentally altered … [the] command economic system and the power structure between the centre and localities', leading to a 'dramatic degrading of the … coherence of the state' (Jia and Lin 1994: 8). Accordingly, they insist that research must 'go beyond either the totalitarian model that essentially treats the Chinese state as a monolithic entity, or the bureaucratic model that has so far limited its discussion of the "pluralization" of Chinese politics to bureaucratic infighting at the central ministerial level' (Jia and Lin 1994: 7). This is precisely what this book does.

The second predictable objection is that power has been re-centralised under President Xi, making a state transformation analysis redundant. Yes, the argument goes, the party-state did become fragmented and incoherent after 1978, but Xi's anti-corruption crackdown, tightening of party discipline, and stiffening of party control over public and private organisations means that power has now been firmly re-centralised. This objection misunderstands both our argument and Xi's behaviour. The state transformation approach does *not* imply that fragmentation, decentralisation and internationalisation are a unidirectional or teleological process towards dissolution, such that any evidence of a reversal in these processes falsifies the thesis. As explicitly stated earlier, we seek to surmount this binary framing, wherein power is seen either as entirely dispersed or as entirely centralised. We have created a framework capable of understanding how power is exercised in a transformed party-state: through a dynamic, evolving process within a Chinese-style regulatory state. We emphasise the steering mechanisms available to top leaders and their capacity to react to, and try to rein in, wayward behaviour. Xi Jinping has not dismantled this system. On the contrary: his actions involve activating the very steering mechanisms we identify. His tightening of party discipline, his streamlining of the cadre responsibility system and his creation of coordinating bodies are examples *par excellence* (Ahlers and Stepan 2017; Johnson, Kennedy and Qui 2017). Rather than changing the rules of the game, Xi is best understood as a particularly forceful player in the contested process that still characterises policy-making and implementation in the Chinese-style regulatory state.

The preceding discussions (and the following chapters) cite extensive evidence from the Xi era to underscore that the Chinese-style regulatory state is still in operation. An important aspect of continuity is the system's sheer scale: there are some 40 million CCP cadres, 500,000 in leadership positions at some level, including 900 at the centre, 2,500 in ministerial or provincial-level posts, 39,000 at the prefectural level and 446,000 at county level (Goodman 2014: 68). The idea that Xi can single-handedly direct these individuals, take all decisions of any importance, or control in detail the party-state's outputs, strains credibility. Many Chinese officials openly admit this. One group of experts told us: 'Lots of Western analysts think President Xi says, "do this", and everyone does that. But that's not true … There's still controversy. One strongman cannot change all that' (Interviewees E13 2018). Another interviewee says: 'Western countries think Xi controls everything … but leaders can't control the whole thing … This is not true' (Interviewee A30 2018). Ministry of State Security officials concur: 'the Western perception [is] that China is such a unified country … [In reality] it is like other countries: it is internally differentiated. Different groups, different parties, different voices … [Top leaders must] respond to all these voices … the government cannot make totally one voice' (Interviewees A27 2018).

It is not even clear that Xi can control the many LSGs that he now ostensibly chairs. His role is now defined so 'extensive[ly]' that 'it may exceed anyone's span of effective control' (Lampton 2015: 762). As one State Council official puts it, for one person to control these various committees, 'we would need a superman, a god. The problem is, we don't have a god' (Interviewee A28 2018). Moreover, this apparent centralisation has nonetheless 'resulted in policies that are not adequately specified or implemented and in erratic and inconsistent policy commitment' – indeed, 'policy-making has become *more* erratic' and even 'broken'; despite Xi's strong personal commitment to structural economic reform, 'not one of [his] economic reforms has been an obvious success' (Naughton 2016: 40, 41, emphasis added). This is not least because, even where decisions are promulgated centrally, implementation must still 'contend with the diverging interests of multiple government, party, and company actors – many of whom view new reforms as threatening a status quo from which they have long profited' (Leutert 2016: 99; also Zhang, Zhang and Liu 2017). The party-state's fragmentation and decentralisation have not somehow been reversed overnight. Indeed, as one MFA-linked expert insists, 'centralisation and fragmentation is happening at the same time' (Interviewee A01 2018). Xi's PLA reforms, for example, have compounded 'the long-standing fragmentation of CCP organisational leadership' by further separating the military from civilian oversight (You 2017a). Above, we noted evidence of provincial governments' continual defiance of central directives. Xi was still purging wayward cadres as late as 2018, five years into his rule, with one source suggesting it would take another five years to root out the Jiang Zemin faction stymieing his administration (SinoInsider 2018).

Thus, Xi's consolidation of power does not represent a reversion to a 'totalitarian' model of monolithic statehood, but rather a tightening of central steering mechanisms within the Chinese-style regulatory state: 'there is no dramatic change' in policymaking processes (Interviewee A20 2018). Chinese experts describe Xi's mode of governance in terms that perfectly match our conceptualisation. He does not simply issue orders top-down, but must accommodate forces from below – the many 'different departments that have different positions and different voices' that 'come together to make pressure on the government', compelling the government to 'respond ... to bring all these opinions together' – arbitrating between them to develop a loose policy framework (Interviewees A27 2018; also Interviewee A01 2018). Xi and other top leaders specify 'basic principles' and broad targets, but ministries and local governments must still interpret these, enacting more detailed policies (Interviewees A10 2018). Xi 'gives you only a sense of direction. Then you have to develop all the details on how to implement it ... China still lacks a grand strategy' (Interviewee A24 2018). The tightening of central steering mechanisms, particularly disciplinary ones, makes it far harder for subordinates to ignore national frameworks, but the sycophancy this induces also creates a perverse side effect. 'Different departments guess what is Xi's preference' and their desire to demonstrate their 'political correctness' often involves creative or even outlandish behaviour at odds with top leaders' intentions, requiring subsequent clarification: thus, the system still works through 'trial and error' (Interviewee A24 2018). As one MFA official notes: 'it's our political system: the leader says something; the departments will carry out the orders even more radically than the leader intended ... it is not easy for him to predict the consequences of implementation. It is not easy to control' (Interviewee A20 2018). This extends to junior officials trying to 'show their loyalty' by making bellicose statements that 'make Western countries angry ... It's not about international politics, it's domestic politics. But it has an influence on other countries' (Interviewee A30 2018).

Evidence that the Chinese-style regulatory state persists under Xi ranges from the petty to the profound. In April 2015, Xi called for a 'toilet revolution' to improve the presentation and hygiene of public washrooms. Eighteen months later, the central government had to rein in local governments, which had splurged US$3bn on new facilities, doubtless enriching many state-linked construction firms (NPR 2018). This is a classic illustration of how vague slogans from top leaders are rapidly interpreted in ways that support local agendas (in this case, local cadre-capitalists' addiction to debt-fuelled infrastructure spending), smuggling in sectional interests under the cover of demonstrating loyalty to the central leadership. A more serious example is the BRI, which is Xi's signature foreign policy initiative and even written into the CCP constitution. The idea of the BRI, and the loose policy frameworks that have emerged around it, are not top-down grand strategies but the result of bottom-up lobbying processes, driven by the cadre-classes embedded in local governments and SOEs (Summers 2016; Jones and Zeng 2019). These actors did not wait for policy frameworks to be developed after Xi's vague 'one belt, one road' slogan emerged in 2013, but immediately began interpreting the slogan by kick-starting pre-existing economic and regional projects. Central guidelines have also failed to steer activity subsequently, with no correlation between levels of provincial activity and their inclusion in formal policy plans, or between locations of outbound investment and the various corridors identified in official frameworks (Jones and Zeng 2019). The Chinese government's own data also reveal extensive violation of basic Chinese laws and regulations on BRI investments (CAITEC, SASAC and UNDP China 2017). Thus, influencing, interpreting and even ignoring persist under Xi, even within his signature foreign policy framework, as we will also show in our case study chapters.

2 | State Transformation and the South China Sea

[T]he Western perception [is] that China is such a unified country ... [But, really] it is like other countries. It is internally differentiated: different groups, different parties, different voices ... In terms of the South China Sea, there are dovish departments, like the Ministry of Foreign Affairs, which tend to negotiate or [promote] dialogue with claimant parties; but there are some hawkish agencies, like the military, or the coastguard, or the law enforcement authorities ... [which] try to have a much tougher policy ... They have different interests; it's natural ... Western media are saying, 'President Xi is so strong; there is only one voice'. But ... the government cannot make totally one voice. The only possible way is to bring all these opinions together.

Analyst, Chinese Ministry of State Security
(Interviewees A27 2018)

The Korean peninsula aside, the sovereignty disputes in the South China Sea (SCS) are widely regarded as the most serious security flashpoint in East Asia. Realist lenses dominate the discussion, with analysts predicting that the SCS will be where Sino-US rivalry finally erupts into war (Klare 2001; Kaplan 2014). Parallels are drawn to World Wars I and II: analysts label the SCS 'the Mitteleuropa of the twenty-first century' (Kaplan 2014: 182), warning that small disputes may lead to major conflagration, as with the assassination of Archduke Ferdinand in 1914 (Hayton 2014: xvi). Even critical theorists see SCS clashes as a case of Chinese 'territorial expansion', expressing a clash between China's 'Westphalian' conception of sovereignty and the USA's 'globalist' one (Rolf and Agnew 2016).

The SCS is also seen as emblematic of China's wider conduct, making it a doubly important case study. Seen as a weathervane of China's 'global aspirations' (Hendrix and Bateman 2017), China's behaviour there will reveal whether it 'intend[s] to play by the rules of the game or challenge them' (Hayton 2014: xvii). As China's maritime conduct has allegedly become much more 'assertive' under Xi Jinping, this 'seaward expansion' is interpreted as a 'grand strategy' or 'grey zone strategy' intended 'to alter the status quo without resorting to war' (Kaplan 2014: 63; Erickson and Martinson 2019: 2). This is generally said to involve the tight coordination of party-state actors in a 'salami-slicing' strategy, exploiting China's rising power to annex the SCS slice by slice, turning it 'into an internal bastion sea' (Hendrix and Bateman 2017). The multiple actors involved are depicted as 'tools' of this top-down strategy (Glaser and Funaiole 2019: 191). In some accounts, this 'secret strategy' is so well planned that it extends over a full century (Pillsbury 2014).

However, as with our other case studies, reality troubles these 'realist' interpretations. If realists are correct that the SCS 'is all about power; the balance of power mainly' (Kaplan 2014: 18), we might expect to see a steady rise in confrontational incidents as Chinese power has grown. Yet as Figure 2.1 and Table 2.1 show, there is no such correlation. The most confrontational incidents occurred decades ago, in 1974 and 1988, when China's still-weak naval forces seized territory from Vietnam. More recent changes in the territorial status quo have been relatively modest: the discovery of Chinese naval markers at Mischief Reef in 1994 and the

Table 2.1 *Maritime incidents in the SCS, 2010 to October 2019*

	Incidents	Incidents involving Chinese vessels	Fishing-related	Number of vessels involved	Of which Chinese
2010	2	2 (100%)	2 (100%)	17	15 (88%)
2011	6	6 (100%)	3 (50%)	63	50 (79%)
2012	3	3 (100%)	3 (100%)	27	17 (63%)
2013	5	4 (80%)	4 (80%)	26	11 (42%)
2014	7	7 (100%)	5 (71%)	166	141 (85%)
2015	17*	15 (88%)	16 (94%)	62	29 (47%)
2016	16*	13 (81%)	15 (94%)	76	47 (62%)
2017	6	3 (50%)	6 (100%)	28	4 (14%)
2018	2	1 (50%)	1 (50%)	7	4 (57%)
2019	4*	2 (50%)	4 (100%)	7	1 (14%)

Note: * includes at least one incident with an unknown number of vessels, involving imprecise data.
Source: CSIS (2019).

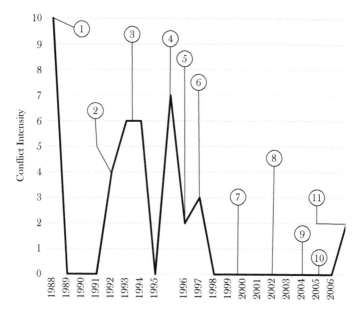

1. China seizes Paracel Islands from Vietnam
2. China's Law on Territorial Sea refers to 'historic rights' in SCS.
   ASEAN issues Declaration on the SCS
3. 1994-5: Vietnamese coastguard repels Chinese survey ships
   interfering with seismic surveys; China de-escalates
4. Chinese installations found on Philippines' Mischief Reef
5. China adopts UNCLOS. Beijing protests Vietnamese
   auctioning of oil blocs
6. Vietnam repels Chinese survey ship
7. 1999-2000: Sino-Vietnamese border demarcation agreements
8. China-ASEAN Declaration on Code of Conduct in the SCS
9. Sino-Vietnamese-Philippine agreement on joint oil exploration
10. Joint Sino-Vietnamese patrols
11. China protests Vietnamese oil deals, then de-escalates

Note: Conflict intensity is rated as follows: 10 = military clashes/ violent
territorial change; 8 = confrontations involving military forces;
7 = peaceful territorial change; 6 = confrontations involving civilian forces;
4 = significant legal, diplomatic or civilian incidents; 2 = minor incidents;
0 = deliberate de-escalation, diplomatic breakthrough, or no notable incident.
Where intensity shifts notably within a single year, space is added on
the horizontal axis.

Figure 2.1 South China Sea conflict intensity
Source: Authors' estimation, based on publicly available sources.

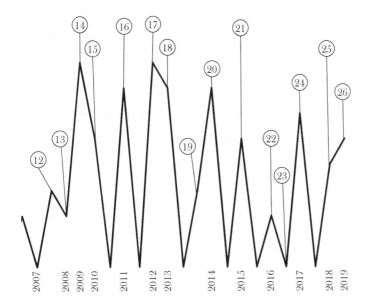

12. China arrests Vietnamese fishermen and blocks oil exploration, but Philippine surveys proceed without comment
13. China and Vietnam protest Philippine claims in SCS
14. China's UNCLOS declaration initiates regional tensions. Chinese ships confront USNS Impeccable off Hainan
15. 2010–11: US involvement emboldens Philippines and Vietnam, inflaming regional tensions; de-escalation follows
16. Chinese maritime law enforcement ships clash with Vietnamese and Philippine survey vessels. Chinese Foreign Ministry de-escalates
17. Scarborough Shoal incident. Spats over oil exploration. PLA establishes Sansha garrison. Hainan issues new SCS regulations, sparking diplomatic protests
18. Philippines launches UNCLOS suit versus China. Thomas Reef incident. Chinese diplomats de-escalate
19. Hainan's new fishing regulations spark regional protests
20. Chinese oil rig placed in waters disputed with Vietnam, sparking major crisis. Chinese diplomats de-escalate
21. Chinese island-building starts, sparking international protests
22. Chinese island-building continues but Chinese diplomats de-escalate. Minor law-enforcement clashes. PLAN establishes bilateral arrangements with US to avoid at-sea incidents
23. China-ASEAN Framework Agreement on Code of Conduct in the SCS
24. Sino-Indonesian law-enforcement standoff at Natuna Island. China protests Vietnamese oil-drilling
25. China protests Vietnamese oil drilling
26. Vietnam suspends oil drilling, claiming China threatened violence

Figure 2.1 (cont.)

transfer of Scarborough Shoal from overlapping Chinese/Philippine control to exclusive Chinese control in 2012 – led by coastguard vessels, not
the People's Liberation Army Navy (PLAN). Figure 2.1 also demonstrates
the erratic nature of Chinese conduct, with conflict escalating and de-
escalating, often within the space of a single year. As Santicola remarks,
China's record displays 'consistent inconsistency . . . an almost incompre-
hensible level of unpredictability . . . [and a] lack of any discernible strategy' (Santicola 2014). The idea that China has become more aggressive
under Xi is also problematic. Many Chinese policies, like consolidating
control over Chinese-held land features, contesting fishing grounds and
exploring for hydrocarbons, predate Xi (Chubb 2019), while maritime
sea confrontations have declined sharply since their peak in 2014–16.

Part of the explanation is that, far from being consistently expansionist, China is often reactive to rival claimants' conduct and, since
2012, US intervention. For example, clashes after 2009 were a reaction
to Vietnamese and Malaysian claims under the ambit of the 1982
United Nations Convention on the Laws of the Sea (UNCLOS), the
intensification of Vietnamese fishing, and Vietnamese and Philippine
seismic surveys in contested areas (Fravel 2015; Jakobson 2015).

However, this chapter argues that the deeper cause of China's
'consistently inconsistent' conduct in the SCS is the impact of state
transformation and the emergence of a Chinese-style regulatory state.
Building on crucial contributions made by other scholars, we draw
attention to the multiple Chinese actors at work in the SCS and their
often poorly coordinated behaviour (e.g. Chung, Chien-peng 2004;
ICG 2012; Jakobson 2014). These include: various national ministries;
the navy; maritime law enforcement agencies (MLEAs); state-owned
enterprises, especially the national oil companies; and local government agencies in Hainan province. However, unlike other accounts,
which discuss these actors atheoretically or use an unsatisfactory
'bureaucratic politics' model (e.g. Long 2016),[1] we deploy the state
transformation approach, situating China's SCS behaviour as part of
wider developments in Chinese policymaking. This demonstrates that
state transformation is shaping China's foreign and security policy
conduct even in an area of 'hard' security.

The chapter comprises five sections, following the method outlined
in Chapter 1. The first describes how state transformation has

---

[1] For a critique, see Chapter 1.

expanded the number of actors within this policy domain to over twenty by the 2000s. The second section identifies the regulatory policy framework and coordination mechanisms through which leaders seek to steer their behaviour in the SCS. It draws attention to the infamous 'nine-dash line' and the vague injunction to strike a balance between maintaining stability and upholding China's maritime rights, and the lack of coherent coordination mechanisms or legal frameworks. The subsequent sections explore how different actors behave in practice. Through a roughly chronological treatment, we show how their attempts to influence, interpret and ignore China's vague SCS policy guidelines can explain some of the important incidents included in Figure 2.1, and largely account for the crescendo of regional confrontations over the last decade. The final substantive section considers developments under Xi, who has recognised the problems arising from state fragmentation and sought to overcome them. However, his efforts have only been moderately successful – though they have managed to dampen regional tensions in practice.

The conclusion assesses the extent to which China's erratic conduct can be understood as a 'strategy'. We argue that Chinese behaviour has not been carefully planned, but evolves in a largely ad hoc manner, lurching between extremes within Beijing's loose and permissive policy guidelines. Although the overall trajectory has undoubtedly led to China consolidating its grip on the SCS, precisely because the end goal was not weighed up against competing policy objectives and resolved into a coherent strategy, this has come at great and unanticipated cost.

China's Maritime Actors and Institutions

This section describes how state fragmentation, decentralisation and internationalisation have pluralised the actors operating within the SCS. By the 2000s, around twenty different maritime agencies had some role here, many overlapping, while Hainan's local government had also acquired substantial powers. Meanwhile, MLEAs initially developed for purely domestic administrative duties became internationalised.

The fragmentation of Chinese maritime policymaking and implementation, arising from many piecemeal reforms, is summarised in Table 2.2, which lists the agencies involved prior to major reforms in

Table 2.2 *Chinese maritime agencies as of 2013*

Name	Main responsibilities
National-level entities – major players	
People's Liberation Army Navy (PLAN)	Maritime defence
Ministry of Foreign Affairs (MFA)	Represents China internationally; negotiates with rival claimants
Ministry of Land and Natural Resources (MLNR)	Sets policy on use of natural maritime resources, e.g., hydrocarbons
• State Oceanic Administration (SOA)	Makes and enforces policies relating to research, exploitation and protection of marine resources; operates China Marine Surveillance (CMS), an MLEA
• China Geological Survey	Oversees maritime geological surveys
• State Bureau of Survey and Mapping	Maps Chinese territory, including at sea
Ministry of Agriculture's Bureau of Fisheries Administration (BFA)	Sets and enforces fisheries policy; operates Fisheries Law Enforcement Command (FLEC), an MLEA
Ministry of Transportation	
• Maritime Safety Administration (MSA)	MLEA responsible for maritime safety, including inspection of vessels and facilities
• Rescue and Salvage Bureau's China Marine Search and Rescue Centre	Rescue and salvage operations

Ministry of Public Security	Responsible for maritime border security
• Border Control Department	
• China Maritime Police Bureau (CMP) *	MLEA concerned with criminal matters, e.g., smuggling
China National Offshore Oil Company (CNOOC)	Allocates offshore blocks for hydrocarbon exploration and exploitation

National-level entities – minor players

Ministry of Environment	Maritime environmental protection
Ministry of Health	Food security of marine products
Ministry of Education	Coordinates international cooperation on marine science and technology
Ministry of Science and Technology	Marine science and technology
National Development and Reform Commission (NDRC)	Economic planning including marine development; must approve major investments, including marine construction projects
State-owned Assets Supervision and Administration Commission	Oversees centrally owned SOEs; controls sea salt industry
National Tourism Administration	Oversees touristic travel by sea, including to SCS
General Administration of Customs (GAC) Anti-Smuggling Bureau	MLEA responsible for combating land and maritime smuggling
National Weather Bureau	Maritime surveillance for weather forecasting
State Quality Inspection Commission	Regulating marine products

Table 2.2 (*cont.*)

Name	Main responsibilities
State Administration of Work Safety	Security of oil production
Cultural Relics Bureau	Protection of undersea relics
Forestry Bureau	Protection of marine life
Subnational entities	
Hainan provincial government	Legally governs all Chinese territory in the SCS. Empowered to issue maritime regulations within ambit of national law. Controls functional maritime units, e.g., customs, maritime safety administration, public security. Oversees maritime economic development, notably tourism and fisheries. Maintains provincial MLEAs
County/municipal governments	Maintains the most local MLEAs and maritime militia units *

Note: * Under joint command of Central Military Commission.
Sources: Bickford, Holz, and Velluci (2011: 64–6); Wang, Gang (2011: 3); Tseng (2013: 30–1); Xiong and Li (2013); Dong (2018).

2013 (considered in this chapter's penultimate section). As different agencies have contradictory mandates, this entails conflict among party-state apparatuses. For example, the State Oceanic Administration (SOA) was tasked with preserving China's marine resources and environment, but hydrocarbon exploitation and fisheries are controlled by the Ministry of Land and Natural Resources (MLNR) and Ministry of Agriculture (MoA). The SOA complains that, since 'fisheries is related to business, [the MoA] are very powerful in terms of policy. We feel very far away from the centre of policymaking' (Interviewee A31 2018). This fragmentation is widely recognised as problematic within China itself, leading to many calls for rationalisation. Notably the SOA – which has wide-ranging *de jure* responsibilities but, as a mere vice-ministerial agency, little de facto power (Interviewee A07 2018; Interviewee A24 2018) – has 'been pushing for a ministry of ocean affairs for many years', but was thwarted by other agencies' resistance (Interviewee A31 2018). The confusion and overlap between different maritime agencies became especially notorious with respect to the various MLEAs, which until 2013 were widely nicknamed the 'five dragons stirring up the sea' (see Table 2.3), for reasons discussed below.[2]

Table 2.3 *China's maritime law enforcement agencies to 2013*

Responsibilities/Agency	CMS	MSA	FLEC	CMP	GAC
Environmental protection	✓	✓	✓	✓	
Protecting maritime rights and interests	✓		✓	✓	
Inspecting vessels		✓	✓	✓	
Port management	✓				✓
Anti-smuggling				✓	✓
Fishing ground management	✓	✓			
Internal maritime security	✓			✓	
Maritime patrol	✓		✓	✓	✓

Source: Wang, Gang (2011: 4).

---

[2] The 'five dragons' were: China Maritime Surveillance (CMS), the Ministry of Transport's Maritime Safety Administration (MSA), the Ministry of Agriculture's Fisheries Law Enforcement Command (FLEC), the Ministry of Public Security's China Maritime Police (CMP) and the General Administration of Customs (GAC).

Decentralisation has also clearly transformed SCS policymaking and implementation. Administrative control over China's maritime territory was devolved to provincial governments in 1992, which swiftly enabled corruption, criminality and quasi-autonomous maritime behaviour (Segal 1994: 328). Legally, all Chinese land features in the SCS are part of Hainan province. Hainan is known as a particularly freewheeling province, having served – rather disastrously – as a testbed for pro-market reforms in the 1980s (Brødsgaard 2009). Legal experts regard it as a 'very bizarre' province, whose party-state bosses are frequently chided for disobeying central instructions (Interviewee A07 2018). Provincial governments view their maritime domains primarily as resources for local capitalist development, and have competed ferociously to exploit fisheries, 'creating overcapacity and duplicating efforts' (Jakobson 2014: 34), aided by the full decentralisation of many relevant agencies: Hainan's Marine and Fishery Department reports exclusively to the provincial governor, not the MoA (Xiong and Li 2013). In pursuit of local economic objectives, Hainan officials lobby for central support while stretching their local autonomy to breaking point, typically '"report[ing their behaviour] after the fact" rather than seek[ing] preapproval' (Jakobson 2014: 34).

Finally, internationalisation has also transformed many formerly domestic agencies into international maritime actors. The 'five dragons', for example, were initially all domestic law enforcement agencies, operating exclusively around China's coastal waters. However, as China's maritime activity has expanded into the SCS, their reach has extended, bringing them into contact – and often conflict – with the trawlers, coastguards and navies of rival claimants, and even the US navy (see Figure 2.1 and Map 2.1). The same applies for Hainan's 'maritime militia'. These militia are overwhelmingly fishermen, who receive basic training from the PLAN and ship upgrades and subsidies from local Hainan governments in exchange for leading fishing expeditions or occasionally supporting PLAN-led operations. This has empowered fishermen to engage in confrontational behaviour in pursuit of fishing grounds, putting trawlers on the front lines of major incidents with other states.

However, other internationalising agencies have pursued a more peaceful approach. For instance, the Maritime Safety Administration (MSA) tries to avoid SCS conflicts and has participated in transnational governance networks with other states' coastguards, including the US-led West Pacific Naval Symposium, the Container Security Initiative, the International Maritime Organisation's International Ship and Port Facility Security Code programme and the Japanese-led Regional Cooperation Agreement on Combating Piracy and Armed Robbery Against Ships in Asia (Li 2010). Similarly, the SOA has promoted 'blue partnerships', establishing ties with agencies in over fifty countries, signing over thirty bilateral agreements, and collaborating on ten projects with Southeast Asian counterparts in its latest five-year plan (2016–20) (Chen 2018). The SOA has established a 'joint committee' with its Southeast Asian equivalents to promote cooperation, including three joint research centres, high-level technocrat exchanges and joint fieldwork (Wang 2018). These activities frequently continue even when other agencies are harshly confronting one another (Interviewees A26 2018).

Regulating Chinese Conduct in the South China Sea

This section describes the mechanisms used to coordinate this remarkably broad range of actors in the SCS. As anticipated in the theoretical framework developed in Chapter 1, we do not perceive a carefully planned strategy, specifying clear objectives and roles. Rather, reflecting actual dynamics, contending actors and interests are accommodated within a loose policy framework, centred on the nebulous nine-dash line (9DL) and an injunction to strike a 'balance' between maintaining stability (*weiwen*) and protecting China's maritime rights (*weiquan*). Top leaders also use various coordinating bodies, but these have historically been confused, weak or inactive. Accordingly, the actors described above have enjoyed a high degree of latitude to interpret China's vague national policy, as subsequent sections demonstrate in detail.

Chinese conduct in the SCS is shaped by two loose policy guidelines. The first is China's claim to 'historic rights' within the 9DL (see Map 2.1). As Hayton (2014: ch. 2) compellingly documents, historically, the SCS was not 'owned' or even governed by any state but, in response to Western imperial predation and domestic nationalism, Chinese governments and nationalists began asserting sovereignty claims over the area in the early twentieth century. These claims gradually extended southwards and, in 1947, the Chinese government formally adopted a map drafted by a nationalist cartographer in 1936, adapting an initial 11-dash line into a 9-dash line. This map has gradually become ingrained into official and

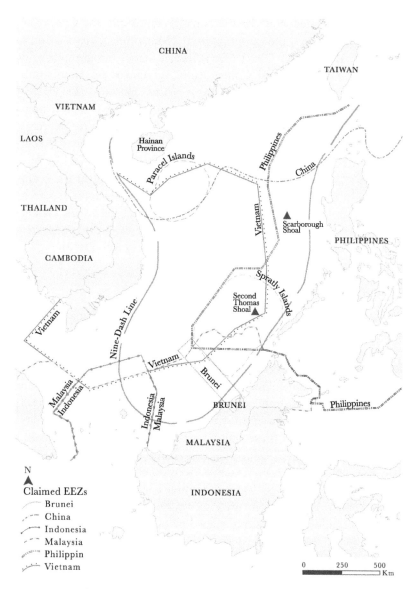

Map 2.1 South China Sea

popular consciousness in China, despite the fact that it was not used in
a formal diplomatic context until 2009, as part of the submission by the
Ministry of Foreign Affairs (MFA) to the United Nations Commission on
the Limits of the Continental Shelf.

Table 2.4 *UNCLOS regulations*

Type of feature	Attendant maritime right
Land	12 nautical mile (nm) territorial sea plus 200 nm exclusive economic zone (EEZ)
Rocks ('which cannot sustain human habitation or economic life of their own')	12 nm territorial sea
Low-tide elevations ('a naturally formed area of land which is surrounded by and above water at low tide but submerged at high tide')	None, unless it is within 12 nm of land/rock, in which case they may be used to establish baselines of the territorial sea/EEZ.

Note: 'Territorial sea' means full sovereignty over waters, seabed and airspace, similar to terrestrial sovereignty. EEZ means a state enjoys exclusive rights to exploit, economically and scientifically, the waters and seabed and may also construct artificial islands, but must allow 'other internationally lawful uses of the sea' by others, including overflight, the laying of submarine cables and pipelines, etc., and is also responsible for conservation, e.g., to prevent overfishing. 'Innocent passage' is guaranteed to all vessels through each of these zones. All other maritime space is designated 'high seas', which are not under the jurisdiction of any state.
Source: United Nations (1982).

Exactly what the 9DL means is open to wide interpretation. As one Chinese legal scholar remarks, 'no one really knows what it means' (Interviewee A11 2018). There are at least three competing interpretations, even among legal experts (Interviewee A33 2018). A minimalist interpretation, compatible with UNCLOS, to which China is a state party, would be that China claims sovereignty over all the land features within the 9DL and attendant rights over oceanic areas, as specified in UNCLOS, which vary with the nature of these features (see Table 2.4). This would still permit creative interpretation over the status of particular features.[3] However, a maximalist interpretation of the 9DL, obviously incompatible with UNCLOS,

---

[3] The Philippines' 2013 suit against China in the International Court of Arbitration included an effort to have five of eight Chinese-held features defined as low-tide elevations and the rest as rocks, in order to limit the extent of Chinese control, which would otherwise lie within the Philippines' EEZ.

might be that the entire area, land and sea, somehow 'belongs' to China. Although such claims are rarely made publicly, except by Chinese hyper-nationalists, some parts of the Chinese party-state apparatus certainly behave as though they believe this, as we shall see. A third, mid-range interpretation is that China has unspecified 'historic rights' within the 9DL. The State Council (2016) explicitly stated this when responding to the outcome of an International Court of Arbitration case brought by the Philippines. What 'historic rights' actually means is unclear, and Chinese legal scholars argue that the State Council's statement made it even murkier (Interviewee A07 2018). Notwithstanding vague and dubious references to 'customary international law', the claim is ultimately grounded in a baseless[4] notion that China administered the entire 9DL area before the predations of others and, consequently, states now wishing to exploit fishing grounds or hydrocarbon resources should cooperate with China.

The sheer vagueness of these claims carries the risk of serious conflicts with other littoral states, but the Chinese government appears unable to clarify the claims, given the domestic interests at stake. The 9DL is provocative in its own right: as a Chinese government advisor admits, referring to the MFA's inclusion of a 9DL map in its 2009 UN submission, 'from 2009 the SCS heated up. The direct reason is the 9DL' (Interviewee A24 2018). Moreover, a lack of clarity around territorial waters, or exclusive economic zones (EEZs), inevitably entails friction over economic exploitation, law enforcement and maritime defence. Rival claimants consistently ask China to clarify the scope of its claims, which would provide a baseline for negotiations. However, as legal experts note, 'The Chinese government ... does not make a clear definition of the 9DL' (Interviewee A08 2018). It 'doesn't have a clear view of the 9DL' and 'won't define it specifically' (Interviewee A09 2018).

Realists often gloss this as deliberate 'strategic ambiguity', designed to help China advance its geopolitical objectives. However, this ignores the way in which the 9DL continually embroils China in regional conflicts and incites US intervention, both contrary to Beijing's wider diplomatic agenda. It also fails to situate the 9DL within wider practices within China's transformed party-state. As explained in Chapter 1, policy

---

[4] See Hayton (2014: ch. 2; 2019).

guidelines are often left vague in order to accommodate incompatible interests. As Ministry of State Security researchers state, 'it's really difficult [to specify the 9DL], not because the Chinese government doesn't want to do so, but because it's really difficult to bring all these different opinions together' – even under Xi Jinping (Interviewees A27 2018). Policymakers also fear alienating nationalists, who are often whipped up by powerful groups like the navy lobby. A State Council researcher observes: 'the government denies that the SCS is a core interest, but many Chinese people think it is' (Interviewee A25 2018). As one legal expert puts it: 'the rulers are afraid of the people ... they fear they will lose their jobs' (Interviewee A08 2018). Thus, the 9DL reflects our conceptualisation of the state as a 'condensation' of contradictory socio-political forces (Jessop 2016: 54).

This is further reflected in the second form of regulatory guidance: the injunction to balance between maintaining stability (*weiwen*) and protecting China's maritime rights (*weiquan*). Exactly when this guideline emerged is unclear: Feng Zhang (2020) argues that it has been implicit policy since the 1990s, while Chubb (2019) dates its adoption to 2008. In any case, the injunction to balance between these objectives is at best aspirational and at worst downright contradictory. As one state-linked researcher notes, in the context of sovereignty disputes, *weiwen* and *weiquan* are often 'conflicting objectives' (Interviewee A25 2018). Accordingly, as an MFA advisor points out, asserting both simultaneously is 'a contradiction. You cannot "balance" them' (Interviewee A12 2018). Instead, as an MFA researcher states, actual behaviour swings back and forth between the two objectives: 'in practice sometimes we put the priority on safeguarding rights, and sometimes ... on maintaining stability ... it is dynamic' (Interviewee A20 2018). Moreover, the lack of implementing guidelines means that, in practice, it is up to China's various maritime agencies to interpret these contradictory imperatives; accordingly, the exact balance at any given moment is not a result of precise, top-down decision-making, but rather the behaviour of fragmented, decentralised and internationalised actors (Jakobson 2014).

This problem is naturally exacerbated by the sheer vagueness of the maritime rights being protected. Given the lack of clarity over the 9DL, 'there is no clear meaning of "safeguarding rights" ... Different departments ... come to different understandings of safeguarding rights' (Interviewee A20 2018). Agencies which benefit from

a maximalist interpretation thus enjoy considerable autonomy to pursue it, with the cover that they were merely implementing *weiquan*
(Jakobson 2014). Agencies seeking to avoid conflict in the SCS must
struggle to deal with the fallout and restore emphasis on *weiwen*. This
guideline thus entails not a harmonious balance, but rather constant
struggles and potentially wild oscillations, which goes a long way to
explaining the erratic behaviours described in Figure 2.1.

Importantly, this has not changed substantially under President Xi.
Much has been made of a speech Xi gave in July 2013, which supposedly stressed China's maritime rights, ushering in an era of Chinese
aggression in the SCS. Yet, as a State Council researcher observes,
although Xi 'put more attention on safeguarding sovereignty
rights . . . *at the same time* he . . . still emphasised maintaining stability'
(Interviewee A20 2018, emphasis added). There was still no clear guidance on what this meant in practice (Jakobson 2014). One maritime
official told the International Crisis Group that 'you won't find anyone
who knows what it really means' (ICG 2015: 9). Interpretations of what
Xi's speech meant for policy actors ranged from a modest shift towards
maintaining rights to total disregard for other nations' claims and interests (Yamaguchi 2014). Thus, reflecting the regulatory-state model, Xi's
words still required interpretation by other party-state actors. As an
MFA scholar notes, Xi provided 'only an overall signal: "we need
to take a more proactive role in maritime issues". Then different organisations begin to make their own recommendations or [engage in] policy
planning' (Interviewee A01 2018). Another State Council researcher
concurs: Xi's statements were 'only an idea – no plan . . . He only
gives you a sense of direction. Then you have to develop all the details
on how to implement it . . . If there was a *strategy*, we would be more
balanced and not become so extreme' (Interviewee A24 2018, original
emphasis).

The situation is further exacerbated by the lack of a clear legal or
institutional framework to guide maritime actors. Chinese legal scholars
widely bemoan the lack of a 'basic law' to govern maritime issues,
resulting in 'quite fragmented' governance (Interviewee A07 2018).
One expert claims to have documented over 5,000 different maritime
laws and regulations, with 'power [being] divided among different
ministries', with 'not very clear' lines of responsibility (Interviewee A08
2018). 'So many departments', national and subnational, 'have jurisdiction involving sea issues; they pass different [regulations and] so

create many conflicts with each other' (Interviewee A09 2018). This entails 'many [legal] shortcomings and loopholes', permitting contradictory behaviour, which is exacerbated by the lack of any clear hierarchy or control mechanism, such that 'coordination between those agencies and departments [is] confused' (Interviewee A07 2018). Top leaders tried to improve coordination through the short-lived Leading Small Group (LSG) for Safeguarding Maritime Rights, created in 2012 and abolished in 2018 (discussed later in this chapter). Until then, the only coordinating mechanism was the Foreign Affairs LSG which, as noted in Chapter 1, was of dubious efficacy, meeting 'only infrequently, if ever' before its own abolition in 2018 (Shirk 2014: 404). In the years of peak SCS confrontation, Christensen (2013: 25) noted a lack of evidence that this LSG had met 'often' or even 'at all'. Its then director, State Councillor Dai Bingguo, 'complained [that] no one listened to him when he tried to coordinate the [other agencies] with interests in the SCS' (Shirk 2014: 404).

The decision-making framework for non-routine SCS matters is also unclear. Sometimes, maritime actors will need permission or resources from the centre to pursue their agendas, or need conflicts among them to be resolved, necessitating intervention from senior leaders. The latter may also need to make ad hoc decisions in response to other claimants' behaviour. However, even China's most knowledgeable experts, enjoying strong insider connections, 'cannot tell what kind of decision-making circle is formed' in these situations (Interviewees A10 2018). Senior government advisors suggest that rather than the routine use of LSGs or other coordinating bodies, decisions reflect bottom-up lobbying efforts, involving only ad hoc consultation with other agencies, if any (Interviewees A06 2017). Accordingly, they primarily see Xi's role as arbitrating between competing attempts to influence from below (Interviewee A01 2017). Hence, as Hayton (2014: 253) argues, 'Chinese policy is less likely to be the result of a considered summation of reasoned arguments than the unpredictable result of an agglomeration of lobbying campaigns'.

Overall, then, what is most striking about China's SCS policy framework is not the presence of a sinister grand strategy but rather the absence of clearly specified objectives and the extreme permissiveness of the guidelines. At most, they describe a very general set of principles: that China's overall position in the SCS should be defended, ideally without creating too much instability. This is not a strategy in any meaningful sense of the word: it does not express a clearly defined goal, then specify concrete steps needed to realise it, authoritatively assigning resources and roles to particular actors. Rather, this approach reflects the Chinese-style regulatory state in action. Top leaders describe guidelines, specified only vaguely to accommodate contending interests, but others must then interpret these, and try to influence policy outcomes within this framework. The vagueness of key terms, and the limited presence and efficacy of coordinating institutions, affords considerable scope for quite extreme interpretations, as actors can always claim that they were 'protecting China's maritime rights', thereby evading disciplinary action except in the most egregious circumstances (Jakobson 2014: 32). The lack of clear decision-making structures also enables fragmented agencies to influence major decisions, while a lack of institutionalised consultation means that 'balanced' outcomes are not assured.

As the rest of this chapter shows, in practice, this entails continuous struggle over policy direction, with outcomes shifting back and forth from *weiwen* to *weiquan* over time. The net result may be considered a favourable outcome for the Chinese-style regulatory state: ultimately, China's grip on the SCS has certainly tightened, without provoking war. However, this approach to SCS policy has undeniably harmed China's wider diplomatic agenda. The assertive conduct of some Chinese actors has provoked increasing tensions, and sometimes serious crises, with other claimant states. This has undermined Beijing's relations with Southeast Asian countries, with many analysts accusing China of trying to divide and weaken ASEAN. It has also provoked 'soft balancing' by the Philippines (from 2012–18) and Vietnam, involving additional military spending and international legal clashes. Chinese activities have also drawn the US directly into the SCS issue, backed by other Western allies in its freedom of navigation operations. These outcomes were neither foreseen nor desired. They emerged not as a result of a carefully planned strategy, which necessarily involves trading off objectives, but rather from a very loosely governed process of policy formation and implementation.

Maritime Actors and the Struggle between 'Stability' and 'Rights'

Chinese policy analysts typically label the agencies that seek to uphold stability (*weiwen*) in the SCS as 'doves', while those who emphasise China's maritime rights (*weiquan*) are called 'hawks'

(Interviewee A01 2017; Interviewee A24 2018). We prefer to avoid this shorthand because, while useful, it can also be misleading. For example, the MFA is typically described as 'dovish', but the MFA also submitted China's 9DL to UNCLOS in 2009, responded vehemently to the Philippines' International Court of Arbitration suit, and has lately practised aggressive 'wolf warrior diplomacy'. Accordingly, we discuss the contending agendas of SCS actors in turn, highlighting their internal contradictions where appropriate, and tracing how their struggles entailed changes in Chinese conduct over time.

The Ministry of Foreign Affairs: Promoting Stability, Losing Influence

As China's main diplomatic interface with other countries, the MFA has a standard interest in interpreting SCS policy guidelines in a peaceful direction. It evaluates proposed actions in the SCS in terms of their likely impact on 'neighbourhood diplomacy', and generally promotes moderation in internal policy battles (Interviewee A01 2018). The MFA represented China in the UNCLOS talks and led the domestic effort to ratify and implement the Convention. Its public interpretation of the 9DL is a minimalist one: China claims only those rights to which it is entitled under international law (Beckman et al. 2013: 429). The MFA also tends to emphasise the pursuit of stability, leading diplomatic efforts to soothe SCS tensions, including negotiating with ASEAN the 2002 Declaration on a Code of Conduct in the SCS and thereafter the Code of Conduct itself. As Figure 2.1 shows, the MFA is also frequently involved in de-escalating tensions sparked by others, alongside the Chinese Communist Party's (CCP) International Liaison Department, which was crucial in repairing ties with Vietnam after 2014.

However, as noted in Chapter 1, the MFA is a relatively weak agency, as well as being constrained to defend actors engaged in a more maximalist interpretation of the centre's policy guidelines. As one MFA-linked scholar laments, 'it is not in charge of SCS policy. It's [responsible for] implementation of policy, coordination, and also [for] send[ing] out the official position on this issue', but is too 'weak' to compel other actors to line up behind its preferred approach (Interviewee A01 2018). Thus, although the MFA may act in accordance with UNCLOS, 'key elements ... [such as] the military, the oil companies and southern coastal provinces ... continue to act on the basis that China maintains a historic territorial claim to the whole sea' (Hayton 2014: 119). The MFA is thus often bypassed in practice by other maritime actors who 'lack international experience and do not always realise – or care – how their actions affect China's dealings with other countries' (Jakobson 2014: 15). As the country's main diplomatic mouthpiece, the MFA is frequently compelled to excuse the behaviour of these actors, and also to reflect the general line set out in SCS policy guidelines. This explains its 2009 UNCLOS submission, and its subsequent statements about 'historic rights' and international law, which were apparently intended to provide cover for more aggressive agencies, yet undermined the MFA's stated commitments to the UNCLOS framework.[5]

The waxing and waning of MFA influence corresponds to the general contours of China's SCS behaviour. The early 1990s saw increasing tensions in the SCS, particularly involving Chinese oil companies in waters contested with Vietnam, and peaked with the Philippines' discovery in 1995 of a Chinese installation on Mischief Reef. The MFA, apparently caught unawares, initially claimed the base had been constructed by FLEC, then later admitted it had been built by low-ranking PLAN officers without official authorisation (Hayton 2014: 86; see also Chung, Chien-peng 2004: ch. 6; Fravel 2015). The strong regional backlash against these moves led the MFA to argue that the supportive environment needed for China's 'peaceful development' was at risk, requiring a strong reorientation around stability maintenance. For several years, the MFA was ascendant in the SCS policy space, leading to the 2002 ASEAN–China Declaration. However, the MFA's efforts continued to be troubled by other actors, including Hainan's bureau of fisheries, which has administered Mischief Reef since 1995 (You 2017b: 13), and which aggravated regional tensions through 1998–9 by continuing to upgrade facilities there (Chung, Christopher 2004: 243–7, 272–5). Moreover, as we shall see, from the mid-2000s, more

---

[5] For instance, in 2014 the MFA defended the presence of a Chinese oil rig in waters claimed by Vietnam by arguing that it was in Chinese territorial waters. This was only plausible if nearby Triton Island was considered Chinese territory, but since this is disputed with Vietnam and would create overlapping EEZ claims, UNCLOS obliges China to proceed cautiously (Thayer 2014a). Similarly, in 2016 the MFA protested Indonesia's arrest of Chinese fishermen off Natuna island (within Indonesia's EEZ) by asserting they were in 'traditional fishing grounds', which also contradicts UNCLOS provisions (Denyer 2016).

aggressive actors were gradually empowered, leading to a shift towards asserting maritime rights. During this period, MFA officials complain of being steadily marginalised from decision-making (Interviewee A01 2018). By around 2012, insiders report, the MFA 'had very little influence', with 'a very small group decid[ing] how to deal with SCS issues'; 'the MFA only received orders and then did it. They had less power to decide how to do it' (Interviewee A24 2018).

The PLA Navy: Lobbying for Resources

The PLAN is typically seen as a 'hawkish' entity, but again its actual interests and behaviour are more complex. It does interpret Chinese policy guidelines on the SCS more expansively, as this supports its domestic campaign for resources. However, the vagueness of these guidelines does entail difficulties for the navy, while the imperative to maintain stability also limits its aggression.

The PLAN is widely understood to be part of a 'navy lobby', a nationalist military-industrial complex that relentlessly posits maritime security threats and lobbies for additional funding (Kardon and Scobell 2015). The navy lobby ties the PLAN's fate directly to China's capitalist development by presenting it as the guardian of China's overseas trade, investment and workforce, a role formally enshrined in the PLA's 'new historic missions' in 2004 (Fravel and Liebman 2011: 75). This does not necessarily imply an aggressive outlook: in the Gulf of Aden, for example, this agenda drew the PLAN into networked governance arrangements to tackle piracy, alongside Western navies (Ghiselli 2015).

However, it does suggest a natural interest in interpreting China's SCS policy framework expansively. For the PLAN, the greater China's maritime territory, the louder it can lobby for additional resources (Fravel and Liebman 2011: 58–60; see also Chung, Christopher 2004: 227–30, 255–6). Exactly what this territory comprises, however, is open to interpretation, thanks to the vague 9DL framework. According to You (2017b: 21), most PLAN representatives at a 2013 national security conference stated that UNCLOS limits Chinese claims to land features and surrounding waters. But a sizeable hawkish faction promotes a broader interpretation, invoking vague claims of 'historic rights' (Fravel 2015). The PLAN has also tried to limit UNCLOS's impact on its interests by demanding that vessels seeking 'innocent passage' through China's territorial waters must first request permission, and by opposing foreign navies' innocent passage through China's EEZ. The first demand, which is incompatible with UNCLOS, was incorporated into China's 1992 Law on the Territorial Sea, which transmitted UNCLOS into domestic China law (Fravel 2015).

At times, the PLAN has also lobbied for aggressive policy moves and even made them without central authorisation. However, contrary to the realist hypothesis that Chinese expansionism should rise with its military power, PLAN's autonomy and influence was greatest when China was militarily weak, and during leadership transitions, highlighting the primacy of domestic power struggles. The PLAN's most aggressive action was its 1988 seizure of the Paracel Islands held by Vietnam. To avoid budget cuts in the late 1980s, the PLAN lobbied vociferously around the SCS, eventually securing resources for a build-up in the Spratly Islands (Garver 1992; Yung 2015). The PLAN also successfully lobbied the Central Military Commission to approve the seizure of nine features, but it was a local commander who opened fire on Vietnamese forces, without central authorisation (Fravel 2015). This was China's last overt use of force for territorial expansion.

The PLAN's apparently unauthorised role in annexing Mischief Reef in 1994 was mentioned earlier. Low-ranking naval officers' willingness to build structures there, without high-level approval, partly reflects the looseness of China's policy guidelines – it could easily be glossed as 'protecting maritime rights' – and partly the political context. Jiang Zemin, seeking to consolidate power after succeeding Deng Xiaoping, was building PLA support by permitting a more aggressive foreign policy, not merely in the SCS but also vis-à-vis Taiwan, resulting in a major international crisis (Storey 1999; Chung, Chien-peng 2004: 265–75).[6] After Jiang's position was secure, the MFA was able to row SCS policy back towards maintaining stability (Chung, Chien-peng 2004: 243–7, 272–5).

Less dramatically, but perhaps no less dangerously, China's loose policy framework also leads to frequent confrontations with foreign naval forces, including US vessels. This is a good demonstration of how a lack of clarity creates unintended consequences, and creates problems

---

[6] In exchange for their loyalty, military leaders also secured base visits, higher spending and promotions (Ding 2003; Hsu 2010).

even for apparently 'hawkish' actors. As a retired senior navy officer states, the fact that the 9DL 'is not well defined or clarified' makes it 'very difficult for the Chinese navy to operate in the SCS', because exactly what territory can legitimately be defended is unclear (Interviewee A23 2018). This led, for example, to PLAN's confrontation of the US spy vessels USNS *Bowditch* in 2001, apparently without central authorisation, and USNS *Impeccable* in 2009, as well as serious frictions around US freedom of navigation patrols (Fravel 2015). It is not clear that the PLAN initiated the *Impeccable* incident – civilian law enforcement and militia took the lead – but a PLAN vessel was present and thus clearly aware of, if not supervising the confrontation. Given the *Impeccable*'s location, PLAN's subsequent claim that it was intruding into 'Chinese waters' implied a very expansive definition of this term, demonstrating the risks arising from China's loose policy framework (Glaser and Funaiole 2019: 200).

Such incidents undermine the maintenance of stability, requiring even the PLAN to seek a more 'balanced' approach at times. For instance, to reduce the risks of accidental war, the PLAN has negotiated two codes of conduct with the US navy (Interviewee A23 2018). Tactically, the PLAN also tends to let civilian vessels take a lead in harassing foreign shipping, to avoid direct military-to-military clashes. The PLAN also seems to have increased efforts to professionalise maritime militia units, whose free-wheeling activities often generate serious international frictions, as discussed below (Kennedy and Erickson 2017a). Nonetheless, the military's disconnection from state structures gives it autonomy from China's diplomatic agencies, permitting uncoordinated behaviour that undermines the latter's operations. For instance, through 2010–11, the MFA was struggling to de-escalate mounting tensions in the SCS by promoting a 'new security concept', foregrounding trust-building and cooperation with ASEAN. The PLAN clashed with a Philippine oil survey vessel in March 2011, ruining the whole scheme (Huang 2013: 41).

Chinese Oil Companies: Pushing for Profit

China's national oil companies (NOCs) also favour a maximalist interpretation of China's SCS policy framework. In pursuit of profit, these centrally owned and quasi-autonomous state-owned enterprises (SOEs) have increasingly pursued hydrocarbon exploration and exploitation in disputed areas, sparking repeated conflict with rival claimants. Reflecting the disorderly nature of decision-making in this policy area, the NOCs have secured top-level support for their agenda by bypassing the party-state's diplomatic institutions, leading to a serious crisis in Sino-Vietnamese relations in 2014.

China's energy sector exemplifies the emergence of the Chinese-style regulatory state, creating 'fragmented and uncoordinated' governance (Tunsjø 2013: ch. 2). The NOCs are former production ministries, converted into profit-seeking SOEs. Their chairmen retain vice-ministerial rank and, from 1993 to 2010, no ministerial agency existed to govern the energy sector, allowing the NOCs to effectively self-regulate, using the powers of the ex-ministries (Andrews-Speed 2010: 38–9; Taylor 2014: ch. 5). Even today, policymaking authority remains fragmented across several ministries, with attempts to create a powerful 'super-ministry' thwarted by resistance from the NOCs and others (Chen 2009: 252). China's National Energy Commission, created in 2010, is merely a weak coordinating body. Each of the eighteen different agencies operating in this sector can still issue its own regulations, resulting in 'inconsistent or even contradictory policies' (Andrews-Speed 2010: 41; cf. Taylor 2014: ch. 6). These arrangements afford the NOCs enormous power to pursue their corporate agendas, reflecting the dynamics of influencing, interpreting and ignoring theorised in Chapter 1. As Chen (2009: 254–8) states, the NOCs enjoy 'considerable influence over the government in pursuit of their commercial interests', and the capacity to 'adapt, modify and even subvert' government directives.

Since the early 1990s, NOCs have also internationalised, with significant consequences for China's foreign relations. The NOCs were driven overseas by dwindling domestic supplies, fierce competition and government price controls. This was initially not sanctioned by the government, but after years of NOC lobbying for policy support, Beijing adopted its 'going out' policy in 2000, providing formal support for SOEs to globalise (Houser 2008: 152–3). As latecomers to international markets, however, the NOCs were forced into risky territories shunned by established oil majors, like Iran, Sudan and Myanmar. Statist accounts often suggest that the NOCs were sent by Beijing to accomplish geostrategic goals, but in reality these investments were driven by their corporate interests, rather than by the national interests of the Chinese state (Downs 2008). Given China's fragmented governance structures, the NOCs 'operate abroad largely free of government oversight', with the MFA barely kept informed of their activities, let alone influencing them (Houser 2008: 161). Where national policy and corporate interests do not align, the NOCs are notorious for ignoring the former, sometimes compelling changes in China's foreign policy. For example, from 2007, China National Petroleum Corporation (CNPC) ignored government instructions to stop investing in Sudan, leaving the MFA to clean up the subsequent diplomatic fallout by mediating in Sudan's civil war and despatching peacekeepers. Similarly, from 2011, the NOCs ignored government injunctions to 'slow down' in Iran, forcing the MFA to try to dilute United Nations sanctions on Tehran (Tunsjø 2013: ch. 4).

However, as Chapter 1 noted, the Chinese-style regulatory state does not grant total autonomy to any party-state actor: the NOCs must still operate within broad policy frameworks. Although they can often influence these frameworks, they also interpret them by framing their corporate agendas within them. The NOCs can always claim that their overseas activities are implementing Beijing's 'going out' policy. From the early 2000s, they also exploited top leaders' vaguely expressed concerns about 'energy security' and the 'Malacca dilemma' to rationalise their investments and secure additional policy and financial support.[7] In the SCS, their corporate agendas are framed as reinforcing China's sovereignty claims. For example, China National Offshore Oil Company's (CNOOC) chairman describes his firm's HYSY-981 oil rig as 'mobile national territory' and a 'strategic instrument' for protecting China's maritime rights (quoted in Orlik 2012). Energy sector expert Erica Downs rightly describes such behaviour as an attempt to attract 'financial or other support from the government' by appearing to 'align' the company 'more closely with national interests' (quoted in Orlik 2012).

---

[7] The 'Malacca dilemma' is the fear that China's oil imports are vulnerable in the event of war because they mostly transit through the 'chokehold' of the Malacca Straits. The NOCs have exploited this concern to get backing for otherwise unviable projects, for example, a US$2.4bn China–Myanmar oil and gas pipeline. In reality, the Malacca Straits are not a chokehold (tankers can re-route south of Indonesia – it simply costs more) and NOCs' 'solutions' have feathered corporate nests rather than solving the alleged problem (the Myanmar pipelines, for example, can barely carry 5 per cent of China's energy requirements, are underused, and are vulnerable to attack). See Wirth (2012) and Mayer and Wübbecke (2013: 293–4).

The NOCs are attracted to the SCS by the lure of untapped energy reserves: up to 2.7 billion tonnes of oil and 3.7 million cubic metres of natural gas (Chen 2011: 479–80).[8] This incentivises an expansive interpretation of China's SCS policy framework for these cadre-capitalists. This is especially true for CNOOC, which administers the rights to exploit offshore hydrocarbon blocks in Chinese waters. Since China's coastal oilfields are almost depleted, the SCS is a lifeline. This does not necessarily imply support for reckless aggression: the NOCs need political stability, not armed conflict, to engage in the long-term, capital-intensive investments needed in this sector. Nonetheless, it does imply an inherent motive to interpret China's 9DL expansively, and to invoke China's ill-defined 'maritime rights' when doing so would advance the NOCs' corporate interests. Thus, CNOOC has regularly auctioned off blocks in disputed waters, sometimes ignoring contrary instructions from Beijing, sparking repeated tensions with rival claim-ants, particularly the Philippines and Vietnam (Zha 2001: 582; Chung, Chien-peng 2004: ch. 6; ICG 2012: 12).

The most prominent example of the NOCs driving conflict with neighbouring states came in May 2014, when the mobile HYSY-981 oil rig was placed in waters disputed with Vietnam, triggering a major international crisis. The rig, leased by a CNOOC subsidiary to CNPC, was placed in the Zhongjiannan basin, near the Paracels and within Vietnam's claimed EEZ. HYSY-981 was escorted by dozens of Chinese ships, including seven PLAN and around forty MLEA vessels, over thirty tugs and similar craft, and thirty-four to forty trawlers – part of Hainan's maritime militia (Fravel 2015). While PLAN stood watch, the civilian vessels aggressively shielded the rig from Vietnamese coast-guard ships and trawlers sent to harass it, resulting in several serious collisions and the arrest of thirteen Vietnamese fishermen. Anti-Chinese protests erupted in Vietnam, escalating into violent riots and resulting in at least twenty deaths (Long 2016: 149). HYSY-981 was eventually withdrawn on 15 July, but China's relations with Vietnam and ASEAN were badly soured. The incident was widely interpreted as an example of Xi Jinping's more 'assertive' maritime policy.

However, a state transformation analysis allows us to trace it more accurately to the NOCs' long-standing corporate agendas and the

---

[8] Other estimates are far lower; the sovereignty disputes complicate exploration efforts.

fragmented decision-making processes outlined above. As a senior industry expert points out, even if Xi had ordered CNPC or CNOOC to drill for oil in this area, this would have been impossible if the companies lacked the capacity to do so (Interviewee A29 2018). And yet, this capacity was being developed long before Xi's rise. HYSY-981 emerged from the '863 Programme', launched in 1986, to reduce the NOCs' dependence on foreign technology (Downs 2014). It was developed as part of CNPC's 'Zhongjiannan Petroleum drilling and exploration project', initiated in 2004, with Ministry of Land and Natural Resources approval secured in 2005. Pre-exploration wells were established in 2011, and a site survey completed in 2013 (Xinhua 2014a). The project was largely exploratory, seeking to assess hydrocarbon potential and seabed conditions, and to continue the long-term development of deep-sea drilling capacities (Xinhua 2014b).

Thus, CNPC had been pursuing hydrocarbon exploration in the Zhongjiannan basin for a full decade before May 2014. In 2006, it held failed talks with PetroVietnam to begin joint surveys (Energy Tribune 2006). In 2007, it agreed to lease drilling equipment from the Swiss firm Transocean to deploy in the area, but its plans were dropped under MFA pressure around the 2008 Beijing Olympics (Downs 2014). From 2009 to 2011, tensions escalated as PetroVietnam partnered with Exxon in an exploration and production deal, encompassing areas claimed by China. In response, CNOOC began offering blocks in the area to foreign investors, prompting protests from Hanoi (Jakobson 2014: 24). A turning point came when CNOOC's HYSY-981 rig came online in early 2012, allowing CNPC to drill without help from foreign oil companies, which largely avoided this disputed area. The MFA's subsequent explanation of the May 2014 incident – that it was merely a 'continuation of the routine process of explorations' – was thus grounded in reality (Ministry of Foreign Affairs 2014). As an oil industry expert remarks, the NOCs 'acquired national licenses much earlier to explore in this area. The HYSY-981 rig's deployment was just totally routine for them' (Interviewee A29 2018).

The question remains: why was this provocative act allowed? After all, in previous years, the MFA had successfully restrained CNPC. The incident cannot be ascribed to rogue corporate behaviour: while the NOCs routinely pay the PLAN and MLEAs for protection, an operation on this scale, particularly involving the navy, would require high-level sanction (Interviewee A29 2018). As noted in Chapter 1, unpicking any specific decision within the party-state is virtually impossible. However, our interviewees suggest that the incident was driven by CNPC, which bypassed the MFA thanks to the fragmented decision-making structures discussed above. As noted, from around 2009, the MFA was being eclipsed by more hawkish actors. Sources within the ministry report that CNPC 'strongly proposed' a drilling programme; 'the MFA [was] against that', predicting 'serious consequences' for China's foreign relations, but it was steadily 'marginalised' from decision-making (Interviewee A01 2018).[9] Our informants, including an MFA advisor, report that decision-making at this time was particularly ad hoc, with powerful groups bypassing formal institutions to lobby Xi directly (Interviewee A12 2018; Interviewee A28 2018).[10] Although the NOCs and PLAN probably presented their proposals as expressing Xi's commitment to safeguarding China's maritime rights, reflecting their interpretation of Beijing's loose policy framework, they also downplayed their assertiveness. According to well-informed national maritime officials, the NOCs argued that their drilling site was located close to Chinese baselines in the Paracels, remote from any 'disputed or troublesome' area (Interviewees A26 2018). As one MFA official remarks, 'the Foreign Ministry ... knew [what] the consequences [would be], but the military, CNPC, they did not expect the reaction from the international community. So we had a very serious result' (Interviewee A01 2018).

This interpretation is supported by the incident's timing. A senior Vietnamese diplomat complained that 'There was no signalling. Vietnam is now unable to predict China's behaviour. We are wondering why China acted this way when bilateral relations were good' (ICG 2015: 20). Indeed, the timing was atrocious, coming just before an ASEAN Regional Forum meeting and when negotiations over the China–ASEAN Code of Conduct were making good progress; HYSY-981's deployment thus 'appeared to contradict Chinese policy',

---

[9] The International Crisis Group (ICG 2015: 10–12) suggests that the decision to deploy HYSY-981 was taken at the Maritime Rights LSG, where the MFA was represented by its Department for Ocean and Boundary Affairs, not the Department for Asian Affairs, resulting in limited appreciation of Vietnam's likely response. This explanation, foregrounding the MFA's *internal* fragmentation, is not implausible, but our MFA informants rejected this version of events.

[10] Long (2016: 160) also notes that Xi was still consolidating his power at this time, especially over the PLA, invalidating 'rational, unitary actor' assumptions.

suggesting poor coordination (ICG 2015: 5). Several well-placed informants also report that Vietnam's reaction 'was a big shock for the leadership' (Interviewee A24 2018; also Interviewee A01 2018; Interviewee A12 2018; ICG 2015: 10–12).

This interpretation is also supported by the mad scramble by Chinese diplomats to contain the international fallout in the name of maintaining stability. Although MFA 'spokesmen always had to say to the outside [world] that we had a consistent policy', justifying the rig's deployment, privately it worked intensively with the CCP's International Liaison Department (ILD) and the State Councillor for Foreign Affairs to de-escalate the crisis though bilateral diplomacy (Interviewee A01 2018; see also Long 2016: 156). The ILD's involvement, reflecting extensive ties between the two countries' communist parties, was particularly important (Interviewee A12 2018; Long 2016: 156). The diplomatic agencies also lobbied internally for an early withdrawal of the rig, which occurred on 15 July, a month ahead of schedule. Although official statements cited the survey's early completion and an approaching typhoon, an MFA official reveals that this was merely a 'good excuse', allowing China to 'save face' (Interviewee A01 2018; see also Thayer 2014b).

This fiasco allowed the MFA to regain some lost ground, winning Xi over to a more diplomatic approach to 'get ASEAN back' through 2014–15, resulting in multiple high-level visits, the launch of the Lancang-Mekong Initiative, and a new maritime cooperation fund (Interviewee A01 2018). However, foreign governments rightly perceived Chinese behaviour as highly contradictory. As an Indonesian diplomat commented: 'We are confused. Although we hear from China about peaceful development and that it does not want to be a hegemon, its actions are different' (ICG 2015: 25). This reflects not simply great-power hypocrisy, as the unitary actor assumption might suggest, but rather the transformation of China's party-state.

Hainan Province: Fishing for Trouble

The other cadre-capitalists most responsible for tensions in the SCS are those clustered around the fishing industry of Hainan province. The vast majority of maritime clashes in the SCS concern struggles over fishing grounds. Their steady increase reflects Hainan's continued pattern of ignoring central guidelines to reduce surplus capacity in the local industry, prioritising economic objectives at the expense of regional stability.

Hainan's malignant role stems from the decentralisation of authority over marine economic development, coupled with the province's dependence on primary industries. As noted earlier, the administration of China's coastal waters was devolved to provincial governments in 1992. Since the maritime domain under Hainan's control is sixty times larger than Hainan's landmass, the provincial government is naturally inclined to support a maximalist interpretation of the 9DL, and an assertive approach to maritime rights, as this extends its jurisdiction and thereby the resources at its disposal. This approach is reinforced by the failure of alternative decentralised development strategies. In the 1980s, Hainan island was separated from Guangdong to become a highly experimental testbed for pro-market reforms. Local officials exploited their newfound freedoms through various dubious schemes, generating a short-lived economic boom then a massive crash in 1993–4, leaving Hainan's economy dependent on fishing, agriculture, steel, oil, coal and basic resource processing (Feng and Goodman 1998; Brødsgaard 2009: chs. 1, 4, 5). Efforts to position Hainan as an economic gateway to Southeast Asia also foundered in the 1990s amid ferocious competition from Yunnan and Guangxi (Cheung and Tang 2001). Accordingly, provincial development plans have been channelled towards resource extraction, setting Hainan onto a collision course with neighbouring countries instead.

Because hydrocarbon exploitation is primarily the domain of centrally owned NOCs, Hainan's interests focus on fishing. Hainan has supported the NOCs, courting their investment, lobbying for central funding for hydrocarbon exploration, and bolstering prospecting missions with maritime militia units. This alliance has been reinforced by the appointment of some ex-NOC chairmen as governors of Hainan.[11] However, because fisheries are locally regulated and taxed, this is the primary focus of local cadre-capitalists. As one former Hainan maritime official bemoans, the 'local government is mostly interested in fish ... [it] doesn't really look after the sea except for the fishermen' (Interviewee A15 2018). From the early 1990s, local authorities heavily subsidised state-owned and private fishing companies, generating a tenfold expansion in the trawler fleet from 1988 to 1997, with the

---

[11] For details see ICG (2016:9).

annual catch quadrupling (Zha 2001: 588–91). By 2005, fisheries comprised over 9 per cent of provincial GDP (Brødsgaard 2009: ch. 4). Hainan's 2005 development plan sought to triple maritime-derived GDP by 2020, to over 30 per cent of provincial GDP, a target increased in 2010 to over 35 per cent by 2015 and 40 per cent by 2020 (ICG 2012: 22; Li 2019: 631–2). The annual growth target for fisheries was set at 13.8 per cent (Zhang, Hongzhou 2019: 145).

This rapid over-expansion quickly exhausted Hainan's coastal waters, creating a crisis for the industry, with local elites fearing mass unemployment and social unrest (Interviewee A14 2018; Interviewee A15 2018). To avert this, the provincial government increased subsidies for fuel and the upgrading of local trawlers to enable them to traverse the rougher, deeper waters of the SCS. Other coastal provinces took similar steps, producing a dramatic shift from near-shore fishing (90 per cent in 1988) to offshore (36 per cent by 2002) (Zhang, Hongzhou 2012: 10, 14–16; 2019: 133). In 1985, just thirteen small boats regularly fished near the Spratly Islands; by 2013, 700 large vessels did so (Zhang, Hongzhou 2019: 133–4). This has directly precipitated the vast majority of international clashes in the SCS, as Chinese fishermen tussle with trawlers or coastguards from other claimant states. In 1989–2010, Hongzhou Zhang (2012: 1) documented 380 such incidents, involving over 750 vessels and 11,300 fishermen. From 2010 to October 2019, another 68 incidents occurred, involving 479 vessels, 87 per cent of which were fishing-related (see Table 2.1). Thus, what statists parse as a 'Westphalian' conflict over territorial sovereignty is better understood as an over-accumulation crisis in Hainan's marine industry, which spills over to *all* surrounding maritime areas, generating clashes with Korea, Japan and Taiwan, *not* just SCS claimants (Zhang 2016; Zhang and Bateman 2017).

This occurs because Hainan has persistently ignored central edicts to reduce fishing, thereby causing China to violate its international obligations. The MoA has committed China to the Food and Agriculture Organisation's 1995 Code of Conduct for Responsible Fishery, enacting its strictures into domestic laws in 1995 and 2000, and further regulations in 2002 (Ferraro 2014). This was regarded as a way to fulfil China's responsibilities under UNCLOS to conserve fisheries resources (Interviewee A07 2018). However, reflecting the Chinese-style regulatory state, national rules only established broad objectives. They required tougher licensing and quota systems to reduce annual catches, but left detailed interpretation and implementation to local governments.

Subnational governments like Hainan, however, circumvented the regulations, resulting in outcomes opposite to those intended in Beijing. In 1999, the MoA introduced a zero-growth policy in fisheries but, as the data just cited show, the fishing fleet actually boomed (Zhang 2012: 9–10, 12–14). In 2002, the MoA launched a drive to reduce surplus capacity, seeking to remove 30,000 vessels and 200,000 fishermen from the industry. However, as local governments were left responsible for compensating owners and managing the economic fallout, they had little incentive to comply, and capacity actually increased again (Ferraro 2014: ch. 5). Hainan and others tolerated the existence of 'black fleets' of illegal trawlers and subsidised trawler upgrades, allowing their total capacity to increase even if the number of vessels fell, generating an 'underreported boom' in the annual catch (Zhang and Wu 2017: 220–1). Since 1999, to curtail overfishing, the MoA has imposed an annual June-to-August moratorium on fishing in the SCS above 12 degrees north. But Hainan has not only failed to enforce it strictly (Interviewee A11 2018); it has regularly organised and subsidised large-scale expeditions during the moratorium period, resulting in clashes with rival claimants (Zha 2001: 585; Hayton 2014: 242; Zhang and Wu 2017: 220–1).

Rather than faithfully implementing central government diktat, as unitary state assumptions would lead one to expect, local cadre-capitalists prioritised their patron–client ties to private or state-owned fishing interests (Brans and Ferraro 2012; Ferraro 2014). As one legal expert flatly states: 'they want money ... they ignore the laws to make money' (Interviewee A07 2018). The head of a Chinese fisheries nongovernmental organisation concurs: 'The [local] government knew that [many trawlers] were illegal ... [but] they want them to make a living. So the government did not drive them out' (Interviewee A19 2018). Local law enforcement capacities were kept very weak, and mostly directed towards harassing foreign vessels, rather than implementing internal regulations (Interviewee A15 2018; Interviewee A19 2018). This local resistance eventually forced the MoA to capitulate, announcing a pro-growth fisheries policy in 2010 (Zhang and Wu 2017: 221). In 2016, the MoA issued fresh plans to suppress overcapacity, slash subsidies and tackle non-compliance, but implementation yet again fell to resistant local governments (Zhang, Hongzhou 2019: 147–8).

Hainan has also exercised its authority to interpret national laws in ways that support its local fishing industry, sparking further conflict with neighbouring states. It has issued at least twelve sets of regulations on the SCS, ostensibly to implement national laws. These include regulations asserting Hainan's authority over half of the SCS, requiring foreign vessels to seek State Council approval to fish in Hainan-administered waters, and demanding that non-Chinese vessels transiting the area first notify Hainan (Jakobson 2014: 16; Li 2019: 634). Although this sea-grabbing generates backlash from rival claimants, the central government is often caught unawares, because it is rarely consulted before such regulations are issued. For example, in November 2012, new Hainanese regulations authorised provincial MLEAs to board, detain or expel foreign ships within 12 nm of Chinese islands, sparking protests from Hanoi, Manila and Washington. Although the MFA asked Hainan to amend or withdraw the regulations, it was ignored (Wong 2018: 748–9). As one State Council analyst notes, given decentralisation, it is a routine matter for provinces to interpret national laws; most of the time, central agencies 'don't even hear [about it]'. But in the SCS, this often 'creates turmoil and sends a very bad signal to the outside world', which tends incorrectly to 'aggregate' local initiatives into a perceived top-down strategy (Interviewee A25 2018).

Hainan has also partnered with MLEAs to support the fishing industry, drawing them into defending fishermen's 'historic rights' and rebuffing the 'illegal invasion' of rival trawlers (Interviewee A18 2018). It has equipped long-range trawlers with Beidou radio systems enabling them to summon coastguard vessels to their aid. Furthermore, Hainan's district governments have enthusiastically sponsored maritime militias, which bolster fishing expeditions to contested waters (Kennedy and Erickson 2017b; 2017c; 2017d). Both the MLEAs and militias have clashed directly with other countries' fishing and coastguard vessels, sparking international incidents. This clear political support means that 'fishing captains know they can take greater risks, because they know they are going to be bailed out. So they know they can push the limits fairly strongly' (Denyer 2016). This extends to breaking Chinese laws and regulations. For example, trawlers routinely deactivate their Beidou tracking system to poach outside of the 9DL, while in 2012 fishermen refused MLEA instructions to withdraw from Scarborough Shoal following a confrontation with the Philippine authorities. As Zhang (2016: 66–7) notes, although this behaviour is frequently seen as directed by Beijing, in reality, 'the [central] Chinese government cannot control the fishermen'.

Finally, the Hainan government has used influencing and interpreting strategies to promote its expansionist approach, discursively and institutionally. Exploiting China's vague sovereignty claims, provincial elites frequently make high-profile visits to disputed islands and promote tourism to bolster China's claims symbolically. For example, in 2011 Hainan declared the SCS islands open to tourism, catching the National Tourism Authority unawares and sparking diplomatic protests from Vietnam (ICG 2012: 23–4; Huang 2013: 42). Hainan's rulers have found willing partners among SOEs in the cruise industry which, like the oil and fishing sectors, faces intense competition and the dwindling of suitable coastal sites due to environmental degradation (Gong 2018: 306–11).

Hainan has also been 'very active' in lobbying for the bureaucratic and physical upgrading of local government units within the SCS, most notably the Sansha administration on Woody Island in the Paracels (Interviewees A06 2017). Sansha was finally upgraded to a municipality in June 2012, with formal jurisdiction over the Paracels, Scarborough Shoal and Macclesfield Bank – which, since these features are claimed by Vietnam and the Philippines, provoked international outrage (Cronin and Dubel 2013: 16). Hainan then devoted RMB26bn to upgrading Sansha's infrastructure, while lobbying Beijing for more resources, receiving support from several opportunistic SOEs, including CNOOC (Jakobson 2014: 33–4; Li 2019: 635–7). The Sansha administration has, predictably, drafted provocative plans to expand fishing and tourism, and unilaterally announced in March 2017 that structures would be built on several disputed features, sending the MFA scrambling to suppress the statement (Wong 2018: 747–8).

Hainan is clearly an extremely canny game-player within the Chinese-style regulatory state. Although it has blatantly ignored some important regulations, it mostly operates within party-state frameworks, lobbying relentlessly to frame local cadre-capitalist interests and agendas as a way to advance national-level policy. This enables substantial local initiative, but can also shape specific national decisions. For example, the upgrading of Sansha, long promoted by Hainan, was approved by the central government as a means to retaliate against Vietnam's new maritime law. Possibly the crowning achievement of Hainan's influencing and interpreting strategy was Xi Jinping's 2013 visit to the province, during which he praised the maritime militia for protecting China's maritime rights. Nonetheless, while provincial elites must always keep one eye on the centre, it is clear that the capacious nature of the 9DL and the *weiquan/weiwen* framework allows Hainan to take a more aggressive line than many Chinese diplomats would prefer.

The Coastguards: 'Five Dragons Stirring up the Sea'

Before 2013, China had five different national-level maritime law enforcement agencies: China Maritime Surveillance (CMS), the Ministry of Transport's Maritime Safety Administration (MSA), the Ministry of Agriculture's Fisheries Law Enforcement Command (FLEC), the Ministry of Public Security's China Maritime Police (CMP) and the General Administration of Customs (GAC). Their competitive scramble for resources and power from the early 2000s led directly to rising conflict in the SCS.

Like the PLAN, MLEAs have a clear motive in supporting maximalist interpretations of China's SCS policy framework because this extends their jurisdiction and thus bolsters their demand for larger budgets. Unsurprisingly, then, 'China's paranaval forces seemingly regard the 9DL as a boundary of Chinese jurisdiction', taking enforcement actions well beyond the remit prescribed in UNCLOS (Glaser and Funaiole 2019: 190; also Hayton 2014: 146). Similarly, these agencies have 'promoted safeguarding rights (*weiquan*) at the expense of maintaining stability (*weiwen*)' (Zhang, Feng 2020: 786).

The MLEAs' growth is strongly correlated with the surge in conflicts in the SCS from the mid-2000s (see Figure 2.1). Although maritime clashes, like the HYSY-981 incident, are often attributed to Xi's more 'assertive' policy after 2012, the expansion in MLEA forces actually pre-dated this by a decade. In the 1980s and 1990s, China's MLEAs were weak, resulting in very few maritime clashes. In this period, Hainanese officials were 'upset and depressed' because they lacked the capacity to 'back up ... their fishermen', who were being 'attacked' by rival claimants' coastguards, prompting them to lobby for central government funding (Interviewee A19 2018). Beijing finally initiated a ship-building campaign in 1999, which began in earnest in 2004 (Hickey, Erickson and Holst 2019: 112).

This triggered a mad scramble for resources, with MLEAs competing to be seen as the boldest defenders of China's 'maritime rights'. As one Chinese expert recalls, MLEAs 'tried to show, "look at what I have done, I have defended the national interest – now give me more ships and personnel!"'. Law enforcement tried to grab more resources from the central government to justify their existence. It was also for their [officials'] personal interest – to get promoted' (Interviewee A33 2018). At this time, 'the agencies were not integrated ... every agency ... had their own interests' (Interviewees A06 2017), which mostly revolved around securing 'higher budgets to buy law enforcement vessels' (Interviewee A12 2018). Their fragmented, overlapping jurisdictions and lack of legal clarity fuelled this rivalry, since 'it wasn't clear who should or should not respond to incidents at sea', or how, thus creating space for ambitious 'egotists' to outdo their rivals (Interviewee A21 2018), with junior officials engaging in adventurism without prior approval (Interviewee A33 2018). Reportedly, the slogan then circulating among the MLEAs was 'grab what you can on the sea, and divide the responsibilities between agencies afterwards', 'demonstrating the considerable latitude ... they enjoy[ed]' (ICG 2012: 19).

That their conduct was fuelling clashes with neighbouring countries' oil-prospecting and fishing vessels was widely recognised within China itself. By around 2008/9, Chinese experts were calling the MLEAs 'five dragons stirring up the sea' (Interviewee A12 2018; also Jakobson 2014: 28), while scholars openly denounced their 'profit-making law enforcement' (Wang 2015: 49). This is a clear instance of internationalisation, whereby agencies created purely for domestic purposes – in this case, coastal law enforcement – become embroiled in international disputes. For example, FLEC was involved in the standoff with the Philippine navy at Scarborough Shoal in 2012, resulting in the forcible transfer of de facto control to China, as well as confrontations with Indonesia's coastguard (Erickson and Kennedy 2015). The dismayed MFA, which has no authority over the MLEAs, could only react to such incidents, hastening to 'try to calm things down' (Interviewee A33 2018).

These negative impacts of state transformation on China's foreign relations were apparently noted at the highest levels of the party-state, prompting demands for reform. From the mid-2000s, Chinese leaders and policy experts began calling for the 'five dragons' to be reined in, but in the short term this only intensified their competitive struggles. In 2003, the Chinese Society of Oceanography proposed creating a single maritime agency under the State Council. In 2004, the State Council demanded 'enhanced coordination' and joint operations, suggesting that the MFA make 'recommendations' on the matter, but this went nowhere (Yung 2015). In 2006, President Hu called for 'coordinated planning of the domestic and international overall situation', 'with the goal of reining in uncoordinated policy actors that were harming China's image' – but again, no real action ensued (Chubb 2019). Calls for an integrated coastguard, made as early as 2007 by maritime police instructors, were being echoed by delegates in the Chinese People's Consultative Committee by 2012. But all of these reform attempts 'faltered because the relevant agencies [did] not want to relinquish their power' (ICG 2012: 18). If anything, concern that the MLEAs might eventually be merged only spurred them to behave more aggressively so as to 'assert dominance within the [prospective] organization's command structure' (Hickey, Erickson and Holst 2019: 114). As a scholar at China's Maritime Police Academy observed, MLEAs under 'central and local governments ... [were] greedy and anxious to seek power, success and instant benefits ... competing for financial budgetary investment' by positioning themselves as the '"main body" in marine rights protection' and exploiting 'institutional chaos ... such as vague power allocation, overlapping rights protection, redundant construction [of ships] and internal coordinating friction' (He 2014).

Xi's Reforms: Activating Regulatory Mechanisms

By the time Xi Jinping became China's paramount leader in 2012, the disparate set of actors and behaviours described above had seriously damaged China's relations with much of Southeast Asia. As one provincial foreign affairs official recalls, actions were being 'taken by individual agencies or different departments, out of concern for their own interests' with 'fragmented and uncoordinated' decision-making resulting in outcomes 'that are actually detrimental to China's interests' (Interviewee A16 2018). In a sign that Xi recognised the problems caused by state transformation, he introduced several institutional reforms designed to rein in wayward policy actors. However, the form and practical implementation of these changes show that, contrary to the widespread view of Xi as a centralising strongman who controls everything in China, regulatory-style governance actually continues under his leadership. His reforms sought to bolster the coordination mechanisms that steer diverse, disaggregated actors, coupled with more novel attempts to counter state fragmentation by amalgamating several MLEAs. However, in a sign that even Xi cannot always get his own way, the new coordinating mechanisms have failed, while MLEA integration remains a work-in-progress, seven years on.

Xi took three main steps to improve the coordination of maritime actors. First, in 2012, when he was still vice-president, he established an LSG for the Protection of Maritime Rights, which he chaired personally. The LSG reportedly included officials from the State Oceanic Administration, the navy, and the Ministries of Foreign Affairs, Public Security, Agriculture, and Land and Natural Resources (Jakobson 2015; Yung 2015). As an MFA advisor notes, its creation tacitly acknowledged that fragmented actors were 'seek-[ing] their own interests in the SCS area by taking some actions without permission of the central government', requiring more 'unified decision-making ... particularly in the disputed areas' (Interviewee A12 2018). However, this was clearly not a break from regulatory-state governance, but rather a move within it. As Chapter 1 explained, LSGs are a core mechanism of the Chinese-style regulatory state. According to insiders, the Maritime Rights LSG, 'can't be an agency that decides anything ... they do not make policy'; the LSG merely serves as a forum for leaders to 'listen to others, bottom up ... to get feedback from different agencies' and mediate inter-agency conflict (Interviewees A17 2018). Xi's role was thus still to arbitrate between competing interests within the party-state (Interviewee A01 2017). Moreover, the Maritime Rights LSG does not actually seem to have functioned particularly frequently or well. Even senior government advisors on the SCS were unconvinced that it met regularly or was used systematically for decision-making or even crisis management (Interviewees A06 2017; Interviewees A10 2018; Interviewee A20 2018). National maritime officials report that the LSG 'never sent out invitations', meeting perhaps only once annually, largely to collate suggestions from below (Interviewees A26 2018). It remained possible for agencies to bypass the LSG and lobby Xi directly – as seems to have happened in the HYSY-981 fiasco (Interviewee A20 2018). Perhaps reflecting this failure, this

LSG was abolished in 2018, its duties shifting to the new CCP Foreign Affairs Commission (Interviewee A21 2018).

Arguably, the main impact of the Maritime Rights LSG's formation was symbolic, communicating an imprecise tweak in the balance between *weiwen* and *weiquan*. Some insiders suggest that it was intended to 'send a signal about the importance of this issue', rather than to create a unified decision-making structure (Interviewees A17 2018). This gels with the supposedly greater emphasis placed on maritime rights by Xi's July 2013 speech. As noted earlier, the speech was actually rather vague and still reiterated the need to balance *weiwen* and *weiquan*, requiring continued interpretation of what remained a vague policy framework.

However, as Jakobson (2014) shows, Xi's apparent emphasis on *weiquan* emboldened hawkish interests to pursue and promote their agendas, framing these as ways to implement the general-secretary's ill-defined will. To the consternation of the MFA, the navy proposed the fortification of Chinese-held features in the SCS, claiming that it was necessary to protect China's maritime rights against Philippine and Vietnamese aggression. Xi's sign-off in late 2013 unleashed a massive, PLAN-led island-building campaign, generating profound alarm across the Asia-Pacific and in many Western capitals (Interviewee A01 2018; also You 2017b). This concession to the navy lobby echoed those made by Jiang Zemin during his own delicate leadership transition.[12] China's MLEAs also intensified their aggressive activity, knowing that it would be hard for anyone to discipline them when they acted in the name of *weiquan* (Jakobson 2014). Hainan exploited this opening too to issue several provocative maritime regulations, including a document claiming that it administered half of the SCS (Downs 2014). And, as we saw earlier, the NOCs and their allies secured approval for the HYSY-981 operation, provoking a full-scale international crisis.

These developments illustrate the remarkable power of Chinese-style regulatory governance, but also its non-strategic nature. Xi did not

---

[12] A possible sign of the extent of the concessions extracted by the PLA in exchange for loyalty to Xi is that his September 2015 promise to the USA that the SCS islands would not be militarised was subsequently broken, with military installations built atop several Chinese-held features between 2016 and 2019. Although most commentators saw this as proof of China's premeditated malignance, it is also possible that Xi had not anticipated breaking this pledge when he made it.

define any new objective or plan, or revolutionise how maritime policymaking and implementation were organised. Nor did he change China's SCS policy framework; he only vaguely suggested a rebalancing within it. As Chinese experts note, his *weiquan* talk was 'only an overall signal' which 'different organisations' still had to interpret (Interviewee A01 2018). Xi provided 'only an idea … a sense of direction', not a 'strategy': 'different departments guess[ed] what is Xi's preference', with their desire to demonstrate 'political correctness' generating 'extreme' interpretations (Interviewee A24 2018). This also reflects the powerful interests at stake, which were willing to exploit any opening to push their expansionist agendas.

Unleashing these interests in an uncoordinated manner further damaged China's international standing. Its ties with most Southeast Asian states soured considerably, especially with Vietnam, which turned to the USA and Japan for diplomatic and military assistance, and the Philippines, which also looked to Washington and sued China in the International Court of Arbitration. Chinese behaviour also prompted international condemnation from European states and Australia, some of which joined the USA in freedom of navigation operations to oppose Chinese aggression. This alarming response apparently allowed dovish forces to urge greater emphasis on *weiwen*, resulting in a de-escalation of tensions through 2015–16 (Townshend and Medcalf 2016: 4, 12).

Xi's second attempt to improve coordination was to mandate the creation of a State Oceanic Commission (SOC), with the SOA as its main administrative agency. Reflecting regulatory-style governance, the SOC was not intended to be a super-ministry. Instead, much like an LSG, it was envisaged as a 'trans-department coordinating body' (Yung 2015). Policymaking authority would remain dispersed among multiple member agencies – the SOA and the Ministries of Agriculture, Transport, Environment and Science and Technology – equally ranked agencies which could not command one another, while critical maritime actors like the PLAN were not even included. Furthermore, these agencies effectively ignored Xi's instructions to coordinate their activity. According to national maritime agency officials, 'the SOC was never actually formed … [The] SOA favoured forming the SOC and wanted to coordinate the other maritime agencies, but other agencies didn't support that' (Interviewees A26 2018). Analysts in a key think tank concur: 'the SOC hasn't been functioning effectively in terms of maritime policy coordination [because] it does not have the power or authority to do such coordination' (Interviewees A17 2018). Some experts complain that the SOA, as a vice-ministerial agency, was simply too junior to manage other, ministerial-level departments (Interviewee A07 2018; Interviewee A24 2018). However, even upgrading the SOA to ministerial level in 2018 did not solve the problem, because equally ranked units cannot issue instructions to one another. As an MFA analyst points out, 'even now, there is still no powerful department to manage this field' (Interviewee A20 2018). The SOC's failure reflects the deeper problems of state fragmentation, which Chinese leaders – Xi clearly being no exception – routinely try to address by creating coordinating bodies of dubious efficacy. As the MFA analyst observes, the SOC failed 'because they wanted to integrate so many different departments, but they had no clear plan how to reform it. They just put together the different branches, then ... began to consider how to merge them together ... So, China still faces the same problems as before' (Interviewee A20 2018).

Xi's third – and most substantial and innovative – reform was to merge several MLEAs into a single China Coastguard (CCG). However, even this has not been fully successful in surmounting the problems of Chinese-style regulatory governance. The integration plan was announced at the National People's Congress (NPC) in March 2013 but, as so often, the decision provided 'few details', being 'more a statement of policy shift than offering substantive guidance' (Morris 2019: 80). The State Council had to interpret this shift, but its June 2013 circular was also rather vague, merely specifying broad areas of activity (Morris 2019: 80–1). Serving maritime officials openly bemoaned the 'inherent inadequacy' of these plans, criticising their 'unclear reform objectives', and their 'disconnection [from] practice' (Dong 2018: 8). The CCG merged four of the 'five dragons' – CMS, FLEC, CMP and GAC – but, reflecting continued state fragmentation and decentralisation, the MSA and all subnational MLEAs were excluded, with the CCG merely directed to 'coordinate' local maritime law enforcement (Morris 2019: 80–1). The CCG thus lacked direct control of provincial fisheries and maritime surveillance units routinely involved in 'rights protection' operations, which had expanded considerably in the preceding decade of resource-grabbing (Hickey, Erickson and Holst 2019: 111, 118). The CCG was also given a confused dual command structure: the SOA was administratively in charge, but the

Ministry of Public Security (MPS) would provide 'operational guidance'.

Rather than swiftly resulting in a new, coherent agency, Xi's poorly planned reforms triggered fresh power struggles between the CCG's constituent agencies and personnel. Rivalry between the SOA and MPS over the CCG's leadership immediately surfaced, while the three other maritime agencies involved also dragged their feet, being reluctant to relinquish authority and resources (Jakobson 2015; also Li 2018: 5–6). As one provincial maritime official told us, their employees 'don't want to combine', worrying about losing *guanxi* (networks) and their career progression (Interviewee A15 2018). There were also practical barriers arising from their past competition: they had different internal command structures, radio systems, training regimens, base facilities and vessels, with highly specialised ships still emerging from the commissioning pipeline (Yu 2015; Wen and Li 2016; Hickey, Erickson and Holst 2019: 127, 119; Morris 2019: 83–5).

Accordingly, in the five years after Xi ordered the CCG's creation, in practice the four 'dragons' largely functioned as separate agencies 'doing different law enforcement projects in the SCS' (Interviewees A06 2017). In 2014, a Chinese scholar characterised the situation as 'superficial combination but separation in nature' (Wang 2015: 49; see also Jakobson 2014). Four years later, another reported: 'the formation of the CCG is still on the road. There is still a long way to go' (Dong 2018: 8). Our interviewees confirmed that the CCG's integration 'has not been carried out' (Interviewee A07 2018), and had 'failed' (Interviewee A24 2018), describing it as 'really slow' and 'painful' (Interviewees A17 2018). 'The different branches still belong to the former boss ... It is still the beginning stage of the reorganisation ... They have not really realised an integrated coastguard' (Interviewee A20 2018). An official in one of the agencies involved stated flatly: 'it's not successful. It's still in progress five years later ... We are not really combined' (Interviewee A15 2018). Another senior official agrees: 'they have still not completely unified' (Interviewee A21 2018). Experts despaired at the lack of progress, suggesting a unified CCG would not be attained for another five to ten years (Interviewee A07 2018), or even 'a generation' (Interviewee A15 2018).

The failure of the 2013 plans led to yet another change in July 2018, whereby command of the CCG shifted from the SOA to the CMP. This put the CCG under the People's Armed Police and thus, ultimately, the Central Military Commission, prompting concern that it was being 'militarised' (e.g. Martinson 2019). However, a state transformation lens reveals a different interpretation: the shift in command was a recognition of the failure of the 2013 reforms, and the outcome of a contingent power struggle. As one MFA analyst observes, 'Xi … [had] no clear idea about how to reform the coastguard. He paid little attention to [it]'. The shift in command to the CMP 'means [that] the leader also realises the failure of the reform' (Interviewee A20 2018). As Martinson (2019: 101) notes, the CMP's leadership was 'never a given'. Indeed, it was a weak candidate, given its origins as a 'coastal and riverine force not known for the seamanship of its members' (Hickey, Erickson and Holst 2019: 123). The CMP seems to have won out for two main reasons. First, it successfully grabbed vessels initially commissioned by rival MLEAs and the PLAN, while also ordering its own ships, and undertook missions previously done exclusively by other agencies (Martinson 2019: 97–8, 93). Secondly, the CMP's well-established command and training systems provided much-needed clarity to the CCG's internal chaos. The CMP's academy became the main training route for CCG officers, and CMP personnel began embarking on other agencies' vessels, becoming a de facto 'spine' for the new organisation (Martinson 2019: 93, 99). Finally, given the continued absence of a coherent framework of maritime law, the CMP was the only agency enjoying a clear right to board vessels in the course of law enforcement – though even this arises from a Hainanese regulation rather than national law (Martinson 2019: 102–3).

Although imposing military structures may appear to resolve the CCG's internal chaos definitively, as Chinese experts point out, the truth is again more complex. They argue that integrating civilian and military personnel will be very difficult (Li 2018), and could yet fail, resulting in its branches being separated again (Interviewees A26 2018). They also worry that the CCG's relocation to the party-state's military wing will make its deployment 'more sensitive', constraining its practical operations (Interviewee A24 2018). Moreover, China's law and regulations still lag well behind institutional transformations, making it impossible for the CCG to conduct coherent law enforcement operations (Xu 2017; Zhao 2018). Although an NPC Standing Committee decision further clarified the scope of the CCG's work in June 2018, as Yang Huanbiao (2019: 15) of the People's Armed Police (PAP) command college complains, these guidelines are still 'too general and vague'. Legally, law enforcement responsibilities remain fragmented across the CCG, the Ministries of Agriculture, Environment, and Natural Resources, and subnational agencies. The CCG's duties are still not linked to particular laws and no guidance exists as to what sorts of enforcement actions are permitted in what kind of maritime area (e.g. territorial sea versus EEZ); crucially, there is still no clarity over how the CCG should behave in disputed waters (Yang 2019: 15–16). This demonstrates that, even with the CCG's supposed 'militarisation', the vagaries of China's 9DL framework will continue to shape Chinese conduct in practice. Furthermore, although the CMP – and thus, presumably, the CCG – is legally mandated to cooperate with the PLAN in defensive warfare and peacetime search-and-rescue operations, coordination between the PLAN and CCG is 'still in its infancy' with 'many problems in the actual operation' (Zhao 2017: 25; see also Yang and Li 2017: 11).

In the short run, at least, the practical effect of this rather shambolic reform process seems to have been to dampen tensions in the SCS. As an MFA analyst states, the integration process, while incomplete, has affected maritime agencies' 'willingness to safeguard [maritime] rights. They will be very cautious ... If there is some wrongdoing during implementation, they could completely lose their job, because they are in the process of reorganisation'. Ironically, the incomplete merger has produced 'stricter discipline' because units must worry about the reaction of their old 'boss' but also the new CCG leadership: 'that means twice as much discipline ... they are afraid of doing some wrongdoing ... they couldn't take strong actions' (Interviewee A20 2018). An instructor at China's PAP academy confirms that, as a result of the reforms and lack of legal clarity, 'China's maritime forces are hesitant and indecisive [even] in ... circumstances in which they should use force' (Zhao 2017: 27). Units of the CCG still lack clear guidance on what they can and cannot do at sea, including their rights to self-defence or to board vessels (Tang and Wang 2018; Zhao 2018). Combined, these factors may explain why, since the CCG's putative formation in 2013, there has not been a single recorded instance of CCG units using force to board foreign vessels, notwithstanding some episodes where warning shots were fired to scare off trawlers involved in illegal fishing (Morris 2019: 86). A 2016 study of maritime rights operations at Scarborough Shoal found that vessels remained 'subordinate to different sub-offices and law enforcement corps', rather than being unified, but were now behaving 'moderately' (Li, Yongji 2016:57). The tapering-off of investment in new law enforcement ships since 2017 (see Hickey, Erickson and Holst 2019: 129) – investment which had done so much to fuel earlier inter-agency rivalry – also provides fewer incentives for aggressive resource-grabbing.

Conclusion

This chapter has explained Chinese behaviour in the SCS using the state transformation approach outlined in Chapter 1. This behaviour is 'consistently inconsistent', oscillating between aggressive and pacific, or even being both simultaneously, denoting a 'lack of any discernible strategy' (Santicola 2014). We traced this behaviour to transformations in China's party-state and the emergence of regulatory-style governance in the SCS issue area. State transformation has produced a fragmented, decentralised and internationalised set of maritime agencies which, rather than being directed by a coherent strategy, are steered by largely ineffective coordinating bodies, within a very loose policy framework comprising the ill-defined 9DL and an injunction to 'balance' between maintaining stability (*weiwen*) and protecting China's maritime rights (*weiquan*).

Chinese conduct reflects struggles within this loose policy framework, which requires constant interpretation by maritime actors to translate into concrete behaviour. At times, diplomatic forces promoting *weiwen* and a minimalist definition of the 9DL are ascendant. This explains periods of relative peace and stability in the SCS, most notably from the mid-1990s to the mid-2000s. Subsequently, however, these forces were steadily marginalised by rivals promoting *weiquan* and a maximalist definition of the 9DL. Drawing in part on the behaviour of rival claimants and the USA, they were able to accrue greater power and resources and to influence and interpret Beijing's policy framework in ways that served their interests and agendas. At times, ignoring behaviour is also apparent, particularly in Hainan's disrespect for national-level attempts to curb overfishing, supported by unruly and self-interested maritime law enforcement actors. The navy and oil lobbies have also worked hard to secure top-level support for their bottom-up agendas, with the ill-fated HYSY-981 expedition symbolising their influence. Beijing's diplomats have struggled to re-emphasise *weiwen*, scrambling to dampen tensions after provocative actions by their more powerful rivals. However, this action has been increasingly reactive and short-lived, with continued oscillations between aggressive and pacific behaviour not masking the overall trend towards greater 'assertiveness'.

One question is whether this approach has served Beijing's foreign policy objectives. We have rejected claims that Chinese behaviour in the SCS signals a carefully calibrated 'salami-slicing' tactic. There is little evidence that the current situation reflects the enactment of a detailed plan, specifying clear objectives and allocating roles and resources appropriately. As this chapter has shown, China's position has instead advanced in fits and starts, through disaggregated struggles, lobbying efforts and ad hoc decision-making. A useful analogy might be drawn to Deng Xiaoping's aphorism about 'crossing the river while feeling for the stones'. There is a broad direction of travel, but the precise goals and methods to attain them are unclear, requiring constant experimentation and adjustment. In the SCS, the broad goal is to enhance (or at least not degrade) China's position in the SCS; but many different behaviours and projects – often rather self-serving – are tolerated in pursuit of this, given the loose guidance provided by the 9DL and the *weiwen/weiquan* framework.

But has the river been crossed? In some respects, China's position is undeniably stronger today than in the late 1980s. Although it has not taken any additional features in the SCS, except Scarborough Shoal, China has certainly consolidated its grip on those it controls, using land reclamation and military installations, while its naval and paranaval power has undoubtedly increased. However, this has come at a considerable cost, precisely because China lacks a conventional grand strategy. A coherent strategy would have weighed up the benefits of consolidating Chinese sovereignty claims in the SCS with the likely damage to China's wider geopolitical interests, notably the need to retain good relations with Southeast Asian states and avoiding giving the USA and Japan an opening to cultivate an anti-Chinese coalition. Instead, China's experimental governance has had the opposite effects. As a State Council analyst laments, 'China has no maritime strategy, even now – never'; if it did, 'we would be more balanced, and not become so extreme … China still lacks a grand strategy' (Interviewee A24 2018).

This chapter also explored Xi Jinping's impact on the mode and outcomes of China's foreign and security policy governance. Xi clearly did not revolutionise this issue area but was instead a particularly powerful participant in Chinese-style regulatory governance.

Although it is often suggested that Xi is personally responsible for China's maritime aggression since 2012, this chapter showed that the dynamics underpinning this behaviour were present for many years before hand. The struggle for fishing grounds that sparks most international incidents in the SCS had been building since the early 1990s, fuelled by the decentralisation of authority to Hainan's cadre-capitalists. Battles over oil exploration go back to the early 2000s, with the NOCs initiating their prospecting in the disputed Zhongjiannan basin in 2004. That same year, when Xi was just a provincial leader in Zhejiang, also saw the start of intensifying rivalry among the 'five dragons'.

If Xi did not create these conflictual dynamics, nor did he fundamentally transform China's governance approach in the SCS. His influence was instead felt through the mechanisms of regulatory-style governance. His apparent emphasis on maritime rights tilted a balance that important actors were already upsetting, though it certainly encouraged them to push their agendas even more aggressively. The ad hoc, poorly institutionalised nature of decision-making apparently allowed some of the parties to circumvent diplomatic actors, notably in the HYSY-981 fiasco, while continued decentralisation and fragmentation allowed the 'five dragons' and Hainan considerable leeway. Xi's efforts to tackle the problems arising from state transformation demonstrate that even this 'strongman' operates within the logic of regulatory statehood. Xi's new coordinating bodies failed to cohere decision-making, while his efforts to create a unified coastguard remained partial and incomplete some seven years later. Fundamentally, the main contours of China's SCS policy framework remain unchanged: the 9DL and an injunction to balance between rights-protection and stability-maintenance. With the partial exception of MLEAs, the actors in this domain remain largely fragmented, decentralised and internationalised, without a clear or coherent decision-making process.

This implies that conflict could easily escalate in the future. Since 2014, a certain unplanned equilibrium has emerged, with PLAN's island-building restoring a new kind of 'stability' in the SCS, while the MLEAs have been tempered by incomplete reform efforts. However, the current balance between stability and rights could shift again. The current position is not institutionally embedded, and the policy framework remains vague and open to interpretation. It remains to be seen, for example, whether the CCG's cautious approach will continue once it is finally cohered. As PAP instructor Xinshuang Zhao (2017: 27) observes, the lack of legal clarity may make the CCG 'hesitant and indecisive' today, but it can equally permit 'the abuse of force ... escalating the situation of marine disputes'.

3 | Chinese Non-Traditional Security Governance in the Greater Mekong Subregion

In recent decades, non-traditional security (NTS) issues – including climate change, terrorism, organised crime, pandemics and cybersecurity – have risen up the international security agenda. These issues are typically depicted as transboundary, and thus beyond individual states' capacities to manage alone, requiring new forms of transnational cooperation. Powerful states and international organisations have consequently extended their 'governance frontiers'[1] into source-countries' territories to manage such issues, while also seeking to reshape how states manage these problems by refashioning domestic state apparatuses and inserting them into transnational governance networks (Hameiri and Jones 2015).

Rising powers – especially China – are often seen as resisting this development, given their fervent commitment to state sovereignty (Ginsburg 2010; Laïdi 2012), thus undermining effective responses to NTS problems (Patrick 2010; 2014). One oft-cited example is the 2003 SARS epidemic. Chinese authorities initially suppressed news of the SARS outbreak in Guangdong in 2002, allowing it to spread internationally. Even after Beijing admitted the problem, Chinese authorities took two months to fully cooperate with global containment efforts. Observers blamed the negative consequences – including 774 deaths in thirty-seven countries – on China's outdated, 'Westphalian' attachment to national sovereignty (Stevenson and Cooper 2009). This complaint was repeated in early 2020, as many – notably US President Trump – blamed the spread of COVID-19 on China's opaque and uncooperative response to the virus.

Conversely, this chapter argues that China's commitment to non-interference has actually softened considerably since the early 2000s, notwithstanding its COVID-19 response; moreover, Chinese agencies

---

[1] 'Governance frontier' refers to the de facto governance reach of state institutions, which may not coincide with a state's notional borders (Hameiri 2009).

are gradually extending their governance frontiers beyond China's borders to manage NTS threats. Chinese policymakers and scholars have reconceptualised security and sovereignty in line with the trans-nationalisation of China's economy, and transformed party-state apparatuses have increasingly moved to tackle threats to China's capitalist development at home and abroad. The outcomes of these interventions reflect the interaction between this internationalisation of the party-state and forces in the societies targeted by Chinese initiatives.

We demonstrate this using case studies of Chinese efforts to combat narcotics and organised crime in the Greater Mekong Subregion (GMS, see Map 3.1). China's 'reform and opening up' has exposed Chinese society to spillovers of NTS threats from this region, such as drugs, crime and human trafficking emanating from the 'golden triangle'. Having eradicated opium in the 1950s, China is now again a major transit country and end-market for drugs, sparking an HIV/AIDS epidemic and major law and order and public health concerns. The 'going out' of Chinese firms and workers has also made them vulnerable to attack, including on the Mekong River.

In response, Chinese authorities have promoted governance arrangements that reflect the Chinese-style regulatory-state model described in Chapter 1. Over forty different agencies are involved, loosely coordinated by the National Narcotics Control Commission (NNCC), with China's vaguely specified narcotics law contributing to a very fragmented, weakly defined governance arrangement. The NNCC is primarily serviced by China's Ministry of Public Security (MPS), a domestic policing agency, which has increasingly internationalised to tackle narcotics, creating a regional framework to guide agencies across the GMS. However, reflecting China's fragmented and decentralised governance, the MPS is just one actor among many. As our first case study shows, in practice, national and subnational commercial actors control a key part of China's NTS governance – its opium substitution programme (OSP) in Myanmar and Laos – producing outcomes starkly at odds with the MPS's governance framework. The resultant warping of counter-narcotics interventions around local business interests, when coupled with dynamics in target states, has actually exacerbated the drug problem.

Our second case study examines the MPS's own GMS activity in greater depth, exploring the extension of its governance frontier through the creation of Chinese-led multinational river patrols from 2011, and the establishment of a new international organisation in

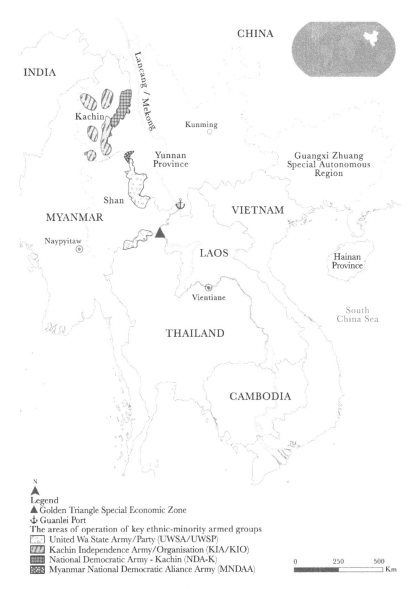

Map 3.1 The Greater Mekong subregion

2017. Reflecting China's slow, somewhat reluctant move away from non-interference in states' internal affairs, these activities are more limited, tentative and evolving than the long-standing OSP. Data on these operations were also far harder to gather due to the extreme secrecy within China and partner countries. Unlike the OSP, it was impossible to study in any detail how the MPS's interventions are contested within recipient countries. Nonetheless, the case study clearly demonstrates that, as China's economic activity extrudes beyond its borders, formerly domestic agencies are being internationalised to help manage and secure it.

The following sections describe China's changing approach to NTS, relating this to transformations in the party-state; identify the regulatory framework established to manage counter-narcotics in the GMS; and present our case studies.

The Transformation of Security in China

In China, as elsewhere, how security is understood and governed is closely related to wider transformations in the state and political economy (see Hameiri and Jones 2015). As China's economy has transnationalised and its state has fragmented, policymakers' understanding of security has widened beyond traditional military concerns. As NTS issues became securitised, the distinction between domestic and international security has become blurred, and transnational interventions and governance projects are increasingly considered essential to manage border-spanning threats.

Under Mao, China's approach to security was Westphalian. With its borders sealed and negligible overseas economic interests, the Chinese government saw security in territorially bounded terms, seeking regime survival internally and deterring military threats externally. This was coupled with a strong commitment to sovereignty and non-interference as the foundation of international order, first articulated at the 1955 Bandung Conference, where Premier Zhou Enlai played a key role.[2]

From the late 1990s, however, NTS issues began climbing up the agenda, becoming a 'key part of [Beijing's] security strategy' (Arase 2010: 818). This partly reflected growing international concern with NTS, especially after 9/11, but it also reflected China's rapid economic transnationalisation, with NTS threats increasingly seen as imperilling Chinese overseas business interests and the domestic and regional

---

[2] In practice, however, China intervened to support sympathetic revolutionary movements until Mao's death; this was discontinued as part of Deng's 'passive revolution' (Jones 2013).

stability needed for continued capitalist development (Ghiselli 2018: 614). In 2002, President Jiang Zemin officially incorporated NTS into the Chinese Communist Party's (CCP) definition of security at the 18th Party Congress, while the Ministry of Foreign Affairs (MFA) outlined a 'new security concept', declaring that 'transnational problems require transnational cooperation' (quoted in Stieber 2017: 21). This meant tackling NTS issues at their source. As Guo (2015: 363) remarks in a typical assessment: 'Interdiction at the frontier can only partially impede trafficking in people and goods [like narcotics] ... both demand-reduction and interior enforcement in all countries concerned are crucial components of any long-term solution to security problems at the border'. China's 2002 Defence White Paper specifically identified the GMS as crucial for China's security, especially with regard to NTS problems like environmental degradation, drug trafficking and transnational crime (Hensengerth 2009: 5). That year, the MFA also signed the China–ASEAN Joint Declaration on Cooperation in the Field of NTS Issues (Arase 2010: 821).

China's approach to NTS involves two aspects: preventing transnational threats from entering China's territory; and protecting Chinese interests abroad. Both blur the distinction between domestic and external security. Indeed, President Xi's 'holistic national security' concept entirely collapses this distinction, and that between traditional and non-traditional security (Ghiselli 2018: 617). The 2015 National Security Law exemplifies this, stating that 'state security work should plan internal security and external security as a whole, [including] the country's territorial security and citizens, traditional security and non-traditional security, and its own security and common security' (quoted in Stieber 2017: 20).

This is obviously in tension with the principle of non-interference. Superficially, China reiterates its commitment to non-interference while seeking closer international cooperation for mutual benefit (Ghiselli 2018: 612). However, in practice, the limits of traditional inter-governmental cooperation have spurred Chinese agencies to extend their governance frontier into other states' territories, in two primary ways.

The first, reflected in our case study of opium-substitution projects in Myanmar and Laos, has been to promote economic development in NTS hotspots in the hope that this will mitigate NTS threats. China's leadership has long subscribed to an illiberal variant of the 'security–development nexus', dubbed the 'Chinese peace thesis' (Kuo 2012). This views state-directed, infrastructure-led economic development, combined with respect for national sovereignty and a preference for political stability, as underpinning peace and security. For example, Lu Shulin (2015), China's former ambassador to Pakistan, argues that the China–Pakistan Economic Corridor will 'help alleviate poverty, which is the source of terrorism, hence effecting a permanent cure to terrorism'. Similarly, influential party-linked scholars Wang Lei and Hu Angang (2010) maintain that 'countries with high levels of economic development are more likely to achieve social and political stability'. Ergo, the remedy for the ills of (under) development is more development, coupled with the strengthening of state capacity. This conveniently presents China's burgeoning overseas business interests as bolstering security, when in reality their frequently rapacious operations are a key driver of insecurity (Hameiri, Jones and Zou 2019). This view of capitalist development as a stabilising force underscores the CCP's abandonment of Marxism-Leninism and its relentless efforts to depoliticise economic questions since 1979 (Hameiri, Jones and Zou 2019: 477).

China's second response, reflected in our second case study, on transboundary law enforcement efforts, has involved tentative moves away from strict non-interference towards interventionism to defend Chinese economic interests and citizens abroad. Beijing remains leery of liberal interventionism, and still positions itself as a non-interventionist power, reflecting its own experience of foreign imperialism (Kuo 2012; 2015). Increasingly, however, influential Chinese scholars and policy experts have argued that non-interference must be softened to deal with new security threats. For example, Yan Xuetong (2011) argues that non-interference is not feasible for great powers. Su Changhe argues that if countries hosting Chinese interests' investments cannot protect them, this should entail 'limit[s] on [their] national sovereignty', and Beijing must reserve 'the right of unilateral or collective interference or intervention' (quoted in Erickson and Strange 2014: 103). Scholars have developed various euphemistic terms to justify and describe China's growing involvement in other states' internal affairs, such as 'constructive involvement' and 'creative involvement' (Duchâtel, Bräuner and Hang 2014: 18).

These intellectual developments are mirrored in policy changes. In 2004, the People's Liberation Army (PLA) was assigned 'new historic missions', including tackling terrorism and piracy and protecting overseas assets and citizens. China has also increased its commitment to multilateral efforts to pacify hotspots, particularly where its economic interests are engaged. It is now the largest provider of peacekeepers among the United Nations (UN) Security Council's permanent members, fielding 2,600 personnel across ten missions, heavily concentrated in African countries where unrest threatens Chinese investments (Fang, Li and Sun 2018). China has also established an 8,000-strong permanent standby force for UN operations, provided US$100m for African Union peacekeeping, and offered to train 2,000 foreign peacekeepers (Zheng 2017). The PLA has joined counter-piracy operations in the Gulf of Aden and Malacca Straits to defend shipping routes key to China's economy (Khalid 2009; Ghiselli 2015). The PLA has also intervened repeatedly to rescue imperilled Chinese nationals, evacuating 36,000 from Libya in 2011, for example. The 2013 Defence White Paper made the link to China's overseas economic interests explicit, directing the PLA to strengthen its 'overseas operational capabilities such as emergency response and rescue, merchant vessel protection . . . and evacuation of Chinese nationals, and [to] provide reliable security support for China's interests overseas' (Ghiselli 2018: 616).

Notwithstanding these developments, given China's continued reluctance to use military force, its primary focus has been preventive and capacity-building measures, which have dispersed responsibility well beyond the military. For example, State Council regulations issued in 2010 required companies operating overseas to develop risk assessment and management plans, while in 2011 firms were made responsible for the safety of overseas workers. However, reflecting the party-state's fragmentation, oversight of firms' compliance is dispersed across multiple, overlapping agencies, with the MFA playing only a marginal role. Consequently, companies have developed diverse approaches, from cooperation with local law enforcement agencies to hiring private security (Duchâtel, Bräuner and Hang 2014: 44, 35–6, 51). Thus, in a barely coordinated manner, corporate actors are actually innovating much of China's overseas security practice. This is clearly apparent in our first case study. However, as our second case study shows, other, non-military actors are also experimenting with transnational governance arrangements.

State Transformation and China's Counter-Narcotics Governance

Let us now explore how these general developments are expressed in the specific field of counter-narcotics. Although NTS issues are often seen as 'new', in fact the CCP has always heavily securitised narcotics due to their association with China's 'century of humiliation', which began with the Opium Wars (Chin and Zhang 2015: 197). However, how Chinese authorities have sought to tackle narcotics has transformed along with China's political economy and party-state.

Under Mao, Beijing's response reflected the autarchic economy and command-and-control state. The government sealed China's historically porous borders with the Golden Triangle, the main foreign source of narcotics, while harshly repressing domestic drug production and use, including through mass executions. Counter-narcotics efforts were thus part of the CCP's wider 'state-building' campaign – the establishment of strong, centralised control across the national territory and along China's borders (Liang 2014). However, as China's borders reopened in the 1980s to facilitate capitalist development, illicit drugs reappeared in the southwest as traffickers exploited new trade routes and transport infrastructure. An estimated 80 per cent of drugs from the Golden Triangle now end up in China, comprising around 60–70 per cent of domestic consumption (Steinberg and Fan 2012: 272–3; Su 2015: 72–3).

This influx – initially of opium and heroin, and more recently amphetamine-type stimulants – has fuelled major public order and health crises. The number of officially registered drug addicts soared from 148,000 in 1991 to 2.1m by 2013, 61 per cent of whom use opiates, especially heroin; the true figure may be closer to 7m (Li and Zheng 2009: 627; Steinberg and Fan 2012: 278; Su 2015: 76). By 2007, 700,000 addicts were also HIV/AIDS positive (ICG 2009: 14–15). The problem is especially pronounced in Yunnan, where 1.1m of the province's 46m inhabitants are registered drug users, and 85,000 have HIV/AIDS (ICG 2009: 14–15). Some 80 per cent of addicts are said to fund their habit through crime, and an estimated 40 per cent of crime in Yunnan is drug-related (Clarke 2008: 75), rising to 60 per cent in Dehong Prefecture, which borders Myanmar (ICG 2009: 15). Yunnan officials have also become involved in the drug trade. For example, in 1994, almost 200 border officials were detained in a large raid by central authorities (Lintner and Black 2009: ch. 2). Re-sealing the border to prevent drug trafficking is now unthinkable, given the southwest's dependence on cross-border commerce and invest-ment. Accordingly, Chinese agencies have instead tried to manage the problem by extending their governance frontiers into the Golden Triangle, to tackle the issue at source.

The form these efforts take reflects the emergence of the Chinese-style regulatory state. The key institution at the national level is China's National Narcotics Control Commission (NNCC). Chaired by the Minister of Public Security, the NNCC was established in 1991 to coordinate the now forty-one ministries and agencies concerned in some way with counter-narcotics (China Anti-Narcotics Network 2015). The overall policy framework is set by the 2007 Narcotics Control Law, which marked a shift from Maoist 'shock and awe policing tactics' like public executions, drug burnings and rallies, to a 'more bureaucratic ... all round approach' promoting 'inter-agency and intra-agency cooperation, both national and international' (Trevaskes 2013: 229). However, the law merely issues vague instructions to the 'related departments' and urges them to cooperate. Moreover, the NNCC cannot issue direct orders to its constituent agencies but, like all such bodies, exists only for 'coordinating, and giving advice' (NPC 2007). This weakness is compounded by the fact that its main operational unit is the MPS's Drug Control Bureau (DCB), a sub-ministerial agency with just fifty personnel, split across seven divisions (Chin and Zhang 2015: ch. 9). Moreover, insofar as its duties are specified, they overlap with other agencies: it may be responsible for 'organising and carrying out international anti-drug cooperation', but so are judicial authorities, unspecified 'relevant departments' of the State Council, and provincial public security bureaus. Subnational governments were also directed to create local versions of the NNCC. The 2007 law thus establishes a highly fragmented, decentralised policy regime encompassing 'the whole of society' (NPC 2007).

Although Chinese policy documents frequently refer to 'three lines of defence' against narcotics trafficking – the borders, internal check-points, and key domestic transportation hubs (see, e.g., State Council Information Office 2000) – in reality, a fourth line of defence has been established outside of China's borders. Working with the UN Office on Drugs and Crime (UNODC), in the early 1990s the MPS developed the Memorandum of Understanding on Drug Control (Mekong MOU), a governance framework that incorporates China, Cambodia, Laos, Myanmar, Thailand and Vietnam. The Mekong MOU Subregional Action Plan, which has gone through ten iterations since 1995, directs participating agencies to focus on four areas: health, law enforcement, judicial reform and sustainable alternative development (see Table 3.1). The plan also incorporates major international instruments, including UN guidelines on opium substitution (see Table 3.2). Senior officials meet annually to review progress against agreed benchmarks and to agree targets for the following year (UNODC 2017). Effectively, the plan is a form of regulatory regionalism: it defines a policy framework regionally, then directs national and subnational agencies to implement international disciplines at home (Hameiri and Jones 2015). Various Chinese agencies have undertaken bilateral activities to implement the plan (see Table 3.3).

Through this mechanism, Chinese security agencies have extended their governance frontier into the Golden Triangle. For example, from the early 2000s NNCC technicians have engaged in remote surveillance of opium cultivation in Myanmar, combining satellite imaging with direct field observations in cooperation with local police.[3] The NNCC uses these data to press the Myanmar authorities and non-state militias to eradicate opium crops in particular locales (Interviewee D04 2018; Interviewee D12 2018; Interviewee D13 2018; see also Kramer, Jelsma and Blickman 2009: 23). This is allegedly supplemented in some areas by Chinese intelligence officials inside Myanmar, especially Wa state (Interviewee D12 2018). China's People's Armed Police, under the MPS, has also developed close ties with its foreign counterparts, enabling extraterritorial policing operations. From 2011 to 2015 alone, this involved 267 bilateral meetings and 173 joint cross-border operations netting over 4,200 kg of drugs (Ding 2016). According to Myanmar police, Chinese officers may be embedded with them for up to six weeks at a time to direct operations against particular kingpins, bringing to bear their superior equipment and expertise (Interviewee D13 2018). Police and judicial cooperation have also yielded extensive information-sharing and the extraction of dozens of suspects to China, despite the absence of any formal extradition treaty (Interviewee D04 2018; Interviewee D13 2018). As our second case study shows, such cooperation is now being formalised through an MPS-led international organisation.

---

[3] Fieldwork was discontinued in 2015–16 due to armed conflict in Myanmar.

Table 3.1 *The Mekong subregional action plan on drug control*

Health
- Increasing and exchanging research on drug use prevention, harm reduction and treatment.
- Enhancing public health approaches including rehabilitation, legislating for community-based treatment, and education.
- Training and capacity-building.

Judicial
- Training and capacity-building.
- Improving execution of requests for Mutual Legal Assistance, extradition, asset seizure and recovery requests by passing domestic laws, disseminating UNODC software, and establishing a mechanism to cooperate on financial investigations.

Law Enforcement
- Establishing and maintaining border liaison offices and launching cross-border operations.
- Sharing real-time intelligence.
- Providing training and equipment.
- Developing shared standard operating procedures.

Sustainable Alternative Development (AD)
- Developing a joint strategy to improve the health and human security of opium farmers; providing training; dissemination of best practices.
- Integrating AD programmes into national drug control plans by holding regional talks, implementing UN Guiding Principles on AD, and aligning AD with wider development agendas including the Sustainable Development Goals.
- Information sharing.
- Field monitoring.

Source: UNODC (2017).

Table 3.2 *Selected UN guidelines on alternative development*

Instrument/ Paragraph	Guidance
1998 UN General Assembly Political Declaration and Action Plan on International Cooperation on the Eradication of Illicit Drug Crops and on Alternative Development	
18	AD should: 'contribute to the creation of sustainable social and economic opportunities through integrated rural development'; 'improve the living conditions'; 'Contribute to the promotion of democratic values to encourage community participation'; 'Observe environmental sustainability criteria'.
19	Use 'participatory approaches … based on dialogue and persuasion … that include the community as a whole, as well as relevant non-governmental organizations … Local communities and public authorities should develop commonly agreed goals and objectives and commit themselves by community-based agreements'.
24	The 'sustainability of illicit crop reduction' is the 'most important assessment criterion of alternative development'.
2009 Political Declaration and Plan of Action on International Cooperation towards an Integrated and Balanced Strategy to Counter the World Drug Problem	
47	Focus on 'human rights and poverty eradication'.
47(m) and 47(e)	Emphasis on environmental protection.
46, 47f–g	Emphasis on 'proper sequencing' of alternative development and illicit crop eradication.
2014 UN Guiding Principles on Alternative Development	
A2	AD should be part of 'tackling poverty and providing livelihood opportunities'.
A5	AD should involve 'recognising and enforcing property rights, including access to land'.
A6	'Local communities and relevant organisations should be involved in the design, implementation, monitoring and evaluation' of AD schemes.
A7	Civil society should be involved.
A9	'Proper and coordinated sequencing' should be observed, including agreements with smallholders and adequate market access.

Table 3.2 *(cont.)*

Instrument/ Paragraph	Guidance
A10	AD should be part of 'promoting comprehensive development and social inclusion, alleviating poverty and strengthening social development, the rule of law, security and stability ... [and] human rights'.
A11	AD should include environmental protection measures.
A17	AD should be assessed by the scale of 'illicit crop reduction' and wider socio-economic indicators.
B(d)	AD must be 'evidence- and science-based' and should 'promote the diversification of licit crops'.
B(l)	AD should be implemented in 'comprehensive and balanced manner ... to avoid the shifting of illicit crop cultivation domestically'.
B(n)	AD must be implemented in a way that 'respect[s] the legitimate interests and specific needs of the local affected ... population'.

Sources: United Nations (2014); UNODC (2015: Annex I).

However, as we shall see, although the NNCC has tried to 'steer' the forty-one agencies involved in counter-narcotics towards common ends, in practice, Chinese NTS interventions have been poorly coordinated, with other national and subnational actors engaged in often contradictory behaviours. This is especially clear with respect to China's opium substitution programme, the subject of our first case study, where commercial interests have taken the lead, resulting in outcomes quite different to those in MPS-led operations.

China's Opium Substitution Programmes in Myanmar and Laos

China's most enduring and important intervention to combat heroin trafficking is its opium substitution programme (OSP). Opium substitution, also called 'alternative development', has been promoted by the UN and others since the 1970s. It seeks to reduce heroin production by encouraging farmers to grow crops other than opium, using subsidies,

Table 3.3 *Selected Chinese actions to implement the Mekong subregional action plan*

Year	Action
1997	China and Myanmar establish Border Representative Agencies, including local military commanders, to manage border security.
1999–2002	Agreement on Management and Cooperation in China–Myanmar Border Areas established and implemented.
2000	China–ASEAN agreement on Cooperative Operations in Response to Dangerous Drugs. Bilateral MOUs signed with Laos, Myanmar and Thailand.
Early 2000s	China begins remote sensing of opium cultivation in Myanmar. NNCC despatches technicians to conduct field surveys, with cooperation from Myanmar police.
2001	Offices for cross-border counter-narcotics operations with Myanmar established. Activities include monthly officials' meetings, joint operations, the training of hundreds of Myanmar personnel in China, and the provision of law enforcement equipment to Myanmar. Programme later widens to Laotian personnel, with over 100 foreign officers trained annually.
2002	China and ASEAN sign Joint Declaration on Cooperation in the Field of NTS, with drugs topping the list of regional concerns. China's MPS and Myanmar's Ministry of Home Affairs sign a Border Security Cooperation Agreement against trafficking, smuggling and gambling.
2004	PLA replaces People's Armed Police on the China–Myanmar border. Chinese and Myanmar Ministries of Defence sign agreement on border affairs covering border demarcation, transnational crime, terrorism, natural disasters, epidemic diseases, advanced information-sharing on troop movements, and an agreement to re-establish Border Representative Agencies.
2005	MPS and Myanmar's Ministry of Home Affairs agree to enhance border cooperation, especially on drug trafficking and tourism. China provides RMB3m in aid.
2005–6	AusAID and UNAIDS (the Joint United Nations Programme on HIV and AIDS) help to establish training centre for Myanmar, Laotian and Vietnamese police in Yunnan.

Table 3.3 *(cont.)*

Year	Action
2006	China and Myanmar sign Agreement on Prohibition of Illegal Trafficking, Abuse of Narcotic Drugs and Psychotropic Substances.
2008–12	Yunnan and Guangxi host regional HIV/AIDS programme funded by the Australian government, including cross-border training and technical exchanges, monitoring and evaluation of programmes, and public health research.
2015	Judicial cooperation yields 60 extraditions from Myanmar since 2009.

Sources: Sheng (2006: 107); Li and Lye (2009: 264, 270–1); Freeman and Thompson (2011: 74–5); Maung Aung Myoe (2011: 142–3); Steinberg and Fan (2012: 274–5); Chin and Zhang (2015: ch. 9); Interviewee D04 (2018); Interviewee D13 (2018).

enhanced market access, training, tools and equipment. Chinese agencies have promoted opium substitution in Myanmar and Laos since the early 1990s.

This NTS intervention is rarely discussed in the International Relations literature. The few accounts that do exist tend to praise it as a success, and as consistent with China's anti-interventionist principles. For example, Freeman and Thompson (2011: 72–3) claim that 'China's stated foreign policy principle of not interfering ... is closely observed in this intervention [*sic*] model, where government and non-government stakeholder buy-in is considered crucial by the Chinese side', stating that the OSP has been a 'success', reducing 'poppy cultivation ... [and] the supply of heroin'. Trevaskes (2013: 226) likewise claims that 'significant declines in poppy production in Burma [are] due largely to successful crop replacement programmes', while Lin (2017: 699–700), citing NNCC reports from 2007 to 2012, judges the programme to be 'effective' and 'excellent'.

However, as we show, building on our fieldwork and critical empirical studies in political geography (e.g. Su 2015) and political ecology (e.g. Kenney-Lazar, Suhardiman and Dwyer 2018), and reports by civil society organisations, these judgements are quite mistaken. The implementation of China's OSP has been powerfully conditioned by state transformation dynamics, resulting in widespread failure. Although the MPS has established a regulatory framework for the OSP, incorporating UN rules, the programme has actually been controlled by China's commercial bureaucracy, following regulatory-state approaches that decentralise power and resources to subnational actors. This has enabled cadre-capitalists in Yunnan province to hijack the programme to support local agribusiness interests which, when combined with socio-political dynamics in the target states of Myanmar and Laos, has produced outcomes starkly different to those sought in Beijing.

Governing China's Opium Substitution Programme

Reflecting the transformation of the party-state, the key actors in China's OSP have not been central government agencies but subnational governments and state-linked enterprises in Yunnan province. These actors have influenced national policy guidelines and interpreted them in line with local cadre-capitalist interests, hijacking counternarcotics policy to support the transboundary expansion of local agribusinesses. They have also ignored some basic Chinese regulations, and the international soft-law principles to which Beijing is ostensibly committed.

The political economy context is, as always, critical. Being relatively under-developed, Yunnan has the second-lowest income per capita among Chinese provinces, around half the national average (National Bureau of Statistics of China 2019). Roughly a third of Yunnan's inhabitants are ethnic minorities, many with kinfolk in Myanmar and Laos. Historically restive, ruled by warlords and better-connected to Southeast Asia than the rest of China, Yunnan was forcibly directed 'inwards' as part of Mao's state-building project. However, in the reform era, local elites have seen the cultivation of transboundary ties with neighbouring states as Yunnan's main route to capitalist development. Reflecting decentralisation of foreign economic policy, from the early 1980s, local authorities began establishing cross-border trade and investment relations, often without Beijing's permission and sometimes in violation of basic Chinese laws and regulations (Hameiri, Jones and Zou 2019).

Emerging regulatory-governance frameworks also empowered Yunnan. In 1992, the provincial government was designated China's main representative in the Asian Development Bank's GMS integration plan. Yunnan also benefited enormously from the Great Western Development (GWD) programme, a loose policy framework designed to support domestic and transboundary infrastructure development, launched in 2000 after years of lobbying from Yunnan and others. Reflecting the regulatory-state model, these two frameworks established broad guidelines but delegated practical implementation to local actors, which lobbied fervently for funding, investment, infrastructure and policy concessions via personal networks, national working conferences, the National People's Congress and the CCP Congress (Holbig 2004; Summers 2013). The Belt and Road Initiative scaled up this approach, allowing Yunnan to again upload its local schemes into national policy (Summers 2016; Jones and Zeng 2019).

The specific interests of Yunnan's cadre-capitalists have powerfully shaped China's economic engagement with neighbouring Southeast Asia. Yunnan is dominated by the state-backed construction sector, agribusiness and extractive industries. In 2000–15, provincial lobbying within the GMS/GWD frameworks yielded RMB750bn (US$114.9bn) in central government funding for the local construction industry, producing a massive boom in domestic and transboundary infrastructure-building (Hameiri, Jones and Zou 2019: 489). This included large-scale road and railway linkages and the dredging of the Mekong River, which cut Yunnan's maritime export route by 3,000 km (Guo 2007: 57). It also included a China–Myanmar oil and gas pipeline designed to boost Kunming's petrochemicals industry, for which Yunnan province and China National Petroleum Company had jointly lobbied, exploiting Beijing's concerns about 'energy security' (Hameiri, Jones and Zou 2019: 489). Yunnan also made itself a base for the transnational expansion of Chinese hydropower companies (see Chapter 4), and other extractive enterprises, particularly timber and mining firms – all facing dwindling opportunities and tightening regulation domestically, and therefore keen to expand into the untapped frontier markets of Myanmar and Laos. More recently, Yunnan's major local industry, agribusiness, has also expanded transnationally to meet surging demand for agricultural commodities in a context of domestic land shortages (Luo, Donaldson and Zhang 2011).

Yunnan's role in China's OSP is heavily shaped by these agribusiness interests, particularly in the rubber industry. Developed through state-led innovation and support, the rubber sector is often depicted as epitomising socialist resourcefulness, progress and modernity (Sturgeon 2013: 76). Beijing classified rubber as a 'strategic crop', exempting the industry from liberalisation after it joined the World Trade Organization and protecting it with 20 per cent import tariffs (Lu 2017: 736; Dwyer and Vongvisouk 2019: 100). China's biggest rubber firms are all Yunnanese. Although many formerly state-owned firms have been privatised, the largest maintain strong ties to local elites (Lu 2017; Sturgeon 2013).

Reflecting the model outlined in Chapter 1, China's OSP initially emerged through bottom-up influencing mechanisms. Opium substitution in Myanmar was initially pioneered by Menghai County in 1992, then scaled-up into a province-wide scheme as part of Yunnan's Green Drug Prevention Plan in the late 1990s, overseen by the province's Department of Commerce. Provincial elites then lobbied Beijing to resource this plan, resulting in its incorporation into national policy in 2000 (Su 2015: 79; Interviewee E16 2018). Accordingly, by 2003, Yunnan's OSP plantations already covered 36,670 ha in Myanmar and 4,667 ha in Laos, with a reported US$63m spent on the programme by 2004 (Swanström and He 2006: 47; Shi 2008: 23).

Beijing's adoption of Yunnan's policy suggestion resulted not in centralised control but rather regulatory-state mechanisms affording continued local autonomy. The State Council established the 122 Workgroup, headed by the Ministry of Commerce (MOFCOM), to coordinate eighteen different ministries and agencies and incorporate opium substitution into overall economic planning. Reflecting the fragmentation of Chinese governance, the OSP was thus overseen by commercial agencies, not the NNCC. These incorporated a 'market logic into [China's] war on drugs ... highlighting a business-driven mode of development assistance' (Su 2015: 79; also Cohen 2009: 424). In regulatory-state mode, the 122 Workgroup outlined a loose policy framework, proposing measures to encourage agribusinesses to undertake opium substitution, including subsidies, low-interest loans and import tariff waivers, and set targets for the establishment of OSP plantations: 66,670 ha in 2006–10, for instance (Shi 2008: 27). This coverage target is the only way the programme's implementation is measured; there is no attempt to assess the OSP's effects on opium cultivation (Lu 2017: 733), thereby ignoring the UN principles to which the MPS had committed China as part of the Mekong MOU (see Table 3.2).

Moreover, although 'MOFCOM set broad targets ... the operation was implemented by local government' (Interviewee E16 2018). Control over the funding allocated by the Ministry of Finance – initially RMB50m annually, increasing to RMB250m during 2011–15 (Su 2015: 79) – was delegated to Yunnan's Department of Commerce (DOC) (Shi 2008: 23). This regulatory-state approach gave the local cadre-capitalist class enormous leeway to interpret opium substitution policy in ways that benefited local agribusiness interests. Unsurprisingly, therefore, 'the policy objective of drug eradication has been appropriated as a commercial and economic opportunity for Yunnan enterprises to expand their activities into neighbouring territories' (Summers 2013: 165–6). As a Yunnan law enforcement expert notes: 'The project was not only [intended] to help solve the drug problem ... but also to help the companies to make money' (Interviewee E10 2018). A Chinese official puts it even more bluntly: 'They regarded the opium substitution plantations as a form of economic activity ... Now it's a completely economic operation' (Interviewee E15 2018). The process was also 'ridden with cronyism and corruption', with DOC eligibility criteria ensuring that the largest and best-connected firms captured the lion's share of subsidies (Shi 2008: 27–30; Lu 2017: 733). As Yunnan experts observe, 'in the process of implementation ... government officials pursued their own profit and made mistakes'; the OSP became 'a project for some companies to earn money for themselves' (Interviewees E09 2018).

Crucially, as a Chinese expert on the OSP states, 'companies are the most important actors in this programme', and they 'had a lot of autonomy to conduct their operations', with only very weak regulatory oversight (Interviewee E16 2018). Unlike the early 1990s, when projects were largely designed by DOC officials, in the 2000s, decision-making was outsourced to the agribusinesses themselves. They were tasked with approaching local authorities in Myanmar and Laos to negotiate access and secure written confirmation that projects would be based in opium-growing areas; then they applied for DOC support (Interviewee E16 2018; Interviewee F05 2018). Reflecting the rise of the local regulatory state, the DOC's 'major function is to supervise' corporate activity, rather than controlling projects directly (Interviewee E16 2018). Furthermore, the DOC has little real supervisory capacity. As one senior Laotian law enforcement officer put it: 'The Chinese don't have their own people monitoring the companies' (Interviewee F05 2018). The DOC instead relies on feedback from Myanmar and Laotian authorities, affording companies wide latitude in practice (Lu 2017: 734; Dwyer and Vongvisouk 2019: 108; also Interviewee E16 2018; Interviewee F04 2018).

These power relations effectively doomed China's OSP from the outset because key corporate actors' interests drove the scheme away from opium-substitution in practice. The Yunnanese agribusinesses most interested in outward expansion were rubber companies, because rubber demand was then booming just as many of China's rubber trees were reaching maturity and required felling (Cohen 2009: 426). However, rubber is an extremely poor substitute for opium. It grows predominantly below 900 m elevation, whereas almost all opium is grown at altitudes of 800–1,800 m (Chen et al. 2016; UNODC 2019a: 34). In the 2010s, rubber has been pushed into higher altitudes in China, reflecting land shortages, while opium has crept down from the mountains in Myanmar, but the ideal conditions for these crops remain fundamentally different. Consequently, it is intrinsically implausible to persuade opium farmers to switch to rubber. They would either have to move to new land, or rubber plantations would develop independently of any change in opium cultivation. An additional problem with the rubber firms' overwhelming domination is that monocropping makes participating farmers heavily dependent on price fluctuations for a single commodity. When rubber prices fell by 75 per cent from 2011 to 2015, and remained low, the impact was devastating (Dwyer and Vongvisouk 2019: 97).

Ultimately, the way China pursued opium substitution reflects the fragmentation and decentralisation of governance within the transformed party-state. As local Chinese experts put it: 'The central government may tell a local government to do something, but the local government might do something different; and then a company can do something different still' (Interviewees E09 2018). The final outcome of these policies, however, is determined by how these firms interact with socio-political forces within host countries, as we now demonstrate.

China's Opium Substitution Programme in Myanmar

Until 2001, when it was overtaken by Afghanistan, Myanmar (Burma) produced most of the world's opium and heroin. Its share fell from

69 per cent in 2001 to 7 per cent in 2018, with opium cultivation and output shrinking from 105,000 ha and 828 tonnes to 36,100 ha and 520 tonnes (see Figure 3.1). As in Afghanistan, drug production in Myanmar is intimately connected to civil war: in Myanmar's case, the world's longest-running ethnic-minority insurgencies. Many ethnic-minority armed groups (EAGs), operating in Myanmar's borderlands, have financed them-selves through drug trafficking, ever since the USA and Thailand began facilitating the heroin trade in the 1950s to support a Kuomintang army that had retreated from China into Burma's Shan state (McCoy 2003). The Myanmar military (Tatmadaw) has also colluded in drug trafficking by EAGs in ceasefires with the government or local militias allied with the army (Meehan 2011). Opium cultivation is heavily concentrated in the upland regions of Shan, Wa and Kachin states, bordering China, home to ongoing conflicts and well-armed ceasefire groups.

China's OSP has entered this highly complex, conflict-ridden con-text in a fairly reckless manner. Although Myanmar's counter-narcotics authority initially agreed to the programme, implementa-tion was entirely decentralised, with no real oversight or coordin-ation. Chinese agribusiness firms used local brokers to strike deals with army commanders and EAGs, with plantations often established through land-grabbing. The benefits have been concentrated among investors and local elites, while smallholding farmers have suffered

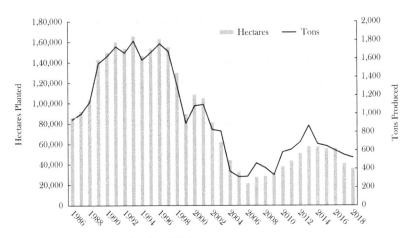

Figure 3.1 Opium production in Myanmar
Sources: UNODC World Drug Report and Southeast Asia Opium Survey, various years.

dispossession, proletarianisation and forced displacement. Coupled with intensifying civil conflict, the result has actually been to *increase* opium production – the opposite of Beijing policymakers' intentions.

The Political Economy Context in Myanmar

The key contextual factors in Myanmar are all closely interrelated: the existence of intense ethnopolitical conflict; the rise of 'ceasefire capitalism' in the borderlands, with Chinese involvement (Woods 2011a); and the fragmentation of authority over land.

Myanmar's drug problem is intimately related to the intense conflict between the centralising, military-dominated state, largely controlled by the ethnic Bamar majority, and ethnic-minority populations in northeastern Myanmar. Separatist insurgencies raged in these areas from the 1950s until the early 1990s, with many EAGs becoming directly involved in the opium trade. The collapse of the Chinese-backed Communist Party of Burma into several ethnically organised militias in 1989 was a key turning point, prompting the then military government to offer these groups ceasefires. In exchange for peace, the EAGs were allowed to retain their arms and control over pockets of territory, formalised in some cases as 'special regions', including lucrative natural resources and border posts. They were encouraged to invest their gains from smuggling and drug trafficking into the formal economy, as part of the regime's shift from state socialism to capitalism (Jones 2014a; 2014b). The military – bolstered by weaponry imported from China – was then deployed against recalcitrant groups, driving yet more into ceasefires. The result was the emergence of 'ceasefire capitalism', with the Tatmadaw and EAGs turning from war to the exploitation of the borderlands' untapped natural resources (Woods 2011a). Ceasefire groups were initially allowed to continue drug production, but government suppression campaigns escalated under the 1999–2014 Narcotic Elimination Master Plan. Nonetheless, drug eradication has always been secondary to the military's main objective: conflict control. Crackdowns largely target non-ceasefire groups and shift according to political dynamics, squeezing oppositional EAGs but allowing loyal militias to continue drug trafficking (SHAN 2006; Meehan 2011; Kramer et al. 2014: 32–4; Meehan 2015; Su 2018).

Chinese and Thai investment has been central to ceasefire capitalism. Yunnan's cadre-capitalists seized on the opportunity to enter this frontier market, with national and provincial SOEs and private firms partnering with the Tatmadaw and (illegally) with EAGs to secure access to timber, gemstones (notably jade), minerals (especially copper and gold), hydropower dam sites and, more recently, agribusiness plantations (Buchanan, Kramer and Woods 2013; Burke et al. 2017). By 2011, two-thirds of Myanmar's inbound foreign investment was concentrated in its resource-rich borderlands (Woods and Kramer 2012: 12). China (including Hong Kong) became, and remains, Myanmar's largest foreign investor, with US$28.7bn approved investment by 2019, 36 per cent of the total (DICA 2019).[4]

Myanmar's ceasefire capitalism is governed – if the term can be stretched this far – in a highly fragmented and quasi-informal manner, making it extremely predatory in practice. The official governance of land and natural resources is fragmented, with responsibilities split across ministries responsible for forestry, environmental conservation and agriculture. Laws, regulations and procedures 'are not only spread across numerous uncoordinated sectoral jurisdictions, but also rife with legal loopholes, special permits, and/or exemptions ... creating a "rule by decree" governance situation conducive to rent-seeking' (Woods 2015: vii). Even after the shift from direct military rule to a civilianised electoral regime in 2011, the government still lacked 'the capacity or political will to ensure that ... foreign investment is properly regulated' (Buchanan, Kramer and Woods 2013: 44). Moreover, central government ministries' writ does not extend into the borderlands, where governance is instead shaped by 'emerging political complexes' between regional military commanders, EAG leaders, local notables, crony-capitalist enterprises and foreign investors (Callahan 2007; Jones 2014b).

Land is especially open to appropriation by powerful social groups. Myanmar's post-independence constitution assigned land ownership to the state, with no legal recognition of customary use rights. Given the country's fragmented and weak governance, in practice this has allowed state-based actors to seize and reallocate land on a discretionary basis. Recent land laws have exacerbated this situation, by empowering all government departments to take charge of 'wasteland', and allowing the Myanmar Investment Commission to override existing land laws to

---

[4] Official figure as of April 2019. The real figures are likely substantially higher because much Chinese investment is never officially recorded or is routed through tax havens.

allocate large-scale, long-term concessions (Woods 2015: 8–10, 20–1). In the period 2010–13 alone, agribusiness concessions increased by 170 per cent, to 2.1 m hectares (Woods 2015: 13). These concessions were largely directed to crony-capitalist enterprises, often to facilitate otherwise illegal logging, but Chinese agribusinesses were also heavily involved in this land-grab, which forcibly displaced many thousands of farmers, particularly in the still heavily forested ethnic-minority states (Woods 2015: 12–14; Woods and Kramer 2012). However, most Chinese concessionaires were not covert loggers but genuine agribusiness investors: Chinese timber companies already enjoy easy access to forested areas through local intermediaries, and the OSP made agribusiness investment profitable (Woods 2015: 39, 42, 45–6). These investors have tended to establish plantations by working with local military commanders, bureaucrats or EAGs, rather than the central government (Woods 2015: 39).

China's Opium Substitution Programme in Northern Myanmar

China's transformed party-state interacted with these contextual dynamics in Myanmar to produce the following outcomes. First, although notionally agreed between national governments, practical implementation of the programme was decentralised and uncoordinated. Second, reflecting Myanmar's fragmented internal governance, China's OSP was highly variegated, depending on individual deals struck with local power-brokers, which typically involved coercive land-grabbing, not the inclusive, consultative approach specified in the UN guidelines to which Beijing was ostensibly committed. Third, implementation and outcomes reflected the foregrounding of business interests and market dynamics, failing to reduce opium cultivation. Finally, China's transformed party-state was an obstacle to Myanmar authorities and civil society actors lobbying for redress.

The implementation of China's OSP in Myanmar was heavily decentralised and thus primarily shaped by the dynamics of state transformation and ceasefire capitalism. Initially, the NNCC approached its Myanmar counterpart, the Central Committee for Drug Abuse Control (CCDAC) to propose the OSP. However, as a former senior CCDAC official notes, after the initial agreement, implementation was devolved to Yunnan-based actors, with no effective oversight, meaning it was hijacked by commercial imperatives (Interviewee D13 2018). As one Myanmar policy expert notes, the central government did not manage the programme, with senior agriculture officials unaware even of its existence. Even today, 'the [Myanmar] government has no idea what the Chinese are doing' and has no strategy to manage external projects (Interviewee D16 2018). A senior, Yangon-based Western diplomat concurs: 'there is no actual coordination' (Interviewee D23 2018).

Instead, Chinese agribusinesses implementing the OSP struck deals with local elites, who were primarily interested in facilitating investment for their own benefit (Interviewee D19 2018). After scouting for suitable land, Chinese firms approached local power-brokers, including township authorities and EAGs – typically through Sino-Burmese middlemen, because foreigners could not legally purchase land. This afforded some leverage to secure benefit-sharing from Chinese investors, but this was monopolised by a 'few people in powerful positions' since 'they're the ones who can supply large areas of land' (Interviewee D20 2018). Township authorities frequently authorised concessions using inaccurate maps showing vacant land, prompting sharp land conflicts with existing land-users, which firms often resolved through illegal land purchases (Interviewee D20 2018). Ethnic-minority armed groups tended to be more helpful partners, using coercion to help establish the plantations. Local civil society actors report that EAGs, including the United Wa State Army (UWSA), the Kachin Independence Organisation/Army (KIO/KIA), the Myanmar National Democratic Alliance Army (MNDAA) and the National Democratic Army-Kachin (NDA-K), all engaged in land-grabbing to establish OSP plantations (Interviewee D08 2018; Interviewee D10 2018; Interviewee D20 2018). The ex-CCDAC official recalls: 'Local government turned a blind eye'; there was 'no intervention at all' and 'corruption at all levels ... [it was] open knowledge to everyone' (Interviewee D13 2018).

This highly fragmented approach produced considerable variation in how OSP plantations were established and operated, but the general approach was extremely exploitative, enriching local elites and investors while farmers were forcibly displaced and proletarianised. For example, the MNDAA used 'land-grabbing and forced labour to establish plantations', forcing peasant farmers to become wage labourers, paid just RMB18 (US$2.60) daily; the Chinese company supplied all the other inputs and took the entire crop, paying the MNDAA a cut (Interviewee D08 2018). The local farmers were unhappy but 'had no voice – they could not compete with the power-holders, the Kokang military and the army. It is jungle rule – you can shoot whoever you want' (Interviewee D08 2018). In UWSA areas, local wage labour was also used (and sometimes forced) to establish plantations, often by converting communal rice paddy fields, turning farmers into day-labourers, while the Chinese again supplied all the other inputs, taking two-thirds of the profits. The UWSA also 'taxed' exports to China (Kramer 2009: 7–9). Local peasants were never consulted (Interviewee D10 2018). Where Wa farmers refused to be proletarianised, Chinese companies illegally imported Chinese workers. As a former UNODC official observes, the OSP thus 'threatens to turn the local people into an underclass of "coolie" labourers' (Renard 2013: 164). The profits were monopolised by local elites and Chinese investors. Local authorities benefited from 'under-the-table dealings with Chinese companies' while 'Chinese industry got cheap rubber' and other agricultural commodities thanks to their monopsonistic power (Interviewee D10 2018). As a local aid worker observes, benefits accrued 'only to the Chinese company ... [and] powerful people in the KIO, the Wa, [and] the NDA-K, [who] have big plantations' (Interviewee D20 2018). The OSP's main impact was thus to 'widen the gap between the haves and the have-nots' (Lanau Roi Aung 2016: 46).

The hijacking of China's NTS intervention by powerful politico-business interests skewed implementation away from the 122 Workgroup's objectives of suppressing narcotics. As the ex-NNCC official remarks, the ostensible 'objective [was] alternative development and opium substitution, but what these Chinese companies did was nothing to do with development, it was purely about business ... They did illegal things also, illegal logging, even drug trafficking' (Interviewee D13 2018). The choice of crops and sites reflected a profit motive, not counter-narcotics objectives. As in Laos (see below), none of the crops promoted – rubber, sugarcane, tea and fruit – are direct substitutes for opium because they grow at lower altitudes. Hence, China's OSP 'is not covering the opium growing areas. It's on paddy fields and orchard-tree growing areas ... virgin soil. So it's not substitution ... it's expanding Chinese farmland into [Myanmar] under the name of that policy' (Interviewee D19 2018). 'They came under the cover of opium substitution, but these are not poppy cultivation areas' (Interviewee D13 2018). Thus, in Wa state, a development worker observed a communal rice paddy, located around 800 m elevation, being seized to establish a rubber plantation

(Interviewee D10 2018). In Kachin, as a local aid worker explains, because 'the opium substitution plantation does not change [farmers'] livelihood; they still depend on poppy plantations', plantation workers continued to farm opium at higher altitudes (Interviewee D20 2018). The crop selection, dictated by Chinese agribusiness's interests, had a particularly devastating impact on Wa state when the rubber price collapsed in 2011, prompting many farmers to abandon the plantations and leaving factories unable to pay suppliers or workers (Su 2016: 18). Many plantations have been left idle, or destroyed and replaced by other crops, while disaffected peasants returned to subsistence agriculture (Interviewee D12 2018; Interviewees E09 2018; Interviewee E12 2018).

China's state transformation and local political economy dynamics thus interacted to make the OSP a failure. According to UNODC estimates, opium cultivation and heroin production actually increased following the OSP's introduction (see Figure 3.1), while NNCC data show corresponding increases in seizures within China (see Figure 3.2). The sharp drops in opium cultivation from the late 1990s to 2003 are attributable to government suppression and, more importantly, key EAGs' own opium bans (see Table 3.4).[5] China's own remote sensing confirmed these findings (Tian et al. 2011). UNODC surveys also reveal government/EAG suppression as the primary reason for the post-2014 downturn in production, followed by bad weather (e.g. UNODC 2014: 67–8; 2015b: 57). The early opium bans were primarily enacted under pressure from Chinese officials, who warned EAGs that they would check progress using remote sensing (Kramer 2009: 22–3, 35; Renard 2013: 150). As a senior Myanmar official of that time comments, 'it was not central [Myanmar] government, it was China's pressure'. Yunnan Public Security officials even helped the UWSA to relocate hundreds of thousands of peasants away from the opium-growing highlands to lowland areas in 2000; the Myanmar government 'knew nothing about this' (Interviewee D19 2018). Myanmar's leading expert on Wa state even alleges that China's Ministry of State Security has intelligence operatives there to identify drug producers,

---

[5] UNODC estimates are contested due to their dubious methodology (Kramer et al. 2014: 20–3). The high figures recorded for the 1980s/1990s are especially disputed, with critics stating that local groups estimate that opium output never exceeded 1,000 tonnes per year and arguing that the figures were inflated to exaggerate the impact of subsequent suppression campaigns (Kramer, Jelsma and Blickman 2009: 14–17, 25).

Table 3.4 *Opium suppression in Myanmar*

Year	Action
1997	National Democratic Alliance Army bans opium in Mongla.
1999 onwards	Myanmar government opium suppression plan targets Shan State and Mongla (1999–2004); eastern Shan, Wa and Danai and Sedun areas of Kachin (2004–9); and Kayah, southern Shan and northern Chin (2009–15).
2003	MNDAA bans opium in Kokang. UNODC declares Kokang Special Regions 1 and 4 opium-free.
2005	UWSA opium ban. UNODC declares Wa Special Region 2 opium-free in 2006.

Sources: Kramer, Jelsma and Blickman (2009: 19); UNODC (2006: 61; 2008: 49).

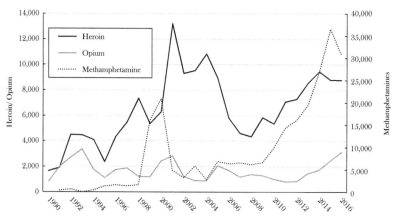

Figure 3.2 Narcotics seizures by Chinese authorities
Source: UNODC (2018).

with Yunnan's Foreign Affairs Bureau then asking the EAGs to suppress the miscreants (Interviewee D12 2018).

There is good reason to believe that China's OSP contributed to the rebound in opium production from 2005 to 2013.[6] The main reasons

---

[6] The primary reason is the breakdown in several important ceasefires in 2009–11, which led conflict actors to increase drug production to raise revenue (or, on the military's part, to tolerate this by pro-government militias). See Meehan (2011).

farmers grow opium are poverty – opium is a lucrative cash crop – and landlessness and tenure insecurity – opium poppies grow at high altitudes on otherwise unproductive land, and produce yields in just three months,[7] an important consideration for farmers who may be displaced by conflict or land-grabbing (Kramer, Jelsma and Blickman 2009: 23; Grimmelmann et al. 2018). The government and EAG opium bans were not sustainable, since they did not resolve these underlying problems. On the contrary, by banning farmers' main source of income and forcibly relocating many peasants, the bans exacerbated these structural drivers of opium cultivation (Kramer, Jelsma and Blickman 2009). At best, the bans displaced cultivation (and sometimes farmers themselves) into other parts of Myanmar's borderlands.

China's OSP only exacerbated this situation, producing uniformly negative assessments among civil society actors. With profits monopolised by Chinese investors and local strongmen, OSP plantations failed to provide farmers with incomes that could rival opium cultivation. Moreover, by fuelling land-grabbing, they exacerbated the land insecurity that also spurs opium cultivation. As a local development worker in Wa observes: 'it's a total failure, because we could not find any alternative livelihood for them ... it is not a success – production just moved to southern Shan' (Interviewee D10 2018). Another suggests that the OSP was simply 'a waste of money' and was 'not effective. You cannot substitute opium with some other crop' (Interviewee D08 2018). Myanmar's leading Wa expert concurs: 'What the [Chinese] companies do in the region is totally hopeless. It's a total waste of time and resources ... no company has succeeded in an opium substitution project' (Interviewee D12 2018). Another civil society activist, a frequent visitor to Wa state, says: 'the project totally failed' (Interviewee E12 2018). In Kachin, a local civil society organisation (CSO) worker observes: 'The opium growing area is not decreasing – it is even increasing. So the policy has failed' (Interviewee D19 2018). Another concurs: the OSP was 'not successful ... Not at all. We just see it as an investment, not poppy substitution' (Interviewee D20 2018). Overall, civil society actors consider China's OSP to be 'a scam ... it's kind of a joke ... not

---

[7] Compare with coffee plants, which take three years to mature and produce a yield, or rubber trees, which take seven years (Kramer, Jelsma and Blickman 2009: 32).

effective to address the real problem or make changes – there are no tangible results' (Interviewees D11 2018).

Myanmar officials generally concur with this assessment, but their domestic power remains limited and their capacity to change Chinese behaviour has been thwarted by state transformation dynamics. A senior Myanmar police officer observes that China's programme started as 'opium substitution but later it just ended up being about their business' interests (Interviewee D04 2018). A senior Ministry of Agriculture official likewise told one of our informants: 'There is no such thing as opium substitution', and no Chinese projects had succeeded (Interviewee D18 2018). Another reports that many Myanmar officials 'really didn't like this programme', while even the NDA-K viewed it as 'a total scam' (Interviewee D16 2018). However, national government officials often cannot control the borderlands directly. Nor, thanks to state transformation dynamics, could they induce Chinese actors to change their behaviour. The ex-CCDAC senior official states that around 2006/7: 'We got very fed up ... and said very bluntly to the Chinese: "this is not the kind of development we want. They [The agribusinesses] are cheating us, and they are cheating you – they are lying to you, telling you they are doing development" ... But these guys are from Beijing, they don't know anything' (Interviewee D13 2018). The CCDAC's interlocutors, the NNCC, explained that they could not help because:

They have no [control over] commerce and agriculture. This is one of the big flaws ... We should have direct access to [officials responsible for] agriculture, rural development ... The NNCC, the Public Security people, they want to help us, but they rely on the private sector, who are not sincere at all ... profit is the main thing [for them] ... [But] NNCC officials said this is the mandate of another ministry. (Interviewee D13 2018)

In addition to fragmentation at the national level, the CCDAC saw decentralisation as another barrier to policy change:

I do not blame the NNCC in Beijing ... [I] blame Yunnan. We are neighbours, we know them well. Beijing lives in another world ... [Yunnan] knows all about us ... [But] they are not sincere .... [The] autonomous provinces ... they listen to Beijing, but they have their own independent way of doing things. (Interviewee D13 2018)

CSOs have encountered identical problems when trying to communicate local farmers' grievances about the OSP to Chinese officials. One relates: 'When we talk to the Yunnan people, they have some idea [about what is really happening]. When we talk to Beijing, they have a very different idea' (Interviewee D18 2018). Similarly, another reports: 'when I met with [officials in] Beijing, they say, "we don't know, it's Yunnan province, that's their decision"' (Interviewee D19 2018). Some civil society actors suggest that some Yunnan officials 'genuinely didn't realise what was going on' (Interviewee D18 2018), reflecting their weak regulatory capacity. Others suggest 'the Yunnan government knows' full well, but simply does not care (Interviewee D19 2018).

Certainly, the Chinese side does not seem to have learned from its mistakes, as these dynamics have continued under Xi Jinping. From 2015, bananas supplanted rubber as the main boom crop. Myanmar civil society groups report that hundreds of thousands of acres have been grabbed for Chinese banana plantations 'in the name of opium substitution', with the active connivance of local authorities, particularly in Kachin state (Interviewee D18 2018). In December 2018, the Kachin state administration found that thirty-six mostly Chinese-backed companies had established illegal plantations covering 70,000–80,000 acres in government-held areas, though CSOs have identified over 100,000 acres of banana plantations in one township alone (Hein Ko Soe and Dunant 2019). Chinese investors have not acquired government permits for their plantations, nor import licences for the new species being used; indeed, the Ministry of Agriculture claims it 'doesn't know [anything] about the banana plantations' (Interviewee D20 2018). Instead, Chinese firms have again partnered with local military, bureaucratic and EAG elites, with farmers pressured to sell their land through poverty or coercion, or being expropriated after being forcibly displaced due to armed conflict (Hein Ko Soe and Dunant 2019). With 'corruption at all levels', local government is 'turning a blind eye', the state governor even claiming that 'it is good for Kachin state, it is reducing opium cultivation' (Interviewee D13 2018). In reality, although Chinese firms 'came under the cover of opium substitution', yet again, 'these are not poppy cultivation areas' (Interviewee D13 2018). Civil society organisations are also alarmed by the Chinese fertilisers and pesticides being used on the plantations, which are associated with soil degradation, livestock poisoning and health problems, including cancer (Interviewee D19 2018). Plantation labourers work without any safety equipment, but at the border, activists report, bananas are handled by people with 'clothes like astronauts', who treat the crops with additional chemicals before they are sold (Interviewee D20 2018). However, CSOs' appeals to the Chinese authorities are falling on deaf ears: 'We have seen no change in policy or scrutinising of the companies' (Interviewee D19 2018). This again exemplifies the weak oversight of Yunnan's outbound agribusiness investments, reflecting local cadre-capitalist elites' interests.

Finally, the OSP has clearly been unable to stem the tide of amphetamine-type stimulants (ATS) into China. In part due to opium suppression, EAGs and pro-government militias increasingly shifted into ATS production from the late 1990s (SHAN 2006; Kramer, Jelsma and Blickman 2009; Lintner and Black 2009). Domestic consumption and trafficking into China have exploded (see Figure 3.2). Ironically, this situation is even worse for Myanmar's peasant farmers because they do not even get the income they used to receive from opium. The chemicals used to produce ATS are overwhelmingly smuggled from China, while Chinese individuals are also said to dominate the industry (Kramer, Jelsma and Blickman 2009: 61; SHAN 2006: 52). Myanmar's police constantly raise this problem in bilateral meetings, to little effect (Interviewee D04 2018). A former CCDAC senior official states that Chinese customs officials 'are not doing their job ... We cannot block the smuggling' because it comes through EAG-controlled areas, 'But the Chinese side is strictly managed – so how can it happen? We think there is a lot of corruption there also' (Interviewee D13 2018). A Western diplomat blames the 'diversity of interests' within China's fragmented party-state, claiming that the MPS's counter-narcotics agenda is undermined by the Ministry of State Security's 'overt' support for the UWSA, which is widely alleged to be involved in ATS production and trafficking. 'You've got two ministries with related interests working at cross-purposes' (Interviewee D23 2018).

In summary, Chinese state transformation dynamics and Myanmar's conflict-ridden political economy have combined to make China's OSP a failure. Rather than tackling an NTS threat, as policymakers in Beijing intended, China's OSP plantations have become part of Myanmar's brutal ceasefire capitalism. Chinese enterprises' conduct clearly violates the international standards to which Beijing has subscribed (see Table 3.2). The companies have also ignored many basic Chinese regulations on outbound investment, including requirements to follow local laws and regulations, ensure 'mutual benefit and win-win', and avoid damaging China's security and bilateral relations (e.g. MOFCOM 2009); general directives to consult local experts and people to ensure that projects are feasible and acceptable (Xinhua 2010); and a specific bilateral treaty which obliges Chinese investors to respect the 'public interest' in Myanmar (Jones and Zou 2017: 752). This not only contributed to the failure of China's NTS intervention, it also intensified anti-Chinese sentiment among populations already suffering dispossession and forced displacement associated with Yunnan firms' logging, mining and hydropower investments (Interviewee D13 2018; Interviewee D16 2018; Interviewee D21 2018).

China's Opium Substitution Programme in Laos

Small, landlocked Laos is not a major drug-producing country. Opium cultivation peaked in 1989 at 42,130 ha, yielding 380 tonnes, before being forcibly suppressed, with the UNODC declaring Laos drug-free in 2006 (Cohen 2009: 425; Windle 2018: 368). Today Laos is mainly a transit country for narcotics, primarily ATS, from Myanmar into China and Thailand (Interviewee F01 2018; Interviewee F04 2018; Stuart-Fox 2007: 171). Nonetheless, from 2004 China's OSP arrived in northern Laos with enthusiastic support from the national government. From 2003 to 2014, the area covered by rubber plantations grew from 900 ha to 261,000 ha (McAllister 2015: 817). In the border provinces, around 100 Chinese OSP plantations were established – 89 per cent between 2005 and 2008, the rubber boom years – comprising one- to two-thirds of all rubber plantations in Laos (Lu 2017: 737–8).

China's OSP had less devastating consequences in Laos than Myanmar, but smallholders still suffered considerable deprivation, and opium cultivation again increased rather than falling. Here, outcomes were shaped by a fragmented one-party state oriented towards attracting large-scale, export-driven foreign investments. While welcoming to Chinese investors, the regime is too divided to secure land, steering Chinese OSP projects towards contract farming rather than the establishment of large plantations. This initially entailed greater benefits for local farmers, but market power imbalances, particularly after the collapse in rubber prices, have led to them being squeezed progressively harder. Over time, smallholdings are being consolidated into large plantations, with benefits increasingly monopolised by elites and smallholders rendered landless (Shi 2015; Dwyer and Vongvisouk 2019). Rather than reducing opium cultivation, this seems to have contributed to its revival. As with Myanmar, the case study first summarises the Laotian context, then traces its interaction with Chinese state transformation dynamics.

The Political Economy Context in Laos

The crucial local factors shaping the outcomes of China's OSP in Laos are the fragmented nature of the Laotian party-state, and its orientation towards large-scale, extractive investment.

Laos has been ruled by the Lao People's Revolutionary Party (LPRP) since 1975. The LPRP initially experimented with Stalinist collectivisation, but local resistance and devastating harvests, coupled with the withdrawal of Soviet aid, impeded implementation. In 1986, the regime moved towards authoritarian capitalism under its New Economic Management Mechanism (Aroonpipat 2017: 51). This has permitted the expansion of private economic activity, though larger enterprises, particularly in the natural resources sector, remain under state control or are run by party-linked elites (Stuart-Fox 2007; Schippers 2017: 101–3). To bolster its domination, the LPRP has courted large-scale foreign investment into these sectors. In the period 2000–11, almost two-thirds of foreign investment went into primary sectors, notably mining and electricity generation (Keovilignavong and Suhardiman 2017: O344; Kyophilavong et al. 2017: 216). This has further intensified Laos's reliance on natural resources, which account for half of its national wealth, a third of economic growth, and over 60 per cent of exports (Howe and Park 2015: 168–9; UNCTAD 2019b). However, the proceeds have flowed overwhelmingly to a narrow LPRP elite, while also helping the state to extend its power over remote regions and ethnic-minority regions (Lu 2017; Sayalath and Creak 2017: 195; World Bank 2017: 7). Although absolute poverty has fallen substantially, 70 per cent of workers remain in (mostly subsistence) agriculture (World Bank 2014: 11).

The regime's land policies are especially important for our purposes. As with extractive megaprojects in mining and hydropower, the regime's 2006 policy of 'turning land into capital' reflects a desire to attract foreign investment into agriculture as part of its drive for 'modernisation' and to build support among, and extend control over, the rural population by turning 'subsistence producers into workers' (Baird 2011: 11; also Creak and Barney 2018: 708). Traditionally, many peasants practise 'swidden-fallow' agriculture, rotating between lowland and upland fields, which the regime has long seen as inefficient and as enabling ethnic minorities to evade state control (Cohen 2009; Lu 2017). Opium substitution is linked to this modernising agenda, since many of these communities have traditionally farmed opium (Cohen 2013). From the 1990s, the government has increasingly seized fallow swidden land, classifying it as 'empty' degraded forest that can be offered to foreign investors (Kenney-Lazar 2018: 685). Peasants, in turn, were encouraged to become plantation labourers.

However, this ostensibly favourable investment context is complicated by the Laotian state's own fragmentation and decentralisation (Lu and Schönweger 2019: 66–9). After the collapse of collectivisation in 1979, provincial governors became increasingly powerful as they developed 'independent' economic strategies. Moreover, as in China, decentralisation led to local officials being made accountable to both central line ministries and local leaders, though they respond primarily to the latter (Yamada 2018: 721). Full central control was apparently re-established in 1991, and there have been several high-profile efforts to curb local corruption (Yamada 2018: 728; see e.g. Stuart-Fox 2007: 173; Creak and Barney 2018: 700). Nonetheless, as in China, 'central level directives are implemented at the provincial and district levels, where they are reinterpreted according to local leaders' own perspectives, capacities and priorities, and often with little feedback to or control from Vientiane' (Lu and Schönweger 2019: 66). Consequently, local and national actors routinely sign land deals with foreign investors without each other's knowledge or approval, creating considerable problems for the companies involved (Barney 2009: 150; Keovilignavong and Suhardiman 2017: O343; Lu and Schönweger 2019). Some rural communities have also managed to exploit these intra-state divisions, and ideological contradictions, to resist land-grabbing (Kenney-Lazar 2018; Kenney-Lazar, Suhardiman and Dwyer 2018).

China's Opium Substitution Programme in Northern Laos

Although Chinese OSP projects were welcomed by national-level officials, the Laotian party-state's fragmentation complicated land acquisition processes, steering investors towards contract farming. Coupled with the problems associated with rubber monocropping, and the price collapse after 2011, this steadily disempowered and dispossessed land-holders while failing to reduce opium cultivation.

The Laotian state provided a highly hospitable legal, regulatory and tax environment for large-scale foreign agribusiness investors, luring Chinese firms with promises of vast, underpopulated land. Yunnanese investors, keen to combine this with OSP subsidies for maximum profit, expected this national backing to translate into smooth oper-ations on the ground. The reality was quite different. Notionally, large-scale land allocations up to 10,000 ha are made by the national Ministries of Planning and Investment, Natural Resources and the Environment, and Agriculture and Forestry, while subnational govern-ments are charged with facilitating projects and allocating land accord-ing to their instructions (McAllister 2015: 823; Lu and Schönweger 2019: 68). However, the Ministry of Natural Resources and the Environment allocated land without consulting local officials or citi-zens, or even checking if the promised land was even available. Accordingly, companies often faced major local resistance when trying to implement nationally authorised projects, in some cases securing no more than a quarter of the land originally promised to them (Lu and Schönweger 2019: 69–72).

While some large plantations were established – notably a massive joint venture between China-Lao Ruifeng Rubber and the Laotian military (Tan 2014: 436) – these problems channelled most Chinese OSP projects towards contract farming. This involves farmers retaining formal control over their land and labour, while the investor provides capital, technology and markets for crops – the so-called '2+3' model (Tan 2014: 436). Initially, this seemed a more inclusive approach entail-ing more widely shared benefits than seen in Myanmar. However, the contracting parties' market power was starkly unequal. In practice, farmers became tied into monocropping arrangements, being forced to sell their crops to Chinese firms at market prices, making them vulner-able to fluctuations (Dwyer and Vongvisouk 2019: 97). The situation was worsened by the creation of local monopsonies, facilitated by Yunnan's narrow eligibility criteria for the OSP, and Laotian officials' preference for large-scale operations, which increase their revenues quickly (Interviewee F03 2018).

Even before the rubber price collapsed, the 2+3 model was not working as promised. Farmers participating in the scheme found themselves impoverished, because rubber trees take five to seven years to produce a yield. This problem was particularly acute because local authorities typically directed Chinese investors towards especially poor and marginal ethnic-minority communities who were unable to show that they were using their fallow land productively (Dwyer and Vongvisouk 2019: 107). Accordingly, from the late 2000s, a '1+4' model emerged, with farmers effectively transferring their land to Chinese companies in exchange for 50–70 per cent of the trees and wages for working on the plantations. However, in practice, a lack of income forced many farmers to sell their trees to the companies. Consequently, de facto enclosures and unofficial, undocumented large land concessions emerged across northern Laos (Dwyer and Vongvisouk 2019: 107).

The 2011 rubber price collapse exacerbated these problems, leading to the consolidation of a dominant Chinese cartel and surging landlessness. The price collapse seriously imperilled the profitability of many plantations. Smaller, less well-connected firms were particularly badly hit, as they enjoyed less state aid and were squeezed by the only rubber processing plant in northern Laos, owned by sector leader Yunnan Rubber (Lu 2017: 740).[8] Accordingly, many smaller firms were forced to abandon or sell their plantations to larger competitors (Interviewee F05 2018). Only the largest firms, enjoying heavy OSP subsidies, remain, with many plantations sitting idle, even though the trees have now matured (Shi 2015: 6; Lu 2017: 740). Having acquired many distressed smallholders and weaker competitors, sometimes in joint ventures with Laotian urban elites, just four firms now control all Laotian rubber exports to China (Shi 2015: 6; Tan 2015: 19; Dwyer and Vongvisouk 2019: 107–9). Smallholders have been forced into wage labour, but the demand is insufficient to absorb the displaced population and many available jobs have gone to migrant workers, leaving local farmers destitute (Lu 2017: 734).

Unsurprisingly, because poverty and landlessness are key drivers of opium cultivation, China's OSP has actually been associated with *increased* output. As in Myanmar, rubber cannot directly substitute opium given the different altitudes at which they grow. Sites for OSP plantations were clearly selected based on their suitability for rubber cultivation, not their potential to substitute opium, thus replacing

---

[8] China does not permit raw rubber imports.

crops grown at lower altitudes, like rice. For example, although Phongsaly province is estimated to produce about 55 per cent of Laos's opium (Liu et al. 2018: 4), only 20 per cent of China's OSP projects are located there (Lu 2017: 737–8). Houaphanh province, another major opium-growing region in Laos's northeast, has no Chinese OSP plantations at all, due to its rugged terrain. By contrast, the UNODC's small OSP project in Laos targets only these provinces, and is also promoting coffee, a more suitable opium-replacement crop (UNODC 2019b). Moreover, as China's OSP plantations reduced incomes and increased landlessness, many farmers have been forced to return to cultivating opium in upland areas. Consequently, from 2007 to 2015, the estimated hectarage of opium farms rose from 1,500 ha to 5,500 ha (UNODC 2015b).

   Another similarity to Myanmar is that the OSP is continuing in a similar vein even under Xi Jinping. Shi (2015: 6) argues that policy-makers in Beijing are noticing the OSP's failure to achieve its intended objectives, resulting in diminishing support. It nonetheless continues due to sustained support from the Yunnan government. After the rubber bust, the OSP shifted to bananas, another poor opium replacement, being grown exclusively in lowland areas (Junquera and Grêt-Regamey 2019: 6). Although China's first banana plantations in Laos were established only in 2010, by 2017 bananas were Laos' biggest export earner, with nearly all exports going to China. Although leasing land – not opium fields, and often formerly rice paddies – to Chinese investors helped Laotian communities to cope with the rubber bust, this came at considerable cost. Thanks to the use of dangerous chemicals and poor workplace safety, in 2016 a staggering 63 per cent of planation workers in northern Laos fell ill over a six-month period, and many local water sources were polluted (Parameswaran 2017). Consequently, in January 2017, the Laotian government banned new banana plantations and announced that existing leases would not be renewed, ending the banana boom (Radio Free Asia 2019). However, the plantations have already cut the land available for subsistence farming, while chemical pollution may make it impossible to resume rice cultivation (Kusakabe and Myae 2019: 597; Radio Free Asia 2019). Accordingly, it seems that many agrarian communities have become locked into plantation-based cash-cropping and associated boom-and-bust cycles, with sugarcane replacing banana from 2017 (Junquera and Grêt-Regamey 2019: 6).

In summary, China's OSP has ultimately been hijacked by the interests of large Yunnanese agribusiness firms while doing little to ameliorate the NTS problem it was established to address. As Dwyer and Vongvisouk (2019: 109) argue, the interests of the 'Chinese agribusiness sector [have prevailed] over public-sector objectives in both China (public-health improvements) and Laos (poverty alleviation)'. This outcome stems directly from state transformation dynamics in China, which allowed Yunnan's cadre-capitalists to direct anti-narcotics resources towards its agribusiness allies, and from the political economy of land use in Myanmar and Laos.

Protecting Chinese Economic Interests and Citizens on the Mekong

Our second case study of China's NTS engagements in the GMS explores Chinese efforts to secure trade and Chinese citizens on the Mekong River. This has involved the growing internationalisation of the MPS, which has led transnational policing operations, recently institutionalised through a new Chinese international organisation. The following sub-sections describe the risks to Chinese interests on the Mekong, explore growing Chinese internationalisation and interventionism in response to these threats, and show how China's extended governance frontier is being institutionalised.

Threats to Chinese Economic Interests and the Internationalisation of China's Police

Following the dredging of the Mekong in the 1990s, Chinese trade on the river grew rapidly, from 500 tonnes in 2001 to 300,000 tonnes in 2010 (Parello-Plesner and Duchâtel 2014: 93). By 2016, the UNODC (2016: 16) estimated that 100,000 tonnes/US$150m of goods, 5,000 vessels and 30,000 people were passing through Yunnan's Guanlei Port every day. The Mekong is especially important for landlocked Yunnan, shortening its trade route to the sea by 3,000 km, and cutting transportation costs by 40–60 per cent (Guo 2007: 57; Erickson and Strange 2014: 114).

However, this exposes Chinese trade and citizens to risks on the Mekong, prompting a steady increase in transnational police intervention from China. Initially, Chinese security agencies – Yunnan's local People's Armed Police (PAP), the military and Yunnan's bureaus for Public Security and State Security – focused on improving relations with their neighbouring counterparts. However, as problems mounted, non-interference began to give way to intervention. For example, in the early 2000s, many casinos opened just inside Myanmar, servicing primarily Chinese clientele. These became hives for organised crime, including drug and people trafficking, with mounting reports that Chinese citizens were being detained, tortured or even murdered for non-payment of gambling debts. In the mid-2000s, the PAP launched cross-border raids into several casinos and shut down others by severing their power supply (Hameiri, Jones and Zou 2019: 487). Though these operations were limited in scope and frequency, they indicated a growing willingness to act transnationally in defence of Chinese citizens.

This escalated following an attack on two Chinese cargo ships on the Mekong on 5 October 2011 when thirteen Chinese crewmembers were murdered and dumped in the river – the biggest-ever attack on Chinese nationals outside of China (Parello-Plesner and Duchâtel 2014: 92). When Thai security forces boarded the ships, they found nearly one million ATS pills worth several million dollars (Howe 2013). Yunnanese authorities immediately halted Chinese shipping on the Mekong, despatching vessels of the Yunnan border police – under the Bureau of Public Security – to escort stranded ships back home (Parello-Plesner and Duchâtel 2014: 94).

The attack prompted widespread public outcry in China and loud demands for intervention to seize the culprits and secure China's international trade. For example, *The China Daily* demanded the establishment of 'a transnational security mechanism at a sub-regional level so that drug trafficking and other organized crimes can be rigorously eradicated ... and personnel and cargo safety along the Mekong can be guaranteed' (quoted in Parello-Plesner and Duchâtel 2014: 95). *The Global Times* suggested that the attack was a 'test [of] the Chinese government's ability to protect its overseas interests' (quoted in Parello-Plesner and Duchâtel 2014: 95). Other publications even suggested that China should station its police forces permanently in the region (Parello-Plesner and Duchâtel 2014: 95). This intense public backlash prompted senior officials, including Premier Wen Jiabao, Minister for Public Security Meng Jianzhu and Defence Minister Liang Guanglie, to take an active interest in the case.

Although the MFA initially led China's response to this international incident, it was quickly displaced by the MPS, reflecting the growing internationalisation of this formerly domestic agency. In late 2011, Liu Yuejin, Director of the MPS's Narcotics Control Bureau, was sent to the Golden Triangle with over 200 Chinese investigators to coordinate a multinational manhunt. The target was the notorious bandit Naw Kham, whose gang had reportedly attacked twenty-eight ships on the Mekong between 2008 and 2011, extracting 'protection money' and hijacking vessels for ransom (Howe 2013; Parello-Plesner and Duchâtel 2014: 93). However, eyewitnesses reported that Naw Kham was actually protecting the Chinese ships in question, which were engaged in drug trafficking; the gang fled upon the arrival of elite Thai forces, who boarded the vessels, following which shots were fired (Howe 2013). Why Naw Kham was accused instead of the Thais is unclear, but one reporter suggested it was because he had attacked Chinese vessels bound for the Chinese-owned Kings Roman Casino in Laos's Golden Triangle Special Economic Zone (Howe 2013). In April 2011, Naw Kham had seized three Chinese ships, ransoming them to the casino owner for US$733,000 (Howe 2013; Parello-Plesner and Duchâtel 2014: 93). According to Howe (2013), it was this attack, and the damage to Kings Roman's business, that put Naw Kham 'on the Chinese government's radar'. While these claims are unverifiable, Chinese authorities, especially in Yunnan, clearly saw Naw Kham's gang as a threat to China's overseas economic interests and people.

Although details remain murky, Chinese police officers reportedly cooperated with their Thai, Laotian and Myanmar counterparts, participating in joint 'clean up' operations and interrogations, including unsuccessful raids in Laos's Boqiao province in December 2011 and in Myanmar in February 2012 (Perlez and Feng 2013; Parello-Plesner and Duchâtel 2014: 96). Liu Yuejin later revealed that Chinese authorities considered using a drone to kill Naw Kham, which would have marked a significant shift in Chinese willingness to use force abroad. However, the idea was dropped in light of the order to capture the bandit alive and also amid concerns about how neighbouring countries might react (Perlez 2013; Parello-Plesner and Duchâtel 2014: 97). Chinese drones were used in the Golden Triangle area, but for surveillance only (Hong

2014). Eventually, on 25 April 2012, Laotian police captured Naw Kham, allegedly following a tip-off from Liu (Parello-Plesner and Duchâtel 2014: 97). He was removed to Kunming with several accomplices to stand trial. This was China's first trial of a foreigner for crimes against Chinese citizens committed outside of China, and the first to feature foreign witnesses (from Thailand and Laos). Naw Kham and two accomplices were found guilty, sentenced to death and, after an unsuccessful appeal, executed in 2013, despite persistently claiming that Thai forces were responsible for the deaths on the Mekong (Parello-Plesner and Duchâtel 2014: 99). These events were portrayed by Chinese authorities, and widely seen, as a 'show of [China's] newfound capacity to mete out justice for crimes against overseas Chinese interests' (Parello-Plesner and Duchâtel 2014: 97), even being dramatised in a popular 2016 movie, *Operation Mekong*.

China's Governance Frontier on the Mekong

Beyond this unusual high-profile operation, MPS officials have also worked to extend China's governance frontier into the GMS, establishing Chinese-led, multinational patrols on the Mekong, which have recently been institutionalised into a new, Yunnan-based international organisation.

The October 2011 attacks spurred the MPS to create a transnational security mechanism to address the threats to China's economic interests. On 31 October 2011, it held a summit with representatives from Myanmar, Thailand and Laos to establish law enforcement cooperation on the Mekong. Under pressure from Zhou Yongkang, the Politburo Standing Committee member responsible for public security, they agreed to establish joint river patrols between Guanlei and Chiang Saen in Thailand, coordinated by an operations centre in Guanlei. The patrols began in December 2011 and have occurred monthly since March 2013 (UNODC 2016: 22). China also pledged capacity-building support for Laos and Myanmar. The rationale of this initiative reflects the new Chinese security thinking described above. As a senior MPS official, on secondment to the Lancang-Mekong Integrated Law Enforcement and Security Cooperation Centre, explains: 'For economic development we have to use the road, the sea, the rivers'; for Yunnan, the riverine route is 'cheaper than the road, and faster'. Xi's Belt and Road Initiative reinforces this, because the 'safety of the

Mekong is connected with the Maritime Silk Road'. The threats on these routes: 'are not only one or two countries' problem – it is the whole world's problem ... By ourselves, we cannot [tackle] it ... If we want to break up crime, it is not for one country or another, we must have cooperation with each other, we need all countries to support each other' (Interviewee E15 2018).

The joint patrols have produced an emergent transnational security governance framework, led by the MPS. Yunnan water police vessels are involved in every patrol, while other states contribute ships on rotation (Interviewees E09 2018; Interviewee E15 2018). An MPS official describes the vessels as operating like 'one police force together' (Interviewee E15 2018). Chinese researchers who have been on the patrols explain that they effectively extend the Chinese police's jurisdiction beyond China's borders, enabling them to arrest suspected criminals, who are then handed over to the local authorities (Interviewees E09 2018). Hotlines have also been established along the river, allowing sailors and local people to contact the police (Interviewee E15 2018). The patrols have often made substantial numbers of arrests and seized large quantities of drugs and other contraband. For example, in 2013 a Sino-Laotian patrol seized 580 kg of ATS tablets worth US$15m (Marshall 2016). In 2016, the patrols reportedly yielded 9,926 arrests, leading to 6,467 drug-related prosecutions, plus the seizure of 12.7 tonnes of drugs, 55.2 tonnes of precursor chemicals and large amounts of firearms and ammunition (Pan and Shi 2017). Banditry on the Mekong has been all but eliminated, although by most accounts this has done little to stem the drug trade (Parello-Plesner and Duchâtel 2014: 100; Marshall 2016; UNODC 2016: 3).

The patrols and associated activities have recently been institutionalised into the new Lancang-Mekong Integrated Law Enforcement and Security Cooperation Centre (LM-LESC). Based in Kunming, the centre was launched in December 2017, following in-principle agreement among the GMS countries in October 2015. It is overseen by a biannual Ministerial Conference on Law Enforcement and Security Cooperation in the Lancang-Mekong River Basin. The LM-LESC is a formal international organisation, headed by a Chinese secretary-general, with each participating country contributing a deputy secretary-general (LM-LESC 2019a). Its Chinese staff are seconded from the MPS (Interviewee E15 2018). The centre's work covers five areas: joint patrols; joint operations; intelligence and investigation support; law enforcement capacity building; and information sharing (LM-LESC 2019b). A senior official at the centre claims the latter part of its work is 'just like Interpol', using the same i247 systems to share intelligence and arrest warrants (Interviewee E15 2018).

The impetus for the centre's formation seems to have been the MPS's desire to convert bilateral talks, capacity-building and declarations into more concrete action on the ground. Although ostensibly regional in scope, the real target is apparently Myanmar. As the senior LM-LESC official states, 'In the joint operations, every country is trying to help Myanmar overcome the drugs problem.' The other participating governments chafe at being corralled by China, saying 'it's not our country ... it's Myanmar'. However, 'If we want to cooperate with Myanmar [alone], it's very difficult': the Myanmar government ostensibly supports cooperation but is leery of practical collaboration and lacks resources. The LM-LESC is thus a way to pressure Myanmar into more meaningful cooperation by drawing its officials directly into institutionalised, transnational networks, backed by resources (Interviewee E15 2018). However, given that narcotics and transnational crime emanating in Myanmar are deeply rooted in political economy and conflict dynamics, it is unlikely that these objectives will be met. This is especially true given that other Chinese actors are contributing to the drivers of these problems, as demonstrated above.

Conclusion

This chapter has shown how state transformation dynamics shape China's management of NTS issues, focusing in particular on the major threat posed by narcotics trafficking in the GMS area, and the risks to Chinese shipping and citizens on the Mekong. The emergence of these NTS issues, and shifting Chinese understandings of security and sovereignty, are clearly bound up with China's shift from autarkic state socialism to authoritarian capitalism. As China's borders have reopened, and as its economy has extruded beyond its borders, new vulnerabilities have emerged, creating pressures for actors at all tiers of the party-state to extend their governance frontiers to manage these problems.

Our first case study, on China's OSP, considered efforts to manage these problems by containing them at source, and clearly demonstrated the impact of state transformation in NTS governance. The national policy framework of opium substitution emerged not top-down but through bottom-up influencing. Reflecting the regulatory-state model, the policy framework was extremely loose, empowering subnational actors to interpret China's OSP according to local cadre-capitalist interests. This resulted in the hijacking of NTS governance by agribusinesses, profoundly skewing its implementation. The precise impacts varied depending on the context in which Chinese actors intervened. While implementation generally involved exploitative, inter-elite pacts, and the ignoring of both UN guidelines (to which China was formally committed) and basic Chinese regulations, it was more predatory and harmful in Myanmar than Laos, due to the more fragmented, conflict-ridden context there. However, in both cases the OSP was associated with an increase in the very problem it was designed to tackle. This outcome, clearly contrary to the intentions of policymakers in Beijing and the work of Chinese security apparatuses, cannot be understood without a state transformation analysis. Furthermore, the problems associated with the OSP are clearly continuing under Xi Jinping, showing how deeply rooted these dynamics are.

Our second case study explored growing Chinese interventionism and attempts to establish formal, transnational security governance arrangements to safeguard Chinese economic interests and citizens abroad. Reflecting the tendency of domestic party-state apparatuses to internationalise, activity in this area has been led by the MPS, not the MFA. Again, this has continued under Xi, with the MPS even founding a new international organisation. The MPS's efforts have arguably been more successful than the OSP, partly reflecting its narrower goals of law enforcement cooperation in a limited riverine space, which does not become as entangled in local socio-political dynamics as the OSP. However, the limits of inter-national cooperation have clearly been reached, with Chinese officials recognising that security problems cannot be tackled without greater intervention in the major source country: Myanmar. Whether this is achievable remains to be seen. Nonetheless, the relentless spread of Chinese economic activity and nationals will certainly draw Chinese security agencies into further interventions across borders, and introduce significant political and diplomatic challenges for the Chinese leadership and central agencies in future.

4 | *China's International Development Financing*

In the last decade, China has become a major provider of international development financing (DF). The precise volume of China's DF is unclear because it withholds detailed information and uses non-standard definitions of aid. However, according to the most authoritative database, AidData (n.d.), from 2000 to 2014 China spent around US$350bn on DF globally, just behind the USA, the world's biggest donor. Since the launch of the Belt and Road Initiative (BRI) in 2013, China is now probably in first place.

China's rapid rise as a DF provider has generated heated debate. Its approach in this area is often seen as a test of its future behaviour: whether China will accommodate itself to existing systems and norms, or seek to reshape the international system to suit its preferences and interests (Reilly 2012: 71). Most observers see Chinese DF as a form of economic statecraft, used to pursue geostrategic ends. Consequently, they focus on divining China's intentions and assessing its impact on other donors, the global aid architecture and development outcomes in recipient countries (Varrall 2016: 21–22). As so often, however, no conclusive evidence has emerged to demonstrate either revisionist or status quo intent. Chinese behaviour sometimes follows, and sometimes undermines, different international norms (see Hameiri and Jones 2018). This is hard to explain if one treats China as a unitary actor, using aid to support a coherent grand strategy.

This chapter breaks this impasse by demonstrating the impact of state transformation on DF policymaking and implementation. Thanks to state fragmentation, authority and policymaking are contested among central agencies in Beijing, notably the Ministry of Foreign Affairs (MFA), Ministry of Commerce (MOFCOM) and the National Development and Reform Commission (NDRC), and major financiers, especially the policy banks. Crucially, DF is also shaped by the state-owned enterprises (SOEs) that implement most projects. They compete fiercely for contracts, are driven by narrow commercial interests, have little regard for Beijing's wider diplomatic objectives and are poorly monitored and regulated by central agencies (Lan 2014: 41–2; Jones and Zou 2017). Because the governance of Chinese DF is systematically biased towards supporting China's economic development, it creates ample opportunities for Chinese companies and recipient governments to manipulate DF to suit their particular interests. Reflecting our regulatory-state model, China's top leaders can steer the disbursement of DF in various ways, but state transformation dynamics militate against coherent, strategic direction of flows for geopolitical purposes.

The concrete impacts of Chinese DF are determined by these dynamics within China and the socio-political structures and conflicts within recipient societies. This chapter demonstrates this through a comparative case study of Chinese hydropower dam projects in Cambodia and Myanmar. Hydropower is a crucial sector for Chinese DF: from 2000 to 2017, around 40 per cent of financing was directed at energy projects, almost 40 per cent of which went to hydropower, second only to coal (Gallagher et al. 2018: 318). In Cambodia and Myanmar, hydropower developments are by far the biggest Chinese DF-funded projects. For instance, financing for Cambodia's Kamchay Dam comprised nearly half of the US$600m of aid received by the country in 2006 (Lyttleton and Nyíri 2011).

The case studies clearly demonstrate our two main claims. First, China's DF projects are generally not planned in a 'top-down' manner by policymakers in Beijing to advance specific geostrategic objectives. Rather, they normally arise 'bottom-up', through the agency of SOEs and recipient-country elites, lobbying within a loose regulatory framework. To be sure, Chinese leaders gave their imprimatur to major projects, expecting them to strengthen bilateral relations with recipient governments. Yet, reflecting the Chinese-style regulatory state, detailed implementation was left to others, resulting in interpreting and ignoring dynamics that sometimes contradicted top leaders' intentions. Secondly, despite these similarities on the Chinese side, outcomes vary enormously between the two cases, which reflects the importance of local socio-political dynamics in co-determining the impact of Chinese DF projects. In Cambodia, dam financing reinforced the domination of the incumbent regime, strengthening bilateral ties. But in Myanmar, it exacerbated social conflict, leading to the suspension of the Myitsone dam project and a severe inter-state crisis. The sections below outline the debate around Chinese development financing, analyse China's DF governance, then present our comparative case studies.

Existing Perspectives on Chinese Development Financing

China's rapidly growing DF has alarmed many observers, with two intertwined concerns particularly prevalent. First, some argue that China is using DF strategically to advance geopolitical objectives, as part of its intensifying hegemonic struggle against the USA and its allies. For example, Cardenal and Aráujo (2013: 151) argue that:

the motivation ... is clearly strategic ... [China partly seeks] to guarantee [its] future supply of raw materials ... [but] infrastructure construction [also] plays a highly strategic role in China's silent world conquest ... [DF projects are] instruments for exercising its soft power ... [and] furthering China's own interests ... to reward loyalty and to seduce the less enthusiastic countries.

Reilly (2013: 142) likewise emphasises China's strategic use of DF to gain access to natural resources. Pan and Lo (2017) view DF as part of an emerging 'neo-tributary' system. The BRI is often described as a 'well thought-out Chinese grand strategy ... [designed] to reclaim its geopolitical dominance in Asia ... [challenge] US dominance and ... create a Chinese-centered order in Asia and beyond' (Bhattacharya 2016: 310). It is supposedly aimed at 'nothing less than rewriting the current geopolitical landscape' (Fallon 2015: 140).

A second, related argument is that Chinese DF is undermining existing global institutions and norms. Some commentators depict the new Chinese-led multilateral development banks (MDBs) – the Asian Infrastructure Investment Bank (AIIB) and the New Development Bank (NDB) – as direct challenges to the US-led World Bank and Japanese-led Asian Development Bank (Zakaria 2014; Renard 2015). From this perspective, China is slowly chipping away at US hegemony by constructing alternative global governance institutions (Beeson and Li 2016; Paradise 2016; Zhou and Esteban 2018). Chinese DF is also said to be undermining global norms, especially those espoused by the members of the Organisation for Economic Co-operation and Development's Development Assistance Committee (DAC) (de Haan 2011; Inada 2013). Some even argue that Chinese DF poses an 'existential aid and investment threat' to Western governments (Copper

2016a: x). This is because, unlike DAC aid, Chinese DF is supposedly offered without economic or political conditions, undermining the pursuit of 'good governance'. China only requires recipients to adopt a 'one China' policy, de-recognising Taiwan (Bräutigam 2009; Mattlin and Nojonen 2015). Beyond that, Beijing has emphasised non-interference in states' domestic affairs ever since Zhou Enlai's 1964 declaration of the 'Eight Principles' governing Chinese aid (State Council 2011; 2014; Copper 2016a: 18). Although some favour China's approach over ineffectual Western aid (Moyo 2009), many others emphasise negative impacts. For well over a decade, commentators have denounced China's 'rogue aid' for propping up corrupt, authoritarian governments (Naím 2007), undermining labour, environmental and social safeguard standards, and neglecting debt sustainability (Copper 2016c: 175; Kaplan 2016).

These two concerns have converged in the 'debt-trap diplomacy' thesis. This is the claim that China is deliberately luring recipient countries into contracting unsustainable debt to finance megaprojects, allowing China to seize control of strategic infrastructure like ports (Chellaney 2017; Pant 2017; Parker and Chefitz 2018). These claims, originating in New Delhi think tanks, have been echoed widely in Western media and policymaking circles (Bräutigam 2020). The most widely discussed case is Sri Lanka's Hambantota Port, which in 2017 was leased for 99 years to a Chinese SOE after Colombo supposedly could not service the Chinese loans used to build it. Scholars and US policymakers claimed that China had deliberately planned this outcome to provide a blue-water base for the Chinese navy (Gopaldas 2018; Hodge 2018; National Review 2018). Similar claims have been made with respect to many other countries.

However, the evidence for both of these lines of argument is sketchy at best. The first claim – that China's DF is strategically directed – is rarely supported by empirical evidence. Quantitative research finds no strong correlation between Chinese DF and countries' natural resource endowments, undermining the claim that DF is used to secure raw materials (Bräutigam 2011: 755; Dreher et al. 2014: 7). Similarly, the implementation of the BRI does not correspond to top-down policy frameworks, let alone 'grand strategy' (Jones and Zeng 2019). Projects are just as likely to be located outside of the six official BRI economic 'corridors' as inside them (Hillman 2018). The 'debt-trap diplomacy' thesis has also been questioned. As we have shown elsewhere in detail, the Hambantota Port was proposed by Sri Lanka, not China; Colombo never struggled to repay its loans from China; and Hambantota Port cannot be used by the Chinese military but will actually host the Sri Lankan navy (Jones and Hameiri 2020). The picture is similar elsewhere. In the Pacific, for example, debt-distressed countries owe most of their debt to sources other than China, and large disbursements are traceable to recipients' requests, not Chinese strategy (Fox and Dornan 2018).

The second claim – that Chinese DF erodes the DAC-led status quo – has also been contested. Bader (2015a), for instance, finds no statistical correlation between levels of Chinese DF and authoritarian regimes' survival. Likewise, the AIIB, far from challenging existing norms, largely duplicates the governance of existing MDBs (Chin 2016; Wilson 2019). Thus, some have argued, the AIIB only reflects China's desire for greater status in global governance, not a wish to overturn established norms (Ren 2016; Wilson 2019). Some even note tentative Chinese convergence on international environmental and social standards (Kirchherr et al. 2017).

As in many other policy areas, then, the evidence is very mixed: Chinese behaviour sometimes seems to indicate a revisionist orientation; sometimes it suggests China's rise is consistent with the status quo. Analysts and policymakers seize on evidence that supports their own perspective, yet the debate remains inconclusive and deadlocked. To break the impasse, we must stop treating China as a unitary actor committed to a single strategy, and instead use the state transformation approach to understand how both kinds of behaviour are generated.

State Transformation and China's International Development Financing

The governance of China's DF has changed dramatically since its foreign aid programme began in the 1950s. Under Mao, decision-making was concentrated in the hands of a few top leaders, who deployed aid strategically to support revolutionary movements and embarrass China's Cold War rivals, the USA and the Soviet Union (Copper 1975). However, China's passive revolution under Deng Xiaoping transformed the nature and governance of Chinese aid. From 1973 to 1979, foreign aid spending fell from 6.92 to 0.89 per cent of the central government budget, and by the 1980s

China had become a net aid recipient (Ohashi 2013: 88; Wang, Ping 2013). Moreover, the purpose of Chinese DF shifted from serving political goals to supporting China's own capitalist development. Before the 1980s, functional ministries were directly tasked with implementing projects in developing countries, reflecting a traditional 'command-and-control' approach. However, with the shift to Chinese-style regulatory statehood in the early 1980s, central agencies retreated from direct implementation to a regulatory role, with implementation subcontracted to profit-making companies, mostly SOEs (Wang 2008: ch. 5). Thus, 'executive administration [gave way] to entities for the coordination and the management of market behaviour' (Zhou 2017: 24).

Chinese DF shifted markedly towards tied 'aid', which seeks to benefit not only recipients but also China's own companies. This makes much Chinese DF hard to classify under DAC's conventional headings of Official Development Assistance (ODA) and Other Official Financing (OOF). Official Development Assistance, or 'development aid', denotes flows that primarily seek to promote recipients' development and welfare, with a grant component of at least 25 per cent and the rest comprising loans at concessional rates (OECD n.d.). China is not a DAC member and does not use these definitions. Although it does distinguish between 'aid' and other flows, it only discloses aggregate totals and rough regional distributions (State Council 2011; 2014). Academics estimate that most Chinese DF does not meet ODA standards, because it often involves non-concessional loans, export credits for the purchasing of Chinese goods and services ('tied aid'), and/or other arrangements benefiting Chinese companies (Bräutigam 2011: 755; Dreher et al. 2016). For example, from 2000 to 2011, only about 11 per cent of Chinese DF to Africa counts as ODA (Strange et al. 2017: 942).

However, we consider it fruitless to try to disentangle Chinese aid from other development assistance, as some have attempted to do (e.g. Kitano 2016; Dreher et al. 2017). In practice, they are typically bundled together, provided by the same banks, and delivered by the same SOEs (Shimomura and Ohashi 2013: 37–8; Economy and Levy 2014). In some cases, such as financing for hydropower dams under the Build, Operate, Transfer model, it is even difficult to distinguish between DF and outbound direct investment (Copper 2016a: 22). Chinese and recipient-country officials also see these flows as part of a single package, even when the sources are different and uncoordinated (Lan 2014). Thus, rather than trying to shoehorn Chinese practices into ill-fitting conceptual boxes, we focus instead on explaining what China actually does, using the looser term 'development financing'.

The Fragmentation of China's International Development Financing

China's DF regime reflects the state transformation dynamics outlined in Chapter 1. Top leaders no longer make detailed decisions about Chinese aid disbursements, but loosely steer a diverse, conflict-ridden set of agencies, which both influence and interpret top-level policy and its implementation. Coordination between these entities is notoriously poor, as Xi Jinping's administration has recognised and tried to address by creating a new aid agency.

Senior Chinese leaders primarily steer DF through broad pronouncements and commitments. The BRI exemplifies this. It emerged from two of Xi's speeches in late 2013, but these lacked detail and it was left to others – commissions, ministries, provincial governments, banks and SOEs – to flesh out what 'one belt, one road' would actually mean in practice (Jones and Zeng 2019). Sometimes, leaders also make specific numerical commitments, like pledges of US$60bn for Africa in 2015 and US$2bn for the Pacific Islands in 2013. However, again, others must decide how – or even whether – these sums are to be delivered. This can generate yawning gaps between pledges and actual disbursements: over 80 per cent in the South Pacific in recent years, for example (Smyth 2018). Non-implementation can even occur when senior leaders back specific projects. For example, despite repeated high-level promises of DF-backed nuclear power plants in Eastern Europe – 'flagship' BRI projects – China's state-owned nuclear companies have yet to develop any, because of profitability concerns (Zhang, Biao 2019). This again underscores the fact, emphasised in Chapter 1, that Xi's rise has not fundamentally changed Chinese policymaking. In other cases, SOEs exploit top-level backing to secure other agencies' cooperation and rapidly push forward. This does not mean that top leaders initiated or planned the projects, or even know much about them, nor that due diligence has been undertaken, or that closer supervision will follow. Project-specific Memoranda of Understanding (MOUs) signed by top leaders with foreign governments often simply rubber-stamp bottom-up initiatives. As one MFA researcher reveals, 'Before a state visit, leaders' staff will ask the embassy [in that country] whether there are projects that could be announced and agreed in order to have something to show for it. Then they'll sign MOUs' (Interviewee B01 2018).

In practice, the power to interpret, implement and influence Chinese DF lies with diverse party-state apparatuses with contending interests and agendas. The NDRC, China's macro-economic planning agency, plays an important role in translating top leaders' vague pronouncements into more detailed policy platforms. For example, it led on BRI planning, consulting provincial governments and SOEs before issuing key policy guidelines with other agencies, including MOFCOM and MFA (NDRC, MFA and MOFCOM 2015; NDRC and SOA 2017). However, with the exception of its authority to block any overseas projects worth over US$100m (or US$300m in the natural resources sector), the NDRC lacks control over the other agencies involved in DF. As one official in an NDRC think tank explains, it acts merely as a 'platform for discussion', 'to coordinate different departments', which all 'have their own work areas' and 'have conflicts' between them. The NDRC cannot 'interfere in different ministries', but 'must respect their opinion'; it 'can try to achieve consensus' through negotiations, but 'cannot resolve conflicts by making a [definitive] decision'; only the State Council can do this (Interviewee E05 2018). Hence, NDRC policy frameworks are typically vague, seeking to incorporate rather than resolve competing agendas. Xi's BRI expresses this tendency, with NDRC-led plans remaining extremely loose and being populated by the pre-existing projects and aspirations of provincial governments, ministries, party organisations and SOEs (Jones and Zeng 2019). Furthermore, because the NDRC's main function is steering China's ongoing capitalist development, its primary interest in DF is how it can support this process. Consequently, it explicitly frames the BRI as extending China's 'reform and opening up' (NDRC, MFA and MOFCOM 2015: §I). Specifically, the NDRC sees the BRI as facilitating the relocation of lower-value-added production and industrial upgrading (Summers 2018: ch. 5). Consequently, the NDRC largely serves to entrench the connection between DF and China's commercial imperatives, undermining risk management. As the NDRC think tank researcher admits, 'If we controlled risk strictly, our outbound investment would shrink', which is hard for the NDRC to countenance (Interviewee E05 2018).

This commercial orientation is reinforced by the powerful role of MOFCOM in policymaking, decision-making and regulation. MOFCOM is primarily responsible for China's international economic relations, including DF, which it uses to support Chinese commercial interests (Varrall 2016: 25–6). Officially, foreign governments seeking DF must apply to the economic sections of Chinese embassies, which are staffed by and report to MOFCOM, not the MFA. The primary duty of MOFCOM's embassy personnel is to promote Chinese companies' commercial interests in the country in which they are stationed. Hence, if a Chinese contractor stands to gain work from a prospective 'tied aid' project, they will typically support it, overriding their MFA colleagues, who prefer to evaluate projects in relation to wider diplomatic and political considerations. In Beijing, MOFCOM is supposed to liaise with the MFA and other national-level agencies to decide on applications (discussed later in this chapter). However, in practice, MOFCOM has dominated decision-making, turning to the MFA only as a 'diplomatic problem-solver' when things go wrong (Corkin 2011: 74; see also Varrall 2016; cf. Zhang and Smith 2017). MOFCOM must approve any overseas projects worth between US$100 and US$300m, with smaller sums regulated by subnational Commerce Bureaus. MOFCOM is also primarily responsible for regulating Chinese companies operating overseas. It has repeatedly tightened this regulation, typically in response to serious corporate misconduct and associated diplomatic blowback (see Table 4.1). This suggests that MOFCOM's interest in promoting enterprises' outward expansion vastly exceeds its capacity to ensure that they follow basic Chinese laws. Lan (2014: 41), for example, argues:

MOFCOM has been trying in recent years to improve existing and develop new regulations and standards related to the development and execution of projects. However, like most Chinese government agencies, the analytical capability within MOFCOM is relatively weak, and numbers of personnel working in development aid is low [sic]. It does not have the capacity nor the incentive to analyse the success and failure of the projects it has supported systematically and to develop a coherent aid strategy.

Many other national-level agencies are also involved in DF policymaking and implementation. Various functional ministries and agencies have substantial, independently managed, aid budgets, including the Ministries of Health, Education, Transport, Culture, Agriculture,

Table 4.1 *Changes in Chinese regulations for overseas aid and investment*

Year	Action
2002	MOFCOM issues regulations for evaluating aid projects.
2006	CDB becomes China's first bank to accede to the UN's Global Compact, a voluntary framework encouraging corporate social responsibility (CSR), relating to human rights, labour, environment and anti-corruption.
	State Council issues *Nine Principles on Overseas Investment*, requiring companies to comply with local laws, bid transparently for contracts, protect local labourers' rights and the environment, and implement CSR.
2007	PBC issues *Green Credit Policy and Guidelines*, requiring environmental and social impact assessments (ESIAs) with loan applications and holding banks responsible for supervising clients' performance. Emphasises compliance with host-country standards, not international ones.
	EXIM Bank issues Environmental Policy requiring environmental impact assessments (EIAs) for loans and regular review throughout the project cycle and updates its 2004 *Guidelines for ESIAs of Loan Projects*.
2008	EXIM Bank issues *Guidelines for Environmental and Social Impact Assessment*, requiring ESIAs with loan applications, to include labour issues, land acquisition and migrant protection, empowering the bank to inspect projects and requiring regular reporting from borrowers.
2009	MOFCOM and Ministry of Forestry issue *Guidebook of Sustainable Operations and Exploration of Overseas Forests by Chinese Enterprises*.
2010	State Forestry Administration issues *Guide on Sustainable Overseas Forests Management and Utilization by Chinese Enterprises*.

Table 4.1 (*cont.*)

Year	Action
	MOFCOM, Ministry of Environmental Protection and the Global Environmental Institute issue *Environmental Protection Policies on Chinese Investment Overseas*. Banks develop implementing guidelines.
	CDB issues *EIA Framework for Small Business Loans Projects*, referring to the World Bank's EIA policy and related Chinese laws and regulations.
2012	Banking Regulatory Commission issues updated *Green Credit Guidelines*, requiring banks to ensure that borrowers abide by international norms in addition to host-country laws when investing abroad.
	SASAC issues *Interim Measures for the Supervision and Administration of Overseas Investment of Central Enterprises*, instructing SOEs to adhere to international best practices in implementing EIAs, support host countries' sustainable development and respect local religions and customs.
2013	MOFCOM and Ministry of Environmental Protection issue *Guidelines for Environmental Protection in Foreign Investment and Cooperation*, similar to SASAC's 2012 Interim Measures.
	MOFCOM issues *Regulations of Behaviour in Competition Abroad in the Area of International Investment and Cooperation*, which proposes recording unethical practices (e.g. bribery, collusion) and using this to influence credit allocation.
2014	MOFCOM issues *Measures for the Administration of Foreign Aid and Measures for Overseas Investment Management*.
	NDRC issues *Measures for the Administration of Confirmation and Recordation of Overseas Investment Projects*.
2017–19	NDRC, SASAC, MOFCOM and PBC issue further regulations on outbound investment and reporting thereof.

and Science and Technology (Cheng, Fang and Lien 2012: 6; Kitano 2016: 13; Zhang and Smith 2017). The Ministry of Finance (MoF) sets the budgets for these others agencies, and also tries to regulate Chinese companies overseas by requiring SOEs to demonstrate their projects' financial viability (Feng 2017). Furthermore, policymaking ministries are quite disconnected from funding bodies. Although MOFCOM and other ministries are tasked with disbursing DF, the MoF sets budgets, under the broad guidance of the NDRC, and holds the funds. In the past, the MoF has declined to cooperate with MOFCOM – for example, by refusing to disclose other ministries' aid budgets ahead of the 2011 Foreign Aid White Paper (Zhang and Smith 2017: 2337).

China's policy banks are also important, quasi-autonomous actors. The Export-Import (EXIM) Bank provides the concessional loans that now comprise over half of China's total aid programme (the MoF covers the gap between concessional and commercial rates), plus other forms of DF, like export credits. It has been an especially important financer of overseas hydropower development (Gallagher et al. 2018). The China Development Bank (CDB) – once a purely domestic agency but now thoroughly internationalised – provides non-concessional DF. Essentially, the policy banks provide cheap credit for DF projects, on the condition that it is used to finance contracts with Chinese companies – 'tied aid'. Here, DF governance closely overlaps with the arrangements for outbound investment, which China's policy banks routinely subsidise by providing cheap credit. This further skews Chinese DF towards commercial imperatives. Moreover, despite being policy banks, like state-owned commercial banks, EXIM Bank and CDB have effectively been corporatised, becoming profit-seeking businesses operating with considerable practical autonomy (Ma 1996). Accordingly, they undertake independent risk assessment, rejecting loan applications they consider excessively risky, even where projects have strong political backing (Sanderson and Forsythe 2013: xv, 58–9; Zhang and Smith 2017: 2339). They cooperate on some projects, but compete over others (Bräutigam 2011).

Although the policy banks have increasingly tried to tighten regulation to improve risk assessment and environmental and social safeguards (see Table 4.1), their practical capacity to control the SOEs implementing DF projects remains exceedingly weak. The policy banks still find it 'very difficult to forecast or evaluate political trends in the host country' (Interviewee E06 2018), relying mostly on SOEs' own – frequently overly optimistic – assessments (Interviewee E11 2018). Moreover, while traditional donors and MDBs have many staff in recipient countries to evaluate risks and help shape projects, China's policy banks have none. As one hydropower industry expert observes:

They don't have the expertise to know what's happening on the ground . . . [Instead] they go by the company's business plan, and their [stated] willingness to obey standards laid out by the Chinese government . . . [In some cases] the company doesn't even know what the risks are. They are very new at this. Their exposure to these big risks is often ignored. If the companies miss it, surely the banks are missing even more than that, because when you apply for a loan, you're not going to tell them everything . . . the credit's given without actually knowing the true risks involved. (Interviewee E04 2018)

Moreover, although Chinese regulations direct the policy banks to scrutinise projects during and after implementation, in reality, after loans are granted, 'the NDRC and other Chinese regulatory authorities have no power to evaluate [projects]. They just ask the [implementing] firm to report their financial and other information to the government. But they cannot control or influence . . . the behaviour of these firms' (Interviewee E06 2018). Other experts concur: 'at the operational level, the state banks cannot really regulate those activities. At best, they will not lend out money. They cannot prevent bad things happening [after they have done so]' (Interviewees E13 2018). 'They don't have environmental specialists who can go to project sites and evaluate them . . . [The compliance process is] just paperwork. You submit a report, I mark it, that's it' (Interviewees E01 2018). In August 2017, regulations on overseas projects were tightened yet again because, as the governor of the People's Bank of China stated, some 'do not meet our industrial policy requirements . . . are not of great benefit to China and have led to complaints abroad' (Feng 2017). This suggests a centre still struggling to improve governance, even under Xi Jinping.

This weak regulatory oversight grants enormous power to the companies that implement China's DF projects; indeed, they are arguably the most important actors of all. Although in some sectors, like hydropower, centrally owned SOEs dominate, most implementing SOEs are subnationally owned. As of 2010, 1,296 companies were involved, of which only 85 were centrally owned, accounting for 36 per cent of contracted projects and 45 per cent of labour services (Ohashi 2013: 94). As Zhang and Smith (2017: 2339) argue, SOEs can often direct DF for their own benefit, such that the 'tail wags the dog'. This is thanks largely to the *non*-strategic, recipient-led nature of Chinese DF. Chinese DF is always dispensed at recipients' request: indeed, this is a point of pride for China (Bräutigam 2009). This explains why, despite claims about aid being used 'strategically', to access natural resources, Chinese aid often funds entirely non-strategic projects with no connection to natural resources, like sports stadiums or student dormitories (Bräutigam 2011; Hameiri 2015). The recipient-led process allows SOEs to lobby foreign governments to apply for DF for projects that these SOEs would be well-suited to implement, as a way to secure lucrative overseas contracts (Cheng, Fang and Lien 2012: 8). As discussed, the formal application process is skewed towards helping them. In practice, as our case studies show, the formal process can also easily be bypassed by other government-to-government ties and lobbying, including from provincial governments supporting their SOEs. State-owned enterprises can also approach policy banks directly for DF to support their proposed projects in other countries.

Importantly, as discussed in Chapter 1, these SOEs are not docile instruments of government policy, but quasi-autonomous, corporatised, profit-seeking entities. Their interest lies not in recipient countries' development or welfare, or even China's diplomatic objectives, but in grabbing some of the DF resources committed by top-level leaders. A senior project manager in a large national construction SOE, heavily involved in implementing BRI projects, explains: 'Our company focuses on the commercial perspective. We pursue [our own] benefit. Only if the project has interest for us [do] we do it ... the most important thing is to make money ... For a long time, we have [had] market freedom without serious strings of government' (Interviewee B08 2018). Reflecting the regulatory-state model, top leaders' vague pronouncements or even subsequent, more developed policy platforms are 'just a suggestion – a guide ... The government can just give us the broad direction, but when it comes to the details of projects, it's hard for the government to control everything ... [ultimately] projects are decided by commercial assessments made by SOEs and banks' (Interviewees B03 2018).

Moreover, because the policy banks' regulatory capacity is very weak, SOEs have enormous practical latitude in designing and implementing DF projects. According to Chinese experts, because the firms are state-owned, the policy banks generally believe that, 'even if the project goes badly wrong, eventually they can pay back the loan in different ways' (Interviewees E13 2018). This moral hazard enables the approval of potentially unviable projects. Some large SOEs may evade basic due diligence altogether: 'a lot of SOEs do not need to provide actual collateral [for loans] ... they have credibility because they are big, they are SOEs – that's [taken as] a guarantee they will pay them back' (Interviewee E11 2018). Finally, if a top leader has signalled a desire to improve ties with a recipient government, or backed a specific project, approvals become even easier to acquire (Interviewee E11 2018).

State-owned enterprises also compete fiercely for tied aid contracts. According to a Chinese government survey, 45 per cent of Chinese firms operating overseas see one other as their main competitors, well ahead of local companies or foreign multinationals (CAITEC, SASAC and UNDP China 2017: 94). For example, rival Chinese nuclear companies competed with one another to secure projects in Europe, while major construction firms also vied for the Hambantota Port project (US Embassy 2007; Zhang, Biao 2019). As our construction SOE manager remarks, 'the competition between construction companies is very fierce, so we operate by market principles' (Interviewee B08 2018). Where recipient countries lack tough regulations and/or enforcement capacities – a common occurrence in the developing countries receiving Chinese DF – the imperative to cut costs often means skimping on social and environmental protection. Beijing's own survey data show that, in 2017, among Chinese companies operating in BRI countries, half were neglecting social impact assessments and a third were not conducting environmental impact assessments, and ignorance of local regulations was widespread, despite Chinese laws requiring all companies to follow them (CAITEC, SASAC and UNDP China 2017: 54, 85, 97). Corporate malfeasance has frequently generated a backlash from affected communities, often escalating into bilateral diplomatic crises (Jones and Zou 2017; Zhang and Smith 2017), because these freewheeling SOEs are perceived as 'representatives of official Chinese policy, often resulting in misunderstandings as to China's aid motivations and modalities' (Varrall 2016: 38).

Chinese leaders have recognised and tried to address these problems, though rather ineffectively. MOFCOM, MFA and MoF established a liaison mechanism in 2008, formalised in 2011 as the Inter-Agency Foreign Aid Coordination Mechanism (Cheng, Fang and Lien 2012: 7). By 2012, it included thirty-three agencies (Watanabe 2013: 76). However, there were also rival coordination mechanisms including the Leading Small Groups for Foreign Affairs, Finance and Economy, and the BRI (Varrall 2016). Moreover, as researchers in an NDRC think tank lament:

It's not easy to coordinate ministries ... [Their] goals are diversified and some goals may be in conflict with each other ... Even [between] the MoF and the NDRC there are some areas of overlap, which makes coordination difficult ... [Because DF] covers a lot of countries, sectors and stakeholders, it ... needs some coordinating organisation at the higher level to [do] all the planning and coordinate the different areas. (Interviewees B02 2018)

Chinese scholars also bemoan the 'Chinese government's lack of strategic planning over Chinese investment and aid', describing DF as being 'like a cake, with different agencies struggling and competing with each other [to eat it] ... Different ministers have their own interests and agendas, and do not coordinate with each other' (Interviewees E03 2018).

The central leadership tried again in March 2018, creating the China International Development Cooperation Agency (CIDCA) in an explicit attempt to ameliorate fragmentation and improve coordination over policymaking, implementation and monitoring (Zhang 2018; Interviewee B01 2018; Interviewee B06 2018; Interviewee B09 2018). According to experts close to the process, CIDCA was established to 'make aid more affiliated with the government's broad initiatives' (Interviewee B01 2018), shifting from an exclusively commercial orientation to 'a holistic perspective – [including] ethical goals and development goals too. The new agency will be more like western agencies, not just focused on commercial goals' (Interviewee B04 2018).

However, Chinese experts note that it is 'too early to say' definitively whether CIDCA can reorient Chinese DF or cohere the fragmented party-state (Interviewees E03 2018). It was very slow to form and appoint personnel, with its first act – a vague circular encouraging better risk management when implementing DF projects – coming only in November 2018. One senior MOFCOM think tank official is sceptical that CIDCA will change much:

MOFCOM is not happy to lose the aid function. It accounted for a large proportion of MOFCOM's budget . . . [But] I don't think that moving aid out of MOFCOM will reduce the commercial aspect of aid. MFA wanted to have aid under them. In that case, it would've had more diplomatic considerations. But now it's independent, so it cannot be directly influenced by MFA . . . [Moreover, CIDCA's] first administrator comes from the NDRC [which] shows it retains a commercial focus. (Interviewee B06 2018)

It is also unlikely that CIDCA will do better than existing regulatory agencies in monitoring and evaluating Chinese projects. It has only 100 personnel (Interviewee B06 2018), compared, for example, with the 2,800-strong UK Department for International Development (DfID 2017: 18).[1] And whereas around 1,300 of DfID's staff are based in recipient countries, CIDCA – like the policy banks – currently has no overseas staff, making it dependent on MFA and MOFCOM embassy staff for monitoring projects in-country, an arrangement which has proven inadequate so far. Furthermore, CIDCA's diminutive size suggests that, rather than being a powerful policymaking and implementation body, it is merely intended to be yet another coordinating agency, dependent on other entities' questionable willingness to cooperate. Understandably, a senior Chinese academic involved in CIDCA's establishment process thus argues that 'it's a half-done revolution' (Interviewee B09 2018). Even under 'strongman' Xi, therefore, Chinese DF remains poorly governed. As Chinese experts note: 'Lots of Western analysts think President Xi says "do this" and everyone does it. But that's not true . . . there's still controversy . . . one strongman cannot change all that . . . no matter who is the leader, bureaucracies have their own logic' (Interviewees E13 2018). Finally, CIDCA's remit is very narrow, excluding non-aid forms of DF, that is, most BRI-related flows.

China's Hydropower Sector

Before approaching our case studies, we also need to describe the specific context of the projects involved: China's hydropower sector. Today, the world's biggest hydropower dam companies are Chinese SOEs. As with SOEs more broadly, their internationalisation does not

---

[1] The Department for International Development was merged with the Foreign and Commonwealth Office in 2020.

reflect Beijing's strategic direction, but rather the agency of the companies themselves, which venture outwards 'on their own volition' to seek profits (Bosshard 2009: 45), with weak regulatory oversight.

This process has been shaped by state transformation and market dynamics, domestically and abroad. The sector's origins lie in the Ministry of Electric Power, which was converted into the China State Power Corporation in 1998, then split into several SOEs in 2002, five of which deal with power generation. These firms were then corporatised and made to compete for hydropower dam sites (Magee 2006: 35–8). They faced intolerable domestic market conditions as tough new environmental regulations halted most new projects, spurring them to find business overseas (Zha 2015). Thus, party-state apparatuses initially created for domestic purposes became international actors. For example, Sinohydro was originally the China National Water Resources and Hydropower Development Authority, created in 1949; by 2009 it was a major international company, building dams in over 30 foreign countries (Magee and Kelly 2009: 128).

Chinese companies found lucrative opportunities in developing countries, thanks to the market exit of many Western dam-builders in the wake of mounting environmental protest and the highly critical World Commission on Dams report in 2000 (McDonald, Bosshard and Brewer 2009: S297; O'Neill 2014). While they had built only fifteen dams overseas before 2000, from 2000 to 2014 they built seventy-five (Kirchherr et al. 2017: 529). By 2015, Chinese companies were reportedly involved in over 300 dam projects in seventy-four countries (International Rivers 2015a: 1). When the number of overseas projects became a criterion in SOE managers' cadre evaluations, even firms with little overseas experience were driven to venture abroad and compete ferociously for projects (Tan-Mullins, Urban and Mang 2017: 470).

Their remarkable expansion was aided by their extensive domestic experience, but also by an estimated US$85.7bn in DF from 2000 to 2017 (Tan-Mullins, Urban and Mang, 2017; Gallagher et al. 2018). Chinese dam projects are usually financed by EXIM Bank or CDB, with 66 per cent of all financing coming from China and 22 per cent from host countries (Urban et al. 2016: 234). The main criteria for awarding financing are recipients' repayment capacity and the project's projected profitability (Tan-Mullins, Urban and Mang 2017: 471). Hydropower expansion is thus driven overwhelmingly by commercial dynamics.

Political factors can, and do, affect decisions over whether particular projects are initiated. Yet, as our case studies show, the Chinese government's political direction is usually little more than a broad indication that it seeks good relations with particular governments (Yeophantong 2014; Liu 2016: 4).

Typically, therefore, we do not see DF deployed in the way that commentators adopting unitary-state assumptions suggest, with Chinese strategists deciding to build this or that project in particular countries. Rather, most DF projects originate with SOEs prospecting for business and recipient-country elites seeking economic opportunities. If they are involved at all, top Chinese leaders do little more than support these bottom-up initiatives. It is left to SOEs and recipients to work out the details. Funding bodies and ministries do *not* participate in negotiations with foreign governments over hydropower projects (Tan-Mullins, Urban and Mang 2017: 473). As with the oil companies discussed in Chapter 2, hydropower firms may frame their projects as advancing China's political objectives, to ease approvals and financing, and to bolster managers' promotion prospects (Zha 2015; Interviewee E06 2018). But 'the first and foremost thing for them is profit' (Interviewee E06 2018).

Yet neither the companies nor those responsible for regulating them are adept at assessing projects' costs, benefits and risks or ensuring compliance with Chinese laws and regulations. The feeling that 'the government has their back' allows hydropower companies to invest without adequate risk assessment and management, or even without all the necessary approvals (Interviewee E04 2018). This is true even at home: several firms have been caught initiating dam projects without having carried out environmental impact assessments required by law, for example (TSYO 2011: 12). Abroad, scrutiny is even weaker, meaning the companies' conduct is primarily shaped by the nature of host-state regulation (Tan-Mullins and Mohan 2013; International Rivers 2015a: 18). Some evidence is emerging that Chinese hydropower SOEs are paying greater attention to international standards after the Myitsone dam crisis (Kirchherr et al. 2017), but International Rivers' (2015b) detailed evaluation of seven major SOEs shows a significant, though variable, gap between formal adherence to international and Chinese standards and their lacklustre implementation. Tough competition and the concern to maximise profits mean that, for example, costlier dam designs that could ameliorate negative impacts are rarely considered without pressure from recipient governments or affected populations (Matthews and Motta 2015: 6270).

The result of these dynamics is that the impact of DF is not determined by Beijing's geopolitical planners, but rather by the context-specific interaction between Chinese actors and those in recipient countries. This can generate closer bilateral ties, as in Cambodia's case, or a massive diplomatic crisis, as in Myanmar's case.

China's Development Financing in Action

Cambodia and Myanmar have been significant recipients of Chinese DF and investment for decades. In the hydropower sector specifically, they are, with Laos, the biggest recipients of Chinese financing in Southeast Asia (Matthews and Motta 2015: 6275). Yet, Chinese DF in general, and dam-building specifically, has yielded different results in the two countries, warming China's relations with Cambodia, but undermining those with Myanmar. Each country case study begins with a brief outline of the socio-political context. We then discuss Chinese economic engagement and DF in general, and in the hydropower sector specifically, and explain the political outcomes of specific projects through process tracing.

Cambodia

Cambodia is now often seen as China's staunchest ally in Southeast Asia, even as a 'client state' (Burgos and Ear 2010; Bader 2015b: 5–6). This is a stark turnaround since 1988, when Cambodia's strongman leader Hun Sen described China, which then supported the Khmer Rouge in Cambodia's civil war, as the 'root of all evil' (Bader 2015b: 7). This changed in 1997, when a power-sharing arrangement between Hun Sen's Cambodian People's Party (CPP) and its main rival broke down violently. Although Western states and donors denounced Hun Sen's 'coup' and withdrew development assistance, China extended political and material support (Ciorciari 2015). Hun Sen reciprocated by expelling all Taiwanese diplomats, claiming that they supported his erstwhile partners (Jelders 2012: 88–9).

China's development assistance has steadily increased since then. Establishing the exact quantity committed is problematic, given the lack of transparency and the difficulty in distinguishing DF from investment. The Council for the Development of Cambodia (CDC), the main interface with foreign donors, states that Chinese concessional loans and grants totalled US$2.7bn from 1992 to 2011 (Heng 2016: 1). In 2014, the Chinese government pledged annual aid spending of US$500–700m (Copper 2016b: 22); recent CDC data shows that around US$300m was actually received in 2016–17 and US$250m in 2018. This makes China Cambodia's biggest donor, well ahead of second-placed Japan, which supplied US$120–170m annually in this period (CDC 2018). Furthermore, Chinese investors hold almost a quarter of Cambodia's total foreign direct investment (FDI) stock, well ahead of the South Koreans on 10.7 per cent (CDC n.d.; also Lim 2015; Nyíri 2017: 27). The Cambodian government has reciprocated with diplomatic support for China. It repatriated twenty Uighurs in 2009, contravening its UN Refugee Convention commitments, and has backed China over the South China Sea, scuttling an ASEAN communiqué in 2012. In 2010, the two countries signed a Comprehensive Strategic Partnership for Cooperation.

Most observers argue that this close engagement with Cambodia reflects Beijing's strategic and political considerations, including its desire to weaken ASEAN's position on the South China Sea (Marks 2000: 92; Burgos and Ear 2010: 620). For example, Heng (2016: v–vi) argues: 'China charms Cambodia not for short term economic benefits, but rather for long term strategic and political gains. China is indifferent to Cambodia's limited resources, but finds Cambodia's strategic geographical location vitally important to increase its influence in the region'. Likewise, Dahles (2013) claims that 'Cambodia's assets are limited and rapidly declining. Instead the returns are first and foremost of a political nature, as the ASEAN incident vividly showed'.

However, while this may capture some Chinese policymakers' views, DF in Cambodia does not actually reflect any strategic direction or diplomatic agenda. Rather, it is driven by the activities and interests of many, poorly coordinated Chinese actors, typically focused on commercial objectives. That these activities end up supporting Chinese leaders' strategic objectives owes more to Cambodia's political economy and Cambodian elites' agency than to careful planning in Beijing.

Cambodia's Political Economy and Chinese Development Financing

Cambodian Prime Minister Hun Sen has retained power for over three decades by positioning himself and close allies at the core of a carefully managed patronage and kinship system. Patronage was central to the regime even in its previous, 'communist' guise (1979–93), but became critical during Cambodia's formal transition to market democracy in the late 1980s and early 1990s, which saw offices and state resources dispensed to party, bureaucratic and military elites (see Hughes 2003; Cock 2010). Subsequently, decades of rapid economic growth shifted the locus of patronage networks to the private sector (Cock 2011: 27; Global Witness 2016: 10). Hun Sen has cultivated a group of tycoons, often called *okhnas* (sometimes transliterated as *oknyas*) – an honorary title awarded to anyone donating US$100,000 to the CPP (Ear 2011: 74; Global Witness 2016: 15). The *okhnas* receive economic opportunities, especially government contracts and licences, in exchange for kickbacks for CPP elites and support needed, for example, before elections (Cock 2011; Biddulph 2014: 878). These rents are used to secure the regime's rural electoral heartlands, through direct payments to local headmen, public works and gifts to voters (Hughes 2006; Strangio 2014).

Patronage also secures the allegiance of military commanders and other security forces, like the Bodyguard Unit – Hun Sen's private army – and the Gendarmerie (Chambers 2015). Cambodia's military has 2,200 generals out of a total of 191,000 personnel, indicating the use of rank as a form of patronage, and in 2014, 22 per cent of the national budget, formally and informally, went to the military (Chambers 2015: 194–6). This permits the routine deployment of state coercion and intimidation against regime opponents and voters. The military is also the linchpin of 'a parallel state of centralized governmental control', whereby CPP elites, 'the military, police, and other security forces informally by-pass and are effectively insulated from the decisions of locally elected bodies' (Chambers 2015: 191).

Because the CPP regime's survival depends on supporting and managing a range of venal interests, which often compete for patronage and lucrative opportunities (Milne 2015: 222), aid and investment are crucial. Western aid – comprising, at one point, half of the government's official budget – has supported public services provision, freeing up state resources for patronage (Hughes 2009). However, Western donors have conditioned their support on 'good governance' reforms and even anti-corruption measures (Hughes 2009; Hameiri 2010: ch. 7). Although this hardly challenges CPP rule, it is a constant irritant, especially after 2018 when Hun Sen banned the main opposition party, resulting in stronger Western criticism (see later in this section).

By contrast, China offers DF without conditions, making it easier to harness for patronage purposes. Indeed, while other donors are managed through the CDC, Hun Sen's office handles Chinese assistance directly (Interviewee B22 2018). This allows him to link Chinese-funded projects to CPP patronage networks – for example, by insisting on a role for companies owned by pro-regime *okhnas*. Foreign investment in extractive industries is handled similarly: as Milne (2015: 222) states, 'foreign companies ... apparently have little choice in the matter: dealing with the *oknyas* is part of operating in Cambodia'.

While this enriches pro-regime elites – just three 'economic land concessions' awarded in 2013 yielded an estimated US$1.5bn for the firms involved (Milne 2015: 221) – it also undermines mass CPP support. These schemes often involve the rapacious exploitation of natural resources, entailing often violent and illegal state-backed land-grabbing, frequently at the expense of poor rural communities (Chambers 2015: 194; Milne 2015; Beban, So and Un 2017). Sites for plantations and dams are overwhelmingly allocated in forested areas, which the companies involved can log, making a lucrative windfall. Logging is also often extended, illegally, to adjacent areas, with companies bribing officials to undermine the already lax supervision of Cambodia's forests (Forest Trends 2015; Milne 2015; BenYishai et al. 2016: 11–12). Although this is nothing new (see Biddulph 2014: 878), the scale of such projects has vastly increased in recent years, not least due to Chinese involvement (Forest Trends 2015: 11; Heng 2016: 3). As they have increasingly encroached on the CPP's rural electoral heartland, resentment has escalated into political resistance (Borras and Franco 2013; Brickell 2014; Lamb et al. 2017). And, thanks to the rise of smartphones and the migration of young rural Cambodians into the cities, often to work in the burgeoning garments sector, these predations are now widely recognised, undermining village headmen's grip (Hameiri, Hughes and Scarpello 2017: ch. 4). Thus, in the 2013 national elections, despite the usual rigging and intimidation, the opposition Cambodian National Rescue Party (CNRP) won 55 of 123 seats in the National Assembly. In the July 2017 commune (village) elections the CNRP took 489 of 1,646 communes, up from 40 in 2012.

The CPP's response has been twofold. First, it has sought to improve rural services delivery by reforming the bureaucracy and increasing civil servants' pay (Hameiri, Hughes and Scarpello 2017: 148–51). However, since CPP rule depends on allowing officials to exploit their positions for financial gain, this is unlikely to yield substantial results. Second, then, and more significantly, the CPP has intensified repression. In 2018, the CNRP was dissolved and its leaders imprisoned or forced into exile, allowing the CPP to win every National Assembly seat in the July elections. Surveillance and censorship of the press and social media have escalated (Reporters Without Borders n.d.; Mech 2017). Meanwhile, new regulations have cowed Cambodia's vibrant non-governmental sector by requiring organisations to disclose their funders and abstain from political activity. Ironically, this authoritarian turn has made the CPP leadership even more reliant on the support of tycoons, foreign governments and investors, reinforcing the dynamics that produced this crisis.

Chinese Financing for Hydropower Development in Cambodia

Unusually for Chinese DF, the majority of flows to Cambodia are ODA-like. More usually, however, the bulk has gone into the transportation sector, mainly for building roads and bridges (Ouch, Saing and Phann 2013: 349; BenYishai et al. 2016: 14; Oh 2016: 33). However, the biggest Chinese-financed projects in Cambodia are hydropower dams, most notably the Lower Sesan 2 (LS2) and Kamchay dams, which have been financed through commercial-rate loans (Burgos and Ear 2010: 623; O'Neill 2014: 173). So far, all of Cambodia's hydropower dams have apparently been built and financed by Chinese companies and banks (see Table 4.2).

Below we focus on LS2, Cambodia's biggest operational dam, costing an estimated US$900m. Its development clearly demonstrates the dynamics described above: (a) LS2 was driven by the Cambodian government, not by Beijing or even China's hydropower SOEs; (b) its implementation has been shaped by the intersecting interests of China's hydropower sector and Cambodia's tycoons, to the detriment of affected communities; (c) community and nongovernmental organisations' (NGO) protests, although significant, have been contained by the government and the dam-building company. Cambodia's government thus remains keen on similar Chinese-funded projects. Hence, the specific dynamics in this case have allowed Chinese DF to strengthen the overall bilateral relationship.

Far from being pushed by Beijing, the Cambodian government has pursued large-scale hydropower development for its own reasons since

Table 4.2 *Operational dams in Cambodia (2019)*

Name	Capacity	Constructing company	Finance provider	Estimated cost
Kirirom 1	12MW	China Electric Power Technology Import and Export Corporation	EXIM Bank	US$36m
Kamchay	193MW	Sinohydro	EXIM Bank	US$311m
Kirirom 3	18MW	State Grid Corporation of China	EXIM Bank	US$47m
Stung Atay	120MW	Datang Corporation	Unknown	US$225m
Lower Stung Russei Chrum	338MW	China Huadian	EXIM Bank	US$558m
Stung Tatai	246MW	China National Heavy Machinery Corporation	EXIM Bank	US$540m
Lower Sesan 2	400MW	HydroLancang (Huaneng)	Believed to be CDB	US$900m

Sources: AidData (n.d.); Banktrack (2016); International Rivers (2017); Electricity Authority of Cambodia (2018).

the early 2000s. Initially envisaged as an export industry, the focus subsequently shifted to meeting domestic demand, which is surging due to industrial and urban development. Cambodia's electricity prices are high and volatile due to reliance on imported diesel (Middleton, Matthews and Mirumachi 2015). The Ministry of Infrastructure, Mines and Energy (MIME) estimated in 2013 that at least 20 per cent annual growth in supply was required to stabilise the market (Ham, Hay and Sok 2015: 221). Moreover, to win back rural support, Hun Sen has promised that all villages, and 70 per cent of households, will have access to electricity by 2020 and 2030 respectively. Since 90 per cent of Cambodia's energy production went to serving Phnom Penh in 2016, this would require a vast expansion in domestic output, largely through hydropower dams (Global Witness 2016: 12). A 2003 MIME survey identified sixty possible sites, prioritising fourteen locations (Ham et al. 2013: 22). This survey, and the Cambodian government's dam-building plans, were based on Cold War-era surveys conducted for the US-initiated Mekong Commission (Hirsch 2010; Cronin 2013: 33; Sithirith 2016: 63), and a 1999 ADB report (Baird 2016).

Since Cambodia's government cannot finance these costly projects, it relies on foreign companies, promoting a Build, Operate, Transfer (BOT) model. This entails companies securing loans, building a project, collecting revenue over a fixed period to repay the loan, then transferring the asset to the host government. The BOT model thus shifts financial risk from the government to the corporate sector. To mitigate this, Cambodia has offered investors a highly favourable legal and regulatory regime, including tax breaks, free licences for dam construction and water use, and rapid environmental approvals. It also pledged to guarantee energy purchases and to buy out operating companies in case of *force majeure*. However, before Chinese SOEs' arrival, the Cambodian government was struggling to attract hydropower companies (Middleton, Matthews and Mirumachi 2015).

Chinese SOEs' involvement in the LS2 project reflected this difficulty. Initially, the Cambodian government signed a project MOU with Electricity Vietnam (EVN). In 2008, EVN's subsidiary conducted a feasibility study, project design and resettlement plan. It outsourced the environmental impact assessment (EIA) to a local consultancy and, despite considerable external criticism, it was approved by Cambodia's Ministry of the Environment (MOE) in 2010, following a public request by Vietnam's prime minister to expedite the process (Hav n.d.: 7; Grimsditch 2012; Harris et al. 2015: 19; Baird 2016: 264). Shortly thereafter, however, it transpired that EVN was struggling to raise sufficient finance. In January 2011, EVN announced that Cambodia's Royal Group (RG) company, owned by Kith Meng, Cambodia's richest *okhna*, had taken a 49 per cent share in the project. This was allegedly demanded by Hun Sen, despite the fact that RG had no experience in the energy sector. Rumours circulated that EVN was trying to pull out. In November 2012, after Cambodia's Council of Ministers (COM) had approved LS2, it was announced that the Chinese SOE China Huaneng Group was now the project's largest shareholder, with 51 per cent. Electricity Vietnam was downgraded to a silent partner, holding 10 per cent, while RG retained 39 per cent (Baird 2016: 264).

After lengthy negotiations, a financing deal was agreed between Huaneng, the national utility company Electricité du Cambodge (EDC) and the Hydro Power Lower Sesan 2 Company, which Cambodia's national assembly passed into law in February 2013 (Royal Government of Cambodia 2013; Ren 2015: 4). The dam-building consortium agreed to pay 30 per cent of the project's cost, with the remaining US$547m financed by a fifteen-year bank loan at 6.5 per cent interest. The lender has been kept secret but is thought to be CDB (Harbinson 2015; Harris et al. 2015: 11; Banktrack 2016). Huaneng agreed to own and operate LS2 for forty-five years, far longer than a typical BOT agreement. Electricité du Cambodge pledged to purchase all of the electricity generated for an agreed price, backed by a government guarantee. The government also agreed to buy out the project if it could not be implemented for political reasons (Royal Government of Cambodia 2013). Huaneng's subsidiary, HydroLancang, began construction in 2014, and the dam came online in 2017.

China's involvement in the LS2 project thus reflected the processes outlined earlier in this chapter. First, it was recipient driven. Far from being directed strategically by China, or even a buccaneering SOE, the impetus for LS2 clearly came from the recipient – the Cambodian government, and Hun Sen personally (O'Neill 2014: 182–3). Huaneng/HydroLancang became involved only belatedly, after the project was designed and approved. Exactly how it was drawn in is unclear, but every available source underscores Cambodian agency, not Chinese planning. According to one of our informants, 'it was Royal Group's idea to get the Chinese involved', though it was the Cambodian government that formally approached Beijing (Interviewee B26 2018). Another agreed that Hun Sen approached China after Kith Meng 'asked Hun Sen to find another partner for the project' (Interviewee B12 2018). Others indicate that Chinese support followed Cambodian government lobbying, including through party-to-party ties (Interviewee B16 2018; Interviewee B24 2018).

Secondly, the LS2 project is strongly shaped by the commercial imperatives of Chinese SOEs and financiers. Electricity Vietnam's difficulty in securing financing probably reflected the dubious viability of the dam, given the vast seasonal fluctuations in water flow at the site (Harbinson 2015). HydroLancang therefore bargained very hard to safeguard its bottom line, securing generous tax breaks and legal guarantees to protect its income, which essentially transfer all the risks back onto the Cambodian government. Understandably, traditional MDBs warn that this and similar projects could create fiscal problems in the future (Naren and Chen 2013).

Thirdly, the project's implementation was shaped by the interaction of China's poorly governed DF system and Cambodia's political economy and governance context. HydroLancang's basic approach was to focus exclusively on constructing the dam, ignoring the social and environmental impacts (thereby violating Chinese regulations), while leaving the dirty work to its local partner. This was facilitated by Cambodia's weak regulatory system, which powerful interests like *okhnas*' companies often simply ignore. Cambodia currently lacks an EIA law, though one is supposedly being developed; there are only sub-decrees on specific areas of environmental management (International Rivers 2015b). The project approval process has seven stages, but companies often begin construction after the third step, meaning projects start 'before all of the necessary checks have been completed' (Ham et al. 2013: 27–8). Indeed, from 2004 to 2011, only 5 per cent of 2,000 major development projects had an EIA before starting (Chanthy and Grünbühel 2015: 228–9).

Lower Sesan 2 was unusual insofar as an approved EIA was already in place, though its quality was questionable (Grimsditch 2012; Harris et al. 2015). Independent assessments maintained that its impact on fisheries would be far worse than the EIA claimed, warning that it would reduce fish biomass in the Mekong by 9 per cent (Ziv et al. 2012). The EIA also ignored the impact on fishing and water quality in upstream and downstream villages, which would affect some 22,000 people, who would not be compensated (Ren 2015: 29; Leong and Mukhtarov 2017: 7; Interviewee B19 2018). Lower Sesan 2's environmental protection budget, at US$2.23 m, was just 2 per cent of that for Huaneng's Nuozhadu dam in China (Ren 2015: 29). HydroLancang did nothing to correct these serious shortcomings.

Nor did the Chinese company make any effort to improve the resettlement process, outsourcing it to its local partner. Lower Sesan 2 was Cambodia's first dam to require mass relocation, involving some 5,000, mostly minority-ethnic, people living in its 30,000 ha reservoir area (Chhom n.d.). Cambodia's constitution and land law allow land expropriation only when projects are in the 'national interest' and 'fair and just' compensation is provided, but these terms are not defined.

The 2010 Expropriation Law states that compensation should be based on market or replacement value, but does not specify how to determine this (Harris et al. 2015: 15). Accordingly, the resettlement process was wide open to abuse. Nonetheless, according to several informants, HydroLancang delegated responsibility for resettlement and compensation to RG, while it focused rigidly on constructing and operating the dam (Interviewee B18 2018; Interviewee B26 2018; see also Ren 2015: 6). Complaints directed at the SOE were therefore rebuffed: 'the company says they don't know anything – they just build dams' (Interviewee B12 2018). Unsurprisingly, of seven Chinese dam projects assessed for their adherence to environmental and social standards, LS2 was judged worst (International Rivers 2015b). Huaneng thus ignored many relevant Chinese regulations.

Thanks to weak regulation and RG's powerful position within the Cambodian state, the company was able to displace the villagers at the LS2 site at minimal cost. As no clear guidelines existed, an ad hoc deal was struck with the government, which became part of the overall agreement signed in February 2013 (Ren 2015: 5). This allocated US$41.94m for resettlement and compensation – about one-quarter of the budget for the Nuozhadu dam on a per capita basis (Ren 2015: 23). Each household was to receive an 80 square-metre house on a 1,000 square-metre block, plus 5 hectares of farmland. Royal Group also pledged to construct public buildings, including a school and clinic, and supply rice to villagers for one year. The villagers were not consulted on the compensation package, which MIME approved in 2014. Just one copy was sent to local authorities and commune chiefs (Hav 2018: 5). In 2015, company staff conducted household asset surveys, without prior notice and accompanied by military police. The villagers were made to thumbprint the inventories, ostensibly to confirm their accuracy, but were later told that this also indicated their consent for the compensation and resettlement offer. Those refusing to sign were intimidated and threatened (Harris et al. 2015: 4).

The relocation has threatened the villagers' basic subsistence. These fishing communities were resettled on a major road, 3 km from the river, while the allocated farming land is often rocky and less fertile than their former land (Ren 2015: 20), but the villagers received no training or equipment to compensate for this (Hav n.d.: 23). This contravenes resettlement practice in China and the Chinese government's guidelines for its SOEs, which require funding to be set aside for livelihood support (McDonald, Bosshard and Brewer 2009: S301; Ren 2015: 5). As one villager stated, the relocated communities are 'not very happy with the company because people have very small land compared to the previous community . . . This new area is also increasing [our] insecurity. We lost livestock. In my case, I lost my big buffalo. It might cost around $1,000. The company won't compensate for this' (Interviewee B20 2018). Food insecurity has certainly increased: the villagers now rely on cash purchases and trucked-in water (Interviewee B12 2018; Interviewee B14 2018; Interviewee B20 2018). As few employment opportunities exist, some villagers have been forced to work for logging companies (Interviewee B12 2018; Interviewee B14 2018; Interviewee B18 2018; Interviewee B20 2018). The company also ignored local people's cultural concerns, as the dam flooded ancestral graves important in local religious and community practices (Hensengerth 2017: 99). Again, this violates MOFCOM's 2014 regulations, which require SOEs operating overseas to respect local customs.

While villagers suffered, RG was able to exploit its close ties with the CPP regime to profit enormously from LS2. The huge reservoir covered 16,000 ha of forest (Ren 2015: 16), providing a bonanza for Kith Meng's timber companies. In April 2013, just after the LS2 agreement was signed, they began harvesting luxury hardwood without approval from local authorities or communities (Ren 2015: 6). They also felled trees illegally outside the reservoir area (Blomberg and Phann 2014), a practice that continued until 2017, according to one villager in a resettled community, by which time 'most of the timber [had] been cut down' (Interviewee B20 2018).

Understandably, LS2 has sparked political controversy and resistance, though this was crushed by dominant forces. In 2012, an anti-dam campaigner was elected as commune chief in one affected area (Baird 2016: 259; Sithirith 2016: 70). Villagers also resisted relocation, with 54 per cent refusing to move even as late as 2016, when the dam's construction was already underway (Chhom n.d.: 29–30). Cambodian NGOs, organised into the Rivers Coalition in Cambodia, and international NGOs like International Rivers, launched a campaign against the dam. Villagers wrote dozens of letters to the prime minister, ministers, HydroLancang, RG, the Chinese embassy, the Chinese MFA and the media, but received no replies (Interviewees B21 2018; Interviewee B19 2018). Villagers also travelled to Phnom Penh in 2014 and 2015 to lobby the government, but were ignored (Interviewee B17 2018). Royal Group staff and provincial government personnel told the villagers that the dam would proceed regardless and that the compensation and resettlement package were non-negotiable (Ren 2015: 21). Villagers were told that unless they agreed to the deal they would receive no compensation (International Rivers 2015b: 27). One informant reported the use of bribes to split the community (Interviewee B14 2018).

The government's response to the unrest was to offer improved compensation, rather than halting the dam. In 2015, MIME established Dam Resolution Committees at the national and provincial levels. Unprecedentedly, this included representatives of the affected communities and civil society. However, the committees' mandate was to quickly resolve compensation disputes, not address more fundamental grievances. Participants felt that challenging this narrow focus would endanger their physical safety (Chhom n.d.: 32). The process did improve the compensation scheme, for example by allocating 14 ha of spiritual forest and burial grounds, and US$150 for every flooded grave (Chhom n.d.: 26). But villagers who still resisted faced coercion. Residents of Kbal Romeas Chas village refused to relocate. According to them, officials 'opened the water-gate in 2017 and flooded the area of the village that didn't want to move. They cut the bridge and there was no access from the outside to the village. They closed down the road connection and also the police prevented teachers and emergency support from entering' (Interviewees B21 2018; also reported by Interviewee B14 2018). The villagers were temporarily displaced, but returned after the waters receded. Next, the provincial authorities accused village committee representatives of being opposition activists who were stirring up opposition to the dam. Three were summoned to court, but refused to attend, fearing a rigged hearing and their possible incarceration. Through 2017, the village was practically under siege, with outsiders barred from entering. As of late 2018, villagers' relatives were allowed in, but NGOs were still excluded, and public services remained suspended (Interviewees B21 2018; Interviewee B14 2018).

Clearly, this development project has caused numerous environmental, social and political problems, reflecting the combined pathologies of Chinese DF and Cambodia's political economy. Despite these perverse outcomes, the project has only strengthened Sino-Cambodian diplomatic ties. This is because the negative effects were confined to already marginalised populations while the benefits accrued to tycoons linked to the incumbent regime. Accordingly, Hun Sen remains enthusiastic about Chinese hydropower development assistance. China Southern Power Grid is reportedly involved in developing the mammoth 7,110MW Sambor dam, which would be the first dam on the lower Mekong mainstream.

Myanmar

The results of Chinese dam development in Myanmar contrast starkly to the situation in Cambodia, reflecting the way that China's fragmented party-state apparatuses have interacted with a very different political economy context. For two decades, Myanmar's military regime (1988–2010) depended heavily on Beijing's aid and investment, their close ties often being called *pauk-phaw* (kinship) (Maung Aung Myoe 2011). However, in 2011, following a transition to a constrained electoral regime, bilateral ties were plunged into crisis when the Myanmar government suspended the Myitsone hydropower dam. Chinese investment in Myanmar plummeted by 95 per cent from 2011 to 2014, and Chinese analysts widely bemoaned Myanmar's 'loss' to the West (Sun 2011). Since then, the Chinese government has been scrambling to salvage its battered reputation, despatching companies, charities, think tanks and others to win Myanmar back (Zou and Jones 2020).

Under military rule, China was Myanmar's principal foreign donor, given Western embargoes on the junta and diminished commitments from Japan – historically the country's main foreign benefactor. According to the Myanmar government, from 1989 to 2010 Beijing provided RMB520m in grant aid, RMB15m in debt relief, and RMB46.67bn and US$474.1m in various loan packages (Maung Aung Myoe 2011: 162). In 2010, China pledged a further US$4.2bn in interest-free loans by 2040 for hydropower dams, road and rail links and IT infrastructure projects, and technical assistance for agriculture (Renwick 2014: 77). Partial lists of the projects involved before 2011 are diverse, with many having no conceivable link to Chinese interests, implying that disbursements were, as usual, recipient-driven (Maung Aung Myoe 2011: 162ff; Khine Tun 2015: 180–1). Again as usual, the bulk of Chinese assistance was distributed as tied aid, with an estimated

US$5.38bn of contracts signed by 2008 (Steinberg and Fan 2012: 224). By 2015/16, Myanmar's government owed US$4.3bn to Chinese lenders (Carr 2018: 38). As in Cambodia and more generally, here Chinese DF shades into subsidised SOE investments. Much Chinese investment in Myanmar is either unregistered or routed via tax havens, making its true extent difficult to establish, but official data suggest that it comprised 17 per cent of the realised total from 2000/01 to 2011/12 (Bissinger 2012: 36).

China's assistance to Myanmar is often framed in terms of Chinese 'grand strategy' and geopolitics. Realists frequently depict Myanmar as central to Asia's 'great game' and Sino-Indian rivalry, with Chinese aid and investment being used to woo Myanmar (e.g. Egreteau 2008; Scott 2008; Egreteau and Jagan 2013). In the 1990s, commentators persistently claimed that China was seeking to establish a naval base on Myanmar's west coast. In the 2000s, an oil and gas pipeline was built, linking that coast to China's Yunnan province, ostensibly to enhance China's 'energy security', underscoring Myanmar's supposed strategic value. Today, a deep-sea port and special economic zone at Kyaukphyu, a 'flagship' BRI project, is widely touted – particularly by Indian strategists – as a form of 'debt-trap diplomacy' to lock Myanmar back into China's orbit.

In reality, as in Cambodia, DF in military-ruled Myanmar did not follow any top-down strategic direction from Beijing, but was instead driven by demand from the Myanmar regime and Chinese companies' commercial interests. However, unlike in Cambodia, in this case these dynamics seriously harmed bilateral ties, and China's 'strategic' position, because it intersected with a very different political economy context.

Myanmar's Political Economy and Chinese Development Financing

Myanmar's military regime – initially called the State Law and Order Restoration Council (SLORC), then the State Peace and Development Council (SPDC) – ruled for two decades through harsh repression and economic manipulation. The 1988 coup followed the state's virtual bankruptcy and the collapse of the previous Burmese Socialist Programme Party amid widespread, Western-backed pro-democracy protests and the world's longest running ethnic-minority insurgencies. The State Law and Order Restoration Council quickly liberalised the economy to avert bankruptcy, welcoming Thai and Chinese investors to Myanmar's largely untapped natural resources sector and using the revenues to bolster the army, including with Chinese arms imports. The regime staged elections in 1990, but refused to transfer power to the victors, Aung San Suu Kyi's National League for Democracy (NLD), insisting first on drafting a constitution that would safeguard military interests and manage threats to Myanmar's territorial integrity. Opposition groups and loyalists were corralled into a National Convention process in pursuit of what the regime called 'discipline-flourishing democracy'. But due to NLD resistance, this was abandoned in 1996. Harsh repression followed, eliminating all space for democratic contestation.

As described in Chapter 3, much of the ethnic-minority borderlands were pacified through a combination of coercion and 'ceasefire capitalism' (Woods 2011a). In exchange for truces, the ethnic-minority armed groups (EAGs) were allowed to retain their arms and parts of their territory, and to engage in licit and illicit economic activity. The regime also offered development assistance to ceasefire groups to build roads, schools and clinics, spending US$506m by 2003 (Jones 2014a: 793). To bolster military support and fund the army, SLORC/SPDC also created military-owned companies, which acquired leading interests in heavy industry, mining, consumer goods and other areas. The regime also cultivated so-called 'national entrepreneurs', popularly referred to as 'cronies' – around a dozen business magnates, mostly emerging from smuggling and drugs trafficking, who launched the conglomerates that today dominate Myanmar's economy (Jones 2014b). The junta also hoped to generate wider economic development that would 'consolidate the masses' behind their de-politicising agenda (Jones 2015: 99).

However, the resultant economic growth was not broadly based. Western sanctions deprived Myanmar of the enormous donor support given to Cambodia's CPP government, and limited the resources available for domestic development. This made the regime heavily dependent on Chinese DF and investment. Chinese aid was used to establish joint ventures with, or create new, SOEs, strengthening the sector used by the regime to cultivate elite support (Maung Aung Myoe 2011: 164–5), while Chinese projects in the borderlands have been pivotal in 'ceasefire capitalism' (Woods 2011a; 2011b; Woods and Kramer 2012; Buchanan, Kramer and Woods 2013). However, these projects have overwhelmingly been in the extractive sectors – for example, mining, oil and gas, logging and agribusiness – and often involved violent land-grabbing and forced displacement, followed by militarisation as the army moved to protect project sites. This has generated deep resentment among ethnic minorities who already nurture decades of grievances against the military (Buchanan, Kramer and Woods 2013). Struggles over the profits of these investments have also created ongoing elite-level tensions. Far from pacifying the borderlands, this form of 'development' has therefore only entrenched conflict (Hameiri, Jones and Zou 2019).

Thus, SLORC/SPDC won a rather pyrrhic victory over its enemies. The pacification of the Bamar heartlands and the ethnic-minority borderlands succeeded sufficiently that the regime felt confident to reconvene the National Convention in 2004–7, generating a new constitution in 2008 that was substantially identical to that it had proposed in the early 1990s. This was adopted through a rigged referendum and elections were held in 2010, allowing the army to hand formal governmental power to a 'civilian' successor, led by former general Thein Sein and his Union Solidarity and Development Party (USDP), a creature of the *ancien régime*. This transition has embedded the 'discipline-flourishing democracy' sought by the military, even following the NLD's landslide election victory in 2015. Nonetheless, it did not resolve Myanmar's underlying social conflicts. Several major EAG ceasefires broke down during the transition, as the regime tried to force ethnic-minority militias to assimilate into the army, and armed conflict is now raging across Myanmar's Kachin and Shan states, periodically pushing refugees across the border into China.

Chinese Financing for Hydropower Development in Myanmar

Of the US$36bn in foreign investment approved by Myanmar's regime between 1988 and 2011, a third was for hydropower dams (Buchanan, Kramer and Woods 2013: 33). By 2014, Myanmar hosted forty-two Chinese hydropower projects at varying stages of development – 11 per cent of the total initiated worldwide since 2000 (International Rivers 2014). Their combined value is estimated at US$23bn and they have 'often [come] bundled with loan and development assistance packages' (Yeophantong 2016: 177). According to the Burma Environmental Working Group (BEWG 2017: 48), over 90 per cent of the large dams being developed are under Chinese companies, twenty-three out of twenty-six of which are SOEs. Importantly, for topographical reasons, almost all large-scale dams are located in Myanmar's ethnic-minority states.

Below we focus on the US$3.6bn Myitsone dam, given its pivotal importance in Sino-Myanmar relations. Myitsone, located at the confluence of the Mali and N'Mai rivers in Kachin state, was part of a seven-dam, US$20bn project agreed between the regime and China Power International (CPI) in 2007. Its development clearly demonstrates the dynamics discussed earlier in this chapter: (a) Myitsone was driven by the Myanmar government and CPI's commercial interests, not Beijing's strategic planning; (b) its implementation has been shaped by these interests and agendas, to the detriment of the local population; (c) unlike in Cambodia, because of Myanmar's regime transition, the resultant uproar led to the project being suspended, precipitating a major crisis in Sino–Myanmar relations. Myanmar's governments have subsequently been wary of further Chinese DF, with relations barely defrosting seven years later.

Contrary to the vast majority of academic and media commentary, which depicts hydropower dams as a means for China to extend its strategic reach deep into Myanmar's territory (see Kirchherr 2018), in reality, hydropower development has been driven overwhelmingly by the Myanmar government, not Chinese planners. Myanmar has the lowest per capita energy consumption in Southeast Asia, with 70 per cent of people, including 84 per cent of rural households, having no electricity, and power shortages constituting a major impediment to industrial development (Carr 2018: 24). Addressing this through hydropower development is a long-standing government agenda. The third SLORC/SPDC five-year plan (2004–9) had called for a 2,000MW increase in electricity supply (Myanmar News Agency 2004). As of 2014, hydropower generated 76 per cent of Myanmar's electricity (OECD 2014: 161). The 2014 National Electrification Plan calls for 100 per cent electrification by 2030, requiring US$30–40bn in investment (GOM-NEMC 2015: i).

Beyond developmental objectives, another possible motive for the junta's pursuit of hydropower projects was their potential to weaken ethnic-minority armed groups. Some EAGs have themselves pursued hydropower development as part of ceasefire capitalism (see Snider 2012: 512ff). However, arguably, dam projects can support state counter-insurgency by flooding areas held or used by EAGs, and by leading to the creation of dual-use infrastructure like roads (Magee and

Kelly 2009: 117, 122; Simpson 2013: 141). As with other megaprojects, dam-building is often accompanied by militarisation, extending the army's reach into the borderlands. From 1992 to 2006, the number of army battalions stationed in Kachin state increased from twenty-six to forty-one (KDNG 2007: 44), while the military presence tripled in Shan state in 1988–2007, reaching 120 battalions (SHAN 2006: 9–10). Dams thus arguably formed part of the military's wider appropriation of space and resources from minority populations and EAGs, described as 'simultaneous military state building and resource extraction' (Grundy-Warr and Dean 2011: 100–1). Certainly many ethnic-minority civil society organisations (CSOs) and EAGs believe that dams are being 'used as a weapon' against them, and often protest or militarily resist hydropower development (BEWG 2017: 45–6). The army has repeatedly clashed with Karen insurgents around the Hatgyi and Ywathit dam projects, the United Wa State Army around the Mongton dam, and with Kokang insurgents over the Kunlong dam (Kirchherr, Charles and Walton 2016: 119; Burke et al. 2017: 41; IFC 2017: 34; KHRG and KRW 2018). Hydropower dams thus seem intimately linked to the regime's state-building project. Twelve of Myanmar's twenty-six operational hydropower dams are in conflict zones, as are forty-two of fifty planned projects (Burke et al. 2017: 40).

The harnessing of dams for military state-building was certainly facilitated by governance structures dominated by the junta's top brass. Although energy planning was fragmented across 'more than a dozen government agencies' (Sovacool 2013: 310), 'historically run in relative isolation from one another' (Adam Smith International 2015: 11), two key committees made the critical decisions. The Leading Committee for National Electricity Development was established in 2004 to oversee the energy supply expansion specified in the 2004–9 five-year plan. It was led by junta chairman Senior General Than Shwe, and its work committee, responsible for approving and supervising projects, was led by the prime minister, who was the SPDC's Secretary-2 (Myanmar News Agency 2004). Hydropower projects also had to be approved by the Special Projects Implementation Committee, established in 1990 and also chaired by Than Shwe (Snider 2012: 109–10). The Ministry of Electric Power-1 (MEP), which led on designing and negotiating specific projects, was also headed by a military man, Colonel Zaw Min, until 2012. The process for commissioning dams also required input from the attorney-general and the

Ministries of Agriculture and Forestry, and approval from the Myanmar Investment Commission (for details see Doran 2014: 89–90; Adam Smith International 2015: 113; Min Khaing 2015). However, these arrangements clearly gave the military considerable scope to direct hydropower DF to suit their political objectives.

They were, moreover, unencumbered by any serious environmental or social regulations. The 1984 Electricity Law, which remains in place today, lacks specific regulations for hydropower and, because it was drafted in Burma's state-socialist era, barely mentions private companies or foreign investors (Snider 2012: 777). The 2006 Conservation of Water Resources and Rivers Law also failed to specify regulations for hydropower or procedures to enforce environmental protection (BEWG 2017: 44–5). Environmental and social impact assessments (ESIAs) were not required in Myanmar until 2015, and the National Commission for Environmental Affairs was kept deliberately weak to encourage foreign investment (Yeophantong 2016: 180–1).

Chinese hydropower companies were drawn into Myanmar by the SPDC, rather than being directed by Beijing. The regime needed their assistance because it lacked the finance, expertise and technology to develop projects autonomously. Initially, a senior Myanmar official reveals, the regime sought EXIM Bank loans to acquire equipment for indigenous projects, which the bank granted on condition that Chinese suppliers were used (Interviewee D03 2018). Later, the regime sought to attract Chinese companies to develop larger-scale dams. For example, the Shweli-1 dam was planned by the Myanmar government, with Chinese involvement sought thereafter (Interviewee D03 2018). This 'pull' factor coincided with the market pressures driving Chinese SOEs' overseas contracts. As Yunnan-based experts observe, 'the Myanmar government knew our SOEs were going abroad, so they found a way to approach us' (Interviewees E13 2018).

Unlike the BOT model used in Cambodia, Myanmar's regime drew Chinese SOEs into joint venture agreements. Typically, this involved the MEP taking a 10–15 per cent stake, plus 10–15 per cent of the energy generated for free, plus commercial taxes (after a five-year break) and other levies on interest and contracts. A smaller stake, usually 5 per cent, was allocated to a Myanmar company, typically crony-owned, which was tasked with preparatory construction and resettlement work.[2] The Chinese partner would own the remaining stake and finance the whole project, with the right to sell the remaining output on commercial terms (Adam Smith International 2015: 115; confirmed by Interviewee D03 2018). When offered such opportunities, China's hydropower SOEs sought loans from CDB or EXIM Bank, which they planned to repay from the revenue accrued by importing power to China's industrial heartlands, which were facing growing energy shortages in the mid-2000s. Perversely, this entailed an energy-starved country exporting up to 90 per cent of the electricity generated from Chinese-backed hydropower dams to China itself. Although scholarly analysts denounced these 'odious and colonial' arrangements (Dapice 2015), for the elites involved this seemed like 'win-win' cooperation, since Myanmar paid nothing, but got some free shares and electricity.

This pattern was reflected in the commissioning of the Myitsone dam project. As an exasperated EXIM Bank official told one of our informants, 'the whole idea was not started by the Chinese people', but rather the Myanmar government (Interviewee D19 2018). Japanese surveyors had identified the site's potential in the 1970s, with Myanmar's MEP and Ministry of Agriculture formally developing an outline plan and feasibility study in 2002 (KDNG 2007: 11). As sources close to CPI noted, 'it wasn't new – everyone knew there was a project there, but they needed to find someone to implement [it]' (Interviewees E01 2018). Exactly how CPI was drawn in, and on what terms, remains murky – even the NLD government refused to disclose the details, even to a committee of legislators tasked with reviewing the project (Interviewee D09 2018). However, all of our informants, in Myanmar and China, agreed that the junta had approached Chinese agencies for help. A senior CPI manager told one of our informants that Myitsone was proposed by the Myanmar government (Interviewee D21 2018; also Hinshelwood and Boehler 2012). Sources close to China's hydropower companies allege that Myanmar's senior general, Than Shwe, asked China's Premier Wen Jiabao for help, with others agreeing that Than Shwe had relentlessly badgered Chinese officials to support his pet project (Interviewees E01 2018; Interviewee D17 2018). Others

---

[2] For examples see TSYO (2011: 12, 25, 27, 32–3); Adam Smith International (2015: 84); BEWG (2017: 50); Foran et al. (2017: 625); Kirchherr (2018: 819–20).

suggest that Myanmar's prime minister proposed the project to CPI's vice-president when the latter visited Myanmar (Interviewees E14 2018). Even the project's opponents now see the Myanmar government as its 'primary initiator' (Interviewee D19 2018).

Myanmar's request interfaced neatly with CPI's own commercial interest in overseas expansion. Some of our informants claimed that Premier Wen agreed to Myanmar's request and suggested that CPI get involved (Interviewees E01 2018). If so, this would exemplify the regulatory approach outlined earlier, whereby top leaders may support projects proposed by foreign governments, hoping to strengthen bilateral ties, but they neither initiate them nor take a detailed interest in their implementation. In any case, CPI apparently needed little encouragement, because it was in its commercial interest to engage. In the early 2000s, CPI's domestic energy-generating arms had been rendered loss-making by rising coal prices and electricity price controls, yet rebalancing to hydropower was extremely difficult, given that dam development was being blocked by regulatory scrutiny after a series of scandals (Liu 2008; He and Jiang 2010). Hence, as Chinese experts observe, 'Chinese hydropower companies are looking for overseas projects, they are trying to find an outlet for their engineers and employees, and make money ... On the other side, the Myanmar government is trying to develop – they needed electricity very badly' (Interviewees E14 2018). Or, as the head of one Myanmar government think tank put it succinctly: 'we need, and they want' (Interviewee D07 2018). Company executives may also have been motivated by the regulatory mechanism of cadre evaluation, which drives SOE managers to pursue eye-catching projects and drive up company profits. As Chinese experts close to the company recall, 'CPI wanted to do something big overseas to prove they have the ability ... The motivation is economically driven by the company' (Interviewees E03 2018).

After a five-month site survey in 2006, CPI concluded an MOU with MEP in January 2007 to build seven dams, including one at Myitsone. According to a member of the parliamentary committee established to review the deal, it was CPI that proposed this massive, US$20bn programme, reflecting its thirst for high-profile overseas expansion (Interviewee D09 2018). China Power International hoped that the megaproject would decisively resolve its profit squeeze by increasing its assets from RMB180bn to RMB380bn and boosting its generating capacity from 43,000 to 63,000MW (Hu 2011; Li 2013; Zhu 2014). Following Myanmar's usual approach, the MOU established a CPI-MEP joint venture to implement the project: the Upstream Ayeyawady Confluence Hydel Power Co. Ltd. The terms have never been publicised, but it is widely reported that they mirror the usual 'colonial' joint venture model, with 90 per cent of the power generated destined for China. Asia World, Myanmar's leading crony conglomerate, received a 5 per cent stake in exchange for undertaking preparatory construction work and resettling affected communities (Foran et al. 2017: 625).

The next steps in the process illustrate the very poor DF governance entailed in China's state transformation. China Power International approached EXIM Bank for financing, and the SOE Sinosure for risk insurance, which in turn assessed the project's commercial viability and risk profile (Interviewees E01 2018). According to sources close to CPI, these entities concluded that the 'project was not bankable' but, because it seemed to enjoy high-level political backing, rather than withholding their support, they simply 'tried to avoid all financial risks so they [did not] lose any money' – shifting the risk onto CPI by demanding extensive collateral (Interviewees E01 2018). One of our Myanmar informants met the EXIM Bank official responsible for approving the loan, who disclosed that he had been reassured that the project would proceed smoothly because he had been shown photographs of Myanmar generals playing golf with leaders of the Kachin Independence Organisation, the local EAG. Asked if he had undertaken a conflict sensitivity assessment, the credit advisor had no idea what this was, and asked our informant to send him some relevant tools (Interviewee D19 2018).

Sinosure also seems to have been reassured by the high-level political backing, as it did not insist on CPI taking out insurance; indeed, CPI failed to insure its investments at any stage (Hui 2012; Jiang 2013). According to one expert who interviewed the CPI manager involved, Sinosure told the company that purchasing insurance was optional (Interviewees E01 2018). This is despite the fact that Sinosure had itself assessed Myanmar as a serious investment risk in 2005, calling on investors to purchase insurance (CECIC 2005). This also violated the *Interim Measures for the Liabilities of Central Enterprises for Asset Losses* issued by the State-owned Assets Supervision and Administration Commission (SASAC), which require due diligence from SOEs to avoid losses (SASAC 2008).

Moreover, EXIM Bank and other Chinese agencies authorised the project without CPI first undertaking ESIAs, ignoring several Chinese regulations. China's 2007 *Green Credit Guidelines* require companies to submit EIAs with loan applications, while MOFCOM's (2009) *Measures for Overseas Investment Management* require SOEs to undertake ESIAs to ensure that projects do not damage China's foreign relations or violate international treaties. Chinese Community Party (CCP) Central Committee and State Council guidelines also require SOEs to consult experts and the public to ensure that projects are feasible and acceptable (Xinhua 2010). In 2004, Premier Wen had specifically instructed hydropower companies to improve public relations and foster consensus before implementing projects, and a bilateral China-Myanmar treaty specifically required Chinese investors to respect 'the public interest' (Zhang, Boting 2010).

In reality, CPI proceeded without an ESIA, unimpeded by China's fragmented DF regime. Following approval from EXIM Bank and the NDRC, the State Council signed off on the project in November 2008, and construction began in December 2009, but an EIA was not completed until March 2010. Moreover, this EIA was clearly flawed. China Power International outsourced it to the Changjiang Institute of Survey, Planning, Design and Research, which subcontracted the work to BANCA, a Myanmar consultancy. In October 2009, BANCA (2009) warned that the Irrawaddy Project would cause considerable environmental and social impact, which could not be mitigated in the case of the Myitsone dam specifically. BANCA recommended splitting the dam into two smaller, lower-impact units, plus intensified mitigation efforts. However, CPI ignored this, publishing a final EIA that falsely claimed that BANCA had approved the project (International Rivers 2011).

Furthermore, CPI was able to draw in other, very high-level state agencies and officials to publicly support their work, reflecting their capacity to influence national elites and transplant their commercial interests into national and even international policy frameworks. In 2008, NDRC Director-General Kong Ling Long witnessed the signing of the Myanmar–CPI contract for the Chipwi Nge dam, which would supply energy needed to construct the Myitsone dam (Snider 2012: 273). In March 2009, a high-level Chinese delegation visited Myanmar, signing the Framework Agreement on the Development of Hydropower Resources in the Union of Myanmar. The agreement was inked by Myanmar's minister for energy and the head of China's National Energy Administration, witnessed by Politburo Standing Committee member Li Changchun. The EXIM Bank governor also signed an

MOU on buyers' credit for hydropower dam components with Myanmar's finance ministry (Myanmar News Agency 2009a). Despite being signed by political leaders, giving the impression of top-down strategic leadership, experts close to CPI insist that, in fact, the company had pushed the Framework Agreement from the 'bottom up' (Interviewees E13 2018); 'it's the company behind it that really wants this scenery' (Interviewees E03 2018). Like all SOEs, CPI managers sought to present their profit-seeking behaviour as serving wider Chinese strategic interests 'to earn credit and be promoted in the system' (Interviewees E03 2018). Moreover, 'the company realised that it was a risky project, so the inter-government agreement was a kind of insurance policy for them' (Interviewees E13 2018). Similar declarations followed, including an Agreement on Joint Ventures in Southeast Asian Hydropower Projects, signed by then Vice-President Xi Jinping, and the Joint Venture Agreement on the Development of Chipwi and Laza Hydropower Projects, witnessed in June 2010 by Premier Wen Jiabao (CPI 2009; Myanmar News Agency 2009c; CPI 2010). China's energy minister also visited the Myitsone site in April 2009 (Myanmar News Agency 2009b). Thus, despite violating Chinese regulations, CPI managed to mobilise powerful party-state elites to back its first major overseas venture. This is a clear case of the 'tail wagging the dog', with SOEs directing national policy rather than the other way around.

Chinese negligence was particularly problematic given the scale and location of the Myitsone dam, which had provoked immediate and mounting local opposition. Myitsone was to be the fifth largest dam in the world: it would flood 766 square kilometres, an area the size of Singapore, inundating over sixty villages and displacing 15,000 people (KDNG 2009: 3–4). Its planned output of 3,200–4,100MW would vastly exceed Myanmar's then national supply (a mere 856MW), with some supplied free for domestic consumption, as well as generating over US$550m a year in export revenues (KDNG 2007: 12; O'Connor 2011: 11). However, the local ethnic-minority Kachin population expected to see none of this, as previous hydropower projects had only benefited military and crony-capitalist interests, while the power was routed to army bases or the Bamar cities (Interviewee D07 2018; Interviewee D09 2018; Interviewee D19 2018; also TSYO 2011: 37; KHRG and KRW 2018: 18). Moreover, the Myitsone site plays a key role in Kachin myths and is an important site for Christian worship (KDNG 2007: 10). Accordingly, local villagers and civil society groups began raising objections in 2004, initially to Kachin organisations, then to the SPDC in 2007, and in 2009 to CPI and several Chinese government agencies including the State Council, the NDRC, the Ministry of Environmental Protection, SASAC, the MFA and MOFCOM (KDNG 2009: 14–20). Their letters to the Chinese rightly highlighted that China's own regulations were being flouted. In 2007, a coalition of ninety-eight Myanmar CSOs and twenty-four international organisations sent a 50,000-signature petition to President Hu Jintao and MOFCOM, warning that China's 'official position' of 'peaceful development … is being undermined by the unregulated actions of Chinese corporations', and predicting 'instability and increased refugee flows into China' if proposed dams went ahead (Burma Rivers Network 2007). None of these Chinese agencies responded.

This growing social movement, incorporating civil society activists, churches and youth groups, eventually drew in the Kachin Independence Organisation (KIO). It had initially been reluctant to oppose the Myitsone dam. Following its 1994 ceasefire with the regime, KIO leaders had been drawn deeply into ceasefire capitalism, including extractive investments and hydropower dam-building, often with Chinese involvement. Indeed, they lured the first Chinese hydropower firms to Kachin state, with the KIO's Buga Company becoming a joint venture partner in several dam projects, including Daying-4, Mali Hka and Nam Tabat (Khun Sam 2006; Snider 2012: 130–2; Hennig 2016: 1241). The KIO had also extracted protection money from the Chinese company Datang after menacing its dam site at Tarpein (Interviewee D19 2018; Snider 2012: 146). China Power International later claimed that KIO forces had sought kickbacks from the Myitsone project, but were rebuffed as it was well outside of KIO-held territory (Hinshelwood and Boehler 2012).

However, three interlinked developments eventually drove the KIO to oppose Myitsone. The first was the conflict over the junta's attempt to convert the KIO's militia, the Kachin Independence Army (KIA), into a 'border guard force' under army control, as part of the forced transition to 'discipline-flourishing democracy'. Despite having endorsed the 2008 constitution, the KIO feared relinquishing its forces before the 2010 elections, and resisted the army's demands, along with several other large EAGs. This conflict triggered the takeover of the KIO by a younger generation of officers who had forged ties with local CSOs disillusioned by the old leaders' venal participation in ceasefire capitalism (Brenner 2015). Secondly, the SPDC was also squeezing the KIO economically. Over several years, the regime re-routed the lucrative trade in commodities like timber and jade away from EAG-controlled border posts, mandating the use of government-held routes through Yangon and Naypyidaw. Moreover, borderland investments were increasingly being brokered by regional commanders, pro-regime crony companies and foreign investors, cutting out KIO elites and their clients (Woods 2011a; 2011b; Jones 2014a: 793–4; Woods 2018). This affected hydropower specifically. In January 2011, the government reassigned the contract to develop a dam on the Nam Tabat river from the KIO's Buga Company to a crony firm, Tun Thwin Mining Co., and China Guodian (Snider 2012: 130–2). The regime also tried to squeeze the KIO out of their deal with Datang at the Darpein dam (Hui 2012). Thirdly, the KIO came under mounting pressure from Kachin civil society, which demanded action to protect Kachin interests (Buchanan, Kramer and Woods 2013: 21). Increasingly, the Myitsone dam was presented as an existential threat to the entire Kachin people (Kiik 2016). Accordingly, in 2007, the KIO had written to General Than Shwe and Yunnan's provincial government, opposing Myitsone, though not the six other dams in the Irrawaddy Project (Foran et al. 2017: 625). Chinese agencies again ignored these protests, apparently trusting the SPDC to repress opposition.

Through 2009–10, Kachin opposition mounted, with ten bombs exploding at the Myitsone construction site, injuring Chinese workers and prompting a vicious military crackdown. Around 2,000 villagers were forcibly resettled onto poor-quality land, with rumours circulating that local authorities were embezzling CPI's meagre compensation funds (Kirchherr, Charles and Walton 2016: 111; Foran et al. 2017: 626). In March 2011, the new KIO chairman wrote to China's president, reiterating his opposition to Myitsone on cultural grounds, but also adding that the reservoir would flood 'locations where KIO military centers are stationed', while the Myanmar army would 'invade the KIO area' to secure the other dam sites. He warned that civil war might resume in Kachin state 'because of this hydro power plant project and the dam construction' (Lanyaw Zawng Hra 2011).

Chinese regulators noted this rising opposition but, reflecting the weak oversight of China's DF, took no decisive action against CPI. In 2010, MOFCOM issued a *Notice on Issuing Overseas Security Risk Early Warning and Information Release System on Foreign Investment*

Cooperation, requiring SOEs to minimise risks and losses if warned by the Ministry (MOFCOM 2010). In June 2011, MOFCOM explicitly warned CPI that growing societal opposition could prompt Myanmar's government to target the company, but CPI ignored the warning (Jiang 2012). Nonetheless, MOFCOM did not suspend the project, as it is empowered to do when due-diligence rules are violated (MOFCOM 2009).

Eventually, MOFCOM's predictions came true. In June 2011, a Myanmar army attempt to seize control of the Darpein dam triggered the breakdown of the KIO ceasefire. The KIA immediately blocked access to the Myitsone site, bombing key bridges and attacking supply lines, with Chinese workers fleeing and construction work abandoned (Buchanan, Kramer and Woods 2013: 21; Foran et al. 2017: 626). Meanwhile, crucially, with the shift to a 'discipline-flourishing democracy' in 2010–11, Bamar environmentalists were able to exploit new freedoms of assembly, speech and press to expand the Kachin protest into central Myanmar. By mid-2011, a 'heterogeneous, pro-river, anti-dam coalition' had emerged, backed by Aung San Suu Kyi, which framed Myitsone as part of an 'existential threat to the people of Myanmar by Chinese colonialism' (Foran et al. 2017: 626; see also Kiik 2016; Chan 2017; Lamb and Dao 2017). Initially, the new government pushed back against the protests, but on 29 September 2011, President Thein Sein told parliament that he was suspending the Myitsone project, as a signal that the new, elected government respected the people's will (Foran et al. 2017: 626).

This plunged China–Myanmar relations into deep crisis. This was not simply about Myitsone. Sinophobia had been brewing for years, given Chinese involvement in many predatory investments (Min Zin 2012). Because most Myanmar people saw SOEs not as loosely regulated, profit-seeking firms but rather as arms of the Chinese state, they blamed Beijing for corporate malpractice (Interviewee D07 2018; Interviewee D08 2018; Interviewee D09 2018; Interviewees D11 2018; Interviewee D14 2018). However, it was clearly the Myitsone project that not only consolidated the Kachin opposition and precipitated the breakdown of the KIO ceasefire, but also mobilised widespread societal opposition. The suspension – publicly announced without advance notification to the Chinese – provoked deep alarm in Beijing. Chinese investment slumped from US$1.5bn in 2010 (68 per cent of Myanmar's inward FDI) to just US$70.5m in 2014

(7 per cent) (ASEAN Secretariat 2017). The revived Kachin insurgency threatened existing Chinese investments, including oil and gas pipelines, and the Darpein dam, which was shut down for two years, and also displaced tens of thousands of refugees across the border, causing uproar among their kinsfolk on the Chinese side. Chinese analysts saw the Myitsone suspension as a strategic disaster, arguing Myanmar had been suddenly lost to the West, ruining two decades of careful diplomacy (Sun 2011).

As so often, China's MFA was left carrying the can for the actions of CPI and other DF actors. Despite rules requiring SOEs to consult local embassies before implementing projects, CPI only approached China's ambassador to Myanmar after the project had been suspended (Mclaughlin 2013). The embassy's subsequent pleas to the Myanmar government to restart the project failed, however, and in the longer term the MFA has had to radically change its Myanmar policy, intervening to support the domestic peace process and stabilise the border area (Sun 2017). The MFA also had to launch a costly public diplomacy campaign to try to re-legitimise China's economic presence in Myanmar (Zou and Jones 2020). However, Myitsone remains suspended, with no compensation paid to CPI, and successive Myanmar governments have been leery of new Chinese megaprojects. No new dams have been agreed, and there is widespread societal opposition to existing projects on the basis that they escalate ethnic conflict (ICEM 2017: 18–19). An agreement to build a US$20bn China–Myanmar railway was allowed to lapse in 2014. Work on a US$3bn oil refinery at Dawei was halted in November 2017. Myanmar's 2017–18 debt report clearly showed a decisive shift away from China towards traditional bilateral and multilateral development agencies (Chan Mya Htwe 2018). Even though Aung San Suu Kyi's government eventually committed Myanmar to China's BRI, signing an MOU on a China–Myanmar Economic Corridor in September 2018, progress has been very slow (Jones and Khin Ma Ma Myo 2021). The Kyaukphyu port and special economic zone project, notionally agreed in 2013 then stalled, has been revived in a dramatically downsized form. Central government authorisation for a Chinese-backed, US$8bn New Yangon City project, including new industrial parks, roads and power plants, is also being withheld.

The Chinese leadership itself recognised that this extremely negative outcome stemmed from the fragmented DF governance regime produced by the transformation of China's party-state. SASAC, MOFCOM and the NDRC all reacted by tightening SOE regulation: the measures issued in 2012–14 all stemmed from the Myitsone scandal (see Table 4.1). However, this followed earlier regulatory tightening, which had clearly not solved the problem, and was itself followed by additional regulations, so its impact on SOEs' actual conduct is questionable. Some Chinese SOEs are stepping up their corporate social responsibility activity, but some are also backtracking (Nordensvard Urban, and Mang 2015; Kirchherr et al. 2017). These agencies' efforts are thus simply part of an ongoing struggle within China's transformed, regulatory state.

The central government also activated its disciplinary mechanisms to rein in CPI specifically. A National Audit Office (2015) investigation uncovered extensive regulatory non-compliance at CPI, including 131 projects between 2008 and 2013, worth a combined RMB119.6bn, where the company 'began construction with incomplete procedures or started production illegally'. The CCP's Central Commission for Discipline Inspection (2015a; 2015b) also identified fifty-seven shortcomings at CPI, including violation of government regulations on aid and investment, and criticised senior managers for scapegoating junior staff. This crackdown ended the careers of several executives, including general manager Qizhou Lu, who publicly confessed his errors and retired. However, there was no thoroughgoing purge, which arguably reflected the way that blame for the fiasco could be spread evenly across the entire DF apparatus, all the way to top leaders who had been drawn into supporting CPI's project.

Conclusion

China's DF is often seen as a tool of Beijing's grand strategy and a direct challenge to established donors and global governance norms. The reality is very different, thanks to state transformation dynamics and the rise of the Chinese-style regulatory state. Specific DF projects are clearly not planned by Beijing's geostrategists. At most, senior Chinese leaders signal a general willingness to support DF projects in particular countries – though even then, this support may emerge through bottom-up lobbying by self-interested SOEs and recipient-country elites. In any case, this merely creates a very permissive context for other actors to determine how DF is deployed in practice. The severe fragmentation of China's DF governance further undermines any strategic oversight, such that the actors that shape DF projects most powerfully are those ostensibly tasked only with implementing government decisions: SOEs. As our case studies showed, these companies opportunistically pursue projects that will bring them profit and prestige, lobbying for financial and political support at home. Recipient governments – which are typically the prime movers of specific development projects – also have their own (potentially nefarious) motivations. Thus, far from reflecting careful planning from Beijing, Chinese DF projects are really an amalgamation of very specific corporate and politico-economic interests, enabled by an extremely weak governance system. This facilitates widespread corporate abuses, including the ignoring of Chinese and host-country regulations and negative social and environmental consequences.

Whether these projects advance or harm China's wider diplomatic objectives is ultimately determined by how they intersect with sociopolitical conflicts in recipient countries. Cambodia's CPP regime was able to contain unrest arising from the Chinese-backed LS2 dam, and extract benefits to feed its patronage system – a successful outcome that has deepened Sino-Cambodian ties. However, Myanmar's far more fractious and fragmented context meant that a similar DF project provoked such serious unrest that the project was abandoned and bilateral ties suffered enormously.

Conclusion

The International Relations (IR) debate on China's rise has been at an impasse for at least a decade. On one side, some commentators perceive China as a revisionist power, intent on challenging and transforming the US-led international order; others, however, see China as a status quo or status seeking power, accommodating itself to global norms or seeking only modest tweaks to reflect its growing heft. The trouble is that there is ample evidence of both kinds of Chinese behaviour, enabling analysts and policymakers to cherry-pick or interpret data to suit their preferred argument. Unable to resolve their disagreement on the basis of existing evidence, observers have instead turned to speculating about what China might do in the future, which is unfalsifiable and even more prone to theory-based evidence-making.

We have argued that this problem stems from the assumption that China is a unitary actor, such that its behaviour can be understood to reflect some underlying strategic intent: look at the behaviour, and one can decode what China 'really' wants. Conversely, building on decades of neglected scholarship in the study of Chinese politics, we have shown that, after many years of state transformation – the uneven and contested fragmentation, decentralisation and internationalisation of party-state apparatuses – China cannot reasonably be regarded as a unitary actor. Evidence of revisionist and status quo-supporting behaviour co-exist because different elements of the party-state are pursuing different courses of action simultaneously. The analytical task is not to emphasise one kind of behaviour while sweeping the rest under the carpet. It is to devise a way of understanding Chinese behaviour that can account for its genuine diversity. This had yet to be done by IR scholars or China specialists.

We approached this task by developing and deploying a new theoretical framework, the state transformation approach. This approach is

concerned to understand how states that have undergone fragmentation, decentralisation and internationalisation operate in practice, and
how this generates specific political outcomes. It does not claim that
China, or any other state, is simply a chaotic mess, with no centralised
control. But equally, it suggests that not everything Chinese actors do
overseas can plausibly be traced to the strategic intentions of senior
leaders. Instead, we theorised the replacement of a top-down command-and-control type system by a Chinese-style regulatory state. In
this mode of governance, top leaders do not issue detailed instructions,
allocate resources and intervene directly to ensure that all party-state
actors are doing exactly what they are told. Rather, they set broad (and
often vague) policy parameters, which others must interpret and implement. They have at their disposal a range of mechanisms to help 'steer'
other actors in broadly favoured directions: party doctrine; public
declarations; coordinating bodies; discretionary control of finance
and laws; and, most importantly, the Chinese Communist Party's
(CCP) powers of appointment, appraisal and discipline. All of these
mechanisms have some effect, and they are clearly stronger than those
seen in Western-style regulatory states. Nonetheless, they are open to
influence from 'below', and ostensibly subordinate actors can also
interpret and even ignore these mechanisms. Far from being monolithic, therefore, China's party-state is a contradictory, conflict-ridden
entity, animated by competing interests and constant struggles over the
direction and implementation of policy – including foreign policy. This
is not least because of the emergence of contending cadre-capitalist
groups as part of China's capitalist transformation.

In a further departure from existing scholarship, we also argued that
the outcomes of Chinese policy depended on how these dynamics
intersected with socio-political conditions in other states. Just as
China is not monolithic, nor is any other country. Reflecting their
own political economy context and associated socio-political struggles,
other countries are also conflict-ridden. Reflecting the uneven distribution of costs and benefits associated with Chinese policy interventions,
some forces welcome them, while others resist. The net result depends
on how these interventions are received and contested. In some cases,
very similar Chinese policy thrusts generate wildly different outcomes,
depending on dynamics in the recipient countries involved. This makes
it even less plausible to trace the results of Chinese policy to some
strategic hive-mind in Beijing.

Key Findings

Variation in the Degree of Policy Coherence

As our case studies show, China's foreign policy formation and implementation is very diverse, ranging from situations that seem to demonstrate strong top-down control, to those approaching fragmented chaos, and everything in between. We can explain this full range of outcomes because our model is dynamic, emphasising ongoing struggles within the transformed party-state, and those within recipient states.

However, this raises the question: under what conditions is Chinese behaviour likely to be more or less coherent? As *Fractured China* is necessarily an exploratory study, we did not try to answer this question in advance, not least because preliminary research debunked many obvious hypotheses. Fragmentation is not necessarily confined to 'low politics', as the South China Sea case demonstrates. Nor is geography determinant: even in neighbouring countries like Myanmar, central coordinating mechanisms seem unable to control key actors. Nor is the presence of so-called core interests, which some see as driving China's 'grand strategy' (Goldstein 2020), because – as so often – these are vaguely specified and open to influence and interpretation (Zeng, Xiao and Breslin 2015a). However, we can now inductively identify some broad patterns, which could lend the model predictive power and generate hypotheses to be tested in future research.

In Figure 5.1, the vertical axis denotes the degree to which the interests of powerful actors within the Chinese party-state align. The horizontal axis denotes the extent to which the Chinese-style regulatory state's coordinating mechanisms are deployed and work effectively. Based on this, four scenarios are possible.

In quadrant A, powerful interests' preferences diverge, but the centre's coordinating mechanisms are applied and are generally effective, though not without a struggle. This results in considerable fragmentation and incoherence in practice. The South China Sea case exemplifies this scenario (Chapter 2). Central leaders have set out broad guidelines – the nine-dash line and the *weiquan/weiwen* framework – and established various coordinating mechanisms. However, contending interest groups have pushed different interpretations of these frameworks as they struggle for power and resources. This results

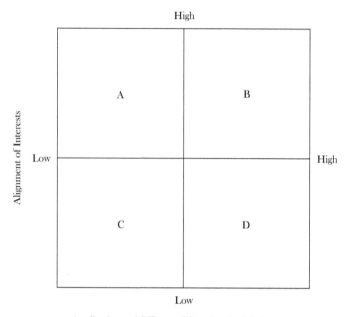

Figure 5.1 Policy coherence in the Chinese-style regulatory state

in incoherent behaviour, with aggressive and diplomatic approaches being pursued simultaneously by different actors. Those bound by unitary actor assumptions wrongly interpret this as intentional, reflecting a sinister strategy of phased annexation, rather than an evolving, conflict-ridden process. While China's position in the South China Sea has strengthened overall, it has done so in an unplanned, rather chaotic manner, and at the expense of China's broader objectives; it has alienated Southeast Asian governments, encouraged anti-Chinese soft balancing, and drawn the intervention of the USA, Japan and others.

In quadrant B, powerful interests align and coordinating mechanisms are applied and are effective, resulting in very smooth and consistent policymaking and implementation, giving the superficial impression of a monolithic, unitary state. China's anti-banditry interventions on the Mekong approximate this scenario (Chapter 3). The brutal killings of Chinese sailors caused a public outcry and galvanised central government action. But Yunnanese authorities and Chinese businesses also had a strong interest in suppressing banditry.

Accordingly, the Ministry of Public Security was easily able to secure their cooperation, resulting in the relatively smooth implementation of transnational law enforcement cooperation. That said, it appears that implementation nonetheless warped around powerful local interest groups, targeting the Naw Kham gang, a major irritant to politically influential businesses, despite *prima facie* evidence that it had actually been in league with the murdered Chinese sailors. Nonetheless, this extrusion of China's governance frontier beyond its national boundaries has been remarkably effective in suppressing banditry along the Mekong river – if not the drug trafficking that seems to have been connected with the initial incident sparking Chinese intervention.

In quadrant C, the interests of important policymaking and implementing agents do not align and coordinating mechanisms are either unused or ineffective, leading to highly incoherent international behaviours. The cases of China's counter-narcotics policy in Myanmar and Laos (Chapter 3), and China's development financing programmes (Chapter 4) both exemplify this rather common scenario. In the counter-narcotics case, China's Opium Substitution Programme was hijacked by Yunnan-based agribusiness companies to support their own cross-border expansion. Their crops were poor substitutes for opium, and the rapacious manner in which their plantations were established perversely led to increased opium production, the opposite of the programme's stated intended goal. The central coordination mechanism, 122 Workgroup, was itself weak and fragmented, resulting in the domination of the Ministry of Commerce at the expense of the Ministry of Public Security, which wanted a greater focus on law enforcement. Similarly, in the case of China's development financing, myriad central agencies with different priorities have been jockeying for influence over policymaking, while implementation was fragmented even further and dominated by state-owned enterprises (SOEs), which compete fiercely with each other over projects, and whose profit-seeking motives are not always aligned with China's wider diplomatic or geopolitical goals.

In quadrant D, coordinating mechanisms are not used or are ineffective, but since powerful agents' interests and agendas align the result is low contestation and relatively consistent international behaviour. Our case studies provide no example for this scenario, but it is a theoretical possibility nonetheless, which may arise in other studies. Importantly, the two variables may change over time, resulting in issue areas moving between the quadrants. For example, central coordination in the South China Sea has tightened significantly in recent years, so arguably this policy issue has moved from quadrant C to A.

More research is needed to better explain the effectiveness or weakness of central coordination, as well as the circumstances that allow issues to shift between quadrants. Nonetheless, this schema provides a useful starting point for generating hypotheses but also for understanding and responding to Chinese behaviour. Different policy domains require different responses, because the problems differ. For example, in the case of development finance, the problem is lack of effective controls, such that working with Chinese agencies to strengthen their oversight could curb the worst excesses and improve developmental outcomes. On the other hand, in other areas, central agencies, or even top leaders, exert greater control over China's international engagements. In these cases, more conventional international responses – deterrence, for example – could be more appropriate.

China's Dangerous Regulatory State

Those who see China as a dangerous revisionist power that needs to be contained or confronted see it as a coherent, strategic actor bent on overturning hegemony. Although we have debunked this conception of China, that does not necessarily mean that it is a harmless international actor. On the contrary, the fractured party-state often engages in highly problematic behaviour – just not for the reasons anticipated by unitary-actor models.

Most observers assume that Chinese foreign policy is made at the top and therefore attribute China's growing international assertiveness in recent years to current 'paramount leader' Xi Jinping (e.g. Fallon 2015). The argument is not baseless, since top leaders' doctrinal shifts and public pronouncements, even if vague, do provide guidance and overall direction for the party-state. However, our case studies show that ostensibly subordinate actors – notably provincial and local governments, and SOEs – are often behind some of the most unsavoury aspects of China's international relations. Their excesses are rarely a result of top-down instructions or strategic planning, but reflect self-interested competition and weak central oversight. In general, these actors are motivated by narrow, often commercial, imperatives, and show scant understanding of, and regard for, Beijing's wider diplomatic or political agendas.

For example, in the South China Sea, Hainan province has played an extremely aggressive role, pushing Beijing's vague policy frameworks to the limit and even ignoring central policy in key areas. The actions of Hainanese fishermen, encouraged and supported by provincial authorities, had a particularly destabilising effect, accounting for the vast majority of international maritime clashes. Similarly, the national oil companies' search for new commercial opportunities ultimately precipitated the crisis in relations with Vietnam in 2014, following the positioning of a Chinese oil rig in contested waters. In Chapter 3, we saw how the interests of Yunnanese agribusinesses hijacked China's national opium-substitution policy. Their rapacious expansion into Myanmar and Laos harmed both smallholder farmers and the environment, and even exacerbated the drugs problem. The hydropower sector's megaprojects in Myanmar and Cambodia were also conducted with little regard for international environmental and social standards. In the case of the Myitsone dam, the blowback against the poorly conceived and executed project was so severe that it continues to undermine China's diplomatic relationship with Myanmar today.

None of these behaviours were planned or intended by top leaders or central agencies, which had in some cases committed China to very different policies, including through international treaties. Oftentimes they are caught unawares, scrambling to contain the fallout and rein in wayward actors. The Myitsone dam fiasco exemplifies this. To clean up the mess created by freewheeling corporate actors, China's Ministry of Foreign Affairs was forced to abandon its long-standing policy of non-interference, intervening in Myanmar's peace process to try to stabilise the borderlands. In the South China Sea, too, central agencies, primarily the PLA Navy, have tried to manage other actors, resulting in fewer maritime incidents, though still within a more fraught regional context.

Moreover, as we have shown, recentralisation efforts may not achieve their intended results, and are often incomplete and temporary, given the usual tussles that characterise the operations of China's transformed party-state. The failure of Xi Jinping to fundamentally transform governance in any of the issue areas we considered is very striking. In the South China Sea, Xi's coordinating mechanisms failed while the China Coastguard remains a work in progress. In non-traditional security, agribusinesses continued to hijack the Opium Substitution Programme under Xi, with bananas and sugarcane succeeding rubber as the boom crop. In development financing, Xi's signature foreign policy, the Belt and Road Initiative, continues to be affected by fragmented governance and corporate self-interest, notwithstanding attempts to improve central coordination (Hillman 2020). All of this underscores that, as many of our Chinese interlocutors constantly stressed, even China's 'new Mao' cannot simply snap his fingers and reverse decades of state transformation. It is just not possible for one man, or even one man and his close allies, to make every important decision in a system as sprawling and complex as the Chinese party-state. Xi has forcefully deployed all the coordinating mechanisms available to any Chinese leader but, while all of these affect the way the system works, none of them can guarantee coherence or compliance. This implies a very different policy response to China's rise than that currently gaining ground in many Western capitals, as we discuss later in this chapter.

The Critical Role of Targets/Recipients

Another key finding of our study is that actors in states play a critical role in shaping the outcomes of China's international engagements. International Relations scholars focus very heavily on what great or rising powers supposedly want and do. As Kenneth Waltz (1979: 72) famously argued, it would be 'ridiculous to construct a theory of international politics based on [weak states like] Malaysia and Costa Rica'. This is only modestly corrected by those studies focusing on weak states' responses to rising powers, such as the 'hedging' literature. Even these studies remain overwhelmingly statist, assuming that foreign policy elites make strategic decisions that then govern their states' external behaviour *tout court* (e.g. Goh 2013). They pay little attention to these states' internal fragmentation, political economy relations, or socio-political struggles that, as we have shown, actually play a determining role in shaping the outcomes of rising powers' policies.

For example, with respect to development financing, we have shown that key megaprojects were not initiated by decision-makers in Beijing but rather by elites in recipient countries (see also Jones and Hameiri 2020). In Chapter 4, we showed that highly controversial hydropower dam projects, which have often been depicted as instruments of Chinese grand strategy, were actually proposed by other governments,

who actively drew Chinese companies and financiers into their countries. Chinese leaders' desire to strengthen ties with their foreign counterparts, combined with the fragmented and weak governance of
China's development financing, created an extremely permissive environment, enabling nefarious interests to benefit and facilitating serious
corporate abuses of human rights and the environment. Yet the outcome differed starkly in our two case studies, Cambodia and
Myanmar, because of these countries' differing socio-political structures and conflicts. The Cambodian People's Party regime was able to
contain resistance to the Lower Sesan 2 dam, while monopolising the
benefits, resulting in warmer ties with Beijing. But in Myanmar, fiercer
social conflict in the context of a fragile regime transition led to the
suspension of the Myitsone dam and a deep crisis in bilateral relations.
To suggest that Beijing strategically controlled either of these outcomes
is clearly fanciful. The only way to understand what happened is to
study how the transformed party-state interacts with disparate social
forces in other countries.

One tentative conclusion, supplying more hypotheses for future
research, is that Chinese engagements are more likely to result in
diplomatic 'wins' for Beijing when partner countries' ruling coalitions
are cohesive, allowing them to manage their uneven flows of costs and
benefits. Where this management fails, or socio-political contestation
intensifies for unrelated reasons, this often seems to generate blowback
for Beijing, as it is now belatedly realising. In Myanmar, China's
fractious party-state could engage in rapacious, poorly regulated
behaviour for decades under military rule. But the unravelling of ceasefire capitalism and spiking conflict amid the 2010–11 transition from
direct military rule led to soaring opposition to Chinese 'colonialism'
and a U-turn by the country's new government. We have seen similar
reversals in Sri Lanka, following President Mahinda Rajapaksa's electoral defeat in 2015, the Maldives, after President Abdulla Yameen was
ousted in 2018, and Malaysia, with the fall of the Barisan Nasional
government in 2018. The return of the Rajapaksa family to power in Sri
Lanka in 2019 and the resurgence of *ancien régime* forces in Malaysia
in March 2020, could change this dynamic again. Chinese policymakers have increasingly realised that they cannot bank on cosy ties
with narrow ruling elites, moving instead to cultivate broader-based
support within partner countries, as well as softening their commitment to non-interference (Zou and Jones 2020). This is another

important way in which a rising power's conduct is shaped by socio-political struggles within other countries.

Lessons for Policymakers

Our findings suggest a rapid rethink is required in how governments, intergovernmental organisations and civil society actors respond to the rise of China. In recent years, many governments, led by the USA, have become overtly hostile towards China. Accusations of widespread Chinese technological theft, unfair economic competition and political interference have abounded, alongside an intensifying Sino-US trade war. In October 2018, American Vice-President Mike Pence argued in a major speech that a 'new Cold War' was in the offing (quoted in Mead 2018). In July 2020, US Secretary of State Mike Pompeo called for democracies to unite against China, and the 'free and open Indo-Pacific' initiative is a thinly concealed effort to generate this unity in Asia. Japan, the USA, the EU and Australia have begun competing explicitly with China's BRI by offering alternative infrastructure financing, though these programmes remain comparatively small-scale at the time of writing. The coronavirus pandemic has only intensified these dynamics, with some Western policymakers seeking to pin blame on China.

To be sure, many of the accusations levelled at China are correct. For example, China's neo-mercantilist industrial practices, though arguably needed to avoid the 'middle-income trap', are potentially devastating for other economies (Holslag 2019). However, many of the current policy responses to China's rise assume that China's international engagements are always strategically directed and coordinated from the top. They therefore attempt to respond in a geostrategic manner, through containment, deterrence and/or hedging. As we have shown, however, the assumption that China is a unitary actor is problematic. Consequently, these policies may not only be ineffective but also counterproductive. If Chinese elites perceive that they are being unfairly blamed for events beyond their control, they are likely to adopt a bunker mentality, seeing the USA and its allies as inevitable enemies, bent on thwarting China's rise regardless of the situation. This is likely to precipitate a tit-for-tat escalation on both sides that could generate major international conflict. In this sense, realist statism becomes a self-fulfilling prophesy, not because it accurately models reality but because it shapes perceptions of it.

The main lesson of our research for non-Chinese policymakers is that there can be no 'one size fits all' policy towards China. Chinese behaviour is not directed by a coherent overall strategy; it genuinely varies across policy domains, reflecting the different actors and interests at stake (and not just those in China), and the presence and efficacy of coordinating mechanisms. It is therefore a mistake to interpret cooperative or positive behaviour in one domain as a mere ruse to disguise an overall sinister grand strategy. Consequently, it is unwise to develop a simplistic, one-eyed policy on China. Difficult as it may be, it is imperative to develop a more sophisticated strategy, recognising variable Chinese behaviour across different issue areas and carefully calibrating policies to encourage the positive and restrain the negative. Our schema in Figure 5.1 may be a useful starting point, though deep and serious analysis will always be required for any given policy domain. This will require China's foreign interlocutors to develop their contacts way beyond one or two ministries in Beijing, encompassing the full range of actors involved in any given area.

For instance, in the area of development financing, some central Chinese agencies have a genuine desire, but limited capacity, to better regulate the conduct of SOEs operating overseas. These agencies are potential allies for foreign governments, international organisations and civil society actors keen to improve the developmental and socio-economic outcomes of Chinese-financed projects. As the nongovernmental organisation Inclusive Development International (2019) argues, the fragmented and disparate regulatory environment actually creates many potential points of entry to promote tougher regulation and redress for negatively affected communities. This is a far more hopeful starting point than a monolithic view of China, which seems bent on a particular strategic course, impervious to any external influence. Similarly, the Asian Infrastructure Investment Bank offers a concrete example of how Western and Chinese officials collaborated to develop a Chinese institution that operates according to high international standards. The vast majority of the bank's projects are also being implemented in partnership with existing multilateral development banks, according to their standards, allowing Chinese practitioners to learn on the job. This is a far more productive outcome than the preferred US policy of boycotting the bank on the grounds that it posed a revisionist challenge to existing institutions.

This further implies that policymakers should consider carefully which Chinese international activities to support and which to resist, rather than treating them all as dangerous and revisionist. Within the huge and fragmented BRI, for example, some projects genuinely benefit recipient populations, while others are harmful. Resisting all BRI projects is as irrational as resisting none of them, and is only likely to antagonise recipient governments, who typically lack meaningful alternatives to Chinese assistance, as well as the Chinese government. Similarly, with respect to non-traditional security, China is not the 'Westphalian' state of old, blocking cooperation in all domains. The Chinese Navy, for example, has played a substantial role in anti-piracy cooperation in the Gulf of Aden. However, international cooperation in the fight against the COVID-19 pandemic collapsed in early 2020, partly because of intensifying US-Chinese rivalry, which immobilised the World Health Organization. These events show the clear risks of perceiving China as a unitary state and approaching every issue through the lens of great power conflict.

Finally, policymakers must develop responses that consider seriously the role of the states and societies with which Chinese actors engage. Too much policy is currently focused on what China does and wants, and how to respond. However, our research shows that dynamics within other countries powerfully shape the outcomes of Chinese activities. Consequently, thinking carefully about how to engage other states and societies can be just as important as understanding China itself. As we have shown, recipient-country elites engage with and support Chinese projects for reasons peculiar to their own political and social circumstances, typically to prop up ruling coalitions and weaken their rivals. These states are also affected by transformative dynamics, though their precise nature and impacts in particular policy domains require careful analysis. Policies seeking to shift these elites' policy positions must take these dynamics into account or be found wanting. For example, alternative opium eradication policies in Laos would have to factor in the Laotian state's reliance upon large-scale, foreign-financed plantations both for patronage and for extending its territorial control over ethnic-minority groups. Interventions that do not gel with elite objectives are likely to remain less attractive than China's offer.

Finally, our research also contains lessons for Chinese policymakers, though these may be even less likely to be accepted. Our findings clearly show that the way China is governed entails behaviours that are genuinely detrimental and internationally provocative. This ought to be accepted and admitted in order to mitigate growing alarm at Chinese behaviour, and to enlist help in enacting reforms to address these problems, where appropriate. However, this is very difficult for Chinese officials for at least two main reasons. First, it would be extremely embarrassing, and contrary to Communist Party ideology, to admit publicly that the central government does not and cannot tightly control the activities of all party-state actors. Chinese officials have admitted this privately in the past. For example, Kurt Campbell (2014), the US Assistant Secretary of State for East Asian and Pacific Affairs under President Obama, recalls 'work[ing] carefully behind the scenes' with Chinese elites to 'untangle the mess created by nationalist and poorly coordinated elements', whose activities 'often caught senior Chinese leaders unawares' and were 'not part of a larger orchestrated strategy'. However, as disciplinary controls have tightened under Xi Jinping, it has probably become harder to admit errors and mistakes, even behind closed doors. Consequently, even Campbell (2014) claims that Chinese behaviour has become 'carefully choreographed' – which, as we have seen, is inaccurate. For policy elites even less interested in nuance, and more interested in promoting confrontation for their own purposes, it is easy to seize on negative Chinese behaviours to posit a dangerous grand strategy at work. This is just one of several negative by-products of Xi's authoritarian clampdown.

A second problem arises from Chinese elites' own ideological blinkers. It is far easier, and more tempting, to attribute backlash and fallout from Chinese engagements to the actions of official adversaries than it is to look hard at one's own conduct and seek to change it. In the case of Myanmar, for example, it is clear that Chinese companies and local officials have behaved in reckless, predatory and illegal ways, seriously antagonising large parts of Myanmar society. However, many Chinese scholars, commentators and elites attributed the eventual backlash against Chinese engagement to a nefarious campaign by US-backed international nongovernmental organisations. This exemplifies a tendency among Chinese elites to view international relations exclusively through the prism of Sino-US rivalry, such that American hands must be behind every setback to Chinese interests – mirroring a similar tendency in Western capitals. Additional ideological constraints emerge from skewed and depoliticised understandings of

China's own development process. As noted in Chapter 4, the inherently conflictual nature of capitalist development is systematically downplayed in Chinese discourse, with economic growth presented as the solution to all ills. This view – falsified by China's own domestic experience, not least in Tibet and Xinjiang – makes it difficult for Chinese elites to recognise how their economic engagement in developing countries can breed social unrest, without any help from outside agitators. Some simply believe that sacrifices are necessary for development, depicting anyone resisting this process as irrational or ignorant. Many insist that China is fundamentally different from Western powers, having itself been a victim of colonialism, and is thus only interested in 'win-win cooperation for mutual benefit', and thus could never be guilty of malfeasance. Ironically, many members of the Chinese Communist Party need to follow Marx's injunction to strip away such ideological thinking and confront with sober senses their real conditions of life and relations with their kind.

A second lesson for Chinese policymakers is that there is an evident need to improve governance in many policy domains, including by departing from the usual regulatory mechanisms. Although statist analysts may deny their existence, senior Chinese elites clearly recognise many of the problems we have exposed, because they have tried to address them. In the South China Sea, for example, Xi Jinping has tried to curb internecine rivalry by creating the China Coastguard, while the new China International Development Cooperation Agency is intended to address the fragmented governance of Chinese development financing. However, the trouble is that even Xi has resorted to mechanisms of dubious efficacy. It seems that every instance of fragmentation is met with calls for a new coordinating body. Such institutions may operate well in a short-term crisis, such as the coronavirus pandemic, when top leaders are closely engaged (see the next section). However, when their attention is more diffused, as is more usually the case, they are often ineffective, typically lacking the authority to resolve conflicts decisively and impose clear, binding decisions on contending party-state apparatuses. Moreover, they often overlap with existing (and presumably failed) coordination bodies, potentially creating additional confusion and allowing opportunists to 'forum shop' for the best venue to advance their agendas. There seems to be real difficulty in fundamentally restructuring the Chinese party-state in a way that abolishes overlapping jurisdictions, establishes clear lines of authority, and creates detailed mandates and instructions. This arguably reflects the way that contending cadre-capitalist interests are managed within the sprawling party-state through endless bargaining and accommodation.[1] However, insofar as this is prioritised over genuine policy coherence, the problems highlighted in this book are likely to continue.

Postscript: State Transformation and COVID-19

As we were finalising this book in early 2020, the world was shaken by the coronavirus pandemic. As we finish this much-delayed conclusion in November 2020, COVID-19 has infected over 47 million people worldwide, killing more than 1.2 million, with no immediate end in sight. The lockdowns imposed by many governments to slow the virus's spread will cause even greater long-term damage. World output is US$6tr lower than expected; global trade and investment are down by 20 and 40 per cent respectively; 500 million jobs are at risk, with 90–120 million pushed into severe poverty; and government spending has increased massively as tax revenues fall, with US$13tr spent in the Group of 20 countries alone (UNCTAD 2020: i–v). All of this began with a disease that originated in China. What might this mean for our understanding of China's rise?

Clearly, the crisis has escalated two pre-existing tendencies: the dissipation of the US-led order and intensifying rivalry between major states. In the early stages of the pandemic, a panel of experts of the World Health Organization (WHO), tasked with evaluating the disease and deciding whether to announce a public health emergency of international concern, was deadlocked as the Chinese and American representatives traded barbs. According to the Australian panellist, rather than acting as dispassionate scientific experts, they represented their own governments' positions, paralysing the organisation and delaying the designation by over a week (Visontay 2020). Subsequently, President Trump lambasted the WHO for deferring to China, calling it the 'Chinese Health Organisation' and halting American funding for the institution, leaving Beijing – which pledged an additional US$2bn – as its biggest donor. The WHO was subsequently marginalised as global cooperation swiftly fragmented into distinctive, often 'zero-sum',

---

[1] For an argument that this explains Xi's failure to enact serious SOE reform, for example, see Zhang, Zhang and Liu (2017).

national efforts. Russia and China have developed their own vaccines, offering these to developing countries. China also engaged in 'mask diplomacy', offering ventilators and personal protective equipment to stricken nations – including some in Europe – while the Trump administration jealously hoarded resources.

However, moving beyond this traditional geopolitical, statist account, the state transformation approach can also shed considerable light on the coronavirus crisis. With few exceptions, Western states have dealt extremely badly with the virus, suffering high levels of death and colossal socio-economic setbacks. Arguably, this reflects their own transformation into regulatory states, which lack the capacity to mobilise the citizenry and organise the production and distribution of key goods and services (McCormack and Jones 2020; Jones and Hameiri 2021). In one sense, President Trump's attempts to blame Beijing for the impact of the 'Chinese virus' were simply an effort to displace this problem, as if the Chinese Communist Party could somehow be responsible for the hollowing out of the US state. In the short term, this has had some traction, with attitudes towards China worsening sharply in the USA and elsewhere. In the longer term, China's greater efficiency in suppressing COVID-19 may well attract some admiration, however grudging, among Western populations.

We can also see that state transformation shaped China's own response to COVID-19, demonstrating the continued utility of our framework. China has rightly been criticised for its sluggish response to the coronavirus outbreak and its limited cooperation with the WHO, which was clearly caused, in part, by the fragmentation and decentralisation of its pandemic preparedness and response system.

This was apparent in interagency rivalry between multiple scientific institutions, which delayed the release of critical information to the WHO. Already by 2 January 2020, the Wuhan-based Chinese Institute of Virology had sequenced the COVID-19 genome. However, on 3 January the National Health Commission instructed all laboratories to destroy their samples of the virus and forbade any publication of results without their approval. The national Centre for Disease Control and Prevention (CDCP) sequenced the genome on 3 January, followed on 5 January by the Chinese Academy of Medical Sciences and the Shanghai Public Clinical Health Center and, on 7 January, by another Wuhan University team. Yet, despite declaring an internal level-one emergency, the CDCP blocked its rival laboratories from releasing their results, and was only bounced into disclosing the genome sequence on 11 January after one team defied the gagging order and published its findings online. Insiders blamed the delay on 'fierce competition' for resources between researchers: the CDCP, seeking to take all the credit, had delayed publication to first verify its own results (Associated Press 2020). During the week-long delay, COVID-19 spread to Thailand.

For two additional weeks, China remained very slow in providing detailed information to the WHO (Associated Press 2020), which reflected the problems of decentralisation. Although China had created a sophisticated national alert system after the 2002–3 SARS outbreak, when local officials had covered up the virus, local officials were still able to subvert its operations in 2019–20 (Pei 2020). Officials in Wuhan and Hubei province again covered up the outbreak to limit its impact on the local economy and their own careers, including by threatening and silencing medical staff (McGregor 2020: 3; Palmer 2020). Moreover, the central institutions tasked with pandemic control lacked the authority to override the provincial executives, who out-ranked the leaders of the National Health Commission, which oversees the national CDCP (McGregor 2020: 4). As a result, when China's top leaders discussed the virus in December 2019, they apparently relied on local reporting that played down the outbreak. Consequently, through early January the central government continually reassured the WHO that the number of cases was very small, with no deaths or evidence of person-to-person transmission. This only changed on 20 January, when the outbreak's severity had become obvious, prompting the central government to lock down Wuhan and admit the existence of community transmission (Rauhala 2020).

The government's own documents openly blamed local officials' non-compliance with central policies for this poor initial response. In early February, Hubei's Commission for Discipline Inspection publicly lambasted local officials for 'Disobeying the unified command and control of epidemic prevention and control, refusing to execute the superiors arrangement [*sic*] . . . Fraud, concealment, misrepresentation, omission and delayed reporting', and engaging in useless 'bureaucratic formalism' (JQK News 2020; Xinhua 2020). Following the commission's threats of instant dismissal for offenders (and immediate promotion for those complying), several senior provincial officials were dismissed, and case reporting suddenly jumped tenfold (Yang and Mitchell 2020). This demonstrated the power of the Chinese-style regulatory state's steering mechanisms, particularly the party's own disciplinary institutions. Similarly, on 26 January, the government established a leading small group under Premier Li Keqiang to take charge of the pandemic situation. These measures apparently brought local officials into line and improved central coordination, shifting China's COVID-19 response from quadrant C to B in Figure 5.1. Its cooperation with the WHO improved rapidly and the party-state moved swiftly to contain the virus. By then, however, Beijing's international reputation was in tatters, and COVID-19 had already spread beyond China. This outcome clearly did not reflect central government intentions, but rather the operation of China's transformed party-state.

References

Note: Interviewees are listed in a separate section at the end. Long URLs have been shortened using Bit.ly.

Acharya, Amitav. 2006. 'Will Asia's Past Be Its Future?' *International Security* 28(3): 149–64.

Acharya, Amitav. 2011. 'Can Asia Lead? Power Ambitions and Global Governance in the Twenty-First Century.' *International Affairs* 87(4): 851–69.

Adam Smith International. 2015. *Institutional and Regulatory Assessment of the Extractive Industries in Myanmar*. Washington, DC: World Bank. https://bit.ly/2PFjiy7.

Agnew, John. 2009. *Globalization and Sovereignty*. Lanham, MD: Rowman & Littlefield.

Ahlers, Anna L., and Gunter Schubert. 2015. 'Effective Policy Implementation in China's Local State.' *Modern China* 41(4): 372–405.

Ahlers, Anna L., and Matthias Stepan. 2017. 'Top-Level Design and Local-Level Paralysis: Local Politics in Times of Political Centralisation.' In *China's Core Executive: Leadership Styles, Structures and Processes Under Xi Jinping*, edited by Sebastian Heilmann and Matthias Stepan, 34–9. Berlin: MERICS.

AidData. n.d. 'China's Global Development Footprint.' AidData: A Research Lab at William and Mary. www.aiddata.org/china.

Aldecoa, Francisco, and Michael Keating, eds. 1999. *Paradiplomacy in Action: The Foreign Relations of Subnational Governments*. London: Frank Cass.

Alden, Chris, and Amnon Aran. 2012. *Foreign Policy Analysis: New Approaches*. London: Routledge.

Andrews-Speed, Philip. 2010. *The Institutions of Energy Governance in China*. Paris: Institut Français des Relations Internationales. https://bit.ly/2Oi0On8.

Ang, Yuen Yuen. 2016. *How China Escaped the Poverty Trap*. Ithaca, NY: Cornell University Press.

Ansell, Chris. 2000. 'The Networked Polity: Regional Development in Western Europe.' *Governance* 13(2): 279–91.

Arase, David. 2010. 'Non-Traditional Security in China-ASEAN Cooperation: The Institutionalization of Regional Security Cooperation and the Evolution of East Asian Regionalism.' *Asian Survey* 50(4): 808–33.

Aroonpipat, Sunida. 2017. 'Governing Aid from China through Embedded Informality: Institutional Response to Chinese Development Aid in Laos.' *China Information* 32(1): 46–68.

Arrighi, Giovanni. 2007. *Adam Smith in Beijing: Lineages of the Twenty-First Century*. London: Verso.

ASEAN Secretariat. 2017. 'ASEANstats Database.' http://aseanstats.asean.org.

Associated Press. 2020. 'China Delayed Releasing Coronavirus Info, Frustrating WHO.' *AP News*, 3 June. https://apnews.com/3c061794970 661042b18d5aeaaed9fae.

Auslin, Michael R. 2013. 'Japan's Response to the Rise of China: Back to the Future?' In *The Rise of China: Essays on the Future Competition*, edited by Gary J. Schmitt, 73–90. New York: Encounter Books.

Bader, Julia. 2015a. 'China, Autocratic Patron? An Empirical Investigation of China as a Factor in Autocratic Survival.' *International Studies Quarterly* 59(1): 23–33.

Bader, Julia. 2015b. 'The Political Economy of External Exploitation. A Comparative Investigation of China's Foreign Relations.' *Democratization* 22(1): 1–21.

Baird, Ian G. 2011. 'Turning Land into Capital, Turning People into Labour: Primitive Accumulation and the Arrival of Large-Scale Economic Land Concessions in Laos.' *New Proposals* 5(1): 10–26.

Baird, Ian G. 2016. 'Non-Government Organizations, Villagers, Political Culture and the Lower Sesan 2 Dam in Northeastern Cambodia.' *Critical Asian Studies* 48(2): 257–77.

BANCA [Biodiversity and Nature Conservation Association]. 2009. *Environmental Impact Assessment (Special Investigation) on Hydropower Development of Ayeyawady River Basin above Myitkyina, Kachin State, Myanmar*. October. Yangon. https://bit.ly/3l3rvb8.

Banktrack. 2016. 'Lower Sesan 2 Dam, Cambodia.' www.banktrack.org/ project/lower_sesan_2_dam.

Barboza, David. 2012. 'Family of Wen Jiabao Holds a Hidden Fortune in China.' *New York Times*, 25 October. https://nyti.ms/3qyiBDF.

Barney, Keith. 2009. 'Laos and the Making of a "Relational" Resource Frontier.' *The Geographical Journal* 175(2): 146–59.

Beban, Alice, Sokbunthoeun So, and Kheang Un. 2017. 'From Force to Legitimation: Rethinking Land Grabs in Cambodia.' *Development and Change* 48(3): 590–612.

Beckman, Robert, Clive Schofield, Ian Townsend-Gault, Tara Davenport, and Leonardo Bernard. 2013. 'Factors Conducive to Joint Development in Asia: Lessons Learned for the South China Sea.' In *Beyond Territorial Disputes in the South China Sea: Legal Frameworks for the Joint Development of Hydrocarbon Resources*, edited by Robert Beckman, Clive Schofield, Ian Townsend-Gault, Tara Davenport, and Leonardo Bernard, 411–41. Cheltenham: Edward Elgar.

Beeson, Mark, and Fujian Li. 2016. 'China's Place in Regional and Global Governance: A New World Comes into View.' *Global Policy* 7(4): 491–9.

BenYishai, Ariel, Bradley C. Parks, Daniel Runfola, and Rachel Trichler. 2016. *Forest Cover Impacts of Chinese Development Projects in Ecologically Sensitive Areas*. Working Paper 32. AidData, College of William and Mary. https://bit.ly/3rD2nKL.

BEWG [Burma Environmental Working Group]. 2017. *Resource Federalism: A Roadmap for Decentralised Governance of Burma's Natural Heritage*. https://bit.ly/38tTNGy.

Bhattacharya, Abanti. 2016. 'Conceptualizing the Silk Road Initiative in China's Periphery Policy.' *East Asia* 33(4): 309–28.

Bickford, Thomas J., Heidi A. Holz, and Frederic Velluci. 2011. *Uncertain Waters: Thinking About China's Emergence as a Maritime Power*. Arlington, VA: Center for Naval Analyses.

Biddulph, Robin. 2014. 'Can Elite Corruption Be a Legitimate Machiavellian Tool in an Unruly World? The Case of Post-Conflict Cambodia.' *Third World Quarterly* 35(5): 872–87.

Bissinger, Jared. 2012. 'Foreign Investment in Myanmar: A Resource Boom but a Development Bust?' *Contemporary Southeast Asia* 34(1): 23–52.

Blomberg, Matt, and Ana Phann. 2014. 'Sesan II Reservoir a Laundry for Illegal Timber.' *Cambodia Daily*, 6 June. https://bit.ly/3t3Iv3K.

Bloomberg. 2012a. 'China's Billionaire Congress Makes its US Peer Look Poor.' *Bloomberg*, 27 February. https://bloom.bg/3cb7F9G.

Bloomberg. 2012b. 'Xi Jinping Millionaire Relations Reveal Fortunes of Elite.' *Bloomberg*, 29 June. https://bloom.bg/38qo4WV.

Borras, Saturnino M., and Jennifer C. Franco. 2013. 'Global Land Grabbing and Political Reactions "From Below."' *Third World Quarterly* 34(9): 1723–47.

Bosshard, Peter. 2009. 'China Dams the World.' *World Policy Journal* 26(4): 43–51.

Branigan, Tania. 2011. 'Chinese Arms Companies "Offered to Sell Weapons to Gaddafi Regime."' *Guardian*, 5 September. https://bit.ly/3uKyZDn.

Brans, Marleen, and Gianluca Ferraro. 2012. 'International Agreements and the Salience of Domestic Politics: Locus, Focus and Gradus. The Case of

Fisheries Policy Reforms in China and Senegal.' *Journal of Comparative Policy Analysis: Research and Practice* 14(1): 9–25.

Bräutigam, Deborah. 2009. *The Dragon's Gift: The Real Story of China in Africa*. Oxford: Oxford University Press.

Bräutigam, Deborah. 2011. 'Aid "With Chinese Characteristics": Chinese Foreign Aid and Development Finance Meet the OECD-DAC Aid Regime.' *Journal of International Development* 23(5): 752–64.

Bräutigam, Deborah. 2020. 'A Critical Look at Chinese "Debt-Trap Diplomacy": The Rise of a Meme.' *Area Development and Policy* 5(1): 1–14.

Brehm, Stefan, and Christian Macht. 2004. 'Banking Supervision in China: Basel I, Basel II and the Basel Core Principles.' *Zeitschrift Für Chinesisches Recht* 4: 316–27.

Brenner, David. 2015. 'Ashes of Co-Optation: From Armed Group Fragmentation to the Rebuilding of Popular Insurgency in Myanmar.' *Conflict, Security & Development* 15(4): 337–58.

Brenner, Neil. 2004. *New State Spaces: Urban Governance and the Rescaling of Statehood*. Oxford: Oxford University Press.

Breslin, Shaun. 2009. 'Understanding China's Regional Rise: Interpretations, Identities and Implications.' *International Affairs* 85(4): 817–35.

Breslin, Shaun. 2013. 'China and the Global Order: Signalling Threat or Friendship?' *International Affairs* 89(3): 615–34.

Brickell, Katherine. 2014. '"The Whole World Is Watching": Intimate Geopolitics of Forced Eviction and Women's Activism in Cambodia.' *Annals of the Association of American Geographers* 104(6): 1256–72.

Brighi, Elisabetta, and Christopher Hill. 2012. 'Implementation and Behaviour.' In *Foreign Policy: Theories, Actors, Cases*, edited by Steve Smith, Amelia Hadfield, and Tim Dunne, 147–67. Oxford: Oxford University Press.

Brødsgaard, Kjeld E. 2009. *Hainan: State, Society, and Business in a Chinese Province*. London: Routledge.

Brown, Kerry. 2018. *The World According to Xi: Everything You Need to Know About the New China*. London: IB Tauris.

Buchanan, John, Tom Kramer, and Kevin Woods. 2013. *Developing Disparity: Regional Investment in Burma's Borderlands*. Amsterdam: Transnational Institute.

Bunge, Mario. 1997. 'Mechanism and Explanation.' *Philosophy of the Social Sciences* 27(4): 410–65.

Burgos, Sigfrido, and Sophal Ear. 2010. 'China's Strategic Interests in Cambodia: Influence and Resources.' *Asian Survey* 50(3): 615–39.

Burke, Adam, Nicola Williams, Kim Joliffe, and Thomas Carr. 2017. *The Contested Areas of Myanmar: Subnational Conflict, Aid, and Development*. San Francisco: Asia Foundation. https://bit.ly/3g17u4y.

Burke, Jason, and Tania Branigan. 2014. 'India–China Border Standoff Highlights Tensions before Xi Visit.' *Guardian*, 17 September. https://bit.ly/329Fsvt.

Burma Rivers Network. 2007. *Open Letter to the People's Republic of China on the Influx of Chinese Dam Building Companies to Burma/Myanmar.* https://bit.ly/3tf9h9U.

Buzan, Barry. 2010. 'China in International Society: Is "Peaceful Rise" Possible?' *The Chinese Journal of International Politics* 3: 5–36.

Buzan, Barry, and George Lawson. 2015. *The Global Transformation: History, Modernity and the Making of International Relations.* Cambridge: Cambridge University Press.

Buzan, Barry, and Ole Wæver. 2003. *Regions and Powers: The Structure of International Security.* Cambridge: Cambridge University Press.

Cabestan, Jean-Pierre. 2009. 'China's Foreign- and Security-Policy Decision-Making Processes under Hu Jintao.' *Journal of Current Chinese Affairs* 38 (3): 63–97.

CAITEC [Chinese Academy of International Trade and Economic Cooperation], SASAC [Research Centre of the State-owned Assets Supervision and Administration Commission], and UNDP [United Nations Development Programme] China. 2017. *2017 Report on the Sustainable Development of Chinese Enterprises Overseas: Supporting the Belt and Road Regions to Achieve the 2030 Agenda for Sustainable Development.* Beijing: Ministry of Commerce. https://bit.ly/3e0hl7Y.

Callahan, Mary P. 2007. *Political Authority in Burma's Ethnic Minority States: Devolution, Occupation and Coexistence.* Washington, DC: East-West Center.

Callinicos, Alex. 2009. *Imperialism and Global Political Economy.* Cambridge: Polity.

Cammack, Paul. 1989. 'Bringing the State Back In?' *British Journal of Political Science* 19(2): 261–90.

Campbell, Kurt. 2014. 'Trouble at Sea Reveals the New Shape of China's Foreign Policy.' *Financial Times*, 22 July. https://on.ft.com/3mNZFk1.

Cardenal, Juan Pablo, and Heriberto Araújo. 2013. *China's Silent Army: The Pioneers, Traders, Fixers and Workers Who Are Remaking the World in Beijing's Image.* Translated by Catherine Mansfield. New York: Crown Publishers.

Carlson, Allen. 2008. *Unifying China, Integrating with the World: Securing Chinese Sovereignty in the Reform Era.* Singapore: National University of Singapore Press.

Carr, Thomas. 2018. *Supporting the Transition: Understanding Aid to Myanmar since 2011.* February. The Asia Foundation. https://bit.ly/2PXHXP3.

CDC [Council for the Development of Cambodia]. n.d. 'FDI Trend.' *Council for the Development of Cambodia*. https://bit.ly/3wQK2Nl.

CDC. 2018. 'The Cambodia ODA Database: Reporting Year 2018.' Cambodian Rehabilitation and Development Board, Council for the Development of Cambodia. http://odacambodia.com/Reports/reports_by_Donor.asp.

CECIC [Chinese Export and Credit Insurance Corporation/ Sinosure]. 2005. 国家风险分析报告 *[The Handbook of Country Risk]*. Beijing: China Financial and Economic Publishing House.

Central Commission for Discipline Inspection. 2015a. '中央第五巡视组向国家电投反馈专项巡视情况 [Fifth Central Inspection Team Gives Feedback to State Power Investment Corporation].' 16 June. https://bit.ly/2PPURi9.

Central Commission for Discipline Inspection. 2015b. '国家电力投资集团公司党组关于巡视整改情况的通报 [Notification of Inspection and Rectification Result for State Power Investment Group Company Party].' 15 September. www.ccdi.gov.cn/yw/201509/t20150915_61936.html.

Cerny, Philip G. 1997. 'Paradoxes of the Competition State: The Dynamics of Political Globalization.' *Government and Opposition* 32(2): 251–74.

Cerny, Philip G. 2010. *Rethinking World Politics: A Theory of Transnational Neopluralism*. Oxford: Oxford University Press.

Chambers, Paul W. 2015. '"Neo-Sultanistic Tendencies": The Trajectory of Civil–Military Relations in Cambodia.' *Asian Security* 11(3): 179–205.

Chan, Chris King-Chi, and Elaine Sio-Ieng Hui. 2017. 'Bringing Class Struggles Back: A Marxian Analysis of the State and Class Relations in China.' *Globalizations* 14(2): 232–44.

Chan, Debby Sze Wan. 2017. 'Asymmetric Bargaining Between Myanmar and China in the Myitsone Dam Controversy: Social Opposition Akin to David's Stone Against Goliath.' *Pacific Review* 30(5): 674–91.

Chan Mya Htwe. 2018. '2017–18 Debt Report Submitted to Pyidaungsu Hluttaw.' *Myanmar Times*, 30 November. https://bit.ly/2RlEPg7.

Chanthy, Sam, and Clemens M. Grünbühel. 2015. 'Critical Challenges to Consultants in Pursuing Quality of Environmental and Social Impact Assessments (ESIA) in Cambodia.' *Impact Assessment and Project Appraisal* 33(3): 226–32.

Chellaney, Brahma. 2017. 'China's Debt-Trap Diplomacy.' *Strategist*, 24 January. www.aspistrategist.org.au/chinas-debt-trap-diplomacy/.

Chen, Dingding, and Jianwei Wang. 2011. 'Lying Low No More? China's New Thinking on the Tao Guang Yang Hui Strategy.' *China: An International Journal* 9(2): 195–216.

Chen, Huafang, Zhuang-Fang Yi, Dietrich Schmidt-Vogt, Antje Ahrends, Philip Beckschäfer, Christoph Kleinn, Sailesh Ranjitkar, and Jianchu Xu. 2016. 'Pushing the Limits: The Pattern and Dynamics of Rubber

Monoculture Expansion in Xishuangbanna, SW China.' *PLOS One* 11(2): e0150062.

Chen, Jie, and Bruce J. Dickson. 2010. *Allies of the State: China's Private Entrepreneurs and Democratic Change.* Cambridge, MA: Harvard University Press.

Chen, Juan. 2017. 'China's Environment Ministry Names and Shames Local Governments, Enterprises Violating Overcapacity Reduction Targets.' *Yicai Global,* 28 December. www.yicaiglobal.com/node/41112.

Chen, Shaofeng. 2009. 'Marketization and China's Energy Security.' *Policy and Society* 27(3): 249–60.

Chen, Wei. 2011. 'Status and Challenges of Chinese Deepwater Oil and Gas Development.' *Petroleum Science* 8(4): 477–84.

Chen, Yue. 2018. 'Welcome Remarks.' Fourth International Workshop on Cooperation and Development in the South China Sea, 27 March. Beijing.

Chen, Zheng. 2016. 'China Debates the Non-Interference Principle.' *Chinese Journal of International Politics* 9(3): 349–74.

Chen, Zhimin. 2005. 'Coastal Provinces and China's Foreign Policy Making.' In *China's Foreign Policy Making: Societal Force and Chinese American Policy,* edited by Yufan Hao and Lin Su, 187–208. Aldershot: Ashgate.

Chen, Zhimin, and Junbo Jian. 2009. *Chinese Provinces as Foreign Policy Actors in Africa.* Occasional Paper 22. Johannesburg: South African Institute of International Affairs.

Chen, Zhimin, Junbo Jian, and Diyu Chen. 2010. 'The Provinces and China's Multi-Layered Diplomacy: The Cases of GMS and Africa.' *The Hague Journal of Diplomacy* 5(4): 331–356.

Cheng, Shuaihua, Ting Fang, and Hui-Ting Lien. 2012. *China's International Aid Policy and Its Implications for Global Governance.* Bloomington, IN: Indiana University Research Centre for Chinese Politics and Business.

Cheung, Peter T. Y., and James T. H. Tang. 2001. 'The External Relations of China's Provinces.' In *The Making of Chinese Foreign and Security Policy in the Era of Reform, 1978–2000,* edited by David M. Lampton. eBook edition. Stanford, CA: Stanford University Press.

Cheung, Tai Ming. 2015. 'The Riddle in the Middle: China's Central Military Commission in the Twenty-First Century.' In *PLA Influence on China's National Security Policymaking,* edited by Phillip C. Saunders, and Andrew Scobell. eBook edition. Stanford, CA: Stanford University Press.

Chhom, Theavy. n.d. *Resettlement from a Village Perspective: Understanding Hydropower Governance from the Ground Up.* Unpublished Report. Phnom Penh: Cambodia Development Resource Institute.

Chin, Gregory. 2016. 'Asian Infrastructure Investment Bank: Governance Innovation and Prospects.' *Global Governance* 22(1): 11–25.

Chin, Gregory, and Eric Helleiner. 2008. 'China as a Creditor: A Rising Financial Power?' *Journal of International Affairs* 62(1): 87–102.

Chin, Gregory T. 2016. 'Asian Infrastructure Investment Bank: Governance Innovation and Prospects.' *Global Governance* 22(1): 11–25.

Chin, Ko-lin, and Sheldon X. Zhang. 2015. *The Chinese Heroin Trade: Cross-Border Drug Trafficking in Southeast Asia and Beyond.* New York: New York University Press.

China Anti-Narcotics Network. 2015. '国家禁毒委成员单位 [Members of the National Narcotics Control Commission].' 24 April. www.nncc626.com/2015-04/24/c_127728721.htm.

Christensen, Thomas J. 2013. 'More Actors, Less Coordination? New Challenges for the Leaders of a Rising China.' In *China's Foreign Policy: Who Makes It, and How Is It Made?*, edited by Gil Rozman, 21–37. New York: Palgrave Macmillan.

Chubb, Andrew. 2019. 'Xi Jinping and China's Maritime Policy.' *Brookings*, 22 January. https://brook.gs/32brjxO.

Chung, Chien-peng. 2004. *Domestic Politics, International Bargaining and China's Territorial Disputes.* eBook edition. London: Routledge Curzon.

Chung, Christopher. 2004. 'The Spratly Islands Dispute: Decision Units and Domestic Politics.' PhD Thesis. Canberra: University of New South Wales, Australian Defence Force Academy.

Ciorciari, John D. 2015. 'A Chinese Model for Patron–Client Relations? The Sino-Cambodian Partnership.' *International Relations of the Asia-Pacific* 15(2): 245–78.

Clarke, Ryan. 2008. 'Narcotics Trafficking in China: Size, Scale, Dynamic and Future Consequences.' *Pacific Affairs* 81(1): 73–93.

Clegg, Jenny. 2009. *China's Global Strategy: Towards a Multipolar World.* London: Pluto Press.

Coats, Dan. 2020. 'There's No Cold War with China – and If There Were, We Couldn't Win.' *Washington Post*, 29 July. https://wapo.st/3e2sxkD.

Cock, Andrew Robert. 2010. 'External Actors and the Relative Autonomy of the Ruling Elite in Post-UNTAC Cambodia.' *Journal of Southeast Asian Studies* 41(2): 241–65.

Cock, Andrew Robert. 2011. 'The Rise of Provincial Business in Cambodia.' In *Cambodia's Economic Transformation*, edited by Caroline Hughes and Kheang Un, 27–49. Copenhagen: NIAS Press.

Coen, David, and Tom Pegram. 2018. 'Towards a Third Generation of Global Governance Scholarship.' *Global Policy* 9(1): 107–13.

Cohen, Paul T. 2009. 'The Post-Opium Scenario and Rubber in Northern Laos: Alternative Western and Chinese Models of Development.' *International Journal of Drug Policy* 20(5): 424–30.

Cohen, Paul T. 2013. 'Symbolic Dimensions of the Anti-Opium Campaign in Laos.' *Australian Journal of Anthropology* 24(2): 177–92.

Collins, Neil, and Jörn-Carsten Gottwald. 2011. 'The Chinese Model of the Regulatory State.' In *Handbook on the Politics of Regulation*, edited by David Levi-Faur, 142–55. Cheltenham: Edward Elgar.

Cooper, Andrew F., and Daniel Flemes. 2013. 'Foreign Policy Strategies of Emerging Powers in a Multipolar World: An Introductory Review.' *Third World Quarterly* 34(6): 943–62.

Copper, John F. 1975. 'China's Foreign Aid Program: An Analysis of an Instrument of Peking's Foreign Policy.' PhD Dissertation, University of South Carolina.

Copper, John F. 2016a. *China's Foreign Aid and Investment Diplomacy, Volume I: Nature, Scope and Origins*. Basingstoke: Palgrave Macmillan.

Copper, John F. 2016b. *China's Foreign Aid and Investment Diplomacy, Volume II: History and Practice in Asia, 1950–Present*. Basingstoke: Palgrave Macmillan.

Copper, John F. 2016c. *China's Foreign Aid and Investment Diplomacy, Volume III: Strategy Beyond Asia and Challenges to the United States and the International Order*. Basingstoke: Palgrave Macmillan.

Corkin, Lucy. 2011. 'Redefining Foreign Policy Impulses toward Africa: The Roles of the MFA, the MOFCOM and China Exim Bank.' *Journal of Current Chinese Affairs* 40(4): 61–90.

Cornago, Noé. 1999. 'Diplomacy and Paradiplomacy in the Redefinition of International Security: Dimensions of Conflict and Co-operation.' *Regional & Federal Studies* 9(1): 40–57.

CPI [China Power International]. 2009. '2009 年度大事记 [2009 Events].' www.cpicorp.com.cn/nddsj/201010/t20101028_127126.htm.

CPI. 2010. '2010 年度大事记 [2010 Events].' www.spic.com.cn/nddsj/2011 11/t20111124_165184.htm.

Creak, Simon, and Keith Barney. 2018. 'Conceptualising Party-State Governance and Rule in Laos.' *Journal of Contemporary Asia* 48(5): 693–716.

Cronin, Richard P. 2013. 'Hydropower Dams on the Mekong: Old Dreams, New Dangers.' *Asia Policy* 16(1): 32–8.

Cronin, Richard, and Zachary Dubel. 2013. *Maritime Security in East Asia: Boundary Disputes, Resources, and the Future of Regional Stability*. Washington DC: Stimson Center. https://bit.ly/2PR4cX3.

CSIS [Center for Strategic and International Studies]. 2019. 'South China Sea Incident Tracker.' Accessed 3 October. https://csis-ilab.github.io/cpower-viz/csis-china-sea/.

Daekwon, Son. 2018. 'I Visited the Chinese-North Korean Border. Here's What I Found.' *National Interest*, 3 October. https://bit.ly/3wOVwkl.

Dahles, Heidi. 2013. 'Why China Charms Cambodia.' *East Asia Forum*, 24 August. https://bit.ly/32asX2O.

Dapice, David. 2015. *Hydropower in Myanmar: Moving Electricity Contracts from Colonial to Commercial*. Cambridge, MA: Ash Center, Harvard Kennedy School. https://bit.ly/3wUE9i3.

de Haan, Arjan. 2011. 'Will China Change International Development as We Know It?' *Journal of International Development* 23(7): 881–908.

Denyer, Simon. 2016. 'How China's Fishermen Are Fighting a Covert War in the South China Sea.' *Washington Post*, 12 April. https://wapo.st/2OPIxOo.

DfID [Department for International Development]. 2017. *Department for International Development Annual Report and Accounts 2016–17*. London: DfID. https://bit.ly/3wPuyJx.

DICA [Myanmar Directorate of Investment and Company Administration]. 2019. *Yearly Approved Amount of Foreign Investment (By Country)*. Naypyidaw. https://bit.ly/3wQPFLt.

Dickson, Bruce J. 2003. *Red Capitalists in China: The Party, Private Entrepreneurs, and Prospects for Political Change*. Cambridge: Cambridge University Press.

Dickson, Bruce J. 2008. *Wealth into Power: The Communist Party's Embrace of China's Private Sector*. Cambridge: Cambridge University Press.

Ding, Shu Yong. 2016. '云南警方5年缴毒近百吨 [Yunnan Police Seized Nearly 100 Tons of Drugs in Five Years].' *Ta Kung Pao*, June 20. https://bit.ly/3tftFI0.

Ding, Shufan. 2003. '一九九〇年代以來的中國黨軍關係 [China's Party–Military Relations Since the 1990s].' *Mainland China Studies* 46(2): 57–80.

Donaldson, John. 2010. 'Provinces: Paradoxical Politics, Problematic Partners.' In *China's Local Administration: Traditions and Changes in the Sub-National Hierarchy*, edited by Jae Ho Chung and Tao-chiu Lam, 14–38. Abingdon: Routledge.

Dong, Jiawei. 2018. '中国海洋执法体制重构路径探析 [Analysis of the Path of China's Maritime Law Enforcement System Reconstruction].' 公安海警学院学报 *[Journal of China Maritime Police Academy]* 17(1): 8–16.

Doran, D. 2014. 'Hydropower in Myanmar: Sector Analysis and Related Legal Reforms.' *The International Journal on Hydropower & Dams* 21(3): 87.

Downs, Erica S. 2008. 'Business Interest Groups in Chinese Politics: The Case of the Oil Companies.' In *China's Changing Political Landscape:*

Prospects for Democracy, edited by Cheng Li, 121–41. Washington, DC: Brookings Institution Press.

Downs, Erica S. 2014. 'Business and Politics in the South China Sea: Explaining HYSY 981's Foray into Disputed Waters.' *China Brief* XIV(12): 6–8.

Dreher, Axel, Andreas Fuchs, Roland Hodler, Bradley C. Parks, Paul A. Raschky, and Michael J. Tierney. 2014. *Aid on Demand: African Leaders and the Geography of China's Foreign Assistance*. AidData Working Paper 3, 1 November. Williamsburg, VA: College of William and Mary. https://bit.ly/3uLUUua.

Dreher, Axel, Andreas Fuchs, Bradley C. Parks, Austin M. Strange, and Michael J. Tierney. 2016. *Apples and Dragon Fruits: The Determinants of Aid and Other Forms of State Financing from China to Africa*. Department of Economics Discussion Paper 620. Heidelberg: University of Heidelberg. https://papers.ssrn.com/sol3/papers.cfm?abstract_id=2855935.

Dreher, Axel, Andreas Fuchs, Bradley Parks, Austin M. Strange, and Michael J. Tierney. 2017. *Aid, China, and Growth: Evidence from a New Global Development Finance Dataset*. AidData Working Paper 46. Williamsburg, VA: College of William and Mary. http://docs.aiddata.org/ad4/pdfs/WP S46_Aid_China_and_Growth.pdf.

Duchâtel, Mathieu, Oliver Bräuner, and Zhou Hang. 2014. *Protecting China's Overseas Interests: The Slow Shift Away from Non-Interference*. Stockholm: SIPRI.

Dwyer, Michael, and Thoumthone Vongvisouk. 2019. 'The Long Land Grab: Market-Assisted Enclosure on the China–Lao Rubber Frontier.' *Territory, Politics, Governance* 7(1): 96–114.

Ear, Sophal. 2011. 'Growth in the Rice and Garment Sectors.' In *Cambodia's Economic Transformation*, edited by Caroline Hughes and Kheang Un, 70–93. Copenhagen: NIAS Press.

Economist. 2018. 'Party Time.' *The Economist*, 15 March. https://econ.st /3dfBibC.

Economy, Elizabeth. 2001. 'The Impact of International Regimes on Chinese Foreign Policy-Making: Broadening Perspectives and Policies ... But Only to a Point.' In *The Making of Chinese Foreign and Security Policy in the Era of Reform, 1978–2000*, edited by David M. Lampton. eBook edition. Stanford, CA: Stanford University Press.

Economy, Elizabeth C. 2018. *The Third Revolution: Xi Jinping and the New Chinese State*. Oxford: Oxford University Press.

Economy, Elizabeth, and Michael A. Levy. 2014. *By All Means Necessary: How China's Resource Quest Is Changing the World*. New York: Oxford University Press.

Egreteau, Renaud. 2008. 'India and China Vying for Influence in Burma: A New Assessment.' *India Review* 7(1): 38–72.

Egreteau, Renaud, and Larry Jagan. 2013. *Soldiers and Diplomacy in Burma: Understanding the Foreign Relations of the Burmese Praetorian State*. Singapore: National University of Singapore Press.

Electricity Authority of Cambodia. 2018. *Report on Power Sector of the Kingdom of Cambodia Compiled by the Electricity Authority of Cambodia from Data for the Year 2017*. Phnom Penh: Electricity Authority of Cambodia. www.eac.gov.kh/site/annualreport?lang=en.

Energy Tribune. 2006. 'PetroVietnam in Beijing.' *GlobalSecurity.org*, 13 September. https://bit.ly/3uJCV7u.

Erickson, Andrew, and Conor M. Kennedy. 2015. 'China's Daring Vanguard: Introducing Sanya City's Maritime Militia.' Center for International Maritime Security, 5 November. https://bit.ly/3uSEqR3.

Erickson, Andrew S., and Ryan D. Martinson. 2019. 'Introduction. "War Without Gun Smoke": China's Paranaval Challenge in the Maritime Gray Zone.' In *China's Maritime Gray Zone Operations*, edited by Andrew S. Erickson and Ryan D. Martinson, 1–11. Washington, DC: Naval Institute Press.

Erickson, Andrew S., and Austin M. Strange. 2014. 'Ripples of Change in Chinese Foreign Policy? Evidence from Recent Approaches to Nontraditional Waterborne Security.' *Asia Policy* 17: 93–126.

Etzioni, Amitai, and G. John Ikenberry. 2011. 'Point of Order: Is China More Westphalian than the West?' *Foreign Affairs* 90(6): 172–5.

Fallon, Theresa. 2015. 'The New Silk Road: Xi Jinping's Grand Strategy for Eurasia.' *American Foreign Policy Interests* 37(3): 140–7.

Fan, Gang. 2000. '论体制转轨的动态过程——非国有部门的成长与国有部门的改革 [On the Dynamic Process of Institutional Transition: The Growth of Non-State Sector and the Reform of State Sector].' 经济研究 *[Economic Research]* 2000(1): 11–21.

Fang, Songying, Xiaojun Li, and Fanglu Sun. 2018. 'China's Evolving Motivations and Goals in UN Peacekeeping Participation.' *International Journal* 73(3): 464–73.

Feng, Chongyi, and David S. G. Goodman. 1998. 'Hainan Province in Reform: Political Dependence and Economic Interdependence.' In *Provincial Strategies of Economic Reform in Post-Mao China: Leadership, Politics and Implementation*, edited by Peter T. Y. Cheung, Jae Ho Chung, and Zhimin Lin, 342–71. Armonk: ME Sharpe.

Feng, Emily. 2017. 'China Tightens Rules on State Groups' Foreign Investments.' *Financial Times*, 3 August. www.ft.com/content/3251987c-7806-11e7-90c0-90a9d1bc9691.

Ferraro, Gianluca. 2014. *International Regimes in China: Domestic Implementation of the International Fisheries Agreements*. Abingdon: Routledge.

Fingar, Thomas. 1987. 'Implementing Energy Policy: The Rise and Demise of the State Energy Commission.' In *Policy Implementation in Post-Mao China*, edited by David M. Lampton, 190–224. Berkeley, CA: University of California Press.

Fishman, Ted. 2005. *China, Inc.: How the Rise of the Next Superpower Challenges America and the World*. New York: Simon and Schuster.

Flemes, Daniel. 2013. 'Network Powers: Strategies of Change in the Multipolar System.' *Third World Quarterly* 34(6): 1016–36.

Foot, Rosemary, ed. 2013. *China Across the Divide: The Domestic and Global in Politics and Society*. New York: Oxford University Press.

Foot, Rosemary. 2014. 'Constraints on Conflict in the Asia-Pacific.' *Political Science* 66(2): 119–42.

Foran, Tira, Laur Kiik, Sullivan Hatt, David Fullbrook, Alice Dawkins, Simon Walker, and Yun Chen. 2017. 'Large Hydropower and Legitimacy: A Policy Regime Analysis, Applied to Myanmar.' *Energy Policy* 110: 619–30.

Forest Trends. 2015. *Conversion Timber, Forest Monitoring, and Land-Use Governance in Cambodia*. Washington, DC: Forest Trends. https://bit.ly/3s9zZzv.

Fox, Rohan, and Matthew Dornan. 2018. 'China in the Pacific: Is China Engaged in "Debt-Trap Diplomacy"?' DevPolicy Blog, 7 November. https://bit.ly/3mMuUvJ.

Fravel, M. Taylor. 2015. 'The PLA and National Security Decisionmaking: Insights from China's Territorial and Maritime Disputes.' In *PLA Influence on China's National Security Policymaking*, edited by Phillip C. Saunders and Andrew Scobell. eBook edition. Stanford, CA: Stanford University Press.

Fravel, M. Taylor, and Alexander Liebman. 2011. 'Beyond the Moat: The PLAN's Evolving Interests and Potential Influence.' In *The Chinese Navy: Expanding Capabilities, Evolving Roles*, edited by Phillip C. Saunders, Christopher D. Yung, Michael D. Swaine, and Andrew N. D. Yang, 41–80. Washington, DC: National Defense University Press.

Fravel, M. Taylor, J. Stapleton Roy, Michael D. Swaine, Susan A. Thornton, and Ezra Vogel. 2019. 'China Is Not an Enemy.' *Washington Post*, 3 June. https://wapo.st/3wSaDcP.

Freeman, Carla, and Drew Thompson. 2011. *China on the Edge: China's Border Provinces and Chinese Security Policy*. Baltimore, MD: Center for the National Interest. https://bit.ly/3g7eNrp.

Friedberg, Aaron L. 1993. 'Ripe for Rivalry: Prospects for Peace in a Multipolar Asia.' *International Security* 18(3): 5–33.

Friedberg, Aaron L. 2005. 'The Future of US–China Relations: Is Conflict Inevitable?' *International Security* 30(2): 7–45.

Friedberg, Aaron L. 2018. 'Competing with China.' *Survival* 60(3): 7–64.

Gallagher, Kevin P., Rohini Kamal, Junda Jin, Yanning Chen, and Xinyue Ma. 2018. 'Energizing Development Finance? The Benefits and Risks of China's Development Finance in the Global Energy Sector.' *Energy Policy* 122: 313–21.

Garnaut, John. 2019. 'Engineers of the Soul: Ideology in Xi Jinping's China by John Garnaut.' *Sinocism*, 19 January. https://sinocism.com/p/engin eers-of-the-soul-ideology-in.

Garver, John W. 1992. 'China's Push through the South China Sea: The Interaction of Bureaucratic and National Interests.' *China Quarterly* 132: 999–1028.

Ghiselli, Andrea. 2015. 'The Chinese People's Liberation Army "Post-Modern" Navy.' *International Spectator* 50(1): 117–36.

Ghiselli, Andrea. 2018. 'Diplomatic Opportunities and Rising Threats: The Expanding Role of Non-Traditional Security in Chinese Foreign and Security Policy.' *Journal of Contemporary China* 27(112): 611–25.

Ghiselli, Andrea. 2021. *Protecting China's Interests Overseas: Securitization and Foreign Policy*. Oxford: Oxford University Press.

Gill, Bates, and James Reilly. 2007. 'The Tenuous Hold of China Inc. in Africa.' *Washington Quarterly* 30(3): 37–52.

Gilpin, Robert. 1981. *War and Change in the International System*. Princeton, NJ: Princeton University Press.

Ginsburg, Tom. 2010. 'Eastphalia as the Perfection of Westphalia.' *Indiana Journal of Global Legal Studies* 17(1): 27–45.

Glaser, Bonnie S., and Matthew P. Funaiole. 2019. 'South China Sea: Assessing Chinese Paranaval Behaviour within the Nine-Dash Line.' In *China's Maritime Gray Zone Operations*, edited by Andrew S. Erickson and Ryan D. Martinson, 189–206. Washington, DC: Naval Institute Press.

Global Witness. 2016. *Hostile Takeover: The Corporate Empire of Cambodia's Ruling Family*. London: Global Witness.

Goh, Evelyn. 2013. *The Struggle for Order: Hegemony, Hierarchy, and Transition in Post-Cold War East Asia*. Oxford: Oxford University Press.

Goldstein, Avery. 2005. *Rising to the Challenge: China's Grand Strategy and International Security*. Stanford, CA: Stanford University Press.

Goldstein, Avery. 2007. 'Power Transitions, Institutions, and China's Rise in East Asia: Theoretical Expectations and Evidence.' *Journal of Strategic Studies* 30(4–5): 639–82.

Goldstein, Avery. 2020. 'China's Grand Strategy under Xi Jinping: Reassurance, Reform, and Resistance.' *International Security* 45(1): 164–201.

GOM-NEMC [Government of the Republic of the Union of Myanmar National Energy Management Committee]. 2015. *Myanmar Energy Master Plan*. Naypyidaw: Government of Myanmar. https://bit.ly/32crqJq.

Gong, Li, Men Honghua, and Sun Dongfang. 2010. '中国外交决策机制变迁研究(1949–2009) [Institutional Changes in China's Foreign Policy Making (1949–2009)].' In 新中国外交60年 *[60 Years of China's Foreign Affairs]*, edited by Zhao Jinjun, 254–68. Beijing: Peking University Press.

Gong, Ting, and Feng Chen. 1994. 'Institutional Reorganization and Its Impact on Decentralization.' In *Changing Central-Local Relations in China: Reform and State Capacity*, edited by Hao Jia and Zhimin Lin, 67–88. Boulder, CO: Westview Press.

Gong, Xue. 2018. 'The Role of Chinese Corporate Players in China's South China Sea Policy.' *Contemporary Southeast Asia* 40(2): 301–26.

Goodman, David S. G. 2014. *Class in Contemporary China*. Cambridge: Polity.

Goodman, David S. G., and Gerald Segal, eds. 1994. *China Deconstructs: Politics, Trade and Regionalism*. London: Routledge.

Gopaldas, Ronak. 2018. 'Lessons from Sri Lanka on China's "Debt-Trap Diplomacy."' Institute for Security Studies, 21 February. https://bit.ly/3mKdhMZ.

Gramsci, Antonio. 1971. *Selections from the Prison Notebooks*. Translated by Quintin Hoare and Geoffrey Nowell Smith. New York: International Publishers.

Gray, Kevin, and Jong-Woon Lee. 2018. 'The Rescaling of the Chinese State and Sino–North Korean Relations: Beyond State-Centrism.' *Journal of Contemporary Asia* 48(1): 113–32.

Grimmelmann, Klaas, Jorge Espinoza, Jana Arnold, and Nike Arning. 2018. 'The Land–Drugs Nexus: How Illicit Drug Crop Cultivation is Related to Access to Land.' *Bulletin on Narcotics* LXI: 75–104.

Grimsditch, Mark. 2012. 'China's Investments in Hydropower in the Mekong Region: The Kamchay Hydropower Dam, Kampot, Cambodia.' Open Development Mekong. https://bit.ly/3g6oWo5.

Grundy-Warr, Carl, and Karin Dean. 2011. 'The Myriad Spaces of Sovereignty, Peace and Conflict in Myanmar/Burma.' In *Reconstructing Conflict: Integrating War and Post-War Geographies*, edited by Scott Kirsch and Colin Flint, 91–114. Farnham: Ashgate.

Gu, Bin. 2017. 'Chinese Multilateralism in the AIIB.' *Journal of International Economic Law* 20(1): 137–58.

Guo, Rongxing. 2015. *Cross-Border Management: Theory, Method and Application*. Berlin: Springer.

Guo, Xiaolin. 2007. *Towards Resolution: China in the Myanmar Issue.* Washington, DC: Central Asia-Caucasus Institute and Silk Road Studies Program.

Habib, Benjamin. 2016. 'The Enforcement Problem in Resolution 2094 and the United Nations Security Council Sanctions Regime: Sanctioning North Korea.' *Australian Journal of International Affairs* 70(1): 50–68.

Hackenesch, Christine, and Julia Bader. 2020. 'The Struggle for Minds and Influence: The Chinese Communist Party's Global Outreach.' *International Studies Quarterly* 64(3): 723–33.

Ham, Kimkong, Samchan Hay, and Thea Sok. 2015. 'The Politics of the Lower Sesan 2 Dam in Cambodia.' In *Hydropower Development in the Mekong Region Political, Socio-Economic and Environmental Perspectives*, edited by Nathanial Matthews and Kim Geheb. eBook edition. Abingdon: Routledge.

Ham, Kimkong, Samchan Hay, Thea Sok, Vichet Sim, and Rasmey Lor. 2013. *Improving Hydropower Project Decision Making Processes in Mekong Basin: Case Studies of Lower Sesan 2 and Kamchay Hydropower Projects, Cambodia.* Phnom Penh: Royal University of Phnom Penh.

Hameiri, Shahar. 2009. 'Governing Disorder: The Australian Federal Police and Australia's New Regional Frontier.' *Pacific Review* 22(5): 549–74.

Hameiri, Shahar. 2010. *Regulating Statehood: State Building and the Transformation of the Global Order.* Basingstoke: Palgrave Macmillan.

Hameiri, Shahar. 2015. 'China's "Charm Offensive" in the Pacific and Australia's Regional Order.' *Pacific Review* 28(5): 631–54.

Hameiri, Shahar, Caroline Hughes, and Fabio Scarpello. 2017. *International Intervention and Local Politics: Fragmented States and the Politics of Scale.* Cambridge: Cambridge University Press.

Hameiri, Shahar, and Lee Jones. 2015. *Governing Borderless Threats: Non-Traditional Security and the Politics of State Transformation.* Cambridge: Cambridge University Press.

Hameiri, Shahar, and Lee Jones. 2016. 'Rising Powers and State Transformation: The Case of China.' *European Journal of International Relations* 22(1): 72–98.

Hameiri, Shahar, and Lee Jones. 2018. 'China Challenges Global Governance? The Case of Chinese International Development Finance and the Asian Infrastructure Investment Bank.' *International Affairs* 94 (3): 573–93.

Hameiri, Shahar, Lee Jones, and John Heathershaw. 2019. 'Reframing the Rising Powers Debate: State Transformation and Foreign Policy.' *Third World Quarterly* 40(8): 1397–414.

Hameiri, Shahar, Lee Jones, and Yizheng Zou. 2019. 'The Development–Insecurity Nexus in China's Near-Abroad: Rethinking Cross-Border

Economic Integration in an Era of State Transformation.' *Journal of Contemporary Asia* 49(3): 473–99.

Hameiri, Shahar, and Jinghan Zeng. 2020. 'State Transformation and China's Engagement in Global Governance: The Case of Nuclear Technologies.' *The Pacific Review* 33(6): 900–30.

Hao, Yufan, and Su Lin, eds. 2007. 中国外交决策: 开放与多远的社会因素分析 [*Chinese Foreign Policy Making: An Analysis of Societal Forces*]. Beijing: Social Sciences Academic Press.

Harbinson, Rod. 2015. 'Cambodian Dam Proceeds despite Opposition over Fish, Ousted Villagers.' *Mongabay*, 17 August. https://bit.ly/2OPKuuc.

Harris, Maureen, Daniel King, Ame Trandem, Ith Mathoura, and Meach Mean. 2015. *Submission to UN Special Rapporteur on the Situation of Human Rights in Cambodia Hydropower Dam Development in Cambodia: Lower Sesan 2 and Stung Cheay Areng Hydropower Projects*. Phnom Penh: EarthRights International, International Rivers, Samreth Law Group and Sesan, Srepok, Sekong Protection Network.

Harris, Stuart. 2014. *China's Foreign Policy*. Cambridge: Polity.

Harrison, Graham. 2004. *The World Bank and Africa: The Construction of Governance States*. London: Routledge.

Hav, Gechhong. n.d. *Resettlement and Sustainable Livelihoods: The Case of the Lower Sesan 2 Dam*. Unpublished Report.

Hav, Gechhong. 2018. 'Women and Dam Development: Negotiation for Better Compensation and Sustainable Livelihood Development.' Master of Arts Thesis. Phnom Penh: Royal University of Phnom Penh.

Hayton, Bill. 2014. *The South China Sea: The Struggle for Power in Asia*. New Haven, CT: Yale University Press.

Hayton, Bill. 2019. 'The Modern Origins of China's South China Sea Claims: Maps, Misunderstandings, and the Maritime Geobody.' *Modern China* 45 (2): 127–70.

He, Haining, and Jiang Yannan. 2010. '三十年低调一朝开启 雅鲁藏布江水电坎坷前传 [The Prequel of Brahmaputra River Hydropower Project, Launch After Thirty Years Low Profile].' *Southern Weekend*, 9 December. www.infzm.com/content/53335.

He, Qinglian. 1998. 现代化的陷阱 [*The Pitfalls of China's Modernization*]. Beijing: Jinri Zhongguo Chubanshe.

He, Xianchen. 2014. '我国海洋维权的现实困境与法治化思考 [Realistic Predicament of China's Maritime Rights and Interests Protection and Reflection on the Rule of Law].' 公安海警学院学报 [*Journal of China Maritime Police Academy*] 13(4): 57–62.

Heath, Timothy R. 2018. *China's New Governing Party Paradigm: Political Renewal and the Pursuit of National Rejuvenation*. Abingdon: Routledge.

Heberer, Thomas, and Gunter Schubert. 2012. 'County and Township Cadres as a Strategic Group: A New Approach to Political Agency in China's Local State.' *Journal of Chinese Political Science* 17(3): 221–49.

Heilmann, Sebastian, and Nicole Schulte-Kulkmann. 2011. 'The Limits of Policy Diffusion: Introducing International Norms of Anti-Money Laundering into China's Legal System.' *Governance* 24(4): 639–64.

Hein Ko Soe, and Ben Dunant. 2019. 'Kachin's Plantation Curse.' *Frontier Myanmar*, January 17. https://frontiermyanmar.net/en/kachins-plantation-curse.

Hendrix, Jerry, and Robert Bateman. 2017. 'Geography and the Coming US–China War at Sea.' *The Diplomat*, 19 May. https://bit.ly/3tg1eK2.

Heng, Pheakdey. 2016. 'Chinese Investment and Aid in Cambodia's Energy Sector: Impacts and Policy Implications.' PhD Thesis. Amsterdam: VU University of Amsterdam.

Hennig, Thomas. 2016. 'Damming the Transnational Ayeyarwady Basin: Hydropower and the Water-Energy Nexus.' *Renewable and Sustainable Energy Reviews* 65: 1232–46.

Hensengerth, Oliver. 2009. *Money and Security: China's Strategic Interests in the Mekong River Basin*. London: Chatham House.

Hensengerth, Oliver. 2017. 'Regionalism, Identity, and Hydropower Dams: The Chinese-Built Lower Sesan 2 Dam in Cambodia.' *Journal of Current Chinese Affairs* 46(3): 85–118.

Hess, Steve, and Richard Aidoo. 2014. 'Charting the Roots of Anti-Chinese Populism in Africa: A Comparison of Zambia and Ghana.' *Journal of Asian and African Studies* 49(2): 129–47.

Hess, Steve, and Richard Aidoo. 2016. 'Charting the Impact of Subnational Actors in China's Foreign Relations.' *Asian Survey* 56(2): 301–24.

Hickey, Joshua, Andrew S. Erickson, and Henry Holst. 2019. 'China Maritime Law Enforcement Surface Platforms: Order of Battle, Capabilities, and Trends.' In *China's Maritime Gray Zone Operations*, edited by Andrew S. Erickson and Ryan D. Martinson, 108–32. Washington, DC: Naval Institute Press.

Hill, Christopher. 2016. *Foreign Policy in the Twenty-First Century*. 2nd ed. Basingstoke: Palgrave Macmillan.

Hillman, Jonathan E. 2018. *China's Belt and Road Is Full of Holes*. CSIS Briefs. Washington, DC: Center for Strategic and International Studies. https://bit.ly/3dg5TpQ.

Hillman, Jonathan E. 2020. *The Emperor's New Road: China and the Project of the Century*. New Haven, CT: Yale University Press.

Hinshelwood, Colin, and Patrick Boehler. 2012. 'Lies, Dam Lies.' *Irrawaddy*, 30 March. www.irrawaddy.com/news/burma/lies-dam-lies.html.

Hirsch, Philip. 2010. 'The Changing Political Dynamics of Dam Building on the Mekong.' *Water Alternatives* 3(2): 312–23.

Ho, Joshua H. 2009. 'Combating Piracy and Armed Robbery in Asia: The ReCAAP Information Sharing Centre (ISC).' *Marine Policy* 33(2): 432–4.

Hobsbawm, Eric J. 1987. *The Age of Empire, 1875–1914*. London: Weidenfeld & Nicolson.

Hobsbawm, Eric J. 1994. *The Age of Extremes: A History of the World, 1914–1991*. New York: Pantheon Books.

Hodge, Amanda. 2018. 'China's Debt-Trap Diplomacy Snares Our Asian Neighbours.' *The Australian*, 12 January. https://bit.ly/3sn2Twd.

Holbig, Heike. 2004. 'The Emergence of the Campaign to Open Up the West: Ideological Formation, Central Decision-Making and the Role of the Provinces.' *China Quarterly* 178: 335–57.

Holslag, Jonathan. 2019. *The Silk Road Trap: How China's Trade Ambitions Challenge Europe*. Cambridge: Polity Press.

Hong, Brendon. 2014. 'How China Used Drones to Capture a Notorious Burmese Drug Lord.' *The Daily Beast*, 17 April. https://bit.ly/3dfkJg6.

Hooghe, Liesbet, and Gary Marks. 2003. 'Unraveling the Central State, But How? Types of Multi-Level Governance.' *American Political Science Review* 97(2): 233–43.

Houser, Trevor. 2008. 'The Roots of Chinese Oil Investment Abroad.' *Asia Policy* 5(1): 141–66.

Howe, Brendan M., and Seo Hyun Rachelle Park. 2015. 'Laos: The Dangers of Developmentalism?' *Southeast Asian Affairs* 2015: 165–85.

Howe, Jeff. 2013. *Murder on the Mekong: A Notorious Pirate, a Global Superpower, and a Mystery in the Golden Triangle*. Audiobook. https://amzn.to/3uLYrsd.

Hsiao, Hsin-Huang Michael, and Cheng-yi Lin, eds. 2009. *Rise of China: Beijing's Strategies and Implications for the Asia-Pacific*. Abingdon: Routledge.

Hsu, Zixuan. 2010. '中國軍事政策的形成機制: 以解放軍海軍之航母計畫為例 [The Formation of Military Policy in China: A Case Study of PLA Navy's Aircraft Carrier].' *Prospect & Exploration* 8(1): 87–96.

Hsueh, Roselyn. 2011. *China's Regulatory State: A New Strategy for Globalization*. Ithaca, NY: Cornell University Press.

Hu, Cui. 2011. '缅战火殃及太平江水电站 [Myanmar Civil War Brings Disaster to Taipingjiang Hydropower Station].' *China Energy News*, 20 June.

Huang, Mike Chia-Yu. 2013. 'Assertive or Reassuring Chinese Presence in Troubled Waters? The Decision-Making Process of Beijing's South China Sea Policy.' *Asia Pacific Perspectives* 11(1): 36–51.

Huang, Yasheng. 2008. *Capitalism with Chinese Characteristics: Entrepreneurship and the State*. Cambridge: Cambridge University Press.

Hughes, Caroline. 2003. *The Political Economy of Cambodia's Transition, 1991–2001*. London: RoutledgeCurzon.

Hughes, Caroline. 2006. 'The Politics of Gifts: Tradition and Regimentation in Contemporary Cambodia.' *Journal of Southeast Asian Studies* 37(3): 469–89.

Hughes, Caroline. 2009. *Dependent Communities: Aid and Politics in Cambodia and East Timor*. Ithaca, NY: Cornell University Press.

Hui, Elaine Sio-ieng. 2016. 'Putting the Chinese State in Its Place: A March from Passive Revolution to Hegemony.' *Journal of Contemporary Asia* 47(1): 66–92.

Hui, Elaine Sio-ieng, and Chris King-chi Chan. 2016. 'The Influence of Overseas Business Associations on Law-Making in China: A Case Study.' *China Quarterly* 225: 145–68.

Hui, Qin. 2012. 'Behind Myanmar's Suspended Dam.' *ChinaDialogue*, 28 March. www.chinadialogue.net/article/show/single/en/4832.

Hung, Ho-Fung. 2016. *The China Boom: Why China Will Not Rule the World*. New York: Columbia University Press.

ICG [International Crisis Group]. 2009. *China's Myanmar Dilemma*. Asia Report 177. Beijing: International Crisis Group.

ICG. 2012. *Stirring Up the South China Sea (I)*. Beijing: ICG.

ICG. 2015. *Stirring Up the South China Sea (III): A Fleeting Opportunity for Calm*. Beijing: ICG.

ICG. 2016. *Stirring up the South China Sea (IV): Oil in Troubled Waters*. Beijing: ICG.

IFC [International Finance Corporation]. 2017. *Baseline Assessment Report – Peace and Conflict. Strategic Environmental Assessment of the Hydropower Sector in Myanmar*. Washington, DC: IFC.

Ikenberry, G. John. 2008. 'The Rise of China and the Future of the West: Can the Liberal System Survive?' *Foreign Affairs* 87(1): 23–37.

Ikenberry, G. John. 2018. 'The End of Liberal International Order?' *International Affairs* 94(1): 7–23.

Ikenberry, G. John, and Darren J. Lim. 2017. *China's Emerging Institutional Statecraft: The Asia Infrastructure Investment Bank and the Prospects for Counter-Hegemony*. Washington, DC: Brookings Institution.

IMF [International Monetary Fund]. 2019. 'World Economic and Financial Surveys: World Economic Outlook Database.' www.imf.org/external/pubs/ft/weo/2019/02/weodata/weorept.aspx.

Inada, Juichi. 2013. 'Evaluating China's "Quaternity" Aid: The Case of Angola.' In *A Study of China's Foreign Aid: An Asian Perspective*, edited by Yasutami Shimomura and Hideo Ohashi, 197–227. Basingstoke: Palgrave Macmillan.

Inclusive Development International. 2019. *Safeguarding People and the Environment in Chinese Investments: A Reference Guide for Advocates.* 2nd edition. Asheville, NC: Inclusive Development International. https://bit.ly/3mQbpCI.

ICEM [International Center for Environmental Management]. 2017. *Regional River Basin Consultations: Key Findings. Strategic Environmental Assessment (SEA) of the Hydropower Sector in Myanmar.* Hanoi: ICEM.

International Rivers. 2011. 'The Myitsone Dam on the Irrawaddy River: A Briefing.' 28 September. https://bit.ly/3ddHwsT.

International Rivers. 2014. 'Dam Building Overseas by Chinese Companies and Financiers.' 12 November. https://bit.ly/3mI41ce.

International Rivers. 2015a. *Benchmarking the Policies and Practices of International Hydropower Companies Part A.* Berkeley, CA: International Rivers. www.internationalrivers.org/resources/9065.

International Rivers. 2015b. *Benchmarking the Policies and Practices of International Hydropower Companies Part B.* Berkeley, CA: International Rivers. https://www.internationalrivers.org/resources/9065.

International Rivers. 2017. 'China Global Dams Database.' 14 December. https://bit.ly/3a7dFAk.

Jakobson, Linda. 2014. *China's Unpredictable Maritime Security Actors.* Lowy Institute. https://bit.ly/3a7Omhs.

Jakobson, Linda. 2015. 'The PLA and Maritime Security Actors.' In *PLA Influence on China's National Security Policymaking*, edited by Phillip C. Saunders and Andrew Scobell. eBook edition. Stanford, CA: Stanford University Press.

Jakobson, Linda, and Dean Knox. 2010. *New Foreign Policy Actors in China.* SIPRI Policy Paper 26. Stockholm: SIPRI.

Jakobson, Linda, and Ryan Manuel. 2016. 'How Are Foreign Policy Decisions Made in China?' *Asia & The Pacific Policy Studies* 3(1): 101–10.

Jarvis, Darryl S. L. 2012. 'The Regulatory State in Developing Countries: Can it Exist and Do We Want it? The Case of the Indonesian Power Sector.' *Journal of Contemporary Asia* 42(3): 464–92.

Jayasuriya, Kanishka. 2001. 'Globalisation and the Changing Architecture of the State: Regulatory State and the Politics of Negative Coordination.' *Journal of European Public Policy* 8(1): 101–23.

Jayasuriya, Kanishka. 2012. 'Breaking the "Westphalian" Frame: Regulatory State, Fragmentation and Diplomacy.' In *Diplomacy and Developing Nations: Post-Cold War Foreign Policy-Making Structures and Processes*, edited by Justin Robertson and Maurice A. East, 39–54. Abingdon: Routledge.

Jelders, Julio A. 2012. 'Cambodia's Relations with China: A Steadfast Friendship.' In *Cambodia: Progress and Challenges Since 1991*, edited by Pou Sothirak, Geoff Wade, and Mark Hong, 81–95. Singapore: ISEAS.

Jervis, Robert. 1991. 'The Future of World Politics: Will it Resemble the Past?' *International Security* 16(3): 39–73.

Jessop, Bob. 1990. *State Theory: Putting the Capitalist State in Its Place*. Cambridge: Polity.

Jessop, Bob. 2002. 'The Political Economy of Scale.' In *Globalization, Regionalization, and Cross-Border Regions*, edited by Markus Perkmann and Ngai-Ling Sum, 25–49. Basingstoke: Palgrave Macmillan.

Jessop, Bob. 2008. *State Power: A Strategic-Relational Approach*. Cambridge: Polity.

Jessop, Bob. 2009. 'Avoiding Traps, Rescaling States, Governing Europe.' In *Leivathan Undone? Towards a Political Economy of Scale*, edited by Roger Keil and Rianne Mahon, 87–104. Vancouver: University of British Columbia Press.

Jessop, Bob. 2016. *The State: Past, Present, Future*. Cambridge: Polity.

Jia, Hao, and Zhimin Lin. 1994. 'Introduction: Changing Central–Local Relations in China: Reform and State Capacity.' In *Changing Central–Local Relations in China: Reform and State Capacity*, edited by Hao Jia and Zhimin Lin, 1–15. Boulder, CO: Westview Press.

Jiang, Da. 2012. '高冲突地区海外投资风险的盲区与应对 [Blindspots and Countermeasures for Overseas Investment Risks in High Conflict Areas].' *Journal of International Economic Cooperation* 4: 58–60.

Jiang, Da. 2013. '中国在缅甸的投资风险评估—中缅蒙育瓦铜矿调研报告 [Chinese Investment Risk Analysis for Myanmar: Investigation Report for Monywa Copper Mine].' *China Economy Report* 6: 105–110.

Joffe, Ellis. 1994. 'Regionalism in China: The Role of the PLA.' In *Chinese Regionalism: The Security Dimension*, edited by Richard H. Yang, Jason C. Hu, Peter H. H. Yu, and Andrew N. D. Yang, 43–58. Boulder, CO: Westview.

Johnson, Christopher K., Scott Kennedy, and Mingda Qui. 2017. 'Xi's Signature Governance Innovation: The Rise of Leading Small Groups.' Center for Strategic and International Studies, 17 October. https://bit.ly/3gefmQ2.

Johnston, Alastair Iain. 1998. *Cultural Realism: Strategic Culture and Grand Strategy in Chinese History*. Princeton, NJ: Princeton University Press.

Johnston, Alastair Iain. 2003. 'Is China a Status Quo Power?' *International Security* 27(4): 5–56.

Jones, Lee. 2013. 'Sovereignty, Intervention, and Social Order in Revolutionary Times.' *Review of International Studies* 39(5): 1149–67.

Jones, Lee. 2014a. 'Explaining Myanmar's Regime Transition: The Periphery Is Central.' *Democratization* 21(5): 780–802.

Jones, Lee. 2014b. 'The Political Economy of Myanmar's Transition.' *Journal of Contemporary Asia* 44(1): 144–70.

Jones, Lee. 2015. *Societies Under Siege: Exploring How International Economic Sanctions (Do Not) Work.* Oxford: Oxford University Press.

Jones, Lee. 2019. 'Theorizing Foreign and Security Policy in an Era of State Transformation: A New Framework and Case Study of China.' *Journal of Global Security Studies* 4(4): 579–97.

Jones, Lee, and Shahar Hameiri. 2020. *Debunking the Myth of "Debt-Trap Diplomacy": How Recipient Countries Shape China's Belt and Road Initiative.* London: Chatham House. https://bit.ly/3uJFNRO.

Jones, Lee, and Shahar Hameiri. 2021. 'COVID-19 and the Failure of the Neoliberal Regulatory State.' *Review of International Political Economy*, DOI: 10.1080/09692290.2021.1892798.

Jones, Lee, and Khin Ma Ma Myo. 2021. 'Myanmar's Response to China's Belt and Road Initiative: From Disengagement to Embrace.' *Asian Perspective* 45(2): 301–24.

Jones, Lee, and Jinghan Zeng. 2019. 'Understanding China's "Belt and Road Initiative": Beyond "Grand Strategy" to a State Transformation Analysis.' *Third World Quarterly* 40(8): 1415–39.

Jones, Lee, and Yizheng Zou. 2017. 'Rethinking the Role of State-Owned Enterprises in China's Rise.' *New Political Economy* 22(6): 743–60.

Joske, Alex. 2020. *The Party Speaks for You: Foreign Interference and the Chinese Communist Party's United Front System.* Canberra: Australian Strategic Policy Institute. https://bit.ly/32cjBUm.

JQK News. 2020. 'Hubei: Severely Punish Those Who Tell Lies, Ignore Human Life, Report Happiness to Superiors and Not Worry.' *JQK News*, 7 February. https://bit.ly/3dct5oB.

Junquera, Victoria, and Adrienne Grêt-Regamey. 2019. 'Crop Booms at the Forest Frontier: Triggers, Reinforcing Dynamics, and the Diffusion of Knowledge and Norms.' *Global Environmental Change* 57: 101929.

Kahler, Miles. 2013. 'Rising Powers and Global Governance: Negotiating Change in a Resilient Status Quo.' *International Affairs* 89(3): 711–29.

Kang, David C. 2003. 'Getting Asia Wrong: The Need for New Analytical Frameworks.' *International Security* 27(4): 57–85.

Kang, David C. 2007. *China Rising: Peace, Power, and Order in East Asia.* New York: Columbia University Press.

Kaplan, Robert D. 2014. *Asia's Cauldron: The South China Sea and the End of a Stable Pacific.* New York: Random House.

Kaplan, Stephen B. 2016. 'Banking Unconditionally: The Political Economy of Chinese Finance in Latin America.' *Review of International Political Economy* 23(4): 643–76.

Kardon, Isaac B., and Andrew Scobell. 2015. 'Reconsidering the PLA as an Interest Group.' In *PLA Influence on China's National Security Policymaking*, edited by Phillip C. Saunders and Andrew Scobell. eBook edition. Stanford, CA: Stanford University Press.

KDNG [Kachin Development Network Group]. 2007. *Damming the Irrawaddy*. http://burmacampaign.org.uk/media/DammingtheIrr.pdf.

KDNG. 2009. *Resisting the Flood: Communities Taking a Stand against the Imminent Construction of Irrawaddy Dams*. https://bit.ly/3wLCqvD.

Keating, Michael. 2013. *Rescaling the European State: The Making of Territory and the Rise of the Meso*. Oxford: Oxford University Press.

Kennedy, Conor M., and Andrew Erickson. 2016. 'From Frontier to Frontline: Tanmen Maritime Militia's Leading Role Pt. 2.' *Center for International Maritime Security*, 17 May. https://bit.ly/3aajOLU.

Kennedy, Conor M., and Andrew Erickson. 2017a. *China's Third Sea Force, The People's Armed Forces Maritime Militia: Tethered to the PLA*. Newport, RI: China Maritime Studies Institute, Center for Naval Warfare Studies, US Naval War College. https://bit.ly/32dFdQ9.

Kennedy, Conor M., and Andrew Erickson. 2017b. 'Hainan's Maritime Militia: China Builds a Standing Vanguard, Pt. 1.' Center for International Maritime Security, 25 March. https://bit.ly/3dX518t.

Kennedy, Conor M., and Andrew Erickson. 2017c. 'Hainan's Maritime Militia: Development Challenges and Opportunities, Pt. 2.' Center for International Maritime Security, 10 April. https://bit.ly/2RAomVL.

Kennedy, Conor M., and Andrew Erickson. 2017d. 'Hainan's Maritime Militia: All Hands on Deck for Sovereignty Pt. 3.' Center for International Maritime Security, 26 April. https://bit.ly/3a95HXj.

Kennedy, Paul. 1988. *The Rise and Fall of the Great Powers*. London: Fontana Press.

Kenney-Lazar, Miles. 2018. 'Governing Dispossession: Relational Land Grabbing in Laos.' *Annals of the American Association of Geographers* 108(3): 679–94.

Kenney-Lazar, Miles, Diana Suhardiman, and Michael B. Dwyer. 2018. 'State Spaces of Resistance: Industrial Tree Plantations and the Struggle for Land in Laos.' *Antipode* 50(5): 1290–310.

Keohane, Robert O. 1984. *After Hegemony: Cooperation and Discord in the World Political Economy*. Princeton, NJ: Princeton University Press.

Keovilignavong, Oulavanh, and Diana Suhardiman. 2017. 'Characterizing Private Investments and Implications for Poverty Reduction and Natural

Resource Management in Laos.' *Development Policy Review* 36(S1): O341–59.

Khalid, Nazery. 2009. 'With a Little Help from My Friends: Maritime Capacity-Building Measures in the Straits of Malacca.' *Contemporary Southeast Asia* 31(3): 424–46.

Khine Tun. 2015. 'China–Myanmar: Toward a More Balanced and Better Neighborhood.' In *Impact of China's Rise on the Mekong Region*, edited by Santasombat Yos, 167–93. Basingstoke: Palgrave Macmillan.

KHRG and KRW [Karen Human Rights Group and Karen Rivers Watch]. 2018. *Development or Destruction? The Human Rights Impacts of Hydropower Development on Villagers in Southeast Myanmar.* June. https://bit.ly/3tkZhw0.

Khun Sam. 2006. 'KIO Promises Better Power Supply for Kachin State.' *The Irrawaddy*, August 25. www.irrawaddy.org/print_article.php?art_id=6097.

Kiik, Laur. 2016. 'Nationalism and Anti-Ethno-Politics: Why "Chinese Development" Failed at Myanmar's Myitsone Dam.' *Eurasian Geography and Economics* 57(3): 374–402.

Kirchherr, Julian. 2018. 'Conceptualizing Chinese Engagement in South-East Asian Dam Projects: Evidence from Myanmar's Salween River.' *International Journal of Water Resources Development* 34(5): 812–28.

Kirchherr, Julian, Katrina J. Charles, and Matthew J. Walton. 2016. 'The Interplay of Activists and Dam Developers: The Case of Myanmar's Mega-Dams.' *International Journal of Water Resources Development* 33(1): 111–31.

Kirchherr, Julian, Nathanial Matthews, Katrina J. Charles, and Matthew J. Walton. 2017. '"Learning It the Hard Way": Social Safeguards Norms in Chinese-Led Dam Projects in Myanmar, Laos and Cambodia.' *Energy Policy* 102(March): 529–39.

Kirshner, Jonathan. 2012. 'The Tragedy of Offensive Realism: Classical Realism and the Rise of China.' *European Journal of International Relations* 18(1): 53–75.

Kitano, Naohiro. 2016. *Estimating China's Foreign Aid II: 2014 Update.* Tokyo: JICA Research Institute.

Klare, Michael. 2001. *Resource Wars: The New Landscape of Global Conflict.* New York: Owl Books.

Kong, Tat Yan. 2018. 'China's Engagement-Oriented Strategy towards North Korea: Achievements and Limitations.' *Pacific Review* 31(1): 76–95.

Kostka, Genia. 2016. 'Command Without Control: The Case of China's Environmental Target System.' *Regulation & Governance* 10(1): 58–74.

Kramer, Tom. 2009. *From Golden Triangle to Rubber Belt? The Future of Opium Bans in the Kokang and Wa Regions.* Amsterdam: Transnational Institute. www.tni.org/files/download/brief29.pdf.

Kramer, Tom, Martin Jelsma, and Tom Blickman. 2009. *Withdrawal Symptoms in the Golden Triangle: A Drugs Market in Disarray.* Amsterdam: Transnational Institute. https://bit.ly/3wQs25z.

Kramer, Tom, Ernestien Jensema, Martin Jelsma, and Tom Blickman. 2014. *Bouncing Back: Relapse in the Golden Triangle.* Amsterdam: Transnational Institute. www.tni.org/en/publication/bouncing-back.

Kuik, Cheng-Chwee. 2016. 'How Do Weaker States Hedge? Unpacking ASEAN States' Alignment Behavior Towards China.' *Journal of Contemporary China* 25(100): 500–14.

Kuo, Steven C. Y. 2012. 'Beijing's Understanding of African Security: Context and Limitations.' *African Security* 5(1): 24–43.

Kuo, Steven C. Y. 2015. 'Chinese Peace? An Emergent Norm in African Peace Operations.' *China Quarterly of International Strategic Studies* 1 (1): 155–81.

Kusakabe, Kyoko, and Aye Chan Myae. 2019. 'Precarity and Vulnerability: Rubber Plantations in Northern Laos and Northern Shan State, Myanmar.' *Journal of Contemporary Asia* 49(4): 586–601.

Kyophilavong, Phouphet, Michael C. S. Wong, Somchith Souksavath, and Bin Xiong. 2017. 'Impacts of Trade Liberalization with China and Chinese FDI on Laos: Evidence from the CGE Model.' *Journal of Chinese Economic and Business Studies* 15(3): 215–28.

Lai, Hongyi, and Su-Jeong Kang. 2014. 'Domestic Bureaucratic Politics and Chinese Foreign Policy.' *Journal of Contemporary China* 23(86): 294–313.

Laïdi, Zaki. 2012. 'BRICS: Sovereignty, Power and Weakness.' *International Politics* 49(5): 614–32.

Lam, Willy Wo-Lap. 2015. *Chinese Politics in the Era of Xi Jinping: Renaissance, Reform, or Retrogression?* Abingdon: Routledge.

Lamb, Vanessa, and Nga Dao. 2017. 'Perceptions and Practices of Investment: China's Hydropower Investments in Vietnam and Myanmar.' *Canadian Journal of Development Studies* 38(3): 395–413.

Lamb, Vanessa, Laura Schoenberger, Carl Middleton, and Borin Un. 2017. 'Gendered Eviction, Protest and Recovery: A Feminist Political Ecology Engagement with Land Grabbing in Rural Cambodia.' *Journal of Peasant Studies* 44(6): 1215–34.

Lampton, David M. 2001a. 'China's Foreign and National Security Policy-Making Process: Is It Changing and Does It Matter?' In *The Making of Chinese Foreign and Security Policy in the Era of Reform, 1978–2000,* edited by David M. Lampton. eBook edition. Stanford, CA: Stanford University Press.

Lampton, David M., ed. 2001b. *The Making of Chinese Foreign and Security Policy in the Era of Reform, 1978–2000.* eBook edition. Stanford, CA: Stanford University Press.

Lampton, David M. 2015. 'Xi Jinping and the National Security Commission: Policy Coordination and Political Power.' *Journal of Contemporary China* 24(95): 759–77.

Lan, Xue. 2014. 'China's Foreign Aid Policy and Architecture.' *IDS Bulletin* 45(4): 36–45.

Lanau Roi Aung. 2016. 'Laiza: Kachin Borderlands – Life After the Ceasefire.' In *Politics of Autonomy and Sustainability in Myanmar: Change for New Hope … New Life?* edited by Walaiporn Tantikanangkul and Ashley Pritchard, 37–55. Singapore: Springer.

Landry, Pierre F. 2008. *Decentralized Authoritarianism in China: The Communist Party's Control of Local Elites in the Post-Mao Era.* Cambridge: Cambridge University Press.

Lanyaw Zawng Hra. 2011. 'Mali Nmai Confluence Dam Project.' Letter to the Chairman of the Communist Party of China, 16 March. www.burmalibrary .org/docs11/KIO-Letter_to_China-red.pdf.

Lardy, Nicholas. 2018. 'Private Sector Development.' In *China's 40 Years of Reform and Development: 1978–2018,* edited by Ross Garnaut, Ligang Song, and Cai Fang, 329–44. Canberra: Australian National University Press.

Lee, Charlotte. 2017. *Training the Party: Party Adaptation and Elite Training in Reform-Era China.* Cambridge: Cambridge University Press.

Legro, Jeffrey W., and Andrew Moravcsik. 1999. 'Is Anybody Still a Realist?' *International Security* 24(2): 5–55.

Leonard, Mark. 2008. *What Does China Think?* New York: PublicAffairs.

Leong, Ching, and Farhad Mukhtarov. 2017. *Locally Informed Definition of Mekong Good Governance.* Singapore: Lee Kuan Yew School of Public Policy.

Leutert, Wendy. 2016. 'Challenges Ahead in China's Reform of State-Owned Enterprises.' *Asia Policy* 21(1): 83–99.

Li, Cheng. 2009. 'The Chinese Communist Party: Recruiting and Controlling the New Elites.' *Journal of Current Chinese Affairs* 38(3): 13–33.

Li, Cheng. 2016. *Chinese Politics in the Xi Jinping Era: Reassessing Collective Leadership.* Washington, DC: Brookings Institution Press.

Li, Chenyang, and Liang Fook Lye. 2009. 'China's Policies Towards Myanmar: A Successful Model for Dealing with the Myanmar Issue?' *China: An International Journal* 7(2): 255–87.

Li, Hak Yin, and Yongnian Zheng. 2009. 'Re-Interpreting China's Non-Intervention Policy Towards Myanmar: Leverage, Interest and Intervention.' *Journal of Contemporary China* 18(61): 617–37.

Li, Lin. 2018. '论我国海上执法力量改革发展的目标 [On Reform and Development Goal of Maritime Law Enforcement Forces in China].' 公安海警学院学报 *[Journal of China Maritime Police Academy]* 17(2): 1–10.

Li, Mingjiang. 2010. 'China and Maritime Cooperation in East Asia: Recent Developments and Future Prospects.' *Journal of Contemporary China* 19 (64): 291–310.

Li, Mingjiang. 2014. 'Local Liberalism: China's Provincial Approaches to Relations with Southeast Asia.' *Journal of Contemporary China* 23(86): 275–93.

Li, Mingjiang. 2019. 'Hainan Province in China's South China Sea Policy: What Role Does the Local Government Play?' *Asian Politics & Policy* 11 (4): 623–42.

Li, Xin. 2012. '"组织化利益" 与 "政治性行动": 国有企业对中国外交政策制定的影响 ["Organizational Interests" and "Political Actions": The Influence of State-Owned Enterprises on Chinese Foreign Policy].' *Journal of International Studies* 3: 163–75.

Li, Xinmin. 2013. '求解密松困局 – 走进缅甸探访伊江水电项目真相 求解密松困局新华社 [Seeking to Solve the Dilemma – Into Myanmar to Explore the Truth about the Myitsone Hydropower Project]', *Economic Information Daily*, 2 September. https://bit.ly/3wRIX80.

Li, Yi, and Fulong Wu. 2012. 'The Transformation of Regional Governance in China: The Rescaling of Statehood.' *Progress in Planning* 78(2): 55–99.

Li, Yongji. 2016. '执法力量整合后的南海维权对策研究 [Research on Countermeasures for Rights Protection Countermeasures in the South China Sea after the Integration of Law Enforcement Forces].' 公安海警学院学报 *[Journal of China Maritime Police Academy]* 15(1): 56–9.

Liang, Bin. 2014. 'Drugs and its Control in the People's Republic of China.' In *The Routledge Handbook of Chinese Criminology*, edited by Liqun Cao, Ivan Y. Sun, and Bill Hebenton, 183–96. Abingdon: Routledge.

Lieberthal, Kenneth. 2004. *Governing China: From Revolution through Reform*. 2nd ed. New York: W. W. Norton.

Lieberthal, Kenneth, and Michael Oksenberg. 1988. *Policy Making in China*. Princeton, NJ: Princeton University Press.

Lim, Alvin Cheng-Hin. 2015. 'Sino-Cambodian Relations: Recent Economic and Military Cooperation – Analysis.' *Eurasia Review*, 30 June. https://bit.ly/3s8ocBq.

Lin, Hongyi. 2017. 'Evaluation on China's Anti-Drug Efforts and Recommendations.' *International Relations and Diplomacy* 5(11): 694–702.

Lintner, Bertil, and Michael Black. 2009. *Merchants of Madness: The Methamphetamine Explosion in the Golden Triangle.* Chiang Mai: Silkworm Books.

Liu, Breeze. 2016. *Business Case Study: Lower Sesan 2 Dam.* Singapore: Lee Kuan Yew School of Public Policy, National University of Singapore.

Liu, Guoli. 2011. *Politics and Government in China.* Santa Barbara, CA: ABC-CLIO.

Liu, Weixun. 2008. '中电投: 发电企业亏损加剧 [China Power Investment: Increasing Losses in Power Generation Companies, Coal-Power Linkage Is Imperative]', EEO.com, 10 April. www.eeo.com.cn/2008/0410/96508.shtml.

Liu, Xiangyu, Yichen Tian, Chao Yuan, Feifei Zhang, and Guang Yang. 2018. 'Opium Poppy Detection Using Deep Learning.' *Remote Sensing* 10(12).

Liu, Zhongmin, and Teng Guiqing. 2006. '20世纪90年代以来国内南海问题研究综述 [A Summary of Domestic Research on South China Sea Since the 1990s].' *Journal of Ocean University of China* 3: 15–19.

LM-LESC [Lancang-Mekong Integrated Law Enforcement and Security Cooperation Centre]. 2019a. 'Organizational Structure.' www.lm-lesc-center.org/pages_57_283.aspx.

LM-LESC. 2019b. 'Security Cooperation.' www.lm-lesc-center.org/list51.aspx.

Loke, Beverley. 2017. 'China's Economic Slowdown: Implications for Beijing's Institutional Power and Global Governance Role.' *Pacific Review* 31(5): 673–91.

Lokshin, Ben, and Anya Shkurko. 2014. *Cross Border Integration in Northeast Asia: A Preliminary Report on Current Research and Data.* Stanford, CA: Shorenstein Asia-Pacific Research Center.

Long, William I. 2011. 'Cross-Border Health Cooperation in Complicated Regions: The Case of the Mekong Basin Disease Surveillance Network.' In *Cross-Border Governance in Asia: Regional Issues and Mechanisms*, edited by G. Shabbir Cheema, Christopher A. McNally, and Vesselin Popovski, 93–121. Tokyo: United Nations University Press.

Long, Yingxian. 2016. 'China's Decision to Deploy HYSY-981 in the South China Sea: Bureaucratic Politics with Chinese Characteristics.' *Asian Security* 12(3): 148–65.

Lu, Juliet N. 2017. 'Tapping into Rubber: China's Opium Replacement Program and Rubber Production in Laos.' *Journal of Peasant Studies* 44(4): 726–47.

Lu, Juliet, and Oliver Schönweger. 2019. 'Great Expectations: Chinese Investment in Laos and the Myth of Empty Land.' *Territory, Politics, Governance* 7(1): 61–78.

Lu, Ning. 2001. 'The Central Leadership, Supraministry Coordinating Bodies, State Council Ministries, and Party Departments.' In *The Making of Chinese Foreign and Security Policy in the Era of Reform, 1978–2000*, edited by David M. Lampton, eBook edition. Stanford, CA: Stanford University Press.

Lu, Shulin. 2015. '中巴经济走廊:'一带一路'的旗舰项目和示范项目 [China-Pakistan Economic Corridor: The Model Project of "One Belt One Road"].' 印度洋经济体研究 *[Indian Ocean Economy Studies]* 4: 50–6.

Luo, Phoebe Mingxuan, John A. Donaldson, and Qian Forrest Zhang. 2011. 'The Transformation of China's Agriculture System and Its Impact on Southeast Asia.' *International Journal of China Studies* 2(2): 289.

Lyttleton, Chris, and Pál Nyíri. 2011. 'Dams, Casinos and Concessions: Chinese Megaprojects in Laos and Cambodia.' In *Engineering Earth: The Impacts of Megaengineering Projects*, edited by Stanley D. Brunn, 1243–65. Dordrecht: Springer Netherlands.

Ma, Jun. 1996. 'China's Banking Sector: From Administrative Control to a Regulatory Framework.' *Journal of Contemporary China* 5(12): 155–69.

Magee, Darrin. 2006. 'Powershed Politics: Yunnan Hydropower under Great Western Development.' *China Quarterly* 185: 23–41.

Magee, Darrin, and Shawn Kelly. 2009. 'Damming the Salween River.' In *Contested Waterscapes in the Mekong Region: Hydropower, Livelihoods and Governance*, edited by François Molle, Tira Foran, and Mira Käkönen, 115–40. London: Earthscan.

Majone, Giandomenico. 1994. 'The Rise of the Regulatory State in Europe.' *West European Politics* 17(3): 77–101.

Marks, Paul. 2000. 'China's Cambodia Strategy.' *Parameters* 30(3): 92–108.

Marshall, Andrew R. C. 2016. 'Led by China, Mekong Nations Take on Golden Triangle Narco-Empire.' *Reuters*, 17 March. www.reuters.com/article/idUKKCN0WH2ZW.

Martinson, Ryan D. 2019. 'Militarising Coast Guard Operations in the Maritime Gray Zone.' In *China's Maritime Gray Zone Operations*, edited by Andrew S. Erickson and Ryan D. Martinson, 92–107. Washington, DC: Naval Institute Press.

Massey, Doreen. 2007. *World City*. Polity: Cambridge.

Matthews, Nathanial, and Stew Motta. 2015. 'Chinese State-Owned Enterprise Investment in Mekong Hydropower: Political and Economic Drivers and Their Implications across the Water, Energy, Food Nexus.' *Water* 7(11): 6269–84.

Mattlin, Mikael, and Matti Nojonen. 2015. 'Conditionality and Path Dependence in Chinese Lending.' *Journal of Contemporary China* 24 (94): 701–20.

Maung Aung Myoe. 2011. *In the Name of Pauk-Phaw: Myanmar's China Policy Since 1948*. Singapore: ISEAS.

Mayer, Maximilian, and Jost Wübbeke. 2013. 'Understanding China's International Energy Strategy.' *Chinese Journal of International Politics* 6(3): 273–98.

McAllister, Karen E. 2015. 'Rubber, Rights and Resistance: The Evolution of Local Struggles against a Chinese Rubber Concession in Northern Laos.' *Journal of Peasant Studies* 42(3–4): 817–37.

McCormack, Tara, and Lee Jones. 2020. 'COVID-19 and the Failed Post-Political State.' *The Full Brexit*, 17 April. www.thefullbrexit.com/covid19-state-failure.

McCoy, Alfred W. 2003. *The Politics of Heroin: CIA Complicity in the Global Drug Trade, Afghanistan, Southeast Asia, Central America, Colombia*. 2nd ed. Chicago, IL: Lawrence Hill.

McDonald, Kristen, Peter Bosshard, and Nicole Brewer. 2009. 'Exporting Dams: China's Hydropower Industry Goes Global.' *Journal of Environmental Management* 90(S3): S294–S302.

McGregor, Richard. 2010. *The Party: The Secret World of China's Communist Rulers*. London: Allen Lane.

McGregor, Richard. 2020. *China's Deep State: The Communist Party and the Coronavirus*. Sydney: Lowy Institute. https://bit.ly/3uSHCMx.

Mclaughlin, Tim. 2013. 'Chinese Ambassador Casts Doubt on Myitsone Resumption.' *Myanmar Times*, 19 July. https://bit.ly/3aakW26.

Mead, Walter Russell. 2018. 'Mike Pence Announces Cold War II.' *Wall Street Journal*, 8 October. https://on.wsj.com/3g658ll.

Mearsheimer, John. 2014a. 'Can China Rise Peacefully?' *The National Interest*, 25 October. https://bit.ly/2RlPtU7.

Mearsheimer, John. 2014b. *The Tragedy of Great Power Politics*. Updated ed. New York: W. W. Norton.

Mearsheimer, John J. 1990. 'Back to the Future: Instability in Europe After the Cold War.' *International Security* 15(1): 5–56.

Mearsheimer, John J. 2019. 'Bound to Fail: The Rise and Fall of the Liberal International Order.' *International Security* 43(4): 7–50.

Mech, Dara. 2017. 'Cambodia's Facebook Crackdown: Police Are Monitoring Site for "Enemies" and "Rebel Movements".' *Phnom Penh Post*, 25 July. https://bit.ly/3apheSH.

Meehan, Patrick. 2011. 'Drugs, Insurgency and State-Building in Burma: Why the Drugs Trade is Central to Burma's Changing Political Order.' *Journal of Southeast Asian Studies* 42(3): 376–404.

Meehan, Patrick. 2015. 'Fortifying or Fragmenting the State? The Political Economy of the Opium/ Heroin Trade in Shan State, Myanmar, 1988–2013.' *Critical Asian Studies* 47(2): 253–82.

Mei, Ciqi, and Margaret M. Pearson. 2014. 'Killing a Chicken to Scare the Monkeys? Deterrence Failure and Local Defiance in China.' *China Journal* 72: 75–97.

Meidan, Michal, Philip Andrews-Speed, and Ma Xin. 2009. 'Shaping China's Energy Policy: Actors and Processes.' *Journal of Contemporary China* 18(61): 591–616.

Middleton, Carl, Nathanial Matthews, and Naho Mirumachi. 2015. 'Whose Risky Business? Public–Private Partnerships, Build-Operate-Transfer and Large Hydropower Dams in the Mekong Region.' In *Hydropower Development in the Mekong Region: Political, Socio-Economic and Environmental Perspectives*, edited by Nathanial Matthews and Kim Geheb. eBook edition. Abingdon: Routledge.

Migdal, Joel S. 2001. *State in Society: Studying How States and Societies Transform and Constitute One Another*. Cambridge: Cambridge University Press.

Miller, Alice. 2015. 'The PLA in the Party Leadership Decisionmaking System.' In *PLA Influence on China's National Security Policymaking*, edited by Phillip C. Saunders and Andrew Scobell. eBook edition. Stanford, CA: Stanford University Press.

Milne, Sarah. 2015. 'Cambodia's Unofficial Regime of Extraction: Illicit Logging in the Shadow of Transnational Governance and Investment.' *Critical Asian Studies* 47(2): 200–28.

Min Khaing. 2015. 'Status of Myanmar Electric Power and Hydropower Planning.' Presentation at Workshop on Sustainable Hydropower Development and Regional Cooperation, 19 January, Naypyitaw. https://bit.ly/3dZjH79.

Min Zin. 2012. 'Burmese Attitude toward Chinese: Portrayal of the Chinese in Contemporary Cultural and Media Works.' *Journal of Current Southeast Asian Affairs* 31(1): 115–31.

Ministry of Foreign Affairs. 2014. 'The Operation of the HYSY 981 Drilling Rig: Vietnam's Provocation and China's Position.' 8 June, Beijing. www.fmprc.gov.cn/mfa_eng/zxxx_662805/t1163264.shtml.

Mitchell, Timothy. 1991. 'The Limits of the State: Beyond Statist Approaches and Their Critics.' *American Political Science Review* 85(1): 77–96.

MOFCOM [Ministry of Commerce]. 2009. '中华人民共和国商务部令2009年第5号 《境外投资管理办法》[MOFCOM Decree 2009/5, "Measures for Overseas Investment Management"].' www.mofcom.gov.cn/aarticle/b/c/200903/20090306103210.html.

MOFCOM. 2010. '商务部关于印发《对外投资合作境外安全风险预警和信息通报制度》的通知 [Notice of the Ministry of Commerce on Issuing the Overseas Security Risk Early Warning and Information Release System of

Foreign Investment Cooperation].' www.mofcom.gov.cn/aarticle/b/g/201
009/20100907152677.html.

Moore, Gregory J. 2007. 'How North Korea Threatens China's Interests:
Understanding Chinese "Duplicity" on the North Korean Nuclear Issue.'
International Relations of the Asia-Pacific 8(1): 1–29.

Moore, Jack. 2014. '1,000 Chinese Soldiers Cross India's Border as Xi
Jinping Visits Region.' *International Business Times*, 18 September.
https://bit.ly/3mLRQLQ.

Moore, Thomas G., and Dixia Yang. 2001. 'Empowered and Restrained:
Chinese Foreign Policy in the Age of Economic Interdependence.' In *The
Making of Chinese Foreign and Security Policy in the Era of Reform,
1978–2000*, edited by David M. Lampton. eBook edition. Stanford, CA:
Stanford University Press.

Morris, Lyle J. 2019. 'Organizing for the Gray Zone: Assessing the
Rights Protection Capabilities of the New China Coast Guard.' In
China's Maritime Gray Zone Operations, edited by Andrew
S. Erickson and Ryan D. Martinson, 77–91. Washington, DC: Naval
Institute Press.

Moyo, Dambisa. 2009. *Dead Aid: Why Aid is Not Working and How There
is a Better Way for Africa*. London: Allen Lane.

Mulvad, Andreas. 2015. 'Competing Hegemonic Projects within China's
Variegated Capitalism: "Liberal" Guangdong vs. "Statist" Chongqing.'
New Political Economy 20(2): 199–227.

Mulvad, Andreas Møller. 2018. 'China's Ideological Spectrum: A Two-
Dimensional Model of Elite Intellectuals' Visions.' *Theory and Society*
47(5): 635–61.

Myanmar News Agency. 2004. 'Formation of Work Committee for Electric
Power Development.' *New Light of Myanmar*, 4 April. www.ibiblio.org
/obl/docs/NLM2004-04-01.pdf.

Myanmar News Agency. 2009a. 'Myanmar, PRC Sign Agreements.' *New
Light of Myanmar*, 26 March. https://bit.ly/3uQR9U1.

Myanmar News Agency. 2009b. 'Chinese Energy Minister Visits Ayeyawady
Confluence Hydropower Plant Project.' *New Light of Myanmar*, 2 April.
www.burmalibrary.org/docs6/NLM2009-04–02.pdf (link obsolete).

Myanmar News Agency. 2009c. 'Vice-Senior General Maung Aye Meets
PRC Vice President Mr Xi Jinping.' *New Light of Myanmar*,
21 December. https://bit.ly/2QlzSU0.

Naím, Moisés. 2007. 'Rogue Aid.' *Foreign Policy*, 1 March. www.foreign
policy.com/articles/2007/02/14/rogue_aid.

Naren, Kuch, and Dene-Hern Chen. 2013. 'Government has 13 Payment
Guarantees for Energy Projects.' *Cambodia Daily*, 24 February.
https://bit.ly/32cFfYl.

National Audit Office. 2015. *The Audit Results of the Financial Revenues and Expenditures of China Power Investment Corporation for 2013.* 28 June, Beijing. www.audit.gov.cn/en/n746/n752/n771/c80977/part/41468.doc.

National Bureau of Statistics of China. 2019. 'National Data.' http://data.stats.gov.cn/english/easyquery.htm?cn=E0103.

National Review. 2018. 'China's Debt-Trap Diplomacy.' *National Review*, 3 July. https://bit.ly/2Rsp1Z3.

Naughton, Barry. 2016. 'Shifting Structures and Processes in Economic Policy-Making at the Centre.' In *China's Core Executive: Leadership Styles, Structures and Processes Under Xi Jinping*, edited by Sebastian Heilmann and Matthias Stepan, 40–5. Berlin: MERICS.

NDRC [National Development and Reform Commission], MFA [Ministry of Foreign Affairs], and MOFCOM [Ministry of Commerce]. 2015. 'Vision and Actions on Jointly Building Silk Road Economic Belt and 21st-Century Maritime Silk Road.' 28 March, Beijing. http://en.ndrc.gov.cn/newsrelease/201503/t20150330_669367.html.

NDRC [National Development and Reform Commission] and SOA [State Oceanic Administration]. 2017. 'Vision for Maritime Cooperation under the Belt and Road Initiative.' 20 June, Beijing. https://bit.ly/3teWvrL.

Nexon, Daniel H. 2009. *The Struggle for Power in Early Modern Europe: Religious Conflict, Dynastic Empires, and International Change.* Princeton, NJ: Princeton University Press.

Ng, Teddy. 2018. 'The Shake-Up that Signals China's Push for a Greater Global Role.' *South China Morning Post*, 10 March. https://bit.ly/3a7hO7i.

Nordensvard, Johan, Frauke Urban, and Grace Mang. 2015. 'Social Innovation and Chinese Overseas Hydropower Dams: The Nexus of National Social Policy and Corporate Social Responsibility.' *Sustainable Development* 23(4): 245–56.

Norris, William J. 2016. *Chinese Economic Statecraft: Commercial Actors, Grand Strategy, and State Control.* Ithaca, NY: Cornell University Press.

NPC [National People's Congress]. 2007. 'Narcotics Control Law of the People's Republic of China.' 29 December, Beijing. www.lawinfochina.com/display.aspx?lib=law&id=6604.

NPR. 2018. 'China's "Toilet Revolution" Is Flush with Lavish Loos.' NPR, 3 February. https://n.pr/3siDSC6.

Nyíri, Pál. 2017. 'Investors, Managers, Brokers, and Culture Workers: How Migrants from China are Changing the Meaning of Chineseness in Cambodia.' In *Chinese Encounters in Southeast Asia: How People, Money, and Ideas from China are Changing a Region*, edited by Pál Nyíri and Danielle Tan, 25–41. Seattle, WA: University of Washington Press.

O'Brien, Kevin J., and Lianjiang Li. 1999. 'Selective Policy Implementation in Rural China.' *Comparative Politics* 31(2): 167–86.

O'Connor, James. 2011. *State Building, Infrastructure Development and Chinese Energy Projects in Myanmar.* IRASEC Discussion Paper 10. Bangkok: IRASEC. www.irasec.com/ouvrage.php?id=38&lang=en.

Odgaard, Liselotte. 2007. 'China: Security Cooperation with Reservations.' In *Global Security Governance: Competing Perceptions of Security in the 21st Century*, edited by Emil J. Kirchner and James Sperling, 199–218. London: Routledge.

OECD [Organisation for Economic Co-operation and Development]. n.d. 'Official Development Assistance: Definition and Coverage.' https://bit.ly/3g7l32n.

OECD. 2014. *Multi-Dimensional Review of Myanmar: Volume 2. In-Depth Analysis and Recommendations.* https://bit.ly/3wUSpaS.

Oh, Yoon Ah. 2016. *China's Development Finance to Asia: Characteristics and Implications.* KIEP Working Paper 16–12. Sejong: Korea Institute for International Economic Policy.

Ohashi, Hideo. 2013. 'The Link between Aid and Non-Aid Activities: A Distinguishing Feature of China's Engagement.' In *A Study of China's Foreign Aid: An Asian Perspective*, edited by Yasutami Shimomura and Hideo Ohashi, 82–103. Basingstoke: Palgrave Macmillan.

Oi, Jean C. 1999. *Rural China Takes Off: Institutional Foundations of Economic Reform.* Berkeley and Los Angeles, CA: University of California Press.

O'Neill, Daniel. 2014. 'Playing Risk: Chinese Foreign Direct Investment in Cambodia.' *Contemporary Southeast Asia* 36(2): 173–205.

Orlik, Tom. 2012. 'Picking Apart Nationalist Rhetoric Around China's New Oil Rig.' *Wall Street Journal*, 11 May. https://on.wsj.com/3mJLwED.

Ouch, Chandarany, Chanhang Saing, and Dalia Phann. 2013. 'Impacts of China on Poverty Reduction in Cambodia.' In *Impact of China's Rise on the Mekong Region*, edited by Hossein Jalilian, 297–384. Singapore: ISEAS.

Palmer, James. 2018. 'Nobody Knows Anything About China.' *Foreign Policy*, 21 March. https://bit.ly/3uOZGHo.

Palmer, James. 2020. 'Chinese Officials Can't Help Lying About the Wuhan Virus.' *Foreign Policy*, 3 February. https://bit.ly/3mJgUCZ.

Pan, Jennifer, and Yiqing Xu. 2018. 'China's Ideological Spectrum.' *Journal of Politics* 80(1): 254–73.

Pan, Su-Yan, and Joe Tin-Yau Lo. 2017. 'Re-Conceptualizing China's Rise as a Global Power: A Neo-Tributary Perspective.' *Pacific Review* 30(1): 1–25.

Pan, Yingqiu, and Guang Shi. 2017. 'Forging a Secure Waterway.' *China Report ASEAN*, 22 February. https://bit.ly/2Qm00OR.

Pang, Edgar. 2017. *'Same-Same but Different': Laos and Cambodia's Political Embrace of China*. Singapore: Yusuf Ishak Institute of Southeast Asian Studies. www.iseas.edu.sg/images/pdf/ISEAS_Perspective_2017_66.pdf.

Pant, Harsh. 2017. 'China's Debt Trap Diplomacy.' Observer Research Foundation, 3 August. www.orfonline.org/research/chinas-debt-trap-diplomacy/.

Paradise, James F. 2016. 'The Role of "Parallel Institutions" in China's Growing Participation in Global Economic Governance.' *Journal of Chinese Political Science* 21(2): 149–75.

Parameswaran, Prashanth. 2017. 'What's Behind Laos' China Banana Ban?' *The Diplomat*, 14 April. https://bit.ly/3a7TjH4.

Parello-Plesner, Jonas, and Mathieu Duchâtel. 2014. 'Murder on the Mekong: The Long Arm of Chinese Law.' *Adelphi Series* 54(451): 91–106.

Parello-Plesner, Jonas, and Mathieu Duchâtel. 2015. *China's Strong Arm: Protecting Citizens and Assets Abroad*. Abingdon: Routledge.

Parker, Sam, and Gabrielle Chefitz. 2018. *Debtbook Diplomacy: China's Strategic Leveraging of Its Newfound Economic Influence and the Consequences for US Foreign Policy*. Cambridge, MA: Belfer Center. https://bit.ly/3uNoYWk.

Patapan, Haig, and Yi Wang. 2018. 'The Hidden Ruler: Wang Huning and the Making of Contemporary China.' *Journal of Contemporary China* 27 (109): 47–60.

Patrick, Stewart. 2010. 'Irresponsible Stakeholders? The Difficulty of Integrating Rising Powers.' *Foreign Affairs* 89(6): 44–53.

Patrick, Stewart. 2014. 'The Unruled World: The Case for Good Enough Global Governance.' *Foreign Affairs* 93: 58–73.

Pearson, Margaret M. 2001. 'The Case of China's Accession to GATT/ WTO.' In *The Making of Chinese Foreign and Security Policy in the Era of Reform, 1978–2000*, edited by David M. Lampton, 337–70. Stanford, CA: Stanford University Press.

Pearson, Margaret M. 2005. 'The Business of Governing Business in China: Institutions and Norms of the Emerging Regulatory State.' *World Politics* 57(2): 296–322.

Pei, Minxin. 2016. *China's Crony Capitalism: The Dynamics of Regime Decay*. Cambridge, MA: Harvard University Press.

Pei, Minxin. 2020. 'Coronavirus is a Disease of Chinese Autocracy.' *The Strategist*, 29 January. https://bit.ly/3sdXJCC.

Perlez, Jane. 2013. 'Chinese Plan to Kill Drug Lord with Drone Highlights Military Advances.' *New York Times*, 21 February. https://nyti.ms /3mK3K8T.

Perlez, Jane, and Bree Feng. 2013. 'Beijing Flaunts Cross-Border Clout in Search for Drug Lord.' *New York Times*, 8 April. https://cn.nytimes.com /world/20130408/c08druglord/en-us.

Phillips, Andrew, and J. C. Sharman. 2015. *International Order in Diversity: War, Trade and Rule in the Indian Ocean*. Cambridge: Cambridge University Press.

Pillsbury, Michael. 2014. *The Hundred-Year Marathon: China's Secret Strategy to Replace America as the Global Superpower*. New York: Henry Holt.

Poulantzas, Nicos. 1978. *State, Power, Socialism*. London: New Left Books.

Ptak, Thomas, and Demian Hommel. 2016. 'The Trans-Political Nature of Southwest China's Energy Conduit, Yunnan Province.' *Geopolitics* 21(3): 556–78.

Pu, Xiaoyu. 2017. 'Controversial Identity of a Rising China.' *Chinese Journal of International Politics* 10(2): 131–49.

Putnam, Robert D. 1988. 'Diplomacy and Domestic Politics: The Logic of Two-Level Games.' *International Organization* 42(3): 427–60.

Radio Free Asia. 2019. 'Chinese Banana Plantations in Lao District Leave Locals with Little Land to Farm.' *Radio Free Asia*, 5 March. www.rfa.org /english/news/laos/plantations-03052019144331.html.

Rauhala, Emily. 2020. 'Chinese Officials Note Serious Problems in Coronavirus Response. The World Health Organization Keeps Praising Them.' *Washington Post*, 9 February. https://wapo.st/3uFYg1A.

Reilly, James. 2012. 'A Norm-Taker or a Norm-Maker? Chinese Aid in Southeast Asia.' *Journal of Contemporary China* 21(73): 71–91.

Reilly, James. 2013. 'China and Japan in Myanmar: Aid, Natural Resources and Influence.' *Asian Studies Review* 37(2): 141–57.

Ren, Iris Yaxin. 2015. *Same Company, One River, Two Dams: Using Hydrolancang's China Domestic Practice to Mainstream Biodiversity, Fisheries and Livelihood Protection in the Lower Sesan 2 Dam Project*. Berkeley, CA: International Rivers.

Ren, Xiao. 2016. 'China as an Institution-Builder: The Case of the AIIB.' *Pacific Review* 29(3): 435–42.

Renard, Ronald D. 2013. 'The Wa Authority and Good Governance, 1989–2007.' *Journal of Burma Studies* 17(1): 141–80.

Renard, Thomas. 2015. *The Asian Infrastructure Investment Bank (AIIB): China's New Multilateralism and the Erosion of the West*. Security Policy Brief 63. Brussels: Egmont.

Renwick, Neil. 2014. 'China's Role in Burma's Development.' *IDS Bulletin* 45(4): 70–84.

Reporters Without Borders. n.d. 'Cambodia: Hun Sen's War on Critics.' https://rsf.org/en/cambodia.

Reus-Smit, Christian. 2013. *Individual Rights and the Making of the International System*. Cambridge: Cambridge University Press.

Rice, Susan E., and Stewart Patrick. 2008. *Index of State Weakness in the Developing World*. Washington, DC: Brookings Institution. https://brook.gs/3sjcDqV.

Ripsman, Norrin M., Jeffrey W. Taliaferro, and Steven E. Lobell. 2016. *Neoclassical Realist Theory of International Politics*. Oxford: Oxford University Press.

Robertson, Justin. 2012. 'Introduction: The Research Direction and a Typology of Approaches.' In *Diplomacy and Developing Nations: Post-Cold War Foreign Policy-Making Structures and Processes*, edited by Justin Robertson and Maurice A. East, 1–35. Abingdon: Routledge.

Rolf, Steve, and John Agnew. 2016. 'Sovereignty Regimes in the South China Sea: Assessing Contemporary Sino-US Relations.' *Eurasian Geography and Economics* 57(2): 249–73.

Rosenau, James N. 2003. *Distant Proximities: Dynamics beyond Globalization*. Princeton, NJ: Princeton University Press.

Rosser, Andrew. 2015. 'Contesting Tobacco-Control Policy in Indonesia.' *Critical Asian Studies* 47(1): 69–93.

Royal Government of Cambodia. 2013. *Authorization of Payment Warranty of the Royal Government of Cambodia for the Hydro Power Lower Sesan 2 Company*. 15 February, Phnom Penh.

Sanderson, Henry, and Michael Forsythe. 2013. *China's Superbank: Debt, Oil and Influence – How China Development Bank is Rewriting the Rules of Finance*. Singapore: Wiley.

Santicola, Ryan. 2014. 'China's Consistently Inconsistent South China Sea Policy.' *The Diplomat*, 24 May. https://bit.ly/3a4K6PW.

SASAC [State-Owned Assets Supervision and Administration Commission]. 2008. '中央企业资产损失责任追究暂行办法 国务院国有资产监督管理委员会令 第 20 号, 2008 [Interim Measures for the Investigation of Liability for Asset Loss of Central Enterprises, State-Owned Assets Supervision and Administration Commission Order No. 20, 2008].' 1 October, Beijing. www.gov.cn/gongbao/content/2009/content_1257481.htm.

Sassen, Saskia. 2006. *Territory, Authority, Rights: From Medieval to Global Assemblages*. Princeton, NJ: Princeton University Press.

Saull, Richard. 2012. 'Rethinking Hegemony: Uneven Development, Historical Blocs, and the World Economic Crisis.' *International Studies Quarterly* 56(2): 323–38.

Saunders, Phillip C., and Andrew Scobell. 2015. 'Introduction: PLA Influence on China's National Security Policymaking.' In *PLA Influence on China's National Security Policymaking*, edited by Phillip C. Saunders and Andrew Scobell. eBook edition. Stanford, CA: Stanford University Press.

Sayalath, Soulatha, and Simon Creak. 2017. 'Regime Renewal in Laos: The Tenth Congress of the Lao People's Revolutionary Party.' *Southeast Asian Affairs* 2017: 179–200.

Schippers, Lan Katharina. 2017. 'Aid for Trade as Contested Statebuilding Intervention: The Cases of Laos and Vietnam.' PhD Thesis. London: Queen Mary University of London.

Scott, David. 2008. 'The Great Power "Great Game" between India and China: "The Logic of Geography".' *Geopolitics* 13(1): 1–26.

Segal, Gerald. 1994. 'Deconstructing Foreign Relations.' In *China Deconstructs: Politics, Trade and Regionalism*, edited by David S. G. Goodman and Gerald Segal, 322–55. London: Routledge.

Shambaugh, David. 2013. *China Goes Global: The Partial Power*. Oxford: Oxford University Press.

SHAN [Shan Herald Agency for News]. 2006. *Hand in Glove: The Burma Army and the Drug Trade in Shan State*. Chiang Mai: SHAN. www.burmalibrary.org/docs07/HandinGlove.pdf.

Shearman, Peter. 2014. 'The Rise of China, Power Transition, and International Order in Asia: A New Cold War?' In *Power Transition and International Order in Asia: Issues and Challenges*, edited by Peter Shearman, 8–27. Abingdon: Routledge.

Shen, Simon. 2016. 'Paradiplomacy and Hong Kong: Challenges and Opportunities.' Paper Presented at the International Studies Association, 18 March, Atlanta.

Sheng, Lijun. 2006. 'China-ASEAN Cooperation Against Illicit Drugs from the Golden Triangle.' *Asian Perspective* 30(2): 97–126.

Sheng, Yumin. 2011. *Economic Openness and Territorial Politics in China*. Cambridge: Cambridge University Press.

Shi, Weiyi. 2008. *Rubber Boom in Luang Namtha: A Transnational Perspective*. GTZ, April. http://lad.nafri.org.la/fulltext/1599-1.pdf.

Shi, Weiyi. 2015. 'Rubber Boom in Luang Namtha: Seven Years Later.' Unpublished MS, 27 April. https://bit.ly/2Qph4na.

Shimomura, Yasutami, and Hideo Ohashi. 2013. 'Why China's Aid Matters?' In *A Study of China's Foreign Aid: An Asian Perspective*, 31–51. Basingstoke: Palgrave Macmillan.

Shirk, Susan. 2014. 'The Domestic Context of Chinese Foreign Security Policies.' In *The Oxford Handbook of the International Relations of Asia*, edited by Saadia M. Pekkanen, John Ravenhill, and Rosemary Foot, 391–410. Oxford: Oxford University Press.

Silove, Nina. 2018. 'Beyond the Buzzword: The Three Meanings of "Grand Strategy".' *Security Studies* 27(1): 27–57.

Simpson, Adam. 2013. 'Challenging Hydropower Development in Myanmar (Burma): Cross-Border Activism under a Regime in Transition.' *Pacific Review* 26(2): 129–152.

SinoInsider. 2018. 'Political Risk Watch: China Target 30 Provinces, Gov't Depts. in Post-19th Congress Sweep.' SinoInsider, 4 February. https://bit.ly/3mGU7aW.

Sithirith, Mak. 2016. 'Dams and State Security: Damming the 3S Rivers as a Threat to Cambodian State Security.' *Asia Pacific Viewpoint* 57(1): 60–75.

Slaughter, Anne-Marie. 2004. *A New World Order*. Princeton, NJ: Princeton University Press.

Smyth, Jamie. 2018. 'China's Commitment to the Pacific May Be Overstated.' *Financial Times*, 9 August. www.ft.com/content/5700e93c-9ac6-11e8-9702-5946bae86e6d.

Snider, Eric. 2012. *Electrical Industry of Burma/Myanmar: Online Compendium*. 4th ed. www.burmalibrary.org/docs2/myanmar-elec.pdf.

So, Alvin Y. 2013. *Class and Class Conflict in Post-Socialist China*. Singapore: World Scientific.

Solingen, Etel. 2009. 'Economic and Political Liberalization in China: Implications for US–China Relations.' In *Power and Restraint: A Shared Vision for the US-China Relationship*, edited by Richard Rosecrance and Guoliang Gu, 67–78. New York: Public Affairs.

Song, Zhiyan, and Zhang Feng. 2015. '中国学界的外交决策研究文献综述 [A Literature Review of Chinese Academic Research on Foreign Policy Decision-Making].' *Journal of Beihua University (Social Sciences)* 5: 79–83.

Sørensen, Georg. 2004. *The Transformation of the State: Beyond the Myth of Retreat*. Basingstoke: Palgrave Macmillan.

Sovacool, Benjamin K. 2013. 'Confronting Energy Poverty behind the Bamboo Curtain: A Review of Challenges and Solutions for Myanmar (Burma).' *Energy for Sustainable Development* 17(4): 305–14.

State Council. 2011. *The 2011 White Paper on China's Peaceful Development*. Beijing: State Council of China. http://english.gov.cn/official/2011-09/06/content_1941354.htm.

State Council. 2014. *China's Foreign Aid (2014)*. *White Paper*. Beijing: State Council of China. https://bit.ly/3th21tY.

State Council. 2016. 'Full Text of Chinese Gov't Statement on China's Territorial Sovereignty and Maritime Rights and Interests in S. China Sea.' 12 July, Beijing. https://bit.ly/32cpS2m.

State Council Information Office. 2000. 'Narcotics Control in China.' June, Beijing. http://english.cri.cn/3126/2007/02/07/45@193763.htm.

Statistics Times. 2018. 'Projected GDP Ranking (2019–2023).' 2 April. https://bit.ly/3mNLpYB.

Steinberg, David, and Hongwei Fan. 2012. *Modern China–Myanmar Relations: Dilemmas of Mutual Dependence.* Copenhagen: NIAS Press.

Stevenson, Michael A., and Andrew F. Cooper. 2009. 'Overcoming Constraints of State Sovereignty: Global Health Governance in Asia.' *Third World Quarterly* 30(7): 1379–94.

Stieber, Sabine. 2017. 'Non-Traditional Security in Contemporary Chinese International Relations Thought.' PhD Thesis. Nottingham: University of Nottingham.

Storey, Ian. 1999. 'Creeping Assertiveness: China, the Philippines and the South China Sea Dispute.' *Contemporary Southeast Asia* 21(1): 95–118.

Strange, Austin M., Axel Dreher, Andreas Fuchs, Bradley Parks, and Michael J. Tierney. 2017. 'Tracking Underreported Financial Flows: China's Development Finance and the Aid–Conflict Nexus Revisited.' *Journal of Conflict Resolution* 61(5): 935–63.

Strangio, Sebastian. 2014. *Hun Sen's Cambodia.* Chiang Mai: Silkworm Books.

Stuart-Fox, Martin. 2007. 'Laos: Politics in a Single-Party State.' *Southeast Asian Affairs* 2006: 161–80.

Sturgeon, Janet C. 2013. 'Cross-Border Rubber Cultivation between China and Laos: Regionalization by Akha and Tai Rubber Farmers.' *Singapore Journal of Tropical Geography* 34(1): 70–85.

Su, Changhe. 2007. '国内——国际相互转型的政治经济学：兼论中国国内变迁与国际体系的关系 (1978–2007) [The Political Economy of the Mutual Transition Between Domestic and International: On the Relationship between China's Domestic Changes and the International System (1978–2007)].' *World Economics and Politics* 11: 6–14.

Su, Xiaobo. 2012. 'Rescaling the Chinese State and Regionalization in the Great Mekong Subregion.' *Review of International Political Economy* 19 (2): 502–27.

Su, Xiaobo. 2015. 'Nontraditional Security and China's Transnational Narcotics Control in Northern Laos and Myanmar.' *Political Geography* 48: 72–82.

Su, Xiaobo. 2016. 'Development Intervention and Transnational Narcotics Control in Northern Myanmar.' *Geoforum* 68: 10–20.

Su, Xiaobo. 2018. 'Fragmented Sovereignty and the Geopolitics of Illicit Drugs in Northern Burma.' *Political Geography* 63: 20–30.

Summers, Tim. 2013. *Yunnan – A Chinese Bridgehead to Asia: A Case Study of China's Political and Economic Relations with Its Neighbours.* Oxford: Chandos Publishing.

Summers, Tim. 2016. 'China's "New Silk Roads": Sub-National Regions and Networks of Global Political Economy.' *Third World Quarterly* 37 (9): 1628–43.

Summers, Tim. 2018. *China's Regions in an Era of Globalization.* Abingdon: Routledge.

Sun, Yun. 2011. 'China's Strategic Misjudgement on Myanmar.' *Journal of Current Southeast Asian Affairs* 31(1): 73–96.

Sun, Yun. 2017. *China and Myanmar's Peace Process.* Washington, DC: United States Institute of Peace. https://bit.ly/3dbNiuM.

Swaine, Michael D. 2001. 'Chinese Decision-Making Regarding Taiwan, 1979–2000.' In *The Making of Chinese Foreign and Security Policy in the Era of Reform, 1978–2000*, edited by David M. Lampton. eBook edition. Stanford, CA: Stanford University Press.

Swanström, Niklas, and Yin He. 2006. *China's War on Narcotics: Two Perspectives.* Washington, DC: Central Asia-Caucasus Institute & Silk Road Studies Program, Johns Hopkins University-SAIS.

Taliaferro, Jeffrey W., Steven E. Lobell, and Norrin M. Ripsman. 2009. 'Introduction: Neoclassical Realism, the State, and Foreign Policy.' In *Neoclassical Realism, the State, and Foreign Policy*, edited by Steven E. Lobell, Norrin M. Ripsman, and Jeffrey W. Taliaferro. eBook edition. Cambridge: Cambridge University Press.

Tan, Danielle. 2014. 'Chinese Networks, Economic and Territorial Redefinitions in Northern Lao PDR.' In *Transnational Dynamics in Southeast Asia: The Greater Mekong Subregion and Malacca Straits Economic Corridors*, edited by Nathalie Fau, Sirivanh Khonthapane, and Christian Taillard, 421–52. Singapore: ISEAS.

Tan, Danielle. 2015. *Chinese Engagement in Laos: Past, Present, and Uncertain Future.* Singapore: Institute of Southeast Asian Studies. www.iseas.edu.sg/images/pdf/trends_in_sea_2015_7.pdf.

Tang, Zhengang, and Wang Zhongyuan. 2018. '新体制下海警海上维权武力使用初探 [A Preliminary Study on the Use of the Maritime Police Force to Protect Maritime Rights].' 公安海警学院学报 *[Journal of China Maritime Police Academy]* 17(6): 23–6.

Tan-Mullins, May, and Giles Mohan. 2013. 'The Potential of Corporate Environmental Responsibility of Chinese State-Owned Enterprises in Africa.' *Environment, Development and Sustainability* 15(2): 265–84.

Tan-Mullins, May, Frauke Urban, and Grace Mang. 2017. 'Evaluating the Behaviour of Chinese Stakeholders Engaged in Large Hydropower Projects in Asia and Africa.' *The China Quarterly* 230(June): 464–88.

Tanzi, Alexandre, and Wei Lu. 2018. 'Where Will Global GDP Growth Come from in the Next Five Years?' *Bloomberg*, 28 October https://bloom.bg/3uFYJAS.

Taylor, Brendan. 2018. *The Four Flashpoints: How Asia Goes to War.* Melbourne: La Trobe University Press.

Taylor, Ian, and Zhengyu Wu. 2013. 'China's Arms Transfers to Africa and Political Violence.' *Terrorism and Political Violence* 25(3): 457–75.

Taylor, Monique. 2014. *The Chinese State, Oil and Energy Security.* Basingstoke: Palgrave Macmillan.

Teiwes, Frederick C., and Warren Sun. 2008. *The End of the Maoist Era: Chinese Politics during the Twilight of the Cultural Revolution, 1972–1976.* Armonk, NY: Routledge.

Tellis, Ashely J. 2013. 'China's Grand Strategy: The Quest for Comprehensive National Power and its Consequences.' In *The Rise of China: Essays on the Future Competition*, edited by Gary J. Schmitt, 25–52. New York: Encounter Books.

ten Brink, Tobias. 2013. 'Paradoxes of Prosperity in China's New Capitalism.' *Journal of Current Chinese Affairs* 42(4): 17–44.

Teschke, Benno. 2003. *The Myth of 1648: Class, Geopolitics, and the Making of Modern International Relations.* London: Verso.

Thayer, Carlyle A. 2014a. 'China's Oil Rig Gambit: South China Sea Game-Changer?' *The Diplomat*, 12 May. https://bit.ly/3wQKQlo.

Thayer, Carlyle A. 2014b. '4 Reasons China Removed Oil Rig HYSY-981 Sooner Than Planned.' *The Diplomat*, 22 July. https://bit.ly/2QliGxU.

Tian, Yichen, Bingfang Wu, Lei Zhang, Qiangzi Li, Kun Jia, and Meiping Wen. 2011. 'Opium Poppy Monitoring with Remote Sensing in North Myanmar.' *International Journal of Drug Policy* 22(4): 278–84.

Tiezzi, Shannon. 2014. 'China, India End Military Stand-Off along Disputed Border.' *The Diplomat*, 1 October. https://bit.ly/32he9PL.

Townshend, Ashley, and Rory Medcalf. 2016. *China's New Passive Assertiveness in Asian Maritime Security.* Sydney: Lowy Institute. https://bit.ly/3dVA3Og.

Trevaskes, Susan. 2013. 'Drug Policy in China.' In *Drug Law Reform in East and Southeast Asia*, edited by Fifa Rahman and Nick Crofts, 221–32. Lanham, MD: Lexington Books.

Tseng, Katherine Hui-Yi. 2013. 'Challenges in Marine Affairs Management under the New Chinese Leadership.' *East Asian Policy* 5 (3): 27–37.

TSYO [Ta'ang Students and Youth Organization]. 2011. *Shweli Under Siege: Dams Proceed Amid War in Burma.* November. www.burmalibrary.org/docs13/Sheweli_Under_Siege(en)-red.pdf.

Tubilewicz, Czeslaw. 2017. 'Paradiplomacy as a Provincial State-Building Project: The Case of Yunnan's Relations with the Greater Mekong Subregion.' *Foreign Policy Analysis* 13(4): 931–49.

Tunsjø, Øystein. 2013. *Security and Profit in China's Energy Policy: Hedging against Risk*. New York: Columbia University Press.

UNCTAD [United Nations Conference on Trade and Development]. 2001. *World Investment Report 2001: Promoting Linkages*. New York: United Nations.

UNCTAD. 2018. 'UNCTADstat.' Accessed 26 January. http://unctadstat .unctad.org.

UNCTAD. 2019a. *World Investment Report 2019: Special Economic Zones*. New York: United Nations.

UNCTAD. 2019b. 'General Profile: Lao People's Democratic Republic.' UNCTAD, 11 July. https://bit.ly/3uFZgTo.

UNCTAD. 2020. *World Investment Report 2020: International Production Beyond the Pandemic*. New York: United Nations.

United Nations. 1982. *United Nations Convention on the Law of the Sea*. New York: United Nations. https://bit.ly/3wMTvW5.

United Nations. 2014. *United Nations Guiding Principles on Alternative Development. General Assembly Resolution 68/196*. New York: United Nations. https://bit.ly/3dgeBV4.

UNODC [United Nations Office of Drugs and Crime]. 2006. *Opium Poppy Cultivation in the Golden Triangle: Lao PDR, Myanmar, Thailand*. New York: United Nations. www.unodc.org/pdf/research/Golden_triangl e_2006.pdf.

UNODC. 2008. *Opium Poppy Cultivation in Southeast Asia: Lao PDR, Myanmar, Thailand*. New York: United Nations. www.unodc.org/pdf/ research/Golden_triangle_2006.pdf.

UNODC. 2014. *South-East Asia Opium Survey 2014: Lao PDR, Myanmar*. New York: United Nations. https://bit.ly/3mTQqit.

UNODC. 2015a. *2015 World Drug Report*. New York: United Nations. www.unodc.org/wdr2015/.

UNODC. 2015b. *South-East Asia Opium Survey 2015: Lao PDR, Myanmar*. New York: United Nations. https://bit.ly/3g6hfhL.

UNODC. 2016. *Mekong River Drug Threat Assessment*. Bangkok: UNODC Regional Office for Southeast Asia and the Pacific. https://bit.ly/2QnG5yJ.

UNODC. 2017. *Partnership, Cooperation and Action in the Greater Mekong Sub-Region: The Memorandum of Understanding (MOU) on Drug Control*. Bangkok: United Nations. https://bit.ly/3dbmbA2.

UNODC. 2018. 'Annual Drug Seizures.' 18 June, New York. https://dataunodc.un.org/drugs/seizures.

UNODC. 2019a. *Myanmar Opium Survey 2018*. New York: United Nations. https://bit.ly/3uR9Sz5.

UNODC. 2019b. 'Alternative Development: Lao People's Democratic Republic.' www.unodc.org/unodc/en/alternative-development/laos.html.

Urban, Frauke, Giuseppina Siciliano, Kim Sour, Pich Dara Lonn, May Tan-Mullins, and Grace Mang. 2016. 'South–South Technology Transfer of Low-Carbon Innovation: Large Chinese Hydropower Dams in Cambodia.' *Sustainable Development* 23(4): 232–44.

US Embassy. 2007. 'Sri Lanka: President's State Visit to China Focuses on Port Project and Other Infrastructure Aid.' Cable 07COLOMBO502_a. 28 March, Colombo. https://wikileaks.org/plusd/cables/07COLOMBO502_a.html.

US Embassy. 2009. 'Charge D'Affaires Protests Harassment of USNS Impeccable in South China Sea.' Cable 09BEIJING600_a. 9 March, Beijing. https://search.wikileaks.org/plusd/cables/09BEIJING600_a.html.

Van Aken, Tucker, and Orion A. Lewis. 2015. 'The Political Economy of Noncompliance in China: The Case of Industrial Energy Policy.' *Journal of Contemporary China* 24(95): 798–822.

van Creveld, Martin. 1999. *The Rise and Decline of the State*. Cambridge: Cambridge University Press.

Varrall, Merriden. 2016. 'Domestic Actors and Agendas in Chinese Aid Policy.' *The Pacific Review* 29(1): 21–44.

Veg, Sebastian. 2019. 'The Rise of China's Statist Intellectuals: Law, Sovereignty, and "Repoliticization."' *The China Journal* 82: 23–45.

Visontay, Elias. 2020. 'Coronavirus Health Emergency Declaration Delayed by a Week, Australian WHO Expert Panel Member Says.' *Guardian*, 20 May. https://bit.ly/3g6hsBz.

vom Hau, Matthias. 2015. 'State Theory: Four Analytical Traditions.' In *The Oxford Handbook of Transformations of the State*, edited by Stephan Leibfried, Evelyne Huber, Matthew Lange, Jonah D. Levy, and John D. Stephens, 131–51. Oxford University Press.

Walker, R. B. J. 1993. *Inside/Outside: International Relations as Political Theory*. Cambridge: Cambridge University Press.

Waltz, Kenneth N. 1979. *Theory of International Politics*. Reading, MA: Addison-Wesley.

Wang, Antao. 2018. 'The Implementation of International Cooperation Framework in the SCS and its Adjacent Sea (2016–2020).' Presentation at Fourth International Workshop on Cooperation and Development in the South China Sea, 28 March, Beijing.

Wang, Cungang. 2012. '当今中国的外交政策：谁在制定？谁在影响？——基于国内行为体的视角 [Chinese Foreign Policy Today: Who Makes It? Who Influences It? The Perspective of Domestic Actors].' *Foreign Affairs Review* 29(2): 1–18.

Wang, Fran, and Cheng Siwei. 2018. 'Local Governments Still Cheating on Debt.' *Caixin Global*, 20 April. https://bit.ly/3g4lomj.

Wang, Gang. 2011. '我国分散的海洋执法体制及其制度根源 [China's Dispersed Model of Marine Law Enforcement and Its Origins].' Paper

Presented at Conference of the Chinese Public Administration Society, Kunshan.

Wang, Hui. 2011. *The End of the Revolution: China and the Limits of Modernity*. London: Verso.

Wang, Jintang. 2015. '中国海警发展战略构想 [Conception on Development Strategy of China Maritime Police].' 公安海警学院学报 *[Journal of China Maritime Police Academy]* 14(2): 48–52.

Wang, Lei, and Hu Angang. 2010. '经济发展与社会政治不稳定之间关系的实证研究-基于跨国数据的比较分析 [An Empirical Study on the Relationship between Economic Development and Social and Political Destabilisation].' *Quishi*, 26 February. www.qstheory.cn/wz/xues/20100 2/t20100226_21587.htm.

Wang, Ping. 2013. 'The Chinese View: Reflection of the Long-Term Experiences of Aid Receiving and Giving.' In *A Study of China's Foreign Aid: An Asian Perspective*, edited by Yasutami Shimomura and Hideo Ohashi, 125–44. Basingstoke: Palgrave Macmillan.

Wang, Xiaodong. 2016. 'China, ASEAN Launch Platform to Control Plant and Animal Diseases.' *China Daily*, 10 September. www.chinadaily.com.cn /world/2016-09/10/content_26760738.htm.

Wang, Yizhou. 2008. 中国对外关系转型30年, 1978–2008 *[Transformation of Foreign Affairs and International Relations in China, 1978–2008]*. Beijing: Social Sciences Academic Press.

Wang, Yizhou. 2011. 创造性介入: 中国外交新取向 *[Creative Involvement: A New Direction in China's Diplomacy]*. Beijing: Peking University Press.

Wang, Yuan, and Simon Zadek. 2016. *Sustainability Impacts of Chinese Outward Direct Investment: A Review of the Literature*. Winnipeg: International Institute for Sustainable Development. https://bit.ly/3sfytLW.

Wang, Yuan-Kang. 2013. *Harmony and War: Confucian Culture and Chinese Power Politics*. New York: Columbia University Press.

Watanabe, Shino. 2013. 'Implementation System: Tools and Institution.' In *A Study of China's Foreign Aid: An Asian Perspective*, edited by Yasutami Shimomura and Hideo Ohashi, 58–81. Basingstoke: Palgrave Macmillan.

Webber, Mark, and Michael Smith, eds. 2013. *Foreign Policy in a Transformed World*. London: Routledge.

Wen, Yucang, and Li Mo. 2016. '海警通信系统建设与发展研究 [The Construction and Development of China Coast Guard's Communication System].' 公安海警学院学报 *[Journal of China Maritime Police Academy]* 15(4):54–8, 67.

Wendt, Alexander. 2004. 'The State as Person in International Theory.' *Review of International Studies* 30(2): 289–316.

Wilson, Jeffrey D. 2019. 'The Evolution of China's Asian Infrastructure Investment Bank: From a Revisionist to Status-Seeking Agenda.' *International Relations of the Asia-Pacific* 19(1): 147–76.

Windle, James. 2018. 'Why Do South-East Asian States Choose to Suppress Opium? A Cross-Case Comparison.' *Third World Quarterly* 39(2): 366–84.

Wirth, Christian. 2012. 'Ocean Governance, Maritime Security and the Consequences of Modernity in Northeast Asia.' *Pacific Review* 25(2): 223–45.

Womack, Brantly. 1994. 'Warlordism and Military Regionalism in China.' In *Chinese Regionalism: The Security Dimension*, edited by Richard H. Yang, Jason C. Hu, Peter H. H. Yu, and Andrew N. D. Yang, 21–41. Boulder, CO: Westview.

Wong, Audrye. 2018. 'More than Peripheral: How Provinces Influence China's Foreign Policy.' *The China Quarterly* 235: 735–57.

Wong, Pak Nung, Kathlene Aquino, Kristinne Lara-de Leon, and Sylvia Yuen Fun So. 2013. 'As Wind, Thunder and Lightning: Local Resistance to China's Resource-Led Diplomacy in the Christian Philippines.' *South East Asia Research* 21(2): 281–302.

Wong, Sue-Lin. 2017. 'China's Border City with North Korea Eases Tourism Curbs – Sources.' *Reuters*, 20 December. https://reut.rs/2OIFuHx.

Woods, Kevin. 2011a. 'Ceasefire Capitalism: Military–Private Partnerships, Resource Concessions and Military-State Building in the Burma–China Borderlands.' *Journal of Peasant Studies* 38(4): 747–70.

Woods, Kevin. 2011b. 'Conflict Timber along the China–Burma Border: Connecting the Global Timber Consumer with Violent Extraction Sites.' In *Chinese Circulations: Capital, Commodities, and Networks in Southeast Asia*, edited by Eric Tagliacozzo and Wen-Chin Chang, 480–506. Durham, NC: Duke University Press.

Woods, Kevin. 2015. *Commercial Agriculture Expansion in Myanmar: Links to Deforestation, Conversion Timber, and Land Conflicts*. London: Forest Trends. https://bit.ly/3gd1hTj.

Woods, Kevin. 2018. 'Rubber Out of the Ashes: Locating Chinese Agribusiness Investments in "Armed Sovereignties" in the Myanmar–China Borderlands.' *Territory, Politics, Governance* 7(1): 79–95.

Woods, Kevin, and Tom Kramer. 2012. *Financing Dispossession: China's Opium Substitution Programme in Northern Burma*. Amsterdam: Transnational Institute.

World Bank. 2014. *Lao Development Report 2014: Expanding Productive Employment for Broad-Based Growth*. Washington, DC: World Bank Group. https://bit.ly/2QlFuxy.

World Bank. 2017. *Lao PDR Economic Monitor: Lowering Risks and Reviving Growth*. Washington, DC: World Bank Group. https://bit.ly/32cB8eQ.

Xinhua. 2010. '中共中央办公厅 国务院办公厅印发《关于进一步推进国有企业贯彻落实'三重一大'决策制度的意见》 [The General Office of the Central Committee of the Communist Party of China and the General Office of the State Council issued "Opinions on Further Promoting the Implementation of the 'Three Majors and One Large' Decision System in State-Owned Enterprises"].' *Xinhua*, 15 July. http://news.xinhuanet.com/fortune/2010-07/15/c_111958679.htm.

Xinhua. 2014a. 'Experts Talk about the Zhongjiannan Drilling Project,' *Xinhua*, 15 July. www.xuanyiltd.com/news/html/?443.html.

Xinhua. 2014b. 'CNPC Ends Drilling off Xisha Islands.' *Xinhua*, 16 July. www.china.org.cn/business/2014-07/16/content_32963102.htm.

Xinhua. 2020. '表格任务重如山、聚集动员喊口号、作秀留痕走过场……揭一揭抗疫中的'形式主义'-新华网 [Tasks to Fill Forms Are as Heavy as a Mountain; Gather to Shout Slogans to Mobilize People; Make a Show to Leave Record as a Mere Formality: Revealing "Formalism" during the Fight against the Virus].' *Xinhuanet*, 12 February. www.xinhuanet.com/fortune/2020-02/12/c_1125565688.htm.

Xiong, Yongxian, and Li Yaqiong. 2013. '南海涉外行政执法的对策研究 [Research on Countermeasures of Administrative Law Enforcement Concerning Foreign Affairs].' *Journal of Hunan Police Academy* 25(1): 86–90.

Xu, Ying. 2017. '我国海警执法武力使用的程序规制 [The Procedural Regulation of the Use of Force by the China Coast Guard].' 公安海警学院学报 *[Journal of China Maritime Police Academy]* 16(5): 1–8.

Yamada, Norihiko. 2018. 'Legitimation of the Lao People's Revolutionary Party: Socialism, Chintanakan Mai (New Thinking) and Reform.' *Journal of Contemporary Asia* 48(5): 717–38.

Yamaguchi, Shinji. 2014. *The Foreign Policy of the Xi Jinping Administration and the Establishment of China's Air Defense Identification Zone*. Tokyo: National Institute for Defense Studies. https://bit.ly/3dfumLM.

Yan, Xuetong. 2011. 'How Assertive Should a Great Power Be?' *New York Times*, 1 April. www.nytimes.com/2011/04/01/opinion/01iht-edyan01.html.

Yang, Huanbiao. 2019. '海警部队执法权设定及运行研究 [Research on the Establishment and Operation of the Law Enforcement Powers of the China Coast Guard].' 公安海警学院学报 *[Journal of China Maritime Police Academy]* 18(1): 11–22.

Yang, Yang, and Li Peizhi. 2017. '中国海警海军融合式发展问题探究 [Research on the Integrated Development of China Coast Guard and Navy].' 公安海警学院学报 *[Journal of China Maritime Police Academy]* 16(1):11–15, 34.

Yang, Yuan, and Tom Mitchell. 2020. 'China Reports Sharp Rise in Coronavirus Cases.' *Financial Times*, 13 February. www.ft.com/content/ac7e94da-4e1c-11ea-95a0-43d18ec715f5.

Ye, Zicheng. 2010. *Inside China's Grand Strategy: The Perspective from the People's Republic*. Edited by Steven I. Levine and Guoli Liu. Lexington, KY: University Press of Kentucky.

Yeophantong, Pichamon. 2014. 'Cambodia's Environment: Good News in Areng Valley?' *The Diplomat*, 3 November. https://bit.ly/3sgJOLX.

Yeophantong, Pichamon. 2016. 'China's Hydropower Expansion and Influence Over Environmental Governance in Mainland Southeast Asia.' In *Rising China's Influence in Developing Asia*, edited by Evelyn Goh, 174–92. Oxford: Oxford University Press.

You, Ji. 2017a. 'Military Reform: The Politics of PLA Reorganisation under Xi Jinping.' In *China's Core Executive: Leadership Styles, Structures and Processes Under Xi Jinping*, edited by Sebastian Heilmann and Matthias Stepan, 46–50. Berlin: MERICS.

You, Ji. 2017b. 'Xi Jinping and PLA Centrality in Beijing's South China Sea Dispute Management.' *China: An International Journal* 15(2): 1–21.

Yu, Wenjin. 2015. '海警舰艇统一训练与人才选拔模式的探讨 [Discussion on the Unified Training and Personnel Selection for China Coast Guard Vessels].' 公安海警学院学报 *[Journal of China Maritime Police Academy]* 14(3): 16–18.

Yung, Christopher D. 2015. 'The PLA Navy Lobby and its Influence over China's Maritime Sovereignty Policies.' In *PLA Influence on China's National Security Policymaking*, edited by Phillip C. Saunders and Andrew Scobell. eBook edition. Stanford, CA: Stanford University Press.

Zakaria, Fareed. 2014. 'China's Growing Clout.' *Washington Post*, 13 November. https://wapo.st/3wMUJk9.

Zeng, Jinghan. 2016. 'Constructing a "New Type of Great Power Relations": The State of Debate in China (1998–2014).' *British Journal of Politics and International Relations* 18(2): 422–42.

Zeng, Jinghan, Yuefan Xiao, and Shaun Breslin. 2015a. 'Securing China's Core Interests: The State of Debate in China.' *International Affairs* 91(2): 245–66.

Zeng, Jinghan, Yuefan Xiao, and Shaun Breslin. 2015b. '中国核心利益 [China's National Interests and Core Interests].' In 国家战略报告：国家利益的拓展与维护 *[National Security Strategy: China's National Interests]*, edited by Honghua Men. Beijing: People's Press.

Zha, Daojiong. 2001. 'Localizing the South China Sea Problem: The Case of China's Hainan.' *Pacific Review* 14(4): 575–98.

Zha, Daojiong. 2015. 'A Political Ecology of Hydropower Development in China.' In *Hydropower Development in the Mekong Region: Political,*

Socio-Economic and Environmental Perspectives, edited by Nathanial Matthews and Kim Geheb. eBook edition. Abingdon: Routledge.

Zhang, Amei, and Gang Zou. 1994. 'Foreign Trade Decentralization and Its Impact on Central–Local Relations.' In *Changing Central–Local Relations in China: Reform and State Capacity*, edited by Hao Jia and Zhimin Lin, 153–77. Boulder, CO: Westview Press.

Zhang, Biao. 2019. 'State Transformation Goes Nuclear: The Case of Chinese National Nuclear Companies' Expansion into Europe.' *Third World Quarterly* 40(8): 1459–78.

Zhang, Boting. 2010. '加强科普宣传促进我国水电开发 [Promote Chinese Hydropower by Scientific Education].' http://blog.sciencenet.cn/blog-295 826-385269.html.

Zhang, Denghua. 2018. 'China's New Aid Agency.' *The Interpreter*, 19 March. www.lowyinstitute.org/the-interpreter/china-s-new-aid-agency.

Zhang, Denghua, and Graeme Smith. 2017. 'China's Foreign Aid System: Structure, Agencies, and Identities.' *Third World Quarterly* 38(10): 2230–346.

Zhang, Feng. 2015. *Chinese Hegemony: Grand Strategy and International Institutions in East Asian History*. Stanford, CA: Stanford University Press.

Zhang, Feng. 2020. 'China's Long March at Sea: Explaining Beijing's South China Sea Strategy, 2009–2016.' *Pacific Review* 33(3): 757–87.

Zhang, Hongzhou. 2012. *China's Evolving Fishing Industry: Implications for Regional and Global Maritime Security*. RSIS Working Paper 246. Singapore: National University of Singapore.

Zhang, Hongzhou. 2016. 'Chinese Fishermen in Disputed Waters: Not Quite a "People's War."' *Marine Policy* 68: 65–73.

Zhang, Hongzhou. 2019. *Securing the 'Rice Bowl': China and Global Food Security*. Basingstoke: Palgrave Macmillan.

Zhang, Hongzhou, and Sam Bateman. 2017. 'Fishing Militia, the Securitization of Fishery and the South China Sea Dispute.' *Contemporary Southeast Asia* 39(2): 288–314.

Zhang, Hongzhou, and Fengshi Wu. 2017. 'China's Marine Fishery and Global Ocean Governance.' *Global Policy* 8(2): 216–26.

Zhang, Jun. 2010. *Transformation of the Chinese Enterprises*. Andover: Cengage Learning.

Zhang, Jun, and Jamie Peck. 2016. 'Variegated Capitalism, Chinese Style: Regional Models, Multi-Scalar Constructions.' *Regional Studies* 50(1): 52–78.

Zhang, Jun, Qi Zhang, and Zhikuo Liu. 2017. 'The Political Logic of Partial Reform of China's State-Owned Enterprises.' *Asian Survey* 57(3): 395–415.

Zhang, Qingmin. 2013. '中国对外关系的国内管理和内外统筹 [Domestic Administration and Intermestic Coordination of Chinese Foreign Relations].' *World Economics and Politics* 8: 117–38.

Zhao, Suisheng. 1994. 'China's Central–Local Relationship: A Historical Perspective.' In *Changing Central–Local Relations in China: Reform and State Capacity*, edited by Hao Jia and Zhimin Lin, 19–34. Boulder, CO: Westview Press.

Zhao, Xinshuang. 2017. '法律视角下海警与海军协同问题研究 [Research on the Cooperation between the Coast Guard and the Navy from the Legal Perspective].' 公安海警学院学报 *[Journal of China Maritime Police Academy]* 16(1): 24–9.

Zhao, Xinshuang. 2018. '海军配合海警维权问题研究 [Research on the Navy's Cooperation with the Coast Guard in Rights Protection].' 公安海警学院学报 *[Journal of China Maritime Police Academy]* 17(1): 26–35.

Zheng, Sarah. 2017. 'China Registers 8,000 Troops for UN Peacekeeping Missions.' *South China Morning Post*, 29 September. https://bit.ly/3dgfCwm.

Zheng, Yongnian. 2004. *Globalization and State Transformation in China*. Cambridge: Cambridge University Press.

Zheng, Yongnian. 2007. *De Facto Federalism in China: Reforms and Dynamics of Central-Local Relations*. Singapore: World Scientific.

Zhong, Longbiao, and Wang Jun. 2007. '从单层博弈到双层博弈：中国外交决策模式的变迁 [From One-Level Games to Two-Level Games: The Evolution of China's Foreign Policy-Making Model].' *World Economics and Politics* 7: 62–8.

Zhong, Yang. 2003. *Local Government and Politics in China: Challenges from Below*. Armonk, NY: ME Sharpe.

Zhou, Baogen. 2003. '中国与国际核不扩散机制的一种建构主义分析 [A Constructivist Analysis of China and the World Nuclear Non-Proliferation Regime].' 世界经济与政治 *[World Economics and International Politics]* 2: 23–7.

Zhou, Hong. 2017. 'China's Foreign Aid Policy and Mechanisms.' In *China's Foreign Aid: 60 Years in Retrospect*, edited by Hong Zhou, 1–48. Singapore: Springer.

Zhou, Li-An. 2010. *Incentives and Governance: China's Local Governments*. Singapore: Gale Asia.

Zhou, Weifeng, and Mario Esteban. 2018. 'Beyond Balancing: China's Approach towards the Belt and Road Initiative.' *Journal of Contemporary China* 27(112): 487–501.

Zhu, Yue. 2014. '"你们什么都可以问"—专访中电投总经理陆启洲 ["You Can Ask Me Everything": Conversation with CPI General Manager Qizhou Lu].' *Finance*, 16 June. http://magazine.caijing.com.cn/2014-06-16/114264680.html.

Ziv, Guy, Eric Baran, So Nam, Ignacio Rodríguez-Iturbe, and Simon A. Levin. 2012. 'Trading-off Fish Biodiversity, Food Security, and Hydropower in the Mekong River Basin.' *Proceedings of the National Academy of Sciences* 109(15): 5609.

Zou, Yizheng, and Lee Jones. 2020. 'China's Responses to Threats to Its Overseas Economic Interests: Softening Non-Interference and Cultivating Hegemony.' *Journal of Contemporary China* 29(121): 92–108.

Interviewees

Interviewee A01. 2017. Scholar Linked to the Chinese Ministry of Foreign Affairs.

Interviewee A01. 2018. Scholar Linked to the Chinese Ministry of Foreign Affairs.

Interviewee A02. 2017. Scholar Linked to the Chinese Ministry of Foreign Affairs.

Interviewees A06. 2017. Government Advisors/Officials of Think Tank Linked to the Chinese Ministry of Foreign Affairs.

Interviewee A07. 2018. Chinese Expert on International Maritime Law.

Interviewee A08. 2018. Chinese Expert on International Maritime Law.

Interviewee A09. 2018. Chinese Expert on International Maritime Law.

Interviewees A10. 2018. Officials in Think Tank Linked to the Chinese Ministry of Foreign Affairs.

Interviewee A11. 2018. Chinese Expert on International Relations and International Law.

Interviewee A12. 2018. Think Tank Official and Advisor to the Chinese Ministry of Foreign Affairs.

Interviewee A14. 2018. Chinese Expert on International Maritime Law and Environmental Protection.

Interviewee A15. 2018. Former Official of Provincial Maritime Bureau.

Interviewee A16. 2018. Former Official of Provincial Foreign Affairs Bureau.

Interviewees A17. 2018. Officials in Think Tank Linked to Chinese Ministry of Foreign Affairs and Maritime Agencies.

Interviewee A18. 2018. Chinese Expert on Hainan Province's Fishing Industry.

Interviewee A19. 2018. Head of Chinese Fisheries Non-Governmental Organisation.

Interviewee A20. 2018. Official of Think Tank Linked to the Chinese Ministry of Foreign Affairs.

Interviewee A21. 2018. Head of Think Tank Linked to Chinese Maritime Agency.

Interviewee A23. 2018. Former Senior Naval Officer and Official in Think Tank Linked to the Chinese Ministry of Foreign Affairs.

Interviewee A24. 2018. Official in Think Tank Linked to China's State Council.

Interviewee A25. 2018. Official in Think Tank Linked to China's State Council.

Interviewees A26. 2018. Officials in Chinese Maritime Agency.

Interviewees A27. 2018. Officials in Think Tank Linked to China's Ministry of State Security.

Interviewee A28. 2018. Official in Think Tank Linked to China's State Council.

Interviewee A29. 2018. Official in Think Tank Linked to China's State Council.

Interviewee A30. 2018. Head of Chinese University-Based Think Tank on International Relations.

Interviewee A31. 2018. Senior Official in Chinese Maritime Agency.

Interviewee A32. 2018. Official in Think Tank Linked to Chinese Ministry of State Security.

Interviewee A33. 2018. Leading Scholar of Chinese Maritime Law and History.

Interviewee B01. 2018. Researcher in Chinese Government Think Tank on Foreign Affairs.

Interviewees B02. 2018. Researchers in a Chinese Government Research Institute on Economic Development.

Interviewees B03. 2018. Researchers in the Chinese Academy of Social Sciences.

Interviewee B04. 2018. Chinese Scholar in a Beijing University, Specialising in China's Foreign Aid.

Interviewee B06. 2018. Researcher in Chinese Government Think Tank.

Interviewee B08. 2018. Project Manager, Large Centrally Owned Chinese State-owned Enterprise, Construction Sector.

Interviewee B09. 2018. Chinese Scholar Specialising in South–South Cooperation.

Interviewee B12. 2018. Cambodian Consultant to Civil Society and Communities on Hydropower Development.

Interviewee B14. 2018. Executive Director of a Cambodian Non-Governmental Organisation in Phnom Penh, Focusing on Environmental Conservation.

Interviewee B16. 2018. Executive Director of a Cambodian Non-Governmental Organisation in Phnom Penh, Focusing on Community and Sustainable Development.

Interviewee B17. 2018. Coordinator of a Cambodian Non-Governmental Organisation, Stung Treng Province, Cambodia.

Interviewee B18. 2018. Leader of a Cambodian Non-Governmental Organisation, Ratanakiri Province, Cambodia.

Interviewee B19. 2018. Community Leader, Ratanakiri Province, Cambodia.

Interviewee B20. 2018. Community Member, Stung Treng Province, Cambodia.

Interviewees B21. 2018. Villagers from Stung Treng Province, Cambodia.

Interviewee B22. 2018. Senior Donor-Funded Advisor to the Cambodian Government.

Interviewee B24. 2018. Senior Manager in an International Non-Governmental Organisation.

Interviewee B26. 2018. Cambodian Scholar and Environmental Expert.

Interviewee D03. 2018. Senior Official, Myanmar's Ministry of Electricity and Energy.

Interviewee D04. 2018. Senior Officer, Drug Enforcement Division, Myanmar Ministry of Home Affairs.

Interviewee D07. 2018. Director of a Myanmar State-Linked Think Tank.

Interviewee D08. 2018. Head of Myanmar Civil Society Organisation Focusing on Rural Development.

Interviewee D09. 2018. Member of Myanmar Parliament's Myitsone Dam Review Committee.

Interviewee D10. 2018. Senior Local Official in International Non-Governmental Organisation in Myanmar.

Interviewees D11. 2018. Senior Officials in Two Myanmar Civil Society Organisations.

Interviewee D12. 2018. Myanmar Expert on Wa State.

Interviewee D13. 2018. Retired Senior Myanmar Counter-Narcotics Official.

Interviewee D14. 2018. Senior Member of Myanmar Parliament, National League for Democracy.

Interviewee D16. 2018. Myanmar-Based Drugs Policy Expert.

Interviewee D17. 2018. Director of Non-Governmental Organisation Focusing on Myanmar's Economic Development.

Interviewee D18. 2018. Director of Myanmar Non-Governmental Organisation Focusing on Economic Development.

Interviewee D19. 2018. Deputy Director of a Myanmar Non-Governmental Organisation.

Interviewee D20. 2018. Senior Official in Myanmar Non-Governmental Organisation Focused on Rural Development.

Interviewee D21. 2018. Former Member of the United Wa State Party Central Committee, Myanmar.

Interviewee D23. 2018. Western Diplomat in Myanmar.

Interviewees E01. 2018. Officials from Chinese Environmental Non-Governmental Organisation.

Interviewees E03. 2018. Researchers in Think Tanks Linked to the Chinese Ministry of State Security and Ministry of Commerce.

Interviewee E04. 2018. China-Based Hydropower Industry Expert.

Interviewee E05. 2018. Senior Researcher in Think Tank Linked to the Chinese National Development and Reform Commission.

Interviewee E06. 2018. Senior Researcher in Think Tank Linked to the Chinese State Council.

Interviewees E09. 2018. Yunnan-Based Experts on China's Relations with the Mekong Region.

Interviewee E10. 2018. Yunnan-Based Expert on Law Enforcement.

Interviewee E11. 2018. Yunnan-Based Expert on China's Relations with the Mekong Region.

Interviewee E12. 2018. Head of International Non-Governmental Organisation Focused on Eliminating Opium.

Interviewees E13. 2018. Yunnan-Based Experts on China's Relations with the Mekong Region.

Interviewees E14. 2018. Experts in a Chinese State-Linked Think Tank.

Interviewee E15. 2018. Official from Lancang-Mekong Integrated Law Enforcement and Security Cooperation Centre.

Interviewee E16. 2018. Chinese Expert on Opium Substitution Projects.

Interviewee F01. 2018. Western Diplomat in Laos.

Interviewee F03. 2018. Senior Official in Vientiane-Based Western International Non-Governmental Organisation.

Interviewee F04. 2018. Laos-Based Official of an International Organisation.

Interviewee F05. 2018. Senior Laotian Law Enforcement Official.

Index

Note: For abbreviations and acronyms see the Glossary on pages xv-xvii.
Page numbers in bold indicate tables and those in italic are figures or maps.
Government departments and other bodies are Chinese unless specified otherwise.

Lightning Source UK Ltd.
Milton Keynes UK
UKHW020828101222
413700UK00031B/639